The Consumer-Oriented Neuropsychological Report

The Consumer-Oriented Neuropsychological Report

Edited by

Carmen G. Armengol, PhD, ABPP
Edith Kaplan, PhD, ABPP
Elisabeth J. Moes, PhD, ABPP

PAR Psychological Assessment Resources, Inc.

Dedication

This book is dedicated to the memory of
John A. Cegalis.

Library of Congress Cataloging-in-Publication Data

The consumer-oriented neuropsychological report/edited by Carmen G. Armengol, Edith Kaplan, Elisabeth J. Moes.
p. cm.
Includes bibliographical references and index.
ISBN 0-911907-35-1
1. Neuropsychological tests. 2. Neuropsychological report writing.
I. Armengol, Carmen G., 1955- II. Kaplan, Edith, 1924- III. Moes, Elisabeth J., 1953-
RC386.6.N48 C65 2001
616.8'0475—dc21 99–050125

Published in 2001 by Psychological Assessment Resources, Inc., Lutz, FL 33549 USA.

9 8 7 6 5 4 3 2 1 Reorder #RO-4710 Printed in the U.S.A.

FOREWORD

This worthy instructional book merits not one but four forewords—one for each group of potential readers who can best profit from it. I offer them all here.

To neuropsychology students:

This book is for you, even though you are not yet seeing patients and writing reports. It will acquaint you with a conceptually challenging and clinically responsible approach to eliciting and comprehending the behavioral manifestations of brain disease. Moreover, this book will give you a practical introduction to the ethical and thoughtful application of techniques and tools used for neuropsychological examinations and human research.

To clinical neuropsychology trainees, interns, and residents:

This book is for you as you begin seeing patients and are confronted with the seemingly overwhelming task of producing reports that will do justice to your patients and satisfy your supervisor or mentor. It is unique in describing, in a clear and easy-to-follow manner, the procedures involved in producing a clinically useful examination report. You will also find it to be constructively thought provoking in that, at each step along the procedural path, it lays out much of the information you will need for making decisions that will effectively take you to the next step. Best of all, for those of you who are struggling with how to write a report, this book gives you an outline to follow, which will serve you now and in all your future professional endeavors.

To teachers, mentors, and supervisors:

This is the instructional book you have been waiting for when teaching your trainees and interns how to think and write as neuropsychologists. Now you can hand them this book and let it do much of your work for you. And if you have a particularly bright and gifted student, the information provided herein will stimulate thinking, arouse curiosity, and bring the student to you with more questions and disputations. But that's the fun of being a supervisor or mentor.

To practicing clinicians:

Which one of us has never wondered about how to formulate the examination questions, what extra-examination information should be obtained, how to present the examination findings to a disparate—or even worse, unknown—audience? Although this book is no substitute for thinking about these kinds of examination and reporting concerns, it provides guidelines that will help direct the thinking and writing of even the most experienced clinicians. The chapters on computerized test applications, writing in the shadow of managed care, and reporting for forensic purposes will be particularly useful to both practicing clinicians, who are just beginning to deal with these issues, and to the many who have been dealing with these issues, but who are still uncomfortable or unsure about how best to respond.

In short, this book will serve many purposes for neuropsychologists at every stage of development and in every kind of clinical practice. Enjoy.

Muriel Deutsch Lezak, PhD, ABPP
Oregon Health Sciences University
Portland, Oregon

CONTRIBUTORS

Carmen G. Armengol, PhD, ABPP
Counseling and Applied Educational
Psychology Department
Northeastern University
Boston, Massachusetts

John T. Capuco, PsyD
Administrator
Acquired Brain Disorders Services
New Hampshire Department of Human Services
Concord, New Hampshire

Margaret Dawson, EdD
Center for Attention and Learning Disorders
Portsmouth, New Hampshire

Wilfrid N. Derby, PhD, ABPP
Private Practice
Manchester, New Hampshire

Paul E. Finn, PhD
Department of Psychology
Saint Anselm College
and Private Practice
Manchester, New Hampshire

James A. Grubman, PhD
Private Practice and Consultation
Montague City, Massachusetts

Richard Guare, PhD
Center for Attention and Learning Disorders
Portsmouth, New Hampshire

William Jamieson, PhD
Angel R. Martínez Associates
Manchester, New Hampshire

Lawrence G. Jasper, PhD
Secure Psychiatric Unit
New Hampshire State Prison for Men
Concord, New Hampshire
and Private Practice
Laconia, New Hampshire

Edith Kaplan, PhD, ABPP
Boston University School of Medicine
Departments of Neurology and Psychiatry
and Suffolk University Department of Psychology
Boston, Massachusetts

Donna Z. Kelland, PhD
Department of Psychology
Center for Forensic Psychiatry
Ann Arbor, Michigan

John Mendoza, PhD, ABPP
Veteran's Administration Medical Center
New Orleans, Louisiana

Elisabeth J. Moes, PhD, ABPP
Suffolk University Department of Psychology,
Harvard University Medical School,
and Director, Neuropsychological Services, Inc.
Brookline, Massachusetts

Dana L. Penney, PhD
Department of Neurology
Lahey Clinic
Burlington, Massachusetts

Jean Pieniadz, PhD
Mansfield Psychotherapy Associates
Burlington, Vermont

M. Melanie Sapienza, PhD
Department of Psychology
York University
Toronto, Ontario, Canada

Joan P. Scanlon, PhD
Private Practice
Nashua, New Hampshire

James E. Taylor, PhD
Associate Clinical Director
Lakeview NeuroRehabilitation Center
Effingham Falls, New Hampshire

Tina M. Trudel, PhD
Department of Psychiatry
Dartmouth Medical School
and Clinical Director
Lakeview NeuroRehabilitation Center
Effingham Falls, New Hampshire

ACKNOWLEDGMENTS

As in all projects of this kind, the assistance and support of others has been invaluable. The editors wish to thank the contributing authors for their hard work, enthusiasm, good humor, and dedication to this book. A special thank you to the anonymous responders to the surveys reported in this book. Their input has been invaluable. Family members have contributed in diverse ways. CA and EM wish to thank Guillermo Armengol for his patience and persistence in keeping the house clean and food on the table during long stretches of this project. EM's mother sent care packages from Holland and has always provided encouragement. EK wishes to thank her son Michael and granddaughter Rachel for being understanding and providing support at critical times. Regina Orama, a talented senior in Psychology at Northeastern University, has been invaluable in the preparation of this manuscript.

Last, but not least, we wish to thank the PAR family for their support with this project. R. Bob Smith III, Chairman and CEO of PAR, has provided a caring and thoughtful presence throughout. Serje Seminoff, President of PAR and our project director, has helped keep us on course. Special thanks go to Sandra Schneider, whose patience, understanding, and hard work brought this book to publication.

Carmen G. Armengol
Edith Kaplan
Elisabeth J. Moes
Boston, Massachusetts
September 2001

CONTENTS

INTRODUCTION

Neuropsychologists are faced every day with the task of summarizing for their clients (i.e., referral sources) a wealth of data, observations, impressions, and recommendations. Most neuropsychologists would agree that producing a concise document that does justice to the complexity of the findings, and yet is readable, is one of the most demanding aspects of their clinical practice.

Despite the clinician's best efforts, recipients of neuropsychological reports are frequently challenged by a document that is either too technical, or provides too much or too little detail. Furthermore, it may not include certain types of information that would have enhanced its usefulness in making decisions regarding a client's disposition, treatment, care, and rehabilitation.

Even reading other neuropsychological reports, we, as neuropsychologists, have been frustrated at times by the effort required to understand how conclusions were reached, what the full clinical picture is, and how we can fill in the gaps or generate applications. Not infrequently we have been asked by colleagues in other disciplines to help decipher the meaning of a report they have received from someone else and to explain how it relates to the diagnostic or treatment process. This book is a response to the need expressed by clinicians and students alike to have guidelines to assist them in their report writing efforts. We believe that making neuropsychological reports more *consumer-oriented* and user-friendly will foster greater understanding and appreciation of the contributions of neuropsychology.

This edited volume had a somewhat atypical origin. It grew out of a group of practicing neuropsychologists who meet on a regular basis for case presentations, peer review, and supervision. The group was conceived of and organized 7 years ago by one of the editors, Dr. Carmen Armengol, with Dr. Edith Kaplan as the designated supervisor and primary discussant of each case. The group met originally in Nashua, NH, at the offices of Dr. John A. Cegalis, a private practitioner and the president of ForThought. Two years later, after the untimely and unexpected death of Dr. Cegalis, the group found a home in the Psychology Department of Saint Anselm College in Manchester, NH, through the hospitality of Professor Paul Finn, then Chair of the Psychology Department, a group member, and a contributor to this volume.

The group centers around the presentation of a case for review and discussion. Group members (licensed clinical neuropsychologists with varying years of experience) receive a sanitized copy of the report in advance from one of the group members together with any pertinent articles the writer has come upon. In addition, the raw data are sent in advance to Dr. Kaplan. Two or three packets of the raw data are also made available at the time of the meeting, together with other supporting materials (e.g., medical reports; computed tomography [CT], magnetic resonance imaging [MRI], or other neuroimages; audio or videotapes when available, etc.). The meeting provides a forum in which constructive feedback is exchanged (from test administration to scoring, to data interpretation, and to formulation of conclusions). Practical suggestions for follow-up recommendations are made, and theoretical questions are raised (e.g., what constitutes *loss of function* for a cognitive domain such as attention; that is, how many different measures must reflect impairment and to what degree of severity). Issues of importance (e.g., professional ethics, how to handle problematic forensic and other situations, etc.) are addressed as they present themselves. The collaborative spirit of the group has extended to sharing resources, test materials, and other types of information. Dr. Kaplan plays an active role in bringing to the group the latest news on test development that she has garnered from her own involvement with The Psychological Corporation and in a number of different collaborative settings.

One of the advantages of the group format (comprising a maximum of 12 to 13 members a year) is that, over time, it has provided perspectives on issues encountered across and within diverse settings (from colleges and universities to acute care hospitals, neurosurgical and psychiatric units, inpatient and outpatient rehabilitation programs, nursing homes, and outpatient practices), and provided consultation to school systems, families, and a variety of referring professionals, agencies, and institutions.

These discussions provided a natural springboard for the development of a book that addresses many of the issues that we grappled with. Hence, all of the contributors, with the exception of Dr. Margaret Dawson (a colleague of Dr. Richard Guare at the Center for Attention and Learning Disorders in Portsmouth, NH) and Dr. John Mendoza (of the VA Medical Center in New Orleans) have, at one time or another, been participants in the New Hampshire Advanced Neuropsychological Case Studies Group.

In the early planning stages of the book, the group was fortunate to have met Dr. Mendoza in New Orleans during the annual meeting of the National Academy of Neuropsychology (NAN). Dr. Mendoza had been involved in developing guidelines for the accreditation of neuropsychologists in Louisiana (the only state board in the United States that recognizes the specialty of neuropsychology) and had been working on formulating guidelines to report writing. In the congenial atmosphere of the New Orleans hotel, we were able to convince Dr. Mendoza to contribute his talents to the book.

The first section of the book deals with broad issues pertaining to defining the practitioner, the consumer, and their interface at the time the referral is initiated. In chapter 1, Drs. Kaplan and Moes review extant guidelines on accreditation and training and the historical events leading to their development. In chapter 2, Drs. Finn, Moes, and Kaplan present data gathered from a national survey of referring professionals or *consumers* of neuropsychological reports (e.g., attorneys, allied health professionals and medical specialists) regarding aspects of neuropsychological reports they have found most and least useful. One of the findings to emerge from the survey is that the recommendations included in most reports represent an area of significant weakness. (This issue is revisited in chapter 8.) In the third chapter, Dr. Armengol stresses the importance of the first contact with the referral source as a means of identifying relevant concerns, obtaining pertinent background information, and assisting referral sources in understanding what a neuropsychological assessment can provide.

The subsequent six chapters deal with the second major content area of the book, that is, general issues pertaining to the report itself: the intended scope of the assessment, collecting background data and collateral information, issues the report should cover, whether and how to include scores, guidelines for writing recommendations and, finally, the use of computerized assessment tools.

In chapter 4, Drs. Armengol and Jamieson address the issue of screening versus comprehensive assessments. This chapter deals with the need to understand concepts such as specificity and sensitivity; the differential diagnostic process; ethical issues generated by the demand for brief, focused assessments; and suggestions on how to handle such demands (e.g., from Health Maintenance Organizations, or HMOs, and other sources). In this chapter, the authors also discuss the professional implications of who decides which tests should be paid for.

In chapter 5, Drs. Jasper and Capuco discuss the importance of historical and behavioral observations as providing the contextual framework within which the assessment is conducted, interpreted, and reported. They offer suggestions on how to obtain necessary information in a comprehensive and time-efficient manner. In chapter 6, Dr. Mendoza provides an overview of the general content areas and structure of a neuropsychological report. In addition, he provides a review and checklist of common pitfalls in data collection, interpretation, organization and reporting. Drs. Pieniadz and Kelland (see chapter 7) review the current controversy regarding inclusion of scores in the report and present results from a nationwide survey of directors of neuropsychology training programs on this issue.

Referral sources that regularly use neuropsychological reports have indicated that recommendations are often too general to be useful. This topic is the focus of chapter 8, by Drs. Armengol, Moes, Penney, and Sapienza, which is devoted to the very practical issue of how to write client-centered recommendations. Drs. Trudel and Taylor (see chapter 9) discuss advantages and limitations of computers in data gathering and interpretation and in reporting results.

The third section of the book provides guidelines to writing reports for specific audiences. In chapter 10, Drs. Scanlon and Grubman address constraints imposed by time demands in the managed care setting and how to write brief, timely, and informative reports. In chapter 11, Drs. Guare and Dawson present guidelines for providing services to the schools and discuss the specific challenges and advantages to working with interdisciplinary teams in the school setting. In chapter 12, Dr. Derby explains the specific requirements of forensic reports.

The final chapter of this book provides sample neuropsychological reports for consumers in diverse settings that illustrate differences in style, content, and format discussed in the preceding chapters. A brief introduction highlights the differences and salient aspects of each type of report. The editors wish to acknowledge the contribution of Dr. Gail Grodzinsky, who graciously provided us with one sample. Other reports were generated by various contributors to this book. We take full responsibility for any modifications that may be perceived as detracting from the originals.

The group's goal throughout the compilation of this book has been, on the one hand, to assist the neuropsychologist in writing a report that adequately takes into account the needs of its intended recipients and, on the other hand, fosters an appreciation of neuropsychology and its clinical applications on the part of the consumer.

1

Who Is a Neuropsychologist?

Edith Kaplan and Elisabeth J. Moes

Introduction

Consumers (e.g., HMOs, physicians, lawyers, insurance companies) have expressed concern about how to identify qualified neuropsychologists for referral purposes. Because neuropsychology has had a brief history of rapid growth during the last 50 years and has only recently received recognition of specialty status by the American Psychological Association (APA), there is as yet no full consensus regarding the appropriate training and background of a neuropsychologist.

This chapter reviews the competency and credentialing criteria formulated by various professional organizations and provides a historical perspective on the factors that have led to their development. This is relevant in the sense that the neuropsychological report should be a reflection of the competency of the professional responsible for the assessment and interpretation of results and not simply a report of the scores obtained on given tests. As Schafer remarked in 1948, "To reason or do research only in terms of scores and score patterns is to do violence to the nature of the raw material" (as cited in Lezak, 1995, p. 147). That is, by virtue of the types of questions implicitly posed (i.e., through test selection and qualitative analysis) to examine for the presence or absence of neuropsychological syndromes or identifiable areas of impaired functioning, the report should reflect the thinking of a well trained neuropsychologist. To this end, the distinctive background, training, and role of the neuropsychologist will be contrasted with the background and focus of professionals in other disciplines (e.g., clinical psychologists, school and educational psychologists, cognitive psychologists, experimental neuropsychologists, psychiatrists, and neurologists).

Early Developments

Prior to the 1940s, clinical psychologists were called upon to differentiate between functional and organic disorders. Their arsenal consisted primarily of instruments such as intelligence tests (e.g., various instruments by Wechsler), the Bender-Gestalt, and projective tests (e.g., Rorschach Inkblot Test). Veterans' hospitals, the largest employer of clinical psychologists after World War II, provided more exposure to patients with explicit neurological deficits than had typically been identified in traditional psychiatric hospitals. Theoretical developments that led to a switch from a behavioral emphasis to cognitive models, as well as animal research seeking to localize the memory engram and, more generally, to establish a neuroanatomical basis for behavior and cognition, set the stage for the emergence of neuropsychology as a discipline. In fact, it was Karl Lashley (as cited in Lezak, 1995) who proposed the term *neuropsychology* in 1936. Assessment of patients with localized lesions (e.g., veterans with injuries sustained during combat and with subsequent development of strokes, tumors, head injuries, cortical and subcortical syndromes, etc.) provided a fertile ground in the United States for diagnosis, test development, research, and single case studies. In dealing with patients with clinical needs, both the skills of a clinical psychologist and the greater research and cognitive focus of the neuropsychologist became combined. The confluence of disciplines that resulted in the emergence of the field of neuropsychology (broadly defined) is well reflected in the fact that "Among the early American founders of neuropsychology, Ralph Reitan was a physiological psychologist, Arthur Benton was a clinical psychologist who became interested in brain function, and Norman Geschwind was a neurologist interested in the brain organization of behavior" (Cytowic, 1996, p. 9). Key figures such as A. R. Luria in Russia, Oliver Zangwill in England, Henri Hécaen in France, Luigi Vignolo and Ennio DeRenzi in Italy, and Kevin Walsh in Australia have been influential in the advancement of the discipline of neuropsychology.

Benton (1987) cites the appearance of two international neuropsychological journals, *Neuropsychologia* in 1963 and *Cortex* in 1964, as providing a consolidating force for the emergence of the discipline of neuropsychology, followed in the late 1960s by the establishment of the International Neuropsychological Society (INS), a multidisciplinary organization. Although this organization started as a small group and for the first few years met simultaneously with the APA conference, a decision was made to hold meetings at a different date in the interest of creating a separate identity. Since then,

INS has met independently and had grown to a membership size of 3,489 by February of 1997. Other journals, such as *The Journal of Clinical Neuropsychology* (now the *Journal of Experimental and Clinical Neuropsychology*) and *The Clinical Neuropsychologist,* subsequently appeared, followed by at least 15 other discipline-specific journals. *The Journal of the International Neuropsychological Society* (JINS) was inaugurated in 1994 as the official organ of INS.

In addition to INS, two new organizations came into being: the National Academy of Neuropsychology (NAN), established in 1975, and the Division of Clinical Neuropsychology (Division 40) of APA, established in 1980. NAN was established in order to address the specifically clinical needs and interests of its members, and in 1985 NAN created its own journal, *Archives of Clinical Neuropsychology*. Division 40 was established through the initiative of INS members (in particular as a result of the efforts of Lou Costa) as a forum for national clinical issues and to move in the direction of having the APA designate clinical neuropsychology as a specialty.

Competency and Credentialing Criteria

In 1978, INS and APA Division 40 established a joint Task Force on Education, Accreditation, and Credentialing of Clinical Neuropsychologists, with Lou Costa, Harold Goodglass, Edith Kaplan, Steven Mattis, Manfred Meier, James Reed, Paul Satz, and Barbara C. Wilson as members. From this Task Force, a number of recommendations for accreditation and credentialing provided the impetus for Manfred Meier to spearhead the establishment of the American Board of Clinical Neuropsychology (ABCN). The ABCN was incorporated in Minnesota in 1984. The initial board was composed of Arthur Benton, Linus Bieliauskas, Thomas Boll, Nelson Butters, Louis Costa, Leonard Diller, Gerald Goldstein, Harold Goodglass, Edith Kaplan, Muriel Lezak, Joseph Matarazzo, Charles Matthews, Steven Mattis, Manfred Meier, Allan Mirsky, Oscar Parsons, Homer Reed, Byron Rourke, Paul Satz, Aaron Smith, Ottfried Spreen, and Barbara C. Wilson. The board members agreed that, in order to be formally seated on the board, each member must pass an examination administered internally by three other board members.

The Task Force also proposed guidelines for doctoral training programs in Clinical Neuropsychology (see Reports of the INS–Division 40 Task Force on Education, Accreditation, and Credentialing, 1987). Five core areas were identified: (a) generic psychology, (b) generic clinical neuropsychology, (c) neurosciences and basic human and animal neuropsychology, (d) specific clinical neuropsychology training, and (e) a doctoral dissertation in clinical neuropsychology. It was recommended that specific neuropsychological training should include (a) clinical neurology and neuropathology; (b) specialized neuropsychological assessment techniques; (c) specialized neuropsychological intervention techniques; (d) an assessment practicum in a university-supervised assessment facility; (e) an intervention practicum in a supervised intervention facility; and (f) a clinical neuropsychological internship (1,800 hours), completed in a 1- or 2-year period. In addition, a postdoctoral year of training in clinical neuropsychology was recommended, to include exposure to didactic training in a number of specified settings (i.e., psychiatric, neurological, pediatric, and general medical patients with neurobehavioral disorders) and participation in clinical activities with neurologists and neurosurgeons.

The Task Force recommendations were, by and large, subsequently incorporated into the eligibility criteria to sit for the ABCN, a free-standing board granting diplomate status. "The creation of the diplomate was to provide a credential which the lay public, attorneys, educators and other consumers of neuropsychological services could recognize" (Bieliauskas & Matthews, 1997).

Eligibility criteria to sit for the ABCN include a doctoral degree in psychology from a regionally accredited institution with licensure to practice in one's state or province and 3 years of supervised experience in neuropsychology (one of which can be predoctoral). Board certification, at the time of this writing, consists of a three-part examination administered after eligibility has been established: a written examination; submission of two case studies with supporting material; and an oral examination including a fact-finding portion, a case review and defense, and a focus on ethics. Pass rates (averaging 65% to 70%) are reported to be comparable with those of other professions (i.e., medical boards and Bar associations; see Bieliauskas & Matthews, 1997).

In 1985, largely through the efforts of Manfred Meier, then-President of the ABCN, an affiliation between ABCN and the American Board of Professional Psychology (ABPP) was established. It should be noted that the ABPP recognizes nine other specialties: Behavioral Psychology, Clinical Psychology, Counseling Psychology, Family Psychology, Forensic Psychology, Health Psychology, Industrial/Organizational Psychology, Psychoanalysis in

Psychology, and School Psychology. The ABPP has been the principal certifying Board for psychology since 1947 (Bieliauskas & Matthews, 1997).

The American Board of Professional Neuropsychology (ABPN) was incorporated in Georgia in 1982, but began more formal examination of neuropsychologists in 1991. The ABPN and ABCN have similar requirements, except that ABPN does not require a written examination. Minimum requirements for applying are 3 years of professional experience in neuropsychology. The ABCN and the ABPN are the only two recognized board-certifying bodies in neuropsychology. The consumer should be aware of the recent proliferation of *vanity boards* that do not have the endorsement of recognized psychological organizations.

New developments include a call by Johnstone and Farmer (1997) for additional training guidelines that emphasize the need for neuropsychologists to be better informed about disability and vocational issues; ecological validity; and interventions, programs, and resources that enhance clinical practice (see chapter 8). These suggestions were superceded in 1998 by the policy statement of the Houston Conference on Specialty Education and Training in Clinical Neuropsychology in Houston, Texas. The aim of the conference was to advance "an aspirational, integrated model of specialty training in clinical neuropsychology" (Hannay et al., 1998) and, thereby, to enhance the uniformity across training programs provided to students of clinical neuropsychology. Participants were recruited from an announcement in the *APA Monitor*, members of APA Division 40 and NAN, and directors of internship training programs.

According to the policy statement, the *knowledge base* with which a neuropsychologist should be familiar includes the following:

1. A generic psychology core (statistics and methodology; learning, cognition, and perception; social psychology and personality; biological bases of behavior; life span development; history; and cultural, individual differences, and diversity).
2. A generic clinical core (psychopathology; psychometric theory; interview and assessment techniques; intervention techniques; professional ethics).
3. Foundations for the study of brain-behavior relationships (functional neuroanatomy; neurological and related disorders including their etiology, pathology, course, and treatment; nonneurological conditions

affecting central nervous system (CNS) functioning; neuroimaging and other neurodiagnostic techniques; neurochemistry of behavior [e.g., psychopharmacology], neuropsychology of behavior).

4. Foundations for the practice of clinical neuropsychology (specialized neuropsychological assessment techniques, specialized neuropsychological intervention techniques, research design and analysis in neuropsychology, professional issues and ethics in neuropsychology, practical implications of neuropsychological conditions).

Core skills with which a clinical neuropsychologist should be familiar include the following:

1. Assessment (information gathering, history taking, selection and administration of tests and measures, interpretation and diagnosis, treatment planning, report writing, providing feedback, recognition of multicultural issues).
2. Treatment and interventions (identification of intervention targets, specification of intervention needs, formulation of an intervention plan, implementation of the plan, monitoring and adjustment to the plan as needed, assessment of the outcome, recognition of multicultural issues).
3. Consultation with patients, families, medical colleagues, agencies, and so forth (effective basic communication, such as listening, explaining, and negotiating; determination and clarification of referral issues; education of referral sources regarding neuropsychological services, such as strengths and weaknesses; communication of evaluation results and recommendations; education of patients and families regarding services and disorders).
4. Research (selection of appropriate research topics, review of relevant literature, design of research, execution of research, monitoring of progress, evaluation of outcome, communication of results).
5. Teaching and supervision (methods of effective teaching; plan and design of courses and curricula; use of effective educational technologies; use of effective supervision methodologies, such as assessment, intervention, and research; acknowledging that the relative weightings of these dimensions may vary from one program to another).

To complete the education and training necessary for independent practice in the specialty of clinical neuropsychology, requirements for a postdoctoral residency (with specific staffing needs and clinical experiences) are delineated. For further information, the reader is referred to Hannay et al. (1998). They allude to the possibility that subspecialties in clinical neuropsychology (e.g., pediatric, geriatric, and rehabilitation neuropsychology) will also be recognized eventually. Finally, "All specialists in clinical neuropsychology are expected to engage in annual continuing education...to enhance and maintain the already established competence of clinical neuropsychologists by updating previously acquired knowledge and skills" (Hannay et al., p. 164). It should be noted that the emphasis is on the maintenance and expansion of an *already established competence*, rather than suggesting that continuing education provides an adequate basis for *respecialization* in neuropsychology. Workshops for programs that do not meet the criteria established by the Task Force or the education and training conference in Houston, Texas, but that, nonetheless, offer *certification* in neuropsychology, provide a questionable basis for neuropsychological training; as such, they are misleading to consumers of neuropsychological services.

It should be emphasized that not all qualified neuropsychologists who would meet eligibility criteria to sit for board certification have done so. There may be a number of factors that have precluded neuropsychologists from seeking diplomate status. Clearly, this does not mean that they are not competent to practice; in the interest of being readily identifiable to the public, it is hoped that these individuals will take the necessary and important final steps to sit for the board examination at the earliest opportunity.

The doctoral (PhD) degree requirement as well as Diplomate Status is essentially limited to Canada and the United States. The practice of clinical neuropsychology differs from country to country. For example, in Italy, virtually all practicing clinical neuropsychologists hold a medical degree and have a specialty in neurology. In some countries, a Bachelor's degree in Psychology qualifies the individual to practice the profession. A Master's degree is now beginning to be recognized in several countries (e.g., Mexico, Spain) as a requirement for specializing in a variety of psychological domains such as family therapy, industrial/organizational psychology, and, more recently, neuropsychology.

The Clinical Neuropsychologist's Perspective in Contrast With Other Disciplines

The neuropsychological report should capture the unique perspective on the client provided by the clinical neuropsychologist. There are a number of professionals who are involved in the assessment and care of children and adults with known or suspected central nervous system (CNS) dysfunction. It might also be pointed out that the INS is essentially a multidisciplinary organization, to which not only psychologists, but also neurologists, speech-language pathologists, and professionals in other disciplines belong. As Cytowic (1996) remarks, "The field itself that we are discussing is called neuropsychology, behavioral neurology, behavioral neurobiology, neuropsychiatry, neuroimmunopsychiatry, and other permutations of these root words" (p. 19). However, in each case, the training and orientation of the professional will differ as a function of the discipline. As a consequence, the information provided will differ accordingly. We therefore need to distinguish between the general subject area and the educational background and training of those whose professional activities relate to the field, broadly defined. In short, a neuropsychological report should reflect the *thinking* of a qualified neuropsychologist who meets the training criteria as described herein.

The education and training conference in Houston also produced the following definition of a clinical neuropsychologist: "A clinical neuropsychologist is a professional psychologist trained in the science of brain-behavior relationships. The clinical neuropsychologist specializes in the application of assessment and intervention principles based on the scientific study of human behavior across the lifespan as it relates to normal and abnormal functioning of the central nervous system" (Hannay et al., 1998, p. 161).

In contrast, clinical psychologists work with clinical populations and have a primary focus on intervention (e.g., therapy, behavioral interventions). They will typically have less familiarity and concern with underlying neural mechanisms and neuropsychological syndromes such as the apraxias, agnosias, aphasias, and other cognitive deficits. Although both clinical psychologists and clinical neuropsychologists may administer tests of intellectual functioning, the clinical psychologist emphasizes the psychosocial aspects. There are, however, different levels of analysis that can be drawn on for understanding and predicting behavior. The clinical neuropsychologist, although sensitive to the psychosocial level of analysis, also provides a detailed description of underlying cognitive functions in relation to neural mechanisms.

Clinical neuropsychological evaluations differ from *psychoeducational* and *school evaluations* in specific and important ways. Psychoeducational evaluations are usually requested when academic problems become evident. Typically, they consist of an assessment of academic achievement using standardized achievement tests, such as the Woodcock-Johnson Achievement Tests (Woodcock, McGrew, & Mather, 2001) and the Wechsler Individual Achievement Test (1992), together with an assessment of general intellectual ability (e.g., various instruments by Wechsler). There is an attempt to determine whether a discrepancy between capacity and attainment is present, to identify academic area(s) that are affected, and to propose suggestions for remediation.

The clinical *neuropsychological evaluation*, in contrast, addresses the underlying cognitive processes that affect performance of functions required for academic development. For instance, a neuropsychological assessment will address various aspects of attention, memory, language, visuospatial, sensorimotor, and interpersonal processing. Importantly, it also investigates executive functions (e.g., prioritizing, planning, inhibiting, cognitive flexibility, and self-monitoring) that are critical in everyday learning and active problem-solving situations. Based on an understanding of these cognitive functions and their dynamic interactions with each other, the clinical neuropsychologist can provide a unique perspective within the educational team to assist the student in maximizing goals. As a professional studying brain-behavior relationships, the clinical neuropsychologist utilizes this information in assessing strengths and weaknesses for diagnosis, clarification of behavioral profiles, and identification of appropriate interventions.

Cognitive psychologists are specifically interested in information processing within normal populations and make little, if any, attempt to trace the flow of information through the nervous system. The brain has little relevance within this level of analysis. Although cognitive psychology has played an important and influential role in the understanding of neuropsychological syndromes, the focus of the two disciplines is on quite different aspects of behavior. *Clinical neuropsychologists*, typically working with clinical populations, attempt to relate cognitive functions to neuropsychological syndromes in order to identify affected neuroanatomical structures and functions; conversely, knowledge of localized pathology and disorders provides a framework within which cognitive, affective, and behavioral symptoms can be identified and further assessed.

Nonetheless, it is important to recognize that no amount of sophistication or refinement in neuroimaging techniques will ever substitute for actual neuropsychological assessment. Specific thoughts and feelings of the individual are always unique to that person and do not have a one-to-one correspondence with demonstrated lesion localization. For example, a person with multiple sclerosis will have multiple lesions on an MRI or CT scan, but this information is not particularly helpful in characterizing the patient's memory, problem-solving skills, or other aspects of cognition, affect, or behavior. To quote once more from Cytowic (1996): "Those who assume that neuropsychological analysis must be inferior to the capacity of computed tomography, magnetic resonance imaging (MRI), or some other technology to identify brain lesions might consider that as autopsy series once revealed brain lesions that went undetected in life, so also do modern technologies expose structural abnormalities that are clinically silent. Imaging is not the final word. It is also a fatal error to assume that function is strictly localized or that discrete lesions on scans are isolated. By this I mean a failure to consider the multiplex character of neurophysiology, diaschisis, reciprocal interaction with anatomically remote areas, and even restoration of function. Furthermore, the behavioral sequelae of cardiac arrest and heart-lung bypass, substrate deficiency, poisoning, and metabolic aberrations exist without any structural footprint at all. Technology has not made the practitioner's intelligence passé. Properly done, neuropsychological analysis remains a powerful tool." (p. 11)

Experimental neuropsychologists and *cognitive scientists* lack the clinical training of the clinical neuropsychologist to treat or assess clinical populations. *Psychiatrists* are medical specialists who have a primary focus on psychopathology. Diagnosis is principally based on the mental status examination (MSE), bioassays, and interviews, and treatment typically involves psychopharmacological and psychotherapeutic interventions. The clinical neuropsychologist, on the other hand, provides an in-depth analysis via an assessment of the interrelationship of cognition and affect, in part to clarify questions of differential diagnosis and in part to better describe the person's capabilities and to make recommendations for treatment. A diagnosis is reached by comparing the person's level of function to age, gender, and education-matched peers and by developing a profile that has diagnostic significance. Ironically, the most common differential diagnosis that neuropsychologists are asked to address in psychiatric settings is that of determining whether a person is depressed, suffers from a dementing disorder, or both (i.e., the old *functional/organic* dichotomy). Developments in the field of neuropsychology have yielded improved assessment techniques and more accurate characterization of these syndromes. Screening tools (e.g., the Bender-Gestalt) are unable to identify reversible dementias or to provide measures that are adequately sensitive to different syndromes. (For further discussion of this issue, see chapter 4; and Lezak, 1995, pp. 160-165).

A subset of psychiatrists identify themselves as neuropsychiatrists. They have established the American Neuropsychiatric Association and the *Journal of the American Neuropsychiatric Association*. Additional journals have emerged such as *Neuropsychiatry*; *Journal of Neuropsychiatry and Clinical Neurosciences*; *Journal of Neurology*; *Neuropsychology and Neuropsychiatry*; *Neuropsychology*; and *Behavioral Neurology*.

Behavioral neurologists are physicians who are also specifically interested in brain-behavior relationships; they have formed the Behavioral Neurology Society. Unlike traditional neurologists, who tend to focus less on higher cortical functions, behavioral neurologists are specifically concerned with neuropsychological syndromes and, in fact, as alluded to earlier, often characterize themselves as neuropsychologists. This raises the distinction of the more broadly defined field of *neuropsychology / behavioral neurology* versus the specific training of the practitioners and researchers, each providing their unique contribution.

For convenience, and by virtue of growing consensus, *clinical neuropsychologists* here refer to psychologists who have specialized training. Clinical neuropsychologists differ from behavioral neurologists in that they are professionally trained as psychologists and are well versed in the development and interpretation of standardized and experimental assessment procedures as well as being involved in qualitative research regarding neuropsychological syndromes (e.g., the Boston Diagnostic Aphasia Examination, Goodglass & Kaplan, 1972). In the words of Sattler (1992) "Neuropsychological assessments increase our understanding of the psychological effects of brain injury" (p. 689). In practice, behavioral neurologists and neuropsychologists complement each other and often work effectively as a team, with one providing a more medical focus and the other a more psychological one.

Conclusion

Neuropsychology can be broadly construed as a field of interest to which many disciplines contribute. Usually, the term clinical neuropsychologist specifically denotes a psychologist who has a background that is consistent with the Houston Conference on Specialty Education and Training in Clinical Neuropsychology. Clinical neuropsychological evaluations and neuropsychological reports are within the province of clinical neuropsychologists.

The ABCN and the ABPN are examining boards that award the Diplomate in Clinical Neuropsychology, so that nonneuropsychologists (i.e., consumers of neuropsychological services) can identify individuals with essential competencies in the field. Rosters of individuals who have been credentialed by the ABCN and the ABPN are available to the public.[1] These lists are periodically updated; however, bear in mind that individuals credentialed since the most recent examination may not have been added to the list yet.

Individuals who are competent and qualified neuropsychologists may not yet have been certified or may be practicing in other countries. In these instances, the consumer must rely on obtaining a copy of that clinician's curriculum vita (CV), the recommendations of others to determine whether the clinician's background and training meet desired criteria, or both. Because this is a cumbersome and unreliable process, it is predicted that consumers in North America will turn more and more to board certification as a marker of competence.

[1]The most recent Directory of Diplomates from the ABCN can be obtained by writing to ABCN, Dept. of Psychiatry (B2954, CFOB), University of Michigan Health Systems, 1500 East Medical Centre Drive, Ann Arbor, MI 48109-0704 (Telephone 734.936.8269). A list of ABCN Diplomates can also be found on the Internet at http://www.med.umich.edu/abcn. For a directory of diplomates of the ABPN, contact Michael J. Raymond, PhD, Executive Director, ABPN, Allied Services, John Heinz Institute of Rehabilitation Medicine, 150 Mundy Street, P.O. Box 2096, Wilkes-Barre Township, PA 18702 (Telephone 717.826.3771). The Internet address for ABPN is http://abpn.net.

2

THE CONSUMER'S POINT OF VIEW

Paul E. Finn, Elisabeth J. Moes, and Edith Kaplan

Introduction

Although much has been written on the development of the specialty of neuropsychology, there is very little information on either the way neuropsychologists communicate their findings or the way neuropsychological reports are perceived by referral sources. This chapter presents the results of a national survey[1] of referral sources that focused on the perceived importance of certain types of information (e.g., personality assessment ratings, or severity of disability) and how the format of a report (e.g., length, information included in the history, data presentation) influences its perceived *user-friendliness* (see Appendix 2-1 at the end of this chapter). The authors were specifically interested in assessing the views of individuals who are familiar with neuropsychological reports; in order to maximize the validity and usefulness of the feedback, a deliberate attempt was made to identify representative referral sources.

The survey also addressed the way a group of neuropsychologists perceive the importance of certain types of data and their presentation, thus allowing the researchers to compare and contrast the views of report writers (i.e., neuropsychologists) with those of *consumers* from different professional specialties. Finally, information obtained from different specialties (e.g., neurologists vs. psychiatrists) was compared to see where

[1]The authors are indebted to Barbara Bartlett, faculty secretary at St. Anselm College, for her assistance with this project.

significant differences in perspective and preferences might exist, with the possibility that reports could be tailored in such a way as to maximize their utility to the referring individual. This could involve eliminating information thought to be redundant, focusing on relevant concerns, and maximizing the ease and efficiency with which data is communicated. In addition, it helps neuropsychologists, as a discipline, to know who our audience is most likely to be, what types of referral questions are most common, and how referring specialties differ in their focus on, and perception of, neuropsychological issues. To the best of the researchers' knowledge, this survey appears to be a first of its kind in attempting to elicit direct feedback from referral sources.

Before presenting the research, it may be helpful to recognize that changes in the profession over the last few decades provide an important historical context within which neuropsychology, as a discipline, is perceived. This is true for providers of neuropsychological assessments and consumers alike, as can be readily ascertained by the change in views as to what constitutes an acceptable level of training for neuropsychologists and the required scope of an assessment (see chapters 1 and 4). Indeed, almost all previous relevant studies have sought to document important characteristics of the discipline. Thus, prior surveys have focused on topics including *the education and training of providers of neuropsychological services* (Goldberg & McNamara, 1984; Golden & Kuperman, 1980; Guilmette, Faust, Hart, & Arkes, 1990; Lubin & Sokoloff, 1983; McCaffrey & Isaac, 1984; Putnam & Anderson, 1994; Sheer & Lubin, 1980; Slay & Valdivia, 1988; Solomon, Hale-Friske, McCaffrey, & Isaac, 1985; Sweet & Moberg, 1990; Sweet, Moberg, & Westergaard, 1996); *typical practice mix*—research, assessment, psychotherapy, teaching, rehabilitation (Guilmette et al., 1990; Putnam & Anderson, 1994; Putnam & DeLuca, 1990; Sweet & Moberg, 1990; Sweet et al., 1996); *typical work settings* (Guilmette et al., 1990; Hartlage, 1985; Hartlage & Telzrow, 1980; Putnam & Anderson, 1994; Sweet & Moberg, 1990); *populations served* (Chelune & Edwards, 1981; Sweet & Moberg, 1990; Sweet, Westergaard, & Moberg, 1995); *salary, average charge for assessments, and income source* (Chelune & Edwards, 1981; Guilmette et al., 1990; Putnam, 1989; Putnam & Anderson, 1994; Putnam & DeLuca, 1990; Sweet & Moberg, 1990); and *the impact of managed care* (Sweet et al., 1995).

In addition, there have been studies of *the average number of assessments performed each month* (Guilmette et al., 1990; Hartlage, 1985; Putnam &

Anderson, 1994; Sweet & Moberg, 1990; Sweet et al., 1996); *the average number of hours spent on each assessment and use of technicians* (Sweet & Moberg, 1990; Sweet et al., 1996); *test instruments commonly used* (Craig, 1979; Goldberg & McNamara, 1984; Guilmette & Faust, 1991; Guilmette et al., 1990; Hartlage & Telzrow, 1980; Retzlaff, Butler, & Vanderploeg, 1992; Sellers & Nadler, 1992; Slick & Craig, 1991; Sweet & Moberg, 1990), *theoretical orientation, figures wielding the greatest influence, or both* (Hartlage, 1985; Retzlaff et al., 1992; Sayette & Mayne, 1990; Sweet et al., 1996), and *journals and books most frequently read and cited* (Sweet & Moberg, 1990; Sweet et al., 1996).

Although these surveys have provided important information about neuropsychologists and neuropsychology as a discipline, they do not address the question of how others perceive neuropsychologists. Now that neuropsychology has developed some degree of maturity as a science and clinical practice, it is appropriate to look outside the confines of our discipline to take into account the perspectives of others, particularly those who have fostered its growth.

The authors were able to locate a few articles that have bearing on the issue of how neuropsychology is perceived by other disciplines. Duffy and Camlin (1995) sent a survey to "all of the 190 directors of adult psychiatry residency training programs in the United States" (p. 291). The survey "was intended to evaluate the respondents' opinions on the validity and identity of neuropsychiatry and of training in that area as a subspecialty" (p. 291). They received responses from 90 directors (a 46% response rate). When asked whether the ability to understand and interpret neuropsychological test results should be a required skill of any graduating psychiatry resident, 80% responded *Yes* and 11% responded *No*. This compares with 49% who thought the ability to interpret a head CT scan should be required, 41% who thought the same for a head MRI, 26% who responded *Yes* for the ability to read an electroencephalogram (EEG), and 20% who thought single proton emission computed tomography (SPECT) scan interpretation should be required. In support of this endorsement of neuropsychological testing, 87% indicated that their program provided a core didactic curriculum in neuropsychological assessment, compared with 80% who provided the same for the neurological examination, and 53% who provided training in neuroimaging. (Despite this level of interest and support, 13% of respondents thought that residents graduating from their program were deficient in their ability to understand and interpret neuropsychological test results.)

Coffey et al. (1995), as members of the American Neuropsychiatric Association Committee on Research, conducted a survey in 1993 of its 227 members as well as the 370 members of the British Neuropsychiatry Association. Of the 597 members contacted, 101 responded (a 16.9% response rate). Respondents were asked to "describe how they conducted standardized diagnostic assessments and to list the instruments they employ to assess a patient's psychiatric, neurologic, and cognitive status. Information was also requested about the respondents' clinical specialty and practice setting, and the demographics of the patient treated" (p. 288). The majority (73.3%) of respondents were psychiatrists, almost a quarter were neurologists, 5% were neuropsychologists, and 16.8% described themselves as *other* (some respondents checked more than one description). Over half (54.5%) indicated that they used some type of cognitive measure to assess clinical outcome in patients with neuropsychiatric illness. Of these, 48.3% indicated that they used formal neuropsychology, although the article did not make clear whether they employed these neuropsychological techniques themselves or whether they obtained a consultation from a neuropsychologist. Over half (56.9%) used the Mini-Mental State Exam (MMSE; Folstein, Folstein, & McHugh, 1975).

In 1996, the Therapeutics and Technology Assessment Subcommittee of the American Academy of Neurology published a report in the journal *Neurology*, entitled "Assessment: Neuropsychological Testing of Adults. Considerations for Neurologists." This report endeavored to describe "the appropriate application and limitations of neuropsychological testing, specific disorders where evaluation is pertinent, and issues surrounding neuropsychological consultation to neurologists" (p. 592). The report was based on "a review of the pertinent literature, opinions, and information from experts in the field of Neurology and Neuropsychology, and input from the Academy of Neurology at large" (p. 592).

After reviewing technical issues in neuropsychological assessment (e.g., the importance of test reliability and validity and the need for demographic corrections), a brief review of specific neurologic disorders followed, with recommendations on the role of neuropsychological assessment in each disorder. A section discussing the potential advantages of neuropsychological assessment was followed by recommendations on when to obtain consultation and prescriptive remarks about what the neuropsychological evaluation should and should not do. For example, the authors concluded that numerical data should be included ("e.g., percentile of performance corrected for age and education," p. 597), and that "brevity in reporting often serves the clinician better than an extended narrative" (p. 597). In addition,

> ...administration of test batteries that are too long or too short to answer the specified questions, failure to recognize the limitations of neuropsychological tests (especially with regard to localization and diagnosis), administration of inappropriate tests or tests without proper standardization, and preparation of unhelpful reports are indications of inadequate preparation. (p. 597)

The report came to a number of controversial conclusions that sparked a flurry of protest letters to the Editor from eminent neuropsychologists. A selection of these, together with the Subcommittee's response, appeared later in the October 1997 issue of *Neurology*. Respondents to the article noted that the report contained inaccurate information and made inappropriate and unduly restrictive comments regarding the practice of neuropsychology, although the general value of neuropsychological testing was also recognized. A discussion of the specific merits and limitations of the report is beyond the scope of this chapter, and the interested reader is referred to the original articles.

The survey discussed in the next section was not designed to elicit feedback from other professionals regarding either the appropriateness of the specific test instruments used by neuropsychologists or the circumstances in which they might consider neuropsychological assessments to be more or less appropriate. Rather, it was an attempt to elicit feedback regarding general aspects of the neuropsychological report in order to be able to highlight preferences and identify the way(s) information obtained by the neuropsychologist can best be conveyed to its audience.

Method

A letter and survey form were mailed to 1,995 full NAN members who were registered in the NAN directory. (Student members and individuals residing outside the U.S. were not included). Each member was asked to return a list of the most representative referral sources he or she used and was invited to complete and return the Neuropsychology Use Survey (NUS; see Appendix 2-1 at the end of this chapter). Of all the directory registrants, 390 members returned a list of referral sources (19.54% return rate), with an average number of 3.1 sources listed (range = 1 to 8), resulting in a total of 1,203 referral sources from 42 different states. Although this rate is lower than those reported in other surveys (which average from 40% to 60% return rates), the fact that specific names and complete addresses of the respondents' top referral sources were requested may have been a deterring factor. Sixty-three NAN members completed the survey as well.

The most frequently identified referral source consisted of neurologists (410), followed by psychiatrists (200); attorneys (116); physiatrists (85); a combination of family practice, general practice, internal medicine (65); surgeons and neurosurgeons (49); physicians, not otherwise specified (36); neuropsychologists (32); rehabilitation medicine alone or with primary medicine (31); and pediatricians (30). The remainder consisted of a large number of different types of allied health professionals (e.g. case managers, rehabilitation counselors, social workers, and a judge) and nine different agencies or institutions. Three respondents failed to include the names of referral sources.

Next, the NUS was sent to each of these referral sources. Of the 1,203 referral sources, 339 returned the survey form (a 28.18% return rate). There is little data on return rates for surveys based on surveys, so it is hard to know how this figure compares with others. The highest return rates by profession were pediatricians (33%), followed by attorneys (32%), neurologists (26%), and surgeons and neurosurgeons (25%).

Using Putnam and DeLuca's (1990) method to summarize geographical distribution, the following results were obtained: North East = 122 (30.3%), North Central = 81 (20.2%), South = 104 (25.9%), and West = 88 (21.9%). Seven (1.7%) of the respondents were not identified by region.

Of the 63 original NAN respondents who completed and returned the NUS, 28 identified themselves as psychologists and 30 described themselves as neuropsychologists; the remaining 5 did not offer a description. Referral sources included 233 physicians and 37 attorneys; the remainder were in health care fields, including 24 psychologists, 13 rehabilitation counselors, 6 social workers, 6 case managers, 3 speech and language pathologists, 3 neuropsychologists, 1 person in special education, and 1 nurse. Nine individuals checked *other* without providing any further specification, and the rest did not check this category. In total, there were 402 respondents to the NUS (63 NAN members and 339 referral sources).

The overall ratio of women to men was approximately 1:3 (107 women and 298 men). The NAN respondents included 20 women and 42 men, with one person providing no gender information (i.e. a ratio of almost 1:2); of attorneys, 5 were women and 32 were men (a ratio of 1:6); and of the remaining health providers 82 were women and 219 were men (a ratio of 1:2.7). Men were older, but only by 5 years on average.

In the present survey, physicians, as a group, represented 69% (N = 233) of the referral sources who completed the survey, followed by attorneys (N = 37, 12.3%) and then referring psychologists (N = 24, 7%).

The responding physicians included 108 neurologists (46%), 36 psychiatrists (15%), 36 other physicians (15%), 31 physiatrists (13%), 12 surgeons (5%), and 10 pediatricians (4%).

Results

In the following section, results are presented according to the various questions asked of the respondents. Because not all respondents replied to every question, the number of respondents in each category is indicated wherever possible.

Respondent Characteristics

As a group, the referral sources appear to have good familiarity with neuropsychological reports. Fully half (51.5%) reported seeing more than 20 reports a year, and an additional 21.59% reported seeing between 11 and 20 reports a year. Only 13.25% see less than 6 reports a year. Of the 37 responding attorneys, 19% reported seeing more than 20 reports a year, but 35% reported seeing less than 6 reports a year. Thus attorneys, as a group, tend to see fewer reports than health care providers. For the physician groups with a sample size greater than 30, 57% of neurologists, 74% of physiatrists, 56% of psychiatrists, and 39% of other physicians reported seeing more than 20 reports a year. For physicians who see less than 6 reports a year, the results are as follows: neurologists, 8%; psychiatrists, 6%; other physicians, 14%. No physiatrist reported seeing less than 6 reports a year. Of the 30 allied health providers, 33% reported seeing over 20 reports a year, whereas 23% see less than 6 reports a year.

Of the 24 referring psychologists, 42% reported seeing more than 20 reports a year. Of the 33 NAN members who specifically identified themselves as neuropsychologists, 56% reported seeing more than 20 reports a year, whereas 17% reported seeing less than 6 reports a year.

When the NAN members were divided into two groups, those who checked *psychologist* and those who checked *neuropsychologist,* and then compared, only a few minor differences emerged. There were disproportionately more male neuropsychologists (83%) than psychologists (57%). There was a nonsignificant tendency for neuropsychologists to disagree more with the statement that reports are appropriately and meaningfully organized (47% stated that this was *rarely* or *never* the case, compared with 19% of psychologists, $p = .063$). There was also a tendency for neuropsychologists to feel that testing tasks are too long and are a hardship for clients ($p = .051$). The only significant difference was that neuropsychologists were less likely to agree that findings should be summarized at the beginning of the report ($p = .022$). In other respects, the two groups were relatively homogeneous.

Overall, 48% of the referral sources based their judgments on work generated by four or more neuropsychologists (51% for attorneys, 43% of allied health, 47% of neurologists, 45% of physiatrists, 40% of psychiatrists, 47% of the physician group, 56% of psychologists, and 85% of neuropsychologists). Only 10% of all referral sources based their views on reports written by just one neuropsychologist. Over 79% of physicians had reviewed over 10 reports in the average year, and 92% had reviewed more than 7 reports.

Neurologists had incorporated neuropsychological findings into their work over a significantly longer period than either physiatrists or general physicians ($F = 4.716$; $p = .000$). Neurologists averaged just over 16 years, compared with psychiatrists (almost 15 years) and surgeons (13.5 years). Others averaged over 10 years, but less than 12 years. More than a third (36%) of the neurologists had used neuropsychological findings for over 20 years, 29% had used them for at least 10 years but not 20 years, and only 10% had done so for 6 years or less. In contrast, a third of the attorneys had incorporated neuropsychological findings for 6 years or less, and 72% had used them for 10 years or less, suggesting that there is increasing interest among this group. On the other hand, 19% reported having used neuropsychological findings in their work for 20 years or more.

The majority of all respondents (61%, $n = 245$) work exclusively with adults, or with both adults and geriatrics, or exclusively with geriatrics. The remaining 39% ($n = 154$) either work exclusively with infants, children, or adolescents, or with a combination of young, adult, and geriatric populations. The percentage of practitioners who see either infants, children, or adolescents (or some combination of these) in at least part of their practice are as follows: pediatricians, 100%, psychologists, 58%; attorneys, 53%; general physician category, 43%; allied health care, 33%; psychiatrists, 28%; neurologists, 24%, physiatrists, 19%; and surgeons, 17%.

Respondents were asked to rate how frequently they referred (on a 5-point scale from *Never*, *Rarely*, *Sometimes*, *Frequently*, to *Always*) for each of the following areas: cognitive screening, lesion localization, differential diagnosis, repeated testing or monitoring of clinical change over time, behavioral management, rehabilitation planning, litigation, competence, educational planning, disability determination, and benefit determination. These ratings were converted into mean scores and then rank ordered. Table 2-1 presents the results for physicians, attorneys, allied health professionals, and psychologists.

In Table 2-1, with the exception of the physicians, the modest sample sizes indicate the need for caution in interpreting results. Across all groups, screening of cognitive functions was the most common reason for referral, followed by retesting to monitor clinical change over time, differential diagnosis, rehabilitation planning, and disability determination. Educational planning, litigation, and behavioral management concerns followed, in that order. Competency assessment, benefit determination, and, finally, lesion localization, were the least commonly cited referral reasons (also in that order).

Referral sources were asked (in an open-ended question) to indicate from which professions they typically request information about the cognitive status of their clients (patients). For multiple responses, only the first two responses were entered, and they are presented in Table 2-2 as first and second entries, based on the order in which they were entered on the survey.

Neuropsychologists and psychologists are predominantly (75% of the time) preferred for the evaluation of cognitive status, with 54% selecting neuropsychologists as their first choice and 18% selecting psychologists. Collectively, they were listed 40% of the time as a second choice. After neuropsychologists and psychologists, the next most frequent referral choices were neurologists and psychiatrists. Neurologists were listed by 7% of the respondents as first choice and by 12% of those who provided a second choice. Psychiatrists were selected as a first choice 4% of the time and as a second choice 15% of the time. Other disciplines (e.g., speech/language pathology, occupational therapy, nursing, teaching, or other medical specialties)

Table 2-1
Rank order of Frequency of Type of Referral to Neuropsychologists by Other Professionals

Type of referral	Physician[a]		Attorney[b]		Allied health[c]		Psychologist[d]	
	Rank	*M*	Rank	*M*	Rank	*M*	Rank	*M*
1. Repeat test/monitor change	1	3.46	6	3.03	7	3.17	3	2.64
2. Screening cognitive functions	2	3.24	3	3.52	1	3.97	2	2.96
3. Differential diagnosis	3	3.20	4	3.19	5	3.33	1	3.00
4. Rehabilitation planning	4	2.99	5	3.13	2	3.90	6	2.28
5. Behavioral management	5	2.79	10	2.50	3	3.47	7	2.27
6. Educational planning	6	2.78	11	2.41	4	3.44	4	2.58
7. Disability determination	7	2.65	2	4.11	6	3.31	5	2.56
8. Competence	8	2.58	9	2.82	8	3.10	10	1.96
9. Litigation	9	2.39	1	4.60	9	2.29	11	1.83
10. Lesion localization	10	2.18	8	3.00	11	2.17	9	2.08
11. Benefit determination	11	2.11	7	3.00	10	2.25	8	2.16

[a]n = 238. [b]n = 33. [c]n = 30. [d]n = 27; includes those who were reported as referral sources and non-NAN members.

Table 2-2
Percentage of Neuropsychologists and Psychologists Selected for Referrals by Other Professionals[a]

Profession (n)	First referral choice				Second referral choice			
	Neuropsychologists	Psychologists	n/N[b]	% Total	Neuropsychologists	Psychologists	n/N[c]	% Total
Surgeon	9	1	10/11	91%	1	2	3/5	60%
Psychologist	6	9	15/23	65%	2	5	7/15	47%
Psychiatrist	16	7	23/29	79%	7	6	13/20	65%
Allied health	10	7	17/27	63%	2	4	6/20	30%
Attorney	16	3	19/33	58%	4	7	11/27	41%
Physician	15	5	20/29	69%	3	4	7/19	37%
Physiatrist	14	8	22/30	73%	3	4	7/26	27%
Pediatrician	1	5	6/7	86%	1	2	2/5	40%
Neurologist	64	10	74/86	86%	3	5	5/37	14%

[a]For assessment of cognitive status. [b]N = number of individuals who provided a first choice. [c]N = number of individuals who provided a second choice.

failed to garner even 1% of the vote as either a first or second choice for cognitive evaluations.

The Neuropsychological Report

When respondents were asked what they considered an appropriate length for a neuropsychological report, many answered with a range; most ranges were small (e.g., 7-9 pages). For statistical purposes, the mean of the range was entered. Ranges were truncated when no upper limits were set (e.g., if 7+ pages was noted, a 7 was entered; this represented only 4 of 357 cases). Finally, with the exception of one specified range of 10 to 50 pages, the highest value was 13 pages; to minimize skewness due to an outlier, a value of 13 pages was assigned to that response. Table 2-3 presents data on the respondents' preferred length for a neuropsychological report. The responses are compared with those of the NAN neuropsychologists to assess for significant differences of opinion.

Table 2-3
Length of a Neuropsychological Report Preferred by Other Professionals

Profession	*n*	Mean length (pages)	*SD*	Significance[a]
Allied health	28	5.5	2.2	*ns*
Attorney	30	6.9	2.8	*ns*
Neurologist	93	4.2	1.9	$p = .000$
Pediatrician	9	4.4	2.6	*ns*
Physiatrist	27	5.8	2.3	*ns*
Physician	35	4.1	2.0	$p = .000$
Psychiatrist	31	4.7	2.4	$p = .04$
Psychologist	49	5.8	2.9	*ns*
Surgeon	11	3.4	1.4	$p = .003$
NAN Member	31	6.4	2.7	—

Note. $F(9, 334) = 7.8, p = .000$
[a]As compared with survey responses of NAN neuropsychologist respondents.

As can be seen from the data presented in Table 2-3, surgeons, neurologists, psychiatrists, and a mixed group of physicians (not belonging to the other three categories) believe that neuropsychological reports should be shorter than neuropsychologists think they should be. Although not reaching statistical significance, it is worth noting that all other groups except attorneys provided a preferred report length that was shorter than that specified by neuropsychologists. Attorneys seem quite satisfied with the length of reports they currently receive.

For purposes of data summary and analysis, respondents were first broken into three broad categories, comprised of the NAN members (n = 64); attorneys (n = 37); and a third category of physicians (n = 231) and other health providers (n = 71), grouped together. In Table 2-4, ratings for all the questions on the survey are listed (with the χ^2 values for each), comparing NAN members, health professionals (providers), and attorneys. Further analyses were then conducted to assess differences between professions and specialties. Gender differences were also analyzed separately. Chi-square values are reported for each survey question.

Overall, based on the findings reported in Table 2-4, there was considerable agreement between the groups. Over 80% of the health providers thought reports are *always* or *frequently* appropriately and meaningfully organized, as did 73% of the attorneys. Respondents agreed that findings should not be summarized at the beginning of the report, and that diagnostic impressions should also be included in the summary. Respondents wanted a list of the tests administered and believed that the specific findings for each test administered are important. (Attorneys were quite emphatic in this regard.) Attorneys were uniformly opposed to the idea of receiving a one page summary, and this was rejected by neuropsychologists and other health providers as well.

Neuropsychologists, in particular, but also other providers, tend to disagree with the notion that graphs and summary tables should only be provided for significant findings, with between 22% and 32% believing that this may sometimes be appropriate; attorneys are more evenly divided on this issue. Respondents are evenly divided in the belief that graphs, summary tables, or both should be provided for *all* tests. Sixty-five percent of health care providers and 72% of attorneys *frequently* or *always* prefer percentiles as a means of score presentation. Generally, respondents agreed that test scores should be provided on a summary sheet (see chapter 7 for a further discussion of the debate as to whether scores should or should not be provided).

Interestingly, whereas most respondents agreed that codes from the ninth revision of the International Classification of Diseases (*ICD-9*; World Health Organization, 1977) are sometimes, but usually not very useful, respondents were divided on the need to include diagnoses from the fourth

Table 2-4
Survey Responses of NAN Members Compared With Those of Referring Attorneys and Health Providers

Item	Profession	Response					χ^2
		Never	Rarely	Sometimes	Frequently	Always	
1. Reports are appropriately and meaningfully organized.	NAN[a]	0.0	3.3	27.9	55.6	13.1	p = .126
	Attorney[b]	0.0	0.0	27.0	59.5	13.5	
	Provider[c]	0.0	1.4	17.1	56.4	24.7	
2. Findings are best summarized at the beginning of the report.	NAN	18.3	46.7	20.0	8.3	6.8	p = .813
	Attorney	13.5	37.8	21.6	18.9	8.1	
	Provider	15.2	37.3	22.4	15.5	9.7	
3. Diagnostic impressions of brain-behavior relationships are best provided in the summary.	NAN	0.0	6.7	16.7	45.0	31.7	p = .721
	Attorney	0.0	3.0	30.3	42.4	24.2	
	Provider	1.0	6.6	19.4	49.1	23.9	
4. I would prefer just the basic findings with no extensive explanations.	NAN	**19.7**	**26.2**	**31.1**	**16.4**	**6.6**	p = .001
	Attorney	**61.1**	**25.0**	**5.6**	**02.8**	**5.6**	
	Provider	**31.9**	**33.9**	**18.0**	**5.6**	**3.7**	
5. A one page summary is sufficient for me.	NAN	**30.0**	**45.0**	**10.0**	**10.0**	**5.5**	p = .001
	Attorney	**72.2**	**22.2**	**5.6**	**00.0**	**0.0**	
	Provider	**37.5**	**30.1**	**17.6**	**10.1**	**4.7**	
6. Listing of tests administered is important.	NAN	4.9	4.9	9.8	19.7	60.7	p = .071
	Attorney	0.0	2.7	5.4	16.2	75.7	
	Provider	1.3	9.3	13.3	24.7	51.3	
7. I need actual test scores.	NAN	**3.3**	**4.9**	**18.0**	**34.4**	**39.34**	p = .000
	Attorney	**2.8**	**2.8**	**22.2**	**16.7**	**55.6**	
	Provider	**7.7**	**23.1**	**22.1**	**18.4**	**28.4**	
8. Tests scores should be presented as percentiles.	NAN	**9.8**	**11.5**	**32.8**	**31.1**	**14.8**	p = .002
	Attorney	**2.8**	**0.0**	**25.0**	**22.2**	**50.0**	
	Provider	**2.8**	**8.3**	**23.4**	**35.9**	**29.7**	

(continued)

Table 2-4 (continued)
Survey Responses of NAN Members Compared With Those of Referring Attorneys and Health Providers

Item	Profession	Never	Rarely	Sometimes	Frequently	Always	χ^2
9. Test scores should be presented as scaled scores.	Nan	9.8	8.2	26.2	27.9	27.9	$p = .086$
	Attorney	8.8	2.9	29.4	17.6	41.1	
	Provider	6.0	17.7	28.6	25.8	21.9	
10. Test scores should be on a summary sheet.	NAN	4.9	11.5	29.5	26.2	27.9	$p = .147$
	Attorney	8.6	2.9	20.0	20.0	48.6	
	Provider	3.9	12.3	18.7	32.7	32.4	
11. Graphs/summary tables for *only* significant findings should be presented.	Nan	**16.4**	**39.3**	**31.1**	**6.6**	**6.6**	$p = .025$
	Attorney	**22.6**	**12.9**	**22.6**	**19.4**	**22.6**	
	Provider	**16.1**	**27.7**	**24.2**	**21.1**	**10.9**	
12. Graphs/summary tables for all tests should be presented.	NAN	8.2	32.8	26.2	16.4	16.4	$p = .359$
	Attorney	8.8	20.6	23.5	14.7	32.4	
	Provider	15.0	25.9	22.0	19.9	17.1	
13. Examples of client responses are important.	NAN	1.7	11.7	31.7	33.3	21.7	$p = .640$
	Attorney	2.9	11.4	20.0	40.0	25.7	
	Provider	4.1	10.5	33.2	37.3	14.9	
14. Specific findings for each test administered are important.	NAN	**1.6**	**18.0**	**26.2**	**29.5**	**24.6**	$p = .001$
	Attorney	**2.9**	**8.8**	**5.9**	**26.5**	**55.9**	
	Provider	**3.1**	**11.6**	**31.4**	**33.1**	**20.8**	
15. The report makes clear how the cognitive functioning translates into an understanding of my clients' needs.	Nan	0.0	3.3	15.0	36.7	45.0	$p = .749$
	Attorney	0.0	2.9	20.6	23.5	52.9	
	Provider	0.3	5.7	18.9	36.5	38.5	
16. Appraisal of personality is important.	NAN	0.0	0.0	21.3	45.9	32.8	$p = .249$
	Attorney	2.9	2.9	20.0	28.6	35.7	
	Provider	1.0	5.7	24.0	39.5	29.7	

(continued)

Table 2-4 (continued)
Survey Responses of NAN Members Compared With Those of Referring Attorneys and Health Providers

Item	Profession	Response: Never	Rarely	Sometimes	Frequently	Always	χ^2
17. Interview of family member(s), significant other, or caregiver(s) is important.	NAN	1.6	3.3	18.0	50.8	26.2	$p = .247$
	Attorney	2.9	0.0	28.6	31.4	37.1	
	Provider	1.7	4.7	31.9	35.9	25.8	
18. A summary of work by others (e.g., physical therapists) is important.	NAN	**0.0**	**11.5**	**29.5**	**41.0**	**18.0**	$p = .000$
	Attorney	**2.9**	**8.6**	**22.9**	**31.4**	**34.3**	
	Provider	**6.7**	**25.9**	**40.1**	**20.9**	**6.4**	
19. A statement of functional capabilities and implications of treatment is important.	Nan	0.0	1.7	8.5	32.4	47.5	$p = .074$
	Attorney	0.0	0.0	2.8	30.6	66.7	
	Provider	1.4	3.4	16.2	38.2	40.9	
20. Recommendations are often too general to be useful.	NAN	5.1	13.6	49.2	32.2	0.0	$p = .401$
	Attorney	5.7	22.9	42.9	28.6	0.0	
	Provider	5.7	25.8	47.7	19.8	1.0	
21. Recommendations are often missing.	NAN	11.7	30.0	43.3	13.3	1.7	$p = .188$
	Attorney	11.4	31.4	34.3	22.9	0.0	
	Provider	21.5	36.4	29.6	11.4	1.0	
22. Recommendations are often very practical and helpful.	NAN		**13.3**	**48.3**	**35.0**	**3.3**	$p = .037$
	Attorney		**0.0**	**44.1**	**38.2**	**17.6**	
	Provider		**8.0**	**35.1**	**43.8**	**13.0**	
23. Ratings of severity or percentage of disability are important.	NAN	**0.0**	**21.7**	**41.7**	**31.7**	**5.0**	$p = .000$
	Attorney	**2.8**	**8.3**	**11.1**	**30.6**	**47.2**	
	Provider	**6.2**	**24.0**	**31.2**	**28.4**	**10.3**	
24. It is imperative that *DSM-IV* diagnoses be included.	NAN	**6.7**	**26.7**	**33.3**	**23.3**	**10.0**	$p=.034$
	Attorney	**5.6**	**2.8**	**38.9**	**27.8**	**25.0**	
	Provider	**10.4**	**28.5**	**27.9**	**17.8**	**15.4**	
25. *ICD-9* codes are useful.	NAN	10.0	31.7	26.7	26.7	5.0	$p = .248$
	Attorney	20.7	20.7	31.0	17.2	10.3	
	Provider	15.9	36.3	28.0	14.2	5.5	

(continued)

Table 2-4 (continued)
Survey Responses of NAN Members Compared With Those of Referring Attorneys and Health Providers

Item	Profession	Response					χ^2
		Never	Rarely	Sometimes	Frequently	Always	
26. Most reports I receive are too long.	NAN	**1.7**	**32.2**	**32.2**	**27.1**	**6.9**	$p = .046$
	Attorney	**25.0**	**38.9**	**22.2**	**11.1**	**2.8**	
	Provider	**15.2**	**33.4**	**26.7**	**17.2**	**7.4**	
27. The vocabulary used tends to be incomprehensibly technical.	NAN	**5.0**	**33.3**	**41.7**	**16.7**	**3.3**	$p = .002$
	Attorney	**11.8**	**38.2**	**29.4**	**17.6**	**2.9**	
	Provider	**24.2**	**42.3**	**24.5**	**7.0**	**2.0**	
28. Testing takes too long and is a hardship on clients.	NAN	13.3	45.0	30.0	11.7	0.0	$p = .645$
	Attorney	17.7	23.5	41.2	14.7	2.9	
	Provider	11.5	39.5	34.8	12.5	1.7	
29. CT and MRI can identify behaviors and functional abilities.	NAN	**44.8**	**29.3**	**17.2**	**8.6**	**0.0**	$p = .006$
	Attorney	**29.0**	**22.6**	**35.5**	**9.7**	**3.2**	
	Provider	**56.7**	**23.9**	**15.9**	**3.1**	**0.3**	
30. Neuropsychological evaluations are critical in rehabilitation/academic planning.	NAN	0.0	3.3	13.3	33.3	50.0	$p = .201$
	Attorney	0.0	0.0	18.5	48.1	33.3	
	Provider	0.3	2.7	25.8	39.9	31.2	
31. Neuropsychological evaluations are instrumental in evaluating the gains made in rehabilitation/academic work.	NAN	**0.0**	**5.0**	**15.0**	**36.7**	**43.3**	$p = .003$
	Attorney	**0.0**	**3.6**	**28.6**	**46.4**	**21.4**	
	Provider	**0.7**	**7.7**	**36.0**	**37.4**	**18.2**	
32. Neuropsychological referrals are limited due to costs.	NAN	**0.0**	**10.0**	**30.0**	**36.7**	**13.3**	$p = .017$
	Attorney	**2.9**	**8.6**	**62.9**	**20.0**	**5.7**	
	Provider	**5.1**	**14.8**	**39.1**	**34.3**	**6.7**	

Note. NAN = Member of National Academy of Neuropsychology; CT = computed tomography; MRI = magnetic resonance imaging. Significant findings appear in bold type.
[a]$n = 63$. [b]$n = 37$. [c]$n = 302$; physicians and other health care providers.

edition of the *Diagnostic and Statistical Manual of Mental Disorders* (*DSM-IV*; American Psychiatric Association, 1994). Examples of actual client responses are popular (especially with attorneys). There is broad agreement that an appraisal of personality is important (67% of the referral sources and 79% of the NAN members rated the importance as *frequently* or *always*). Similarly, interviews of a family member, significant other, or caregiver are considered important.

Somewhat disconcertingly, although half the respondents disagreed with the view that testing takes too long or is a hardship on clients, 35% felt that this was sometimes true, and an additional 13% thought this was frequently the case. The majority of respondents agreed that neuropsychological evaluations are, nonetheless, critical for rehabilitation, academic planning, or both. The majority also agreed that neuropsychological evaluations are instrumental in evaluating the gains made in rehabilitation or academic work. It was generally agreed that cost limits referrals at least *some of the time*; 39% thought this was *frequently* or *always* the case, with neuropsychologists (50%) significantly more inclined to believe this than referral sources (33%).

With respect to Item 15 ("The report makes clear how the cognitive functioning translates into an understanding of my clients' needs"), results were quite favorable. Seventy-five percent of health providers and 75% of attorneys agree that this occurs *frequently* or *always*. In a more specific analysis by specialty of those respondents marking *Frequently* or *Always*, the percentages are as follows (see also Table 2-5): physiatrists, 87%; psychologists, 83%; surgeons, 82%; psychiatrists, 81%; attorneys, 76%; physicians (no specialty noted), 75%; allied health care, 73%; neurologists, 69%; and pediatricians, 60%.

Of the 18 respondents who rated Item 15 as *Rarely* or *Never* (6% of the total number of health care referral sources), 13 were neurologists (out of a total of 16 physicians). It is worth noting that this was not a naive group. Of the group of 18, 15 see more than 11 neuropsychology reports in an average year. All have seen reports by more than one neuropsychologist, with 11 seeing reports from four or more neuropsychologists. On average, they have been using neuropsychology reports for 14 years (SD = 7.9 years). There is a difference by region of the U.S. (North East = 4, 3.6%; South = 3, 3.4%; West = 4, 6%; North Central = 7, 9.9%). The percentages represent the percentage of total respondents for that region who felt that neuropsychological reports do not clarify the relationship between cognitive functioning and the needs of their client.

As a follow-up to this issue, Item 19 asked respondents to rate the importance of including a statement of functional capabilities and implications for treatment. There was substantial agreement (80% of neuropsychologists, 97% of attorneys, and 80% of health providers) that this should be included in the report *frequently* or *always*. Despite this sentiment, respondents agreed that in many cases recommendations are often too general to be useful, or are missing. When present, recommendations are by no means always perceived as practical and helpful. Although over half the referral sources felt that recommendations are (*frequently* or *always*) practical and helpful, a sizeable minority disagreed. Forty-four percent of attorneys and 43% of health providers indicated this is the case only *sometimes* or *rarely*, clearly suggesting room for improvement. (Interestingly, neuropsychologists appear to be significantly more critical of themselves in this regard than are the referral sources, presumably reflecting awareness of an area of weakness.)

An analysis by gender indicated that women were on average 5 years younger than the male respondents and, not surprisingly, had used neuropsychological findings in their work for approximately 4 years less, $p < .001$. They were more likely than men to feel that an interview with a family member is *always* important (39% of women vs. 23% of men, $p = .003$), and that a summary of work by others is *frequently* or *always* important (46% vs. 31%, $p = .005$). They were also significantly more likely to insist on a statement of functional capabilities and implications for treatment (67% vs. 36%, $p = .005$), although this difference is reduced when grouping respondents who felt this is *frequently* or *always* the case (88% vs. 80%). Women are less likely to believe that reports are too long: 14% feel this is *frequently* or *always* the case, compared with 58% who feel this is *rarely* or *never* the case. In contrast, 30% of the men thought reports are frequently or always too long, whereas, 44% felt this was *rarely* or *never* true ($p = .031$). Although there was a significant, $p = .021$, difference between genders in the degree to which neuropsychological evaluations are perceived to be instrumental in evaluating gains made in rehabilitation or academic work (women being slightly more positive), the actual magnitude of the difference was very small. Female health care providers were more likely to disagree with the idea that graphs or tables for only significant findings should be presented, $p = .022$, and were more likely to want graphs and tables for all tests. They also want *DSM-IV* diagnoses. Finally, female health care professionals are more likely to feel that neuropsychological evaluations are critical for rehabilitation planning.

Some items did elicit significant differences among the NAN members, attorneys, and referring health care professionals. Attorneys especially, but other health providers as well, are quite opposed to the idea of omitting extensive explanations. As a group, attorneys tend to want as much information as they can get and are less likely to feel constrained by issues such as cost or length of report. Their primary reason for referral is litigation, followed by disability determination. They want extensive explanations, feel a single page summary is quite insufficient, and are significantly more likely to insist that percentiles always be used. They want specific findings for each test administered and are likely to feel that a summary of work by others is important (65% want this *frequently* or *always* vs. only 27% of other health care providers and 59% of neuropsychologists). Attorneys are likely to see ratings of severity or percentage of disability as much more important than any other group. They are also significantly more likely to feel that it is imperative that *DSM-IV* diagnoses be included. They disagree that reports are too long. They are more likely to think that a CT and an MRI can identify behaviors and functional abilities. They are also more likely than health care referral sources to agree with neuropsychologists that neuropsychological evaluations are instrumental in evaluating the gains made in rehabilitation or academic work.

Given the large sample of neurologists (*N* = 108, or 46% of all physicians and 32% of all referral sources), this group was compared with the other physicians who responded to the survey (*N* = 125). By and large, they were in agreement with their medical colleagues much of the time. The areas of difference are described in Table 2-5. As can be seen, neurologists were more likely to insist on actual test scores and to want graphs or summary tables for all tests. They tended to be slightly more critical in their evaluations of the degree to which neuropsychological reports make clear how the client's cognitive functioning translates into an understanding of their clients' needs.

They were also less enthusiastic than their colleagues about the degree to which recommendations are practical or helpful, or in seeing neuropsychological evaluations as instrumental in evaluating the gains made in rehabilitation or academic work. On the other hand, they agree that reports are appropriately and meaningfully organized, reject the notion of a single page summary, and do not believe that findings should be summarized at the beginning of the report. They want to see a list of the tests administered, prefer percentiles to scaled scores, do not feel that a

Table 2-5
Neurologists Compared With Other Physicians Who Responded to the Survey

Item	Profession	Response: Never	Rarely	Sometimes	Frequently	Always	χ^2
7. I need actual test scores.	Neurologist	4.5	18.2	19.1	20.1	37.3	$p = .002$
	Physician	11.3	29.8	25.8	16.1	16.9	
12. Graphs/summary tables for all tests should be presented.	Neurologist	18.9	16.0	21.7	23.6	19.8	$p = .002$
	Physician	10.2	39.8	20.3	17.8	11.9	
15. The report makes clear how the cognitive functioning translates into an understanding of my client's needs.	Neurologist	1.0	11.2	19.6	37.4	30.8	$p = .054$
	Physician	0.0	2.4	18.5	39.5	39.5	
22. Recommendations are often very practical and helpful.	Neurologist	0.0	8.1	50.5	34.2	7.2	$p = .000$
	Physician	0.0	8.9	22.0	55.3	13.8	
31. Neuropsychological evaluations are instrumental in evaluating the gains made in rehabilitation/academic work.	Neurologist	0.9	9.9	47.7	28.8	12.6	$p = .01$
	Physician	0.0	7.3	28.2	45.2	19.4	

Note. $N = 233$ (108 Neurologists and 125 Other Physicians).

summary of work by others is important most of the time, but believe that interviews with family members or significant others are helpful. Neurologists tended to be somewhat indifferent to *DSM-IV* and *ICD-9* diagnostic codes and do not find the vocabulary used in reports *incomprehensibly technical*. They reject the notion that CT and MRI studies can identify behaviors and functional abilities (although a surprising 15% thought they could, at least some of the time, if not more often).

Table 2-6 addresses physician subgroup data for each of the 32 items. Given the small sample size of some of the groups, results are presented only as percentages. The group of Physicians refers to all MDs not otherwise classified as a neurologist, pediatrician, physiatrist, psychiatrist, or surgeon. What should be noted is the general consistency across physicians for most questions. The data in Table 2-6 are summarized such that the first percentage represents the total percentage of respondents who rated the item *always* and *frequently*. The second percentage includes *always*, *frequently,* and *sometimes*. Further Pearson chi-square analyses compared each physician subgroup with their medical colleagues to identify specific areas of difference. These differences are reported. Due to the relatively small number of respondents in certain comparisons, caution in the interpretation of these results is warranted.

Psychiatrists (n = 35) differed from their colleagues in insisting on the inclusion of *DSM-IV* diagnoses (p = .023; 49% felt they should *always* or *frequently* be included, more than twice as many as their colleagues). Although half (54%) agreed that a CT or an MRI could never identify behaviors and functional abilities, as a group they were less convinced (p = .021) and were more likely to claim that in fact they *could* do so at least *sometimes* (29%), if not *frequently* or *always* (6%).

Physiatrists (n = 31) were significantly more enthusiastic (p = .001) about the recommendations they receive from neuropsychologists than their colleagues, with 87% stating that *frequently* or *always*, these recommendations are often very practical and helpful. They also differed from their colleagues in being more likely (p = .059) to rate neuropsychological evaluations as instrumental in evaluating the gains made in rehabilitation or academic work (74% said this was *frequently* or *always* the case). In other respects, they did not differ from the other groups.

Surgeons (n = 12) comprised only 5% of the total number of physicians who responded. Due to the limited number of respondents in this and the

Table 2-6
Comparison of Neuropsychology Use Survey Responses Among Physician Subgroups

Item	Physician subgroups					
	Neurologist[a]	Pediatrician[b]	Physiatrist[c]	Physician[d]	Psychiatrist[e]	Surgeon[f]
1. Reports are appropriately and meaningfully organized	80% / 98%	90% / 100	81% / 100	81% / 97%	77% / 98%	75% / 92%
2. Findings are best summarized at the beginning	24% / 46%	30% / 70%	30% / 47%	34% / 60%	18% / 36%	50% / 50%
3. Diagnostic impressions...in the summary	76% / 94%	70% / 90%	84% / 97%	61% / 86%	83% / 100	90% / 100
4. I would prefer just the basic findings	20% / 35%	40% / 50%	03% / 29%	14% / 33%	14% / 34%	25% / 33%
5. A one page summary is sufficient for me	20% / 35%	10% / 40%	10% / 39%	17% / 31%	09% / 29%	25% / 50%
6. Listing of tests administered is important	81% / 90%	90% / 90%	65% / 84%	69% / 83%	67% / 89%	58% / 91%
7. I need actual test scores	59% / 78%	60% / 80%	32% / 51%	25% / 56%	37% / 71%	25% / 33%
8. Tests scores should be presented as percentiles	72% / 90%	90% / 90%	77% / 96%	53% / 84%	61% / 79%	50% / 75%
9. Test scores should be presented as scaled scores	50% / 77%	70% / 80%	46% / 78%	40% / 71%	38% / 63%	42% / 67%
10. Test scores should be on a summary sheet	70% / 84%	100%/100%	63% / 85%	63% / 80%	58% / 84%	45% / 54%
11. Graphs/summary tables for *only* significant findings	27% / 50%	70% / 100	33% / 56%	41% / 64%	49% / 67%	18% / 36%
12. Graphs/summary tables for *all* tests	42% / 64%	20% / 50%	19% / 51%	41% / 52%	28% / 47%	36% / 45%
13. Examples of client responses are important	43% / 81%	40% / 100	52% / 86%	57% / 80%	51% / 89%	42% / 80%
14. Specific findings for each test administered	56% / 87%	30% / 70%	40% / 80%	53% / 78%	51% / 85%	33% / 66%
15. The report...understanding...client needs	69% / 87%	60% / 100	87% / 97%	75% / 100	81% / 95%	82% / 100
16. Appraisal of personality is important	64% / 94%	50% / 90%	83% / 100	71% / 97%	66% / 83%	67% / 85%

(continued)

Table 2-6 (continued)
Comparison of Neuropsychology Use Survey Responses Among Physician Subgroups

Item	Physician subgroups					
	Neurologist[a]	Pediatrician[b]	Physiatrist[c]	Physician[d]	Psychiatrist[e]	Surgeon[f]
17. Interview of family member(s)...is important	59% / 92%	90% / 90%	61% / 97%	60% / 100	57% / 88%	67% / 92%
18. A summary of work by others	22% / 58%	40% / 70%	23% / 76%	25% / 75%	26% / 69%	0% / 50%
19. A statement of functional capabilities/implications	65% / 91%	90% / 100%	87% / 100%	69% / 92%	91% / 100%	73% / 91%
20. Recommendations are often too general to be useful	18% / 75%	40% / 80%	07% / 62%	14% / 50%	29% / 64%	33% / 75%
21. Recommendations are often missing	12% / 47%	0% / 30%	07% / 33%	06% / 31%	21% / 42%	33% / 58%
22. Recommendations are often very practical and helpful	43% / 92%	30% / 90%	87% / 94%	72% / 89%	71% / 95%	42% / 84%
23. Ratings of severity or percent disability are important	40% / 67%	30% / 60%	37% / 74%	36% / 64%	47% / 79%	27% / 54%
24. It is imperative that *DSM-IV* diagnoses be included	23% / 49%	20% / 50%	23% / 62%	28% / 54%	49% / 69%	25% / 33%
25. *ICD-9* codes are useful	19% / 41%	0% / 60%	19% / 42%	25% / 56%	22% / 60%	17% / 34%
26. Most reports I receive are too long	27% / 56%	70% / 70%	20% / 47%	22% / 47%	27% / 51%	25% / 67%
27. The vocabulary...incomprehensibly technical	09% / 25%	50% / 70%	10% / 33%	03% / 29%	03% / 29%	17% / 59%
28. Testing takes too long and is a hardship on clients	16% / 51%	30% / 80%	13% / 63%	22% / 33%	11% / 50%	18% / 45%
29. CT and MRI...behaviors/functional abilities	04% / 15%	0% / 0%	06% / 19%	06% / 12%	06% / 35%	0% / 25%
30. Neuropsychological...rehabilitation/academic plan	62% / 96%	70% / 90%	87% / 97%	78% / 97%	74% / 100%	58% / 100%
31. Neuropsychological...evaluating the gains...	41% / 89%	70% / 90%	74% / 90%	64% / 89%	60% / 97%	50% / 50%
32. Neuropsychological referrals are limited due to costs	45% / 81%	80% / 90%	29% / 81%	36% / 83%	29% / 50%	33% / 75%

Note. Items are abbreviated to save space. Complete items are listed in Appendix A. The first percentage in each column represents "Frequently" and "Always" responses. The second percentage represents "Sometimes," "Frequently," and "Always," responses.
[a]n = 108. [b]n = 10. [c]n = 31. [d]n = 36. [e]n = 36. [f]n = 12.

next two groups (i.e., surgeons and pediatricians), the validity of the statistical analyses is limited, and the following results should be seen as likely or possible indications of trends. In comparison with other physicians, fewer surgeons are likely to insist on receiving actual test scores, or to feel as strongly about how they are presented. They are less likely to insist on seeing scores presented as percentiles, or to insist they be presented on a summary sheet. They are more likely to value an interview with a family member or significant other and generally do not care for a summary of work by others. They are more likely to comment that recommendations are *frequently* or *always* missing (33% vs. 11% of other physicians combined).

Pediatricians (n = 10) differed from their colleagues in a number of ways (differences reported for p values less than .05). For example, they strongly endorsed the notion that graphs and tables for *only* significant findings should be presented. Seventy percent felt that reports they receive are *frequently* or *always* too long, although 30% disagreed. They are more likely to feel that the vocabulary used in reports is incomprehensibly technical (50% felt this was *frequently* or *always* the case). On the other hand, they are more likely to reject the notion that a CT or an MRI can identify behaviors or functional abilities (100% said *never* or *rarely*). As was true of other health providers, they have little interest in a summary of work by others. Not surprisingly, 90% thought that an interview with a family member was frequently or always important. Eighty percent thought that referrals are frequently limited due to costs. All respondents wanted a summary sheet with test scores (100% reported that they wanted one *frequently* or *always*).

Physicians who did not fit in the above categories (n = 36) tended to be less likely than other respondents to prefer diagnostic impressions of brain-behavior relations in the summary (although two thirds still felt that they *frequently* or *always* wanted them there, p = .054). They were also less likely to insist on actual test scores (44% indicated that they *rarely* or *never* needed them, p = .057). They are less likely to see recommendations as too general to be useful (p = .039), or to find them missing (p = .009; 70% reported they were *never* or *rarely* missing).

Psychologists who refer to neuropsychologists (n = 22) were compared with all other respondents (excluding the NAN members). They were significantly less likely to feel that diagnostic impressions of brain-behavior relationships are best provided in the summary (p = .017). They felt very strongly (100%) that a statement of functional capabilities and implications for treatment is important (p = .031). They are more inclined to want to see

DSM-IV diagnoses included (39% said *frequently* or *always*, and another 52% said *sometimes*, compared with 33% of others who said *frequently* or *always* and 26% who said *sometimes*, $p = .015$).

The NAN members ($n = 63$) were compared with all other respondents (see Table 2-4). An interesting profile emerged. NAN members are more likely ($p = .017$) to prefer basic findings without extensive explanations (23% rated this *frequently* or *always*) and to insist on actual test scores ($p = .002$). They were significantly *less* likely to want test scores presented as percentiles ($p = .005$) and to want all the data, rather than graphs or tables, for just significant findings ($p = .001$). They differed from others in feeling that a summary of work by others is *always* (18%) or *frequently* (41%) *important* ($p = .001$). They are less likely to find recommendations to be very practical or helpful ($p = .022$), and a somewhat greater number (although still only 37%) think that ratings of severity or percentage of disability are *frequently* or *always* important ($p = .046$). They are more likely than referral sources to feel that reports are too long (33% believe this is *frequently* or *always* the case, $p = .023$) and to believe the vocabulary used tends to be incomprehensibly technical (20% believe this is *frequently* or *always* true, $p = .001$). On the other hand, they are significantly more likely to think neuropsychological evaluations are critical in planning rehabilitation or academic work (83%, $p = .056$) and that such evaluations are instrumental in evaluating gains made in these areas (80% vs. 57% of referral sources say this is *frequently* or *always* true, $p = .000$). Finally, the NAN members were more likely to indicate that referrals are limited due to cost (60% vs. 40% of referral sources, $p = .026$).

Discussion

Insofar as this survey was intended to obtain feedback from referral sources who are thoroughly familiar with the work of neuropsychologists, the results indicate this goal was met. Those who took time to respond are frequent consumers of neuropsychological reports, with over half seeing more than 20 reports a year. Over 90% of the physicians had reviewed more than 10 reports in the last year. Almost half of the referral sources based their judgments on the work of four *or more* neuropsychologists, although 10% based their responses on the work of only one neuropsychologist. The largest group of referral sources, neurologists, had incorporated neuropsychological findings into their work for an average of 16.4 years (*SD* =

8.5 years), and other health care providers had done so for 12.3 years (*SD* = 6.9 years).

Guilmette et al. (1990) found that a combined group of neurologists and neurosurgeons were rated the most frequent source of referrals, whereas psychiatrists were a close second. At that time lawyers ranked sixth, whereas general medical practitioners, psychologists, and other mental health workers ranked third, fourth, and fifth, respectively. Subsequent studies found neurology and psychiatry retaining first and second place both in 1989 and 1996 (Sweet & Moberg, 1990; Sweet et al., 1996). Legal referrals, although in fourth place in 1989, were third in 1996, changing places with rehabilitation referrals. Neurosurgery was consistently in fifth place, followed by psychology in 1989 but overtaken by physiatry in 1996. Various medical specialties, self-referrals, and alcohol or drug related referrals follow. In our study, neurologists, followed by psychiatrists, attorneys, and then physiatrists were most commonly listed by the NAN members as referral sources. These results are consistent with those of Sweet et al. (1996).

The researchers were interested in the reasons referral sources give for referring to a neuropsychologist. In the past, Guilmette et al. (1990) found that in a survey of two groups of self-identified neuropsychologists (the less experienced group relying predominantly on the Wechsler Intelligence Scales, the Bender-Gestalt, and the WRAT), ruling an organic condition in or out was the single most common referral question, regardless of level of training. Assessing a person's capacity to work and educational planning followed. Forensic determination and lesion localization were a distant seventh and eighth on the list.

In this study, differential diagnosis was no longer the primary reason for referral; indeed, for physicians as a group, it was only third in ranked order of frequency. Instead, monitoring change in cognitive functions was the primary reason for referral from physicians, followed by screening of cognitive functions, and only then by differential diagnosis. The fact that neurologists comprised the largest group of physicians may have contributed to this finding. Lawyers are increasingly prone to using neuropsychologists in litigation; the fact that three quarters of the attorneys had used neuropsychological findings only in the last 10 years suggests that there is increasing recognition of the role neuropsychologists have to play in this arena.

Craig (1979) presented results of a survey sent to the Directors of Psychology services at 100 federally funded psychiatric (i.e., Veterans' Administration) hospitals. Of the respondents, 78% (psychologists themselves) felt that psychological tests were able to discriminate between organic and functional disorders, and 12.2% felt that they could not trust psychological test results. At the same time, almost 30% of those doing neuropsychological evaluations in Craig's study had no specialized training whatsoever, 52.5% obtained their training from Reitan's workshops, and only one individual had doctoral (PhD) training in Clinical Neuropsychology. (One individual reported using only one test, the Bender-Gestalt, to make his determinations!) A 10-year follow-up (Slick & Craig, 1991) revealed that 15% of the evaluations were still being performed by individuals with no specialized training of any sort, but there was an increase in instruction provided by graduate schools, and the number of tests available had increased considerably. Despite (or perhaps because of) this minor improvement in training, the overall level of confidence expressed by the Directors of Psychology in the ability of psychological tests to discriminate functional from organic disorders remained comparable with the previous findings (81.7% felt they were useful vs. 18.3% who were neutral or felt the findings were not helpful). Some of the pitfalls in attributing localized lesions to psychiatric patients are examined by Keefe (1995), suggesting one source for the lack of confidence expressed by some of the respondents in the Craig (1979) and the Slick and Craig (1991) studies.

The results of the current study indicate that neuropsychologists are increasingly consulted in order to obtain information about cognitive functioning (and any change occurring therein), rather than to see whether the patient's performance meets some cutoff score that will classify him or her as *organic* or *brain-injured*. It is perhaps interesting, in this regard, to note that lesion localization was the least common reason for referral for all groups. Furthermore, both the NAN members and the referral sources (particularly neurologists) are (with a few exceptions) rather adamant in their insistence on having access to all the test scores. Neurologists and physicians in general (but not psychiatrists) are not particularly interested in the inclusion of *DSM* diagnoses; *ICD* codes interest them even less. One might speculate that this indicates a reluctance to accept the conclusions reached by others without the supporting data, or that they find these diagnostic categories of limited value in and of themselves, or both. This, in turn, could be a result of having seen reports written by inadequately trained neuropsychologists who provide erroneous diagnoses.

As referral sources (physicians as well as attorneys) become more sophisticated about the limitations as well as the advantages of neuroimaging techniques, it is hoped that a better appreciation of the role of neuropsychological evaluations in understanding brain-behavior relationships will develop. This may be one area where neuropsychologists can further highlight the importance of providing a detailed description of the behavior side of the equation through neuropsychological assessment.

Indeed, the majority of respondents were in agreement on most issues, with disagreement on only a few points. Thus, these consumers agreed that reports were appropriately and meaningfully organized, that findings should be at the end and not the beginning of the report, and that a list of tests and test scores should be provided together with specific findings for each one. Percentiles are the preferred method of data presentation, and examples of client responses are popular. Personality assessments are seen as desirable, as are interviews with a family member, significant other, or caregiver. The usefulness of neuropsychological evaluations in rehabilitation and academic settings is affirmed, and most respondents agreed that the reports were successful in clarifying how the client's cognitive functioning translated into an understanding of the client's needs. A statement of the client's functional capacities and implications for treatment is considered highly desirable.

The area of greatest vulnerability appears to lie in the translation of that understanding into specific, useful, and practical recommendations. Recommendations are not uniformly present (surgeons, in particular, noted this). Even when present, they are perceived by a sizeable minority as too general to be useful, or as being neither very practical nor helpful. Neuropsychologists themselves were the most critical in this regard, indicating awareness of a need to address this important issue. The reader may find it helpful to refer to chapter 8 for a discussion of writing recommendations.

Results concerning report length indicated that this is another area of potential concern. On the one hand, neuropsychologists were more inclined than referral sources to agree that most reports they receive are too long. On the other hand, when asked to indicate what they considered an appropriate length for a report, they produced an estimate that was longer than that of all other respondents except attorneys. In this regard, the NAN members differed (significantly) from the majority of referral sources or consumers (neurologists, psychiatrists, physicians as a group, and surgeons).

One reason for the discrepancy may be that health care providers, as a rule, did not feel that a summary of the work of others is necessary (presumably having direct access in any case), whereas neuropsychologists felt strongly that such a summary should be included. (Attorneys and women, regardless of discipline, agreed with the neuropsychologists.) Physicians and surgeons are not interested in test scores or in specific diagnoses, presumably wanting instead just a functional description of the client's abilities and recommendations for treatment. Thus, if one chose to eliminate a review of work by others and simply appended a sheet listing test scores, the chances are that these consumers would feel their needs were being more adequately addressed. Fifty percent of the small sample of surgeons (in definite contrast with other physicians and health care providers) indicated that a one page summary was sometimes (or, more frequently) sufficient.

Physiatrists were generally more positive about the role of neuropsychologists in rehabilitation and were less critical of the recommendations found in reports. One might postulate several reasons for this, including the more active role neuropsychologists in such settings often take in treatment, thus making it more likely that the interventions will be both immediately practical and useful. Also, the philosophy of training of physiatrists in terms of a team approach to rehabilitation may be more conducive to a favorable evaluation of neuropsychologists and their reports. Because treatment plans are generally required in rehabilitation programs, it is perhaps also less likely that recommendations would be omitted altogether.

Women health care providers and attorneys (both males and females combined) responded in surprisingly similar ways on a number of issues. They agree that reports are not too long, they want to include a summary of the work of others, they want to see all the findings, they prefer to see *DSM-IV* diagnoses, and they feel that neuropsychological assessments are critical both in evaluating gains and in rehabilitation planning. These gender and profession-based differences struck the researchers as interesting in light of Carol Gilligan's work (1982) on different relational perspectives (hierarchical vs. inclusive and connected). In the introduction to her book, she makes the point that, although these differences emerged in the course of studying the different *voices* of boys and girls, "this association is not absolute, and the contrasts between male and female voices are presented here to highlight a distinction between two modes of thought...rather than to generalize about either sex" (p. 2). Attorneys (men and women combined) differed from health care providers as a group in being more likely to think that CTs and MRIs can identify behaviors. They were also more likely to want ratings of percentage of disability.

In sum, although referral sources were generally satisfied with the neuropsychological reports they read, a review of the characteristics of each group (provided in the Results section of the study) indicates that contrasts in reasons for referral, content areas, style and type of data presentation, and perceived utility of neuropsychological evaluations do exist. These differences may provide the practitioner with helpful cues in making the reports as user-friendly as possible, targeting specific concerns for discussion or clarification, or both. It is important to bear in mind that sometimes consumers need to be educated about certain issues and that reports often end up with more than one audience (see chapter 8 for a further discussion of this issue). Finally, the survey has identified an area (i.e., writing recommendations that are practical and useful) that is currently perceived as a weakness, not only by regular consumers who clearly value the role of neuropsychologists, but by neuropsychologists themselves. To obtain an even broader perspective, future studies might explore how neuropsychology is perceived by members of a given discipline (e.g., lawyers, neurologists, psychiatrists) as a whole (as opposed to the knowledgeable individuals we targeted).

Appendix 2-1
Neuropsychology Use Survey

Your profession (please check):

☐ physician–specialty ____________________________ ☐ primary care physician

☐ neurologist ☐ psychiatrist ☐ pediatrician ☐ geriatrician ☐ physiatrist

☐ surgeon–specialty ____________________________ ☐ neuropsychologist

☐ psychologist ☐ speech/language pathologist ☐ occupational therapist ☐ physical therapist

☐ rehabilitation counselor ☐ educational specialist ☐ teacher grade_______

☐ social worker ☐ case manager–insurance ☐ attorney ☐ court officer

☐ other (specify) ________________________________

Your gender: ☐ male ☐ female

For your primary work site, what is your zip code? __________________

For approximately how many years have you been using neuropsychological findings in your work?_________

During the average year, about how many neuropsychological reports do you review/use in your professional work: ☐ less than 6 ☐ 6–10 ☐ 11–20 ☐ more than 20

During the average year, approximately how many neuropsychologists have generated reports you have read:
☐ 1 ☐ 2 ☐ 3 ☐ 4 or more

Primary population(s) serviced: ☐ infants ☐ children ☐ adolescents ☐ adults ☐ geriatric

Indicate from which profession(s) you typically request information about the cognitive status of your patients

____

____

____

What do you consider to be an appropriate length for neuropsychological reports?________ (pages)

Please indicate how frequently you refer for each of the following: (Please circle the appropriate number)

	Never	Rarely	Sometimes	Frequently	Always
1. Screening cognitive functions	1	2	3	4	5
2. Lesion localization	1	2	3	4	5
3. Differential diagnosis	1	2	3	4	5
4. Repeated testing/monitoring clinical change over time	1	2	3	4	5
5. Behavioral management	1	2	3	4	5
6. Rehabilitation planning	1	2	3	4	5
7. Litigation	1	2	3	4	5
8. Competence	1	2	3	4	5
9. Educational planning	1	2	3	4	5
10. Disability determination	1	2	3	4	5
11. Benefit determination	1	2	3	4	5
12. Other (explain)	1	2	3	4	5

Appendix 2-1 (continued)
Neuropsychology Use Survey

Please rate the following:

Item	Never	Rarely	Sometimes	Frequently	Always
1. Reports are appropriately and meaningfully organized	1	2	3	4	5
2. Findings are best summarized at the beginning of the report	1	2	3	4	5
3. Diagnostic impressions of brain-behavior relationships are best provided in the summary	1	2	3	4	5
4. I would prefer just the basic finding with no extensive explanations	1	2	3	4	5
5. A one-page summary is sufficient for me	1	2	3	4	5
6. Listing of tests administered is important	1	2	3	4	5
7. I need actual test scores	1	2	3	4	5
8. Test scores should be presented as percentiles	1	2	3	4	5
9. Test scores should be presented as scales scores	1	2	3	4	5
10. Test scores should be on a summary sheet	1	2	3	4	5
11. Graphs/summary tables for only significant finding should be presented	1	2	3	4	5
12. Graphs/summary tables for all tests should be presented	1	2	3	4	5
13. Examples of client responses are important	1	2	3	4	5
14. Specific finding for each test administered are important	1	2	3	4	5
15. The report makes clear how the cognitive functioning translates into an understanding of my client's needs	1	2	3	4	5
16. Appraisal of personality in important	1	2	3	4	5
17. Interview of family member(s), significant other, or caregiver(s) is important	1	2	3	4	5
18. A summary of work by others (e.g., physical therapists) is important	1	2	3	4	5
19. A statement of functional capabilities and implications for treatment is important	1	2	3	4	5
20. Recommendations are often too general to be useful	1	2	3	4	5
21. Recommendations are often missing	1	2	3	4	5
22. Recommendations are often very practical and helpful	1	2	3	4	5
23. Ratings of severity or percent disability are important	1	2	3	4	5
24. It is imperative that *DSM-IV* diagnoses be included	1	2	3	4	5
25. *ICD-9* codes are useful	1	2	3	4	5
26. Most reports I receive are too long	1	2	3	4	5
27. The vocabulary used tends to be incomprehensibly technical	1	2	3	4	5
28. Testing takes too long and is a hardship for clients	1	2	3	4	5
29. CT and MRI can identify behaviors and functional abilities	1	2	3	4	5
30. Neuropsychological evaluations are critical in rehabilitation/academic planning	1	2	3	4	5
31. Neuropsychological evaluations are instrumental in evaluating the gains made in rehabilitation/academic work	1	2	3	4	5
32. Neuropsychological referrals are limited due to costs	1	2	3	4	5

Additional Comments:

3

THE REFERRAL PROCESS

Carmen G. Armengol

Assume that a neuropsychologist receives a call from a college freshman indicating that his Primary Care Physician (PCP) is referring him for an evaluation of possible Attention-Deficit/Hyperactivity Disorder (ADHD). On the face of it, this appears to be a fairly straightforward referral question, so the neuropsychologist goes ahead and schedules an appointment after obtaining the name and phone number of the physician making the referral. She then calls the physician's office, and an assistant agrees to fax her a copy of the referral. Assuming that the insurance company will now pay for services, she proceeds with the evaluation.

In the course of taking a history, she discovers that the student has had several other assessments while in school, suggesting some form of learning disability. (He is rather vague as to the precise nature of his diagnosis, and he cannot remember when the last assessment was performed.) Needless to say, he has not brought copies of any of these prior reports. Furthermore, it is only later, when the neuropsychologist contacts his parents, that she discovers that their alarm about his poor grades and apparent failure to mobilize around the issue led them to consult with friends, who suggested that a neuropsychological evaluation might be helpful. They then instructed their son to see the family physician to ask for a referral to a neuropsychologist (because a referral from the PCP is required by the HMO to which they belong). The mother is particularly concerned that her son is spending more time with "dropouts" and "party animals," but she has not mentioned this concern to her husband, her son, or the family doctor.

The family physician, a busy practitioner who is not very conversant with neuropsychology or the rules of this particular HMO, was nonetheless willing to cooperate in making the referral. When the doctor asked the student about his complaints, he was told that the student has a hard time writing papers and paying attention in class. The physician notes, however, that the young man exhibited flat affect and expressed no obvious concern, shrugging and stating that he was there at his parents' insistence. The physician is concerned about other conditions, such as depression or substance abuse; he also wants to rule out a thyroid condition, as this is prevalent in the family. He has decided to wait for the results of the evaluation and the blood levels before suggesting any further intervention.

Meanwhile, her assessment completed, the neuropsychologist concludes that the student does not have ADHD, as he is able to sustain his attention on a continuous performance task and, when she calls his mother to obtain a clearer developmental history, the mother does not report any attentional problems at home. The neuropsychologist concludes instead, based on a personality measure, that he is dysthymic and has substance abuse issues, which she sees as the underlying cause of his academic problems. Having administered the Wechsler Adult Intelligence Scale, 3rd edition (WAIS-III; Wechsler, 1997a) on which he obtained a Full Scale IQ (FSIQ) at the 34th percentile, and the Wide Range Achievement Test, 3rd edition (WRAT-3; Wilkinson, 1993) where his scores were at a commensurate level, the neuropsychologist has not adequately addressed a possible learning disability in her assessment or report. His mother does mention that in the past he has been diagnosed with a learning disability and promises to mail copies of the reports. Based on the history of prior diagnosis, however, the neuropsychologist adds the history of a learning disability.

She is later upset to discover that her report was sent to a nearby college to which the young man is applying, and it has been rejected because it does not comply with their criteria for defining a learning disability. In addition, the HMO rejects her claim, indicating that they do not cover educational or ADHD assessments, and that neuropsychological testing had, in any event, not been approved. The physician, meanwhile, diagnoses a mild hypothyroid condition. He is neither impressed nor disappointed by the report (having little basis for comparison), but later hears from the mother during one of her visits that the report proved useless in obtaining special accommodations from the college for her son.

Introduction

This scenario, which could befall only a naive or inexperienced practitioner, nonetheless illustrates several important points. The entire fiasco could have easily been avoided had the needs of the client been properly identified at the outset and the appropriate referral information been requested. A discussion with the physician who made the referral would have brought to light his concerns about a possible thyroid condition and depression. In addition, it would have established a personal connection with a chance to explain more specifically what a neuropsychological assessment can provide. Furthermore, on inquiry, the physician would probably have indicated that he had no real experience with the HMO in question and was not sure what they covered. A call to the HMO would have helped to clarify the coverage; the clinical information obtained from the physician might have been helpful in getting the HMO to agree to the assessment on medical grounds. If not, the neuropsychologist would have been able to explain the situation to the parents to see whether they would agree to pay out of pocket. Requesting that the student send records of his previous assessments before his appointment, or at least bring the records with him, would have alerted her to the previous diagnosis of a learning disability and the basis for that diagnosis. This, in turn, would have ensured that she provided a comprehensive assessment of his disability. Asking the young man about his plans for the future and talking with his mother (once he provided a release authorizing this contact) would have suggested the likelihood that the report would be sent to the college. It is always a good idea to contact the colleges, testing agencies, and so forth, from whom special accommodations are going to be requested to ensure that the assessment complies with their requirements and meets their criteria for determining a diagnosis and eligibility. Ultimately, the report could have provided information regarding the student's deficits and specific strengths upon which to capitalize, necessary curriculum and testing modifications, and the extent and types of academic assistance required. This, in turn, may have alleviated some of the concerns and discouragement the student was experiencing, providing the motivation to change his social network, and to interact with less dysfunctional students.

This chapter provides a discussion and overview of issues to consider during the initial referral process in order to maximize the overall success of the assessment from beginning to end. The initial contact sets the stage for a successful first session with the client. At a minimum, the neuropsychologist must determine at the outset whether the referral is appropriate, whether a neuropsychologist is the best person to conduct the evaluation, and who will be financially responsible for the services.

In the early stages of an evaluation, it is important to identify both the *explicit* and the *implicit consumers* to clarify the *implicit* as well as the *explicit* needs of these consumer(s), while at the same time taking the opportunity to (a) identify potential resources for the patient, (b) obtain relevant background information in advance in order to target the assessment as appropriately as possible, (c) ensure reimbursement, and (d) assist referral sources in better understanding the contributions of neuropsychology. It is also important to sort out ahead of time the practicalities and logistics of conducting the evaluation (e.g., duration of sessions, special accommodations, contact person regarding transportation to and from the office in certain instances, etc.). Ultimately, successfully dealing with these issues will translate into a better service to the consumer(s) and an enhanced professional reputation.

Identifying the Consumer(s)

For the purposes of this book, the term *consumer* refers to anyone who has a legitimate interest in the neuropsychological evaluation and who is likely, at some point, to have access to the neuropsychological report. This could be an agency (e.g., an insurance company, HMO, college disability service or student counseling center, state agency for vocational rehabilitation or mental retardation), or an individual (e.g., family member or significant other, case coordinator, lawyer, insurance adjuster or benefits administrator, family physician or nurse, consulting neurologist or psychiatrist, employer, therapist, etc., in addition, most obviously, to the patient). Clearly, this definition goes far beyond the immediate referral source and suggests that in order to successfully address consumer needs, you might first have to do a little detective work to find out who are or are likely to be the consumers of a specific report. But first you might ask, "Why bother?" This is especially true because the network of potential consumers is broad, cannot be anticipated with 100% accuracy, and is typically not contributing to the cost of the assessment.

Hopefully, the above vignette provides an example of what might go wrong if there is no effort to establish in advance exactly who the consumers will be. In that example, even had the assessment of the learning disability been more thorough, the fact that certain institutions develop their own criteria for accepting a diagnosis of a learning disability means that it behooves the examiner to be familiar with these criteria in advance.

In spite of the fact that these criteria may not be considered appropriate in all cases and may need to be challenged (a separate issue to be discussed later), in the meantime, much aggravation, time, and expense can be saved by ensuring that those requirements are met.

Failure to anticipate the needs and requirements of potential consumers (in the broadest sense) ultimately translates into providing less than adequate service to the patient. Furthermore, it seems likely that services to the public are valued according to their perceived utility in meeting the needs and goals of the public. If those services are perceived to have limited usefulness or value, then they will be called upon less frequently. This is a disservice to other neuropsychologists and to the field as a whole, let alone to the many individuals and their significant others who benefit, directly and indirectly, from neuropsychological evaluations and interventions. It is important to remember that neuropsychologists do provide a service; hence, the emphasis in this book on the consumer(s) of that service. In the final analysis, providing good service, as in any field, will, most likely, ultimately benefit the provider in the form of good referrals and reputation.

Other more specific concerns emphasize the need to clarify who the consumer(s) are, because, in some situations, this has a direct bearing on what your relationship to the client will be and the actual nature of your work, your report, or both. This is particularly true in forensic situations, where it is incumbent on the neuropsychologist to clarify in advance whether he or she is being retained as a *litigation consultant* or as an *expert witness* (see chapter 12), or when the neuropsychologist is asked to conduct an evaluation in a context that precludes disclosure of results or providing direct feedback (e.g., in independent medical evaluations or IMEs, or in certain legal or organizational settings). When one of these situations arises, it must be clearly communicated in advance to the examinee or guardian, or both (Binder & Thompson, 1994). It is also incumbent on the neuropsychologist to clarify to a patient when an evaluation is being conducted on behalf of the opposing lawyer in a lawsuit (even when this has already been made abundantly clear to the patient in advance by his or her own legal team). When done in a tactful and businesslike manner, such preliminary remarks should reassure clients that, if they do their best on the tests, they should have nothing to fear from an impartial evaluation. Conversely, if you know that the patient referred to you by another clinician is involved in a lawsuit, then it behooves you to anticipate that, at some point in the future, the opposing attorneys may hire another neuropsychologist to review your work and conclusions, and that, at a minimum, you may be deposed or called to testify regarding your findings. Your test selection should anticipate the types of questions you are likely to be asked in a legal forum (e.g., questions regarding malingering) so that you are a credible expert and, thereby, your conclusions will stand.

In an inpatient setting, when the evaluation is part of a team effort, it is important to make clear to the client and significant others that results will be integrated with those of other team members and most likely discussed and communicated to the client in a team meeting.

Another reason to identify likely consumers in advance is that it provides you with an opportunity to obtain the necessary signed release forms from the examinee while still in your office, rather than necessitating a return visit, or a potential mail delay. In addition, it allows you to discuss with the client any concerns he or she may have regarding release of information and can provide further insights into the client's relationships with others or plans for the future. For example, in the case of a college student who is of age, but whose assessment is being paid for by the parents, it would be important to know in advance if the student does not wish to release the report to the mother and to discuss the best way to resolve this issue in advance.

Clarifying Needs and Expectations

Reimbursement

One thing that should definitely be clarified before spending much time on a referral is the matter of reimbursement. The author has learned from personal experience that what may seem to be an undue focus on financial concerns in the beginning is, in fact, a prerequisite to a clearly negotiated service agreement. A discussion of the way payment will be handled addresses not only the neuropsychologist's need to be paid for the service, but also, importantly, the needs of the patient. No patient would wish to be asked to pay for an evaluation out of pocket when in fact it could, and should, have been paid for by the insurance company. In addition, there is no point in wasting the clinician's time (and that of the referral source) discussing salient clinical concerns when, ultimately, the patient will end up being seen by someone else (e.g., a provider within their network of insurance-approved providers).

Furthermore, one cannot assume that referral sources are equally sensitive to this issue. Some lawyers have been known to refer clients with the assumption that the insurance company will automatically cover the costs, or that the provider accepts Medicaid. In order to avoid any misconceptions, it is a very good idea to explain your reimbursement policy in advance. This should include obtaining written prior authorization (with an authorization number) and written referrals from the appropriate source (often the PCP). Alternatively, as when one is retained by an attorney, it is a good idea to fax a copy of your fee schedule and reimbursement policy in advance, along with your CV, so that retainers and any other fees are clearly understood and submitted in a timely fashion. Similarly, individuals who will pay privately need to understand exactly what is and what is not included in the fee (e.g., whether or not the client feedback session is paid for separately), when to pay, and who to make the check out to. These transactions are a normal part of providing a service to the public, and, although neuropsychologists are not usually trained in standard business practices, the public expects this information to be made available. Whether you deal with these issues personally or through the hospital, a secretary, or a billing person, it is important to have a clear procedure for handling finances if you wish to be perceived as a credible and competent practitioner.

Timeliness

It is a very good idea to ask early during the first referral conversation exactly when the results will be needed, in order to determine whether you can realistically meet the stated deadline, or whether some alternative arrangement can be worked out.

If you are fully booked, and a referring attorney needs an evaluation performed and a lengthy written report completed within the next week (e.g., for submission to the court), the chances are that the conversation can stop right there, unless the attorney believes that there is an alternative way to get around the deadline, or you can somehow juggle your schedule. If, in another example, a parent has delayed setting up an appointment until the last minute and does not have a good appreciation of the time it takes to schedule, perform, and write up an evaluation, you may not wish to put yourself into a position of being unduly rushed. On the other hand, if you are the *remaining hope*, and the stakes are high (e.g., a child's placement and allocation of resources for the next year), you may decide to proceed, with the explicit understanding that you probably will not have a report completed by the time of the school meeting, and that you will not be able to attend, but that you will relay preliminary results, impressions, and recommendations by telephone, or by faxing a brief note to the school psychologist, team leader, or both.

The Patient's Needs

In the vast majority of cases, the patient is the most obvious and immediate intended beneficiary of the neuropsychological assessment. In order to ensure this, specific information gathered during the referral process can be of inestimable value.

Information regarding the patient's cultural and linguistic background is important in determining whether you would actually be the most appropriate person to do the evaluation. Sometimes individuals are naively referred to a bilingual or multilingual examiner even though the examiner does not speak the same language as the patient or have any experience with the patient's culture. It would be more appropriate, at that point, to refer the person to someone who does speak the same language, or to suggest possible avenues for finding such a person (e.g., a clinic that works specifically with that population). In rare cases, a translator may be required; in these instances, finding out who is arranging for the translator, and how, will be important. This author has actually had the experience of being referred someone who spoke Pharsee (Iranian), but who came accompanied to the testing by his sister as the designated translator. This was problematic for several reasons, not least being the fact that he had withheld from his sister an account of being tortured so as not to distress her, even though it caused Posttraumatic Stress Disorder (PTSD) symptoms. The author had to resort to communicating with the patient in private, using gestures and limited English and French on his part.

Similar arguments apply to individuals of a given age. Someone without the training or experience in working with a pediatric population should refer a child to someone who has the appropriate background; conversely, someone who has limited experience assessing older individuals (e.g., for possible dementia or toxicity) may feel more comfortable referring that person to someone who specializes in such cases.

In the latter case, and more obviously in the case of younger children, getting an indication in advance of what the patient's tolerance for testing is likely to be (in terms of time) will be important both in scheduling and in test selection. In addition, it allows for advance clarification of the likely need for, and arrangement of, an approximate number of extra sessions. This provides the caregiver, family member, or parent a realistic expectation of how long the testing will take and facilitates arrangements for transportation and an accompanying individual with sufficient advance notice. Needless to say, the same information should be made available to other examinees (i.e., the length of the session and whether or not the person may need to come back).

Establishing in advance whether there are any physical limitations can also be extremely important. For example, there is an excellent neuropsychologist in the area where the author practices who is fluent in sign language. It is obviously more appropriate to refer a deaf client to that professional rather than to attempt the evaluation oneself. Only when the preferred alternatives are not available should consideration be given to accepting the referral, followed by a careful selection, in advance, of appropriate test materials.

One client who was referred had such significant motor control problems that she found it very taxing and frustrating to write. In fact, this had negatively colored her previous testing experience. Knowing this in advance allowed the examiner to have a laptop ready for her use (which provided a much improved testing environment from the outset for the patient) and to consider in advance which specific tests would provide the information needed while minimizing the patient's need to write or manipulate objects. Finally, although one would hope that most neuropsychologists have offices that are wheelchair accessible, or at least have access to such a space, it may be important to know in advance that the patient is wheelchair bound, just on the off chance that the elevator malfunctions on the day of testing, and the patient or case manager can still be alerted before making a useless trip.

Depending on who the referral source is and the degree of proximity and intimacy with the patient, information regarding the patient's attitude toward the evaluation and any particular prior experiences that may have affected either the patient's expectations or level of cooperation may be elicited. In addition, if the referral is made by, for example, a parent of a student 20 years or older, this, in and of itself, may be a clue to the student's level of responsibility, emotional maturity, shyness, and organizational and follow-through skills. Although a parent may not have the most accurate or extensive knowledge about an older child's current functioning, the parent is often the single best source of information regarding early developmental, social, and educational history (see chapter 5), and the initial contact is an excellent opportunity to start filling in the picture.

Inquiry into the longer-term plans of the examinee (e.g., in the vignette presented earlier, the plan to apply for college) provides valuable insight into how the results of the evaluation are likely to be used and clarifies who the potential consumers may be, as discussed in the previous section. Although the student may not be aware that certain requirements pertain in order to be considered eligible for special accommodations at college, or to sit for national examinations (the student and family may not even be aware of the possibility of obtaining such accommodations), the neuropsychologist should make every effort to be aware of these factors, to point out their implications for the assessment, and, thereby, to incorporate them at the time of testing. It is not the responsibility of the examinee to be aware of these issues; on the other hand, foreseeing the need for specific information in order to facilitate the implementation of recommendations and knowing what appropriate resources are available is the job of the clinician (see chapter 8).

Needs of the Referral Source

The person making the referral needs several things from the neuropsychologist. Most obviously, there is a need to receive the results of the evaluation in a timely fashion. Timeliness depends on a number of factors, depending on who the referral source is, but it is especially in clinical settings that it is important to pinpoint the exact meaning of timeliness in the specific situation. One example would be a patient who needs to be seen preoperatively or who has been admitted to the hospital for a very limited time, with a tentative discharge date already set. The information provided by a neuropsychological evaluation can and should be a critical part of the diagnosis and treatment planning process. Failure to provide information promptly can result in a bottleneck, thus delaying care or, worse, a decision being made by other treatment providers to forgo the results of the neuropsychological evaluation in favor of proceeding with information already available from other sources. Good communication and scheduling is essential in planning for these situations.

If it is not feasible to provide a formal, typed report, a standard note in the patient's chart providing preliminary results and impressions along with a brief consultation to the referring individual (to indicate that the evaluation has been done, the initial impressions and recommendations, and the date when the final report should be expected) is essential. The face-to-face, or voice-to-voice, interaction is extremely helpful and much appreciated in these circumstances; it alerts the referral source to the fact that your evaluation is complete and gives them a chance to ask relevant questions in a time-efficient manner. Although the hospital will still require the report for the record, it is important not to overemphasize the means of communication (i.e., by formal report) at the expense of the purpose of the communication (i.e., to relay your findings and recommendations in a timely fashion).

In outpatient settings, if the patient calls to set up the appointment after being referred by a physician, it is a good idea to ask the date of the follow-up appointment with the physician. If it seems unlikely that you will have a report ready by that time, it is a good idea to let patients know this in advance so that they can relay the message, or, even better, you can call the referral source directly. This not only allows you to obtain further information, but it also enables the referral source to reschedule the follow-up appointment to a later date if the goal is to see the patient after the results of several procedures are available.

Sometimes, a referral source requires specific information regarding a patient's status (e.g., an insurance company requesting an independent medical examination or IME) that follows a particular set of questions and guidelines. Invariably, the agent contacting you will send all the necessary paperwork and information in advance. It is very important to review the information you receive before you meet with the patient so that you are able to provide the specific information requested and to communicate to the patient before the assessment starts that you are not at liberty to release results directly to him or her. In this situation, you have to balance the natural interest and curiosity of the patient against the needs of the referral source, and to do so in an ethical and professional manner requires that expectations be clarified in advance.

Each referral source may have specific preferences and requirements that differ from those of others (see chapter 2 for the results of a national survey addressing some of these issues). If you take the time to clarify these explicitly in advance, the chances of meeting these expectations and needs are significantly enhanced. Simply asking, "Is there anything that would be particularly helpful for you to know or for me to focus on, or that I can do in the way of getting these results back to you?" opens the door for direct feedback and the possibility for negotiation. It signals that you are invested in consumer satisfaction and would not be offended by suggestions or requests. If some requests cannot be accommodated (e.g., an attorney would like you to strike some information from the report), then this needs to be addressed in a tactful but clear way so that the basis for your position is made clear. This, in turn, expands the public's understanding of the rules that guide neuropsychologists in their practice.

A worksheet for gathering the necessary information described in this chapter may be helpful. A sample of such a worksheet is provided in Appendix 3-1.

Appendix 3-1
Referral Worksheet

Client__________________________ Age____ Gender____ DOB____________

SS#____________________ Address____________________________________

____ Phone_______________

1. Direct referral from: __________________________ Date_____________
2. Payment method: ☐ Self ☐ Health insurance ☐ School/agency
   Insurance Carrier and Policy #: ______________________________________
   Beneficiary: Name_____________________________ SS#_________________
3. Results needed by: ________________
4. Linguistic/ethnic considerations: ____________________________________
5. Special needs:
   ☐ Transportation ☐ Escort ☐ Reminders ☐ Other____________________
   (if above marked, specify and describe provisions made to address these needs)
   ____
   ____
6. Handicapping conditions needing accommodation:
   ☐ Sensory ☐ Motor ☐ Other______________________________________
   (if above marked, specify) _______________________________________
   ____
7. Referral to other neuropsychologist indicated? ☐ Yes ☐ No
   (If yes, please describe)____
   ____
8. Person (s) who requested/suggested referral:

	Name	Relationship	Phone	Address
(1)				
(2)				
(3)				

9. Other contacts:

Date	Person	Purpose

Appendix 3-1 (continued)
Referral Worksheet

10. Case coordinator: ______________________________

11. Does person have a guardian? ☐ Yes ☐ No
    Specify: ______________________________

12. Events leading to referral: ______________________________
____

13. Specific presenting problems: ______________________________
____
____

14. Prior evaluation? ☐ Yes ☐ No
    Date of last evaluation: ____________
    Reason for prior evaluation: ______________________________
    Outcome: ______________________________

15. Client's perceived reason for evaluation: ______________________________
____

16. Client's understanding of procedures: ______________________________
____

17. Factors that could potentially influence results:
    Emotional: (anxiety, depression, etc.) ______________________________
    Medical: ______________________________
    Endurance: ______________________________
    Other: ______________________________

18. Current medications: ______________________________

19. Living arrangements:
    ☐ Immediate family ☐ Extended family ☐ Significant other ☐ Alone
    ☐ Supervised living ☐ Assisted living ☐ Long term care facility
    ☐ Shelter ☐ Foster care ☐ Institution ☐ Other ______________

Comments: ______________________________

20. Other comments: ______________________________
____
____
____

4

Screening Versus Comprehensive Neuropsychological Examinations

Carmen G. Armengol and William Jamieson

Introduction

The adequacy and desirability of conducting neuropsychological screening evaluations (or brief, highly focused assessments) for the identification of neuropsychological impairment is a matter that has taken central stage for neuropsychologists in the current climate of managed health care systems. Efficacy and efficiency (i.e., cost-effectiveness) have been raised as the primary motives behind the overwhelming preference for screening evaluations among HMOs (see chapter 10).

These demands have been met with some degree of trepidation by providers of neuropsychological services. Reservations range from how parameters are defined and implemented (i.e., who decides what constitutes efficiency and cost-effectiveness), to the impact of such guiding principles on the quality of assessments, and to the economic repercussions for providers. A survey by Sweet et al. (1995) found that "at least one third of clinical neuropsychologists sampled have experienced reductions in income levels, hourly reimbursements, referral sources, and overall number of referrals secondary to working within a managed care system. Additional concerns include increased paperwork and administrative time" (p. 214). Of the 259 clinicians surveyed, 54% experienced decreased levels of hourly reimbursement, and 25% increased their patient load to maintain their current income. When asked about specific concerns related to the effects of health care reform and managed care on the practice of neuropsychology, 10% wrote in their concerns related to "HMO's use of poorly trained contractors or contract for 'quick' assessments" (p. 216).

In this chapter, a distinction is drawn between screening evaluations that have a legitimate purpose (e.g., for epidemiological research, to identify individuals who require further assessment, etc.), and those that are simply inadequate substitutes for a proper evaluation in order to provide a clinical diagnosis. The authors propose that an alternative to inadequate screening instruments for clinical diagnosis already exists; namely, the hypothesis-testing, process-oriented neuropsychological evaluation. This approach enables the examiner to proceed in a time-efficient manner to evaluate those functional areas that require more careful analysis while spending less time on areas that are intact.

In the remainder of this chapter, technical properties and applications of screening instruments are discussed. Subsequently, guidelines are offered for situations where screening procedures can play an important and useful role.

Scope and Purpose of the Evaluation

To date, neuropsychologists have used screening assessments to answer different types of questions. Historically, the most common question has been simply whether or not brain damage is present (i.e., the functional/organic distinction). This, in large measure, is due to historical views of brain damage as a unitary, global concept (cf. Chapman & Wolff, and Lashley as cited in Lezak, 1995). Several developments in the field, however, resulted in the recognition that brain insult most commonly leads to selective functional impairment (cf. Walsh, 1987), and that the functional manifestations of a syndrome or a lesion identified by neuroimaging techniques vary from person to person (cf. Naeser, Palumbo, Helm-Estabrooks, Stiassny-Eder, & Albert, 1989).

This recognition of the multifaceted, complex nature of brain-behavior relationships has brought about the need to define the appropriate scope of the neuropsychological assessment and report. One example of such efforts is the document prepared by the Massachusetts Statewide Head Injury Program's Professional Collaborative Committee (Morse et al., 1986) regarding what constitutes an acceptable report for this agency's purposes. John Mendoza (see chapter 6) also provides an outline of areas that commonly need to be included. Lezak (1995) provides a description of a neuropsychological evaluation that is comprehensive and emphasizes the assessment of a wide range of functions and variables.

These descriptions can be used as models of a comprehensive neuropsychological evaluation. Such an evaluation results in a wealth of data concerning a wide range of functions; these data can then be integrated to better understand an individual's functional capabilities, to identify likely etiologies, and to provide the foundations for interventions that target areas of difficulty and make the most of the person's strengths.

Screening procedures range from single, very short tests (e.g., Bender-Gestalt, MMSE) to fixed batteries that may take 3 to 4 hours to administer. Benton (as cited in Lezak, 1995, p. 165) proposes that screening procedures be accomplished through a combination of tests that can address both general impairment and specific impairment (e.g., language-related), as well as tests that provide diagnostic signs (e.g., perseveration). The screening process defined in this way is hard to differentiate from a regular evaluation.

Screening instruments have been developed for the purpose of early detection of a multitude of clinical conditions such as learning disorders (e.g., Tramontana & Boyd, 1986; Wilkening, 1987) and dementia (e.g., Blessed, Tomlinson, & Roth, 1968; Folstein, Folstein, & McHugh, 1975). Brief, focused assessments have also been developed to aid in monitoring cognitive changes or in the detection of cognitive dysfunction in individuals already diagnosed with a neurological condition (e.g., Peyser, Rao, LaRocca, & Kaplan, 1990).

It remains customary, unfortunately, to utilize screening instruments primarily for the purpose of *ruling-in* or *ruling-out* the presence of neurological (i.e., organic) involvement. Thus, much of the following discussion will center around issues relating to the criteria used to evaluate the relative efficiency of various screening instruments in determining whether the patient has sustained CNS damage.

Determining Test Efficiency

The diagnostic usefulness of an assessment instrument is predicated on two reciprocal characteristics, namely sensitivity and specificity.

Sensitivity refers to the degree to which an instrument identifies specific characteristics of a person. In answering the question regarding the presence of a neurological or organic disorder, this means identifying those individuals whose functioning is so abnormal (i.e., usually 2 *SD*s below the mean) as to point, in all likelihood, to the presence of brain damage. Thus, hypothetically, a test that identifies 88 individuals out of 100, with known brain damage, would have a sensitivity index of .88. (In this equation, 11% of persons with brain damage will fail to be identified). These individuals may not have been detected simply because the scope of the screening instrument is too narrow to capture their specific deficits. Given the broad range of complexity of cognitive functions, this lack of sensitivity is probably the most common problem encountered among screening instruments designed to detect brain damage.

Some of the identified individuals, on the other hand, may simply belong in the low end of the normal distribution without having suffered brain damage or may be experiencing psychological trauma that has undermined their scores. This raises the counterpart to the issue of sensitivity, namely, specificity.

To the extent that the instrument can differentiate low scorers due to brain damage from low scorers due to other factors (e.g., low education, poor language skills, psychological factors), one speaks of the test's *specificity*. Sensitivity and specificity are equally important from both a theoretical and clinical point of view. Specificity will increase to the extent that confounding variables are adjusted or accounted for. That is, specificity increases to the extent that alternative scenarios that present with the same profile (albeit for very different reasons) are ruled out and to the extent that the false positive rate is reduced. Take, for example, a measure of sustained attention used to identify individuals with a suspected diagnosis of ADHD. The test will not differentiate among people who are sleep-deprived, those who have a seizure disorder, and those who are chronically hypoaroused (e.g., hypothyroid). To claim that the test screens for ADHD, without accounting for those other possibilities, would result in low specificity; that is, a tendency to overdiagnose this condition.

The relationship between a test's specificity and sensitivity is complex but extremely important. Wilkening (1987) provides an illustration of this issue in her review of two screening instruments for children. One, the North Carolina Psychoeducational Screening Test, proved highly sensitive, as it identified 100% of children at-risk for developmental deficits. The false positive rate was 26%; therefore, this is a poor specificity yield. By contrast, the Permanente Medical Group instrument only detected problems in 55%

of the sample when the cutoff score was placed at the 10th percentile. The figure improved to 77% of hits when the cutoff score was at the 20th percentile. False positives were only 2%, regardless of the cutoff criterion utilized. Therefore, using a score at the 20th percentile or less identified 77% of the *at-risk* children (determined independently by more extensive evaluation and follow-up).

Striking a balance along the sensitivity-specificity continuum becomes an important issue, such that an acceptably high percentage of at-risk children are identified, while keeping the number of false positives to a minimum. The ratio can be empirically determined, as indicated earlier. A choice or decision still needs to be made between the two instruments based on what are considered acceptable sensitivity and specificity rates. In this example, one must decide whether the 26% false positive rate (i.e., labeling children incorrectly as developmentally at-risk) is an acceptable trade-off for correctly identifying *all* the children truly at risk. On the other hand, might it be better to *miss* 23% of the at-risk children with the second procedure, but only incorrectly label 2%? The answer clearly depends on the respective implications of being *missed* and *incorrectly labeled*. Some may approach this from a cost-based perspective, others from an emphasis on providing early intervention as soon as possible, and so on. Adjusting the cutoff score for the first procedure might also be attempted in an effort to reduce the false positive rate without unduly impacting the hit rate (i.e., sensitivity).

Chouinard and Braun (1993) did a meta-analysis of the relative sensitivity of certain neuropsychological tests. Their analysis compared choice versus simple reaction time, the Grooved Pegboard with Finger Tapping and Grip Strength, Facial Recognition with Line Orientation, WMS-Visual (delayed) with WMS-Verbal (delayed), the Rey-Osterrieth Figure with Block Design, and Verbal Fluency with Boston Naming Test. In each case, the tests are listed here in order of descending sensitivity, as indicated by their ability to differentiate patient groups with diffuse CNS involvement (e.g., multiple sclerosis [MS], alcoholism, human immunodeficiency virus [HIV] infection, Alzheimer's disease) from a control group. Because the tests reviewed may be differentially sensitive to different patient groups, however, caution must be exercised before assuming that the relative sensitivities hold in all cases. For example, Finger Tapping was found to be more sensitive than the Grooved Pegboard in differentiating MS patients from normals, whereas the opposite finding was obtained with a number of other patient groups.

Chouinard and Braun (1993) also caution that "the greater sensitivity of some neuropsychological screening tests may be due to multidimensionality, complexity, difficulty, reliability, or procedural aspects of the tasks such as their time constraints" (p. 603). For example, the greater sensitivity of the Block Design as compared to the Rey-Osterrieth Figure in differentiating patients with diffuse cerebral injury from controls may be more a function of the respondents' speed of response than of their visuospatial or organizational and planning skills, or both, and memory. Zakzanis, Leach, and Kaplan (1999) provide an analysis of test sensitivity for a number of neurological conditions.

From a practical point of view, there may be situations where it is more important to identify a person at-risk for any particular condition than it is to exclude individuals who, in reality, do not present with this condition, but who are positively identified by the screening instrument. In this case, an instrument's sensitivity (i.e., *how wide the net is*) is given more weight. For example, on National Depression Screening days, the goal of screening is to identify as many people as possible who may be at risk for depression. The goals of such a screening are to heighten awareness of the fact that a person may have a problem, to promote understanding of depression as a disorder, and ultimately, to get those individuals who need it into treatment. The purpose is not to provide a definitive diagnosis for each individual; the assumption is that those who screen positively will be referred for further evaluation.

Ruling-In Versus Ruling-Out: The Issue of Differential Diagnosis

The importance of following up with a comprehensive evaluation after positive identification by a screening procedure when the purpose is clinical (as opposed to epidemiological) cannot be emphasized enough. Wide net approaches to screening are, by nature, designed to rule-in or identify as many individuals who are potentially at-risk as possible. Determining the nature, cause, and treatment of disorders requires an examination of relevant areas of cognitive and emotional functioning, complemented by information gathered through careful interviewing and data obtained from collateral sources.

As an example of the way wide net approaches can be misused, consider the current *epidemic* of ADHD. Following the publication of popular books on ADHD (e.g., Hallowell & Ratey, 1995) and increased media attention to this disorder, many people began to refer themselves to clinics for evaluation, having screened themselves informally with a list of symptoms. It is, unfortunately, not uncommon these days to hear that a person has been placed on medication because the psychiatrist or clinician has simply read the *DSM-IV* criteria for this disorder to the patient, one at a time, and checked off the patient's responses. Little attempt has been made in many cases to make an adequate differential diagnosis (i.e., to rule out other conditions that may give rise to similar symptoms). The authors call this approach to screening the *rule-in* approach. In science, because the natural proclivity of people is to seek confirmatory evidence for their hypotheses, the emphasis is on seeking disconfirmatory data and explanations; that is, to rule a hypothesis *out* rather than *in*. In clinical practice, the failure to adequately evaluate the possible presence of competing disorders can have negative consequences (e.g., prescribing contraindicated medication) or, at the very least, keep the patient from being appropriately diagnosed and treated.

Limitations of the Organic/ Functional Distinction

Lezak (1995) reviews the literature on the Bender-Gestalt test and the various attempts made to improve its sensitivity and selectivity in the detection of brain damage by the introduction of various modifications. For example, McCann and Plunkett (1984) found that when respondents were shown their standard administration drawing together with the stimulus cards and asked to make a new copy (correcting any initial errors), 93% of *organic* patients were identified when compared with normal participants. However, the discrimination between Korsakoff patients and schizophrenics (previously considered a functional disorder) was close to chance. Many tests of cognitive dysfunction are actually quite poor at differentiating psychiatric from neurological disorders; this problem is not unique to the Bender-Gestalt.

A more important question is whether it makes sense to attempt to distinguish between psychiatric and organic conditions, with the implication that they are clearly separable entities. Arguing eloquently against such a distinction, Lishman (1998), in the preface to the third edition of his classic text, *Organic Psychiatry*, states the following:

> ...the biological basis of much of psychiatric disorder is becoming increasingly apparent, so that the dividing line between what may ultimately reflect disturbed cerebral functioning and what is not

> is often hard to discern. This suggests to some that the distinction between organic and nonorganic in psychiatry is destined to become blurred if not entirely obsolete. (p. xv)

In choosing the title *Organic Psychiatry*, Lishman (1998) sought to encompass not only the neurological conditions that affect mental states, but also more general medical conditions (e.g., metabolic and toxic states): "There are psychodynamic, social and cultural aspects of neuropsychiatry to be considered; exploration of conflict must take its place alongside the physical examination in differential diagnosis, psychotherapy alongside pharmacotherapy in treatment" (pp. xiii-xiv). There are, in fact, many disorders in which a psychological reaction coexists with an underlying organic condition (e.g., anxiety and depression in individuals who have sustained head injuries or who notice decline in mental faculties in the early stages of dementia). Attempts to preserve the old distinctions seem increasingly irrelevant to both understanding and treating neuropsychological disorders. An alternative approach would be to focus on identifying and addressing each of the etiological factors contributing to the person's functional profile.

As a further example of the way traditional psychiatric disorders are being reconceptualized, consider schizophrenia. Seidman (1990) relates how he was "brought up" with the optimistic view that schizophrenia was an intrapsychic illness caused primarily by a pathological family environment that could be modified substantially by psychosocial means" (p. 301), only to come to the conclusion that it is, in fact, a neurodevelopmental disorder. Neuropsychological analysis of the specific cognitive difficulties experienced by patients with schizophrenia (e.g., Frith, 1992; Seidman, 1990) contributes important information to the understanding of the mechanisms underlying the disorder, with implications for treatment.

Despite these arguments, the issue of differentiating organic from functional disorders has by no means been laid to rest. For instance, Kane, Parsons, and Goldstein (1985) conducted a study where a number of neuropsychological measures were administered to compare the sensitivity and specificity of the Halstead-Reitan Battery (HRB), the Luria-Nebraska Neuropsychological Battery (LNNB), and the WAIS-R Verbal and Performance IQs in discriminating between brain damaged respondents (mostly head injured and demented) and psychiatric, or *functional,* respondents. Kane et al. specifically excluded schizophrenic patients from their control group, but included others with psychiatric diagnoses ("most typically personality or affective disorders," p. 213) mixed in with medical and *functional neurological* patients (as determined by medical, but not neuropsychological assessment). They concluded that both batteries used were comparable in their ability to identify the presence of brain damage. In addition, they continue, by virtue of the way the analysis was structured, to maintain the necessity of distinguishing between psychiatric and organic disorders.

Later, in a related article, the authors argue that in psychiatric settings, or in settings where the existence of brain damage has not yet been established, tests that can detect brain damage or organic impairment continue to be the most "clinically relevant task faced by a clinical neuropsychologist" (Kane, Goldstein & Parsons, 1989, p. 590). Although one might wish to go beyond such a basic distinction (as discussed later), it is, nonetheless, true that the prognostic implications of depressive symptoms caused by an overwhelming life situation may be quite different from those caused by CNS damage.

Mapou (1988) has provided a critique of the focus in neuropsychology on identifying brain damage versus nonbrain damage, arguing that the field has progressed well beyond such basic (and perhaps spurious) distinctions. He makes the point that too much emphasis is given to test sensitivity and not enough to selectivity and differential diagnosis. Furthermore, in order to be able to design appropriate interventions, both cognitive strengths *and* weaknesses must be delineated. To this end, "it is believed that what an instrument measures and its degree of sensitivity to *specific* [emphasis added] cognitive functions should be evaluated first. An instrument's sensitivity to brain damage is less important, since brain damage is not a unitary phenomenon" (Lezak, as cited in Mapou, p. 272). He further argues that "the unique contribution of the clinical neuropsychologist and, thus, neuropsychological instruments, is to delineate a patient's cognitive function" (p. 272).

Limitations of Screening Tests

It should be emphasized that, although highly sensitive screening instruments may have utility outside the neuropsychologist's office in identifying individuals appropriate for further evaluation, a major shortcoming of single instrument approaches (e.g., Bender-Gestalt, Hooper, Shipley, MMSE) is that each one fails to detect some aspects of brain dysfunction such as the variety of memory disorders, word-finding problems, set, activation issues, visuo-spatial deficits, or a combination (cf. Mapou, 1988; Lezak, 1995, for further discussion of this problem). The Committee on Research of the American Neuropsychiatric Association (Malloy et al., 1997) recognized the limitations of the MMSE, the screening instrument that they endorse most strongly by concluding that "clinicians who employ the MMSE (1) use it as a minimum screening for cognitive dysfunction; (2) employ age- and education-normative corrections, and (3) supplement it with specific measures of spatial functions, delayed memory, and executive abilities" (p. 1890). At this point, one might wonder if a focused neuropsychological evaluation would not be a more cost-effective procedure. Conversely, the LNNB, which takes approximately one hour to administer (tempting some to use it as a screening instrument), has been roundly criticized for numerous methodological shortcomings (Delis & Kaplan, 1983; Spiers, 1981). The main point is that an adequate assessment of neuropsychological functions is not amenable to easy shortcuts. It is sometimes worth reminding consumers that the brain is infinitely more complex and sophisticated than the most advanced computers. Yet, although we do not hesitate to leave a computer in the shop for a day to be repaired, and leave a car for even longer, some consumers appear to balk at the notion that one should spend even an hour examining the human mind.

Another limitation of screening instruments is that they often do not adequately account for demographic variables such as premorbid IQ, education, age, cultural and linguistic background, gender, handedness, and so forth. This can lead to serious errors in classification. For example, a person with a high premorbid IQ may, after sustaining a traumatic head injury, obtain average scores on testing. Furthermore, as Gronwall (1991) reminds us,

> ...*average* should not be mistaken for *normal*, because the patient may have suffered loss of ability from above-average to the average range. Even the traditional *hold* tests may be affected by attentional problems or other factors, such that if scores alone are used as a basis for judging decline in performance, there is a risk of underestimating premorbid abilities. (p. 240)

On a screening instrument that is widely used to detect cognitive impairment, the MMSE (Folstein et al., 1975), a cutoff score of 23 is considered indicative of impairment. Higher cutoff scores have been recommended for specific populations (see Lezak, 1995), a practice not often followed.

Nevertheless, despite proposed adjustments, the fact remains (as described earlier) that the test has a very low ceiling and is unlikely to pick up mild cognitive deficits in above-average individuals.

In a study of 40 patients with MS and 90 demographically matched controls, Heaton, Thompson, Nelson, Filley, and Franklin (1990) compared the MMSE to the Cognitive Capacity Screening Examination (CCSE; Jacobs, Bernhard, Delgado, & Strain, 1977) and the Neuropsychological Screening Battery (NSB; Filley, Davis, & Schmitz, 1989). They found that *none* of the MS patients were detected by the CCSE when a single recommended cutoff score was used. On the expanded HRB, 80% of the patients were noted to have neuropsychological impairments (which include sensorimotor deficits), and 55% were identified as having cognitive impairment. Even when using a less conservative cutoff score on all three instruments (i.e., 1 *SD* below the mean, which also decreases specificity by increasing the number of false positives), individuals with any form of neuropsychological impairment were detected only 28% of the time with the MMSE and only 31% were detected by the CCSE. Although the NSB had a sensitivity of only 72%, it also had a specificity of .75 (i.e., 25% of normal controls were falsely identified).

Aside from the insensitivity of screening instruments in detecting milder deficits, another factor affecting their ability to detect impairment is the impact of age and education on scores obtained by individuals at the lower end of the distribution. By way of illustration, consider the unusual case of a woman of middle European origin who arrived in the U.S. when she was 18 years old. She had a third-grade education and, on arrival in the U.S., obtained employment as a cleaning woman, a job that she held until her retirement. She had led an exceedingly frugal existence, depositing her paychecks in the bank and eating in soup kitchens. Later in life she bought an old and dilapidated rooming house where she lived and rented rooms. Over time, she amassed a very large sum of money. She never mastered English, nor did she speak it with any degree of fluency.

A relative, concerned with her lifestyle, brought her to a psychiatrist, who administered the MMSE, on which she obtained a score of 18. On the basis of this score, which is below the usual cutoff of 23, he promptly pronounced her demented and incompetent to handle her affairs. She was placed in a nursing home.

Her lawyers requested an independent evaluation, which was performed by Dr. Edith Kaplan (personal communication, February 1994).

Questioning the results of the MMSE, she established, using epidemiological corrections reported by Crum, Anthony, Bassett, and Folstein (1993), that the appropriate cutoff score should have been 16 and further concluded that the woman, albeit somewhat eccentric, was nonetheless competent. Crum et al. established that individuals over 80 years old with less than 4 years of education who score in the lower quartile actually pass with scores of 19; those over 85 years old score as low as 15, with a mean score of 19. (Unfortunately, these corrections are rarely used in clinical practice; furthermore, the impact of bilingualism and English as a second language on scores is not known.)

Other researchers have presented data documenting the insensitivity to demographic variables of screening instruments' cutoff scores (Cummings, 1993; Jagger, Clarke, Anderson, & Battcock, 1992; Magaziner, Bassett & Hebel, 1987; Nadler, Richardson & Malloy, 1994; O'Connor et al., 1989; Schwamm, VanDyke, Kiernan, Merrin, & Mueller, 1987). Nelson, Fogel, and Faust (1986) have criticized both the MMSE and the CCSE for lacking sensitivity to milder cognitive deficits, primarily because the ceiling of the tests is too low. Nadler et al. reported a 40% false negative rate with the MMSE in identifying patients who demonstrated mild impairment on formal neuropsychological testing.

Cognitive Screening for Special Populations

Moving beyond single screening instruments designed to detect brain damage, we now turn to screening batteries that have been developed to assess cognitive dysfunction in specific disorders. In cases where there is preexisting understanding of what the most likely areas of dysfunction are, such a screening instrument can be useful in detecting difficulties that may otherwise be missed. This is particularly important when there is a high incidence of cognitive dysfunction that may not be picked up on a routine mental status exam.

One example of a carefully designed instrument is the Multiple Sclerosis Society battery (Peyser et al., 1990). This protocol was constructed by a group of experienced researchers and clinical neuropsychologists with the aim of systematizing data collection in MS clinics and research centers across the nation. Care was taken to minimize fatigue and to avoid tasks requiring motor coordination because these issues are often problematic in individuals with MS. Tasks were selected to tap all major areas of cognitive functioning, at various levels of complexity; parallel forms were constructed to allow for repeated evaluations, a crucial issue in this kind of disorder, with its remitting-relapsing presentations. In this instance, the screening assessment is valuable in addressing the particular needs of the specific population for which it was constructed. Even so, as Heaton et al., (1990) and Minden and Moes (1990) have noted, MS is a disorder that can present with very heterogeneous profiles of impairment. For a given individual whose job and daily functioning are at issue, a more comprehensive evaluation would be appropriate.

This last point is emphasized in a study by White, Heaton, and Monsch (1995), who compared the ability of small, medium, and large neuropsychological batteries in their ability to detect impairment in asymptomatic HIV infected individuals. They concluded that the larger the size of the battery, the more likely it was that early detection of impairment occurred:

> Thus, the tentative conclusion may be reached that there is a modest increase in the risk for NP [neuropsychological] impairment in HIV-1 seropositive asymptomatics, and that impairment is more likely to be detected if a relatively comprehensive NP assessment is utilized. (p. 311)

They caution about the need to correct for possible type 1 errors occurring with multiple comparisons and the desirability of developing smaller neuropsychological batteries of sufficient specificity, sensitivity, and breadth to detect deficits in subgroups of HIV-1 infected individuals. Of course, although that is the ideal, in practice such an instrument does not exist, and one must be cautious not to lock into a particular screening instrument before the full range of potential cognitive impairments has been identified. That is, it is important to ensure that the validation instrument against which the screening battery is being measured is itself of suitable breadth, sensitivity, and specificity to pick up even subtle problems. Mapou (1988) and Butters et al. (1990) provide suggestions related to this issue.

The Importance of Expertise for Screening

One of the purported advantages of screening instruments is that they can be administered by a number of nonneuropsychologists such as clinical psychologists, technicians, psychiatrists, nurses, and so forth. This is an assumption that goes unchallenged more often than not. The implicit assumption behind this argument is that there are tests that can detect cognitive dysfunction with accuracy and sensitivity.

As discussed earlier, it is hard to construct a *one-fits-all* tool that provides the fine-grained ability to predict the presence of neuropsychological dysfunction with a degree of accuracy that even remotely approximates that of, say, a pregnancy kit. Unlike screens for unifactorial biological markers, (e.g., high blood sugar levels or hormonal surges), neuropsychological screening is an exponentially more complex matter.

Central to an appropriate interpretation of the results of a screening test are sensitivity and specificity considerations. In addition, factors, such as education, age, gender, and ethnicity can, as has been seen, greatly influence the significance of results. Thus, a person interpreting results of a screening instrument must, at the very least, be well informed about its psychometric properties (e.g., the impact of varying cutoff scores on the sensitivity and specificity issue and how to correct for demographic variables), as well as the implications of adopting a more or less stringent cutoff criterion.

Aside from having basic knowledge about test instruments in more routine screening situations, *the person interpreting results of screening procedures should ideally be well versed in the varieties of neuropsychological syndromes and have strong diagnostic clinical skills*. This will, hopefully, result in minimization of incorrectly diagnosing some individuals, while missing others with actual deficits. Another advantage would be the ability to explore other potential areas of compromise not covered by screening tests or combinations thereof. This person would have both the knowledge of procedures that would be appropriate additions as issues come up in the course of the brief screening contact and the flexibility to pursue clinical concerns through questions or other procedures not necessarily included in preset screening protocols.

It is precisely at the outset of the diagnostic exercise, when the greatest diagnostic uncertainty exists, that the neuropsychologist's expertise is most needed. Although this may seem counterintuitive at first (i.e., placing the expert at the triage end of the diagnostic spectrum), the logic of such an approach may become more apparent when one considers the central role of a good history in assessment and diagnosis. Franzen and Berg (1989) observe the following:

> The clinical interview itself can be seen as a screening device. It is here that the clinician can begin to gain an understanding of what the problem is (diagnosis) as well as what seems to be causing the problem (etiology)...Also during the interview, the clinician can start generating hypotheses that later can be tested against data. (p. 53)

The importance of testing (rather than relying on just interview data) stems from the fact that patients can be quite unreliable at times in describing their own functioning. Most neuropsychologists will have encountered head-injured or demented individuals who confidently assure them that they have no memory problems or other cognitive deficits, although testing dramatically contradicts their statements. Regardless of this fact, skilled interviewing requires expertise in the intricacies of diagnosis and neuropsychological syndromes in order to be able to ask appropriate follow-up questions. Even the *DSM-IV* decision tree provides an incomplete guide to information-gathering for neuropsychologists.

The Hypothesis Testing (Flexible Battery) Approach as an Alternative to Screening Instruments in Clinical Assessment

Unlike earlier views of what constituted a full neuropsychological evaluation (usually an HRB) and a neuropsychological screening (e.g., a Bender-Gestalt), neuropsychological protocols have become more client-focused and more flexible, thereby accommodating the diagnostic and intervention planning needs of specific consumers. In fact, a recent survey of 279 neuropsychologists (Sweet et al., 1996) has shown that 85% of practicing clinicians use flexible protocols preferentially over fixed batteries.

Within neuropsychology as a field, there are two opposing paradigms, which might be referred to as the actuarial, fixed battery approach, as opposed to the flexible, process approach. In the former (of which the Halstead-Reitan battery is a good example) the argument is made (e.g., Kane, Goldstein, & Parsons, 1989) that a fixed battery ensures that functions are routinely assessed which might otherwise be neglected due to incorrect clinical assumptions. One should be aware that the HRB is a lengthy procedure that can take 8 hours to complete. Furthermore, in areas where impairment is apparent, further assessment with specialized tests might still be needed.

Lezak (1995) notes the following:

> When batteries are used as directed, most patients undergo more testing than is necessary but not enough to satisfy the examination question specific to their problems. Also, like most psychological tests, ready-made batteries are not geared to the patient's handicaps. The patient with a significant perceptual or motor disability may not be able to perform major portions of the prescribed tests, in which case the functions normally measured by the unusable test items remain unexamined. (p. 124)

Lezak (1995) also cites Orsini, VanGorp, and Boone (1988) to the effect that "unless examiners feel free to introduce new assessment techniques into their testing repertory, they cannot take advantage of new knowledge and new developments in the cognitive neurosciences" (p. 124). She concludes that "a ready-made battery may also seem to confer neuropsychological competence on its users, giving false complacency to naive examiners, particularly if it is popular and has accrued a long reference list" (p. 124).

In the process approach, test instruments are selected on the basis of a hierarchy of functions. Thus, if a patient fails to do well on a complex task, a more in-depth analysis occurs by a systematic testing of the variables involved (Kaplan, 1988). If, on the other hand, the patient performs the more complex task without difficulty, it is assumed that simpler tasks need not be administered. (Many tests incorporate this principle by indicating starting levels that are supposed to match the maturational or educational level, or both, of an individual.) A cognitive hierarchy is also assumed, such that failure on, for example, a memory task cannot be assumed to implicate memory functions until underlying functions required for memory (e.g., attention and the specific sensory modality in which the test is given as well as the response system) have also been assessed.

Saling (1994a) argues against the position taken by Wedding and Faust (1989), who contend that "greater overall accuracy is achieved when one adheres 'mindlessly' to actuarial procedures and *never* makes exceptions based on clinical judgment (p. 11)." He cites, for example, a study by Boshuizen and Schmidt demonstrating that "expert medical diagnosticians tend to place a much heavier reliance on clinical information (including history) than novices do despite the vast 'objective' investigative power of modern medicine" (Saling, p. 11).

From this perspective, results from a fixed screening instrument or battery provide no clear advantage over flexible testing when formulating a diagnosis, as the scores they produce typically do not provide sufficient contextual data to allow for the formulation of what are primary versus secondary deficits and may omit information about other critical factors. Once again, information obtained from the history, behavioral observations, testing, and corroborating material (see chapter 5) is critical in differential diagnosis. This information can only be elicited and integrated by a trained and experienced neuropsychologist.

Although this issue is still being debated (e.g., Kane et al., 1989), it is proposed that those using a flexible battery approach rely heavily on information gathered, and, therefore, hypotheses generated in the course of the initial history (modified by data obtained in the course of the examination). The advantage of such an approach is that time to test intact functions can be reduced and more time spent teasing out the variables affecting impaired functions.

Lezak (1995) has commented, "The popularity of ready-made batteries attests to the need for neuropsychological testing and to a general lack of knowledge about how to do it" (p. 123). It is sometimes argued that lack of availability of well trained neuropsychologists in clinical settings necessitates the use of screening instruments administered by nonneuropsychologists. This contention has not been substantiated by any data indicating that a shortage of trained neuropsychologists exists. On the contrary, in his presidential address to the National Academy of Neuropsychology, Barth (1996) commented specifically on the dearth of job announcements for clinical neuropsychologists, concurrent with a significant increase in the number of well trained graduates from programs in neuropsychology. Arguments that well trained neuropsychologists are not available appear cost-motivated (i.e., nonpsychologists cost less) and represent an attempt to replace quality care with less-than-adequate substitutes.

Finally, the assumption that abbreviated assessments (i.e., screenings) actually save money has not been substantiated. No study evaluating the impact (both in terms of outcome for the patient and in terms of monetary savings) of failing to correctly evaluate neuropsychological disorders is known. Such a study would provide an invaluable contribution, especially in the context of the competing pressures to reduce health care costs while maintaining quality of care. In clinical practice, there are many anecdotal situations encountered on an everyday basis that suggest that the costs of misdiagnosis or the failure to diagnose and treat a wide range of disorders can be very costly indeed (in terms of unnecessary therapies or medications, or of needless suffering on the part of the patient).

Guidelines to Using Screening Procedures

Different approaches to screening for neuropsychological syndromes have been proposed. Wilkening (1989) suggests that a variety of available tools for screening children with possible learning disorders can be used with children whose medical or familial history do not place them at risk, whereas a different approach is warranted in the presence of a history positive for risk factors (e.g., prenatal and perinatal complications, infections, etc.). This, of course, presumes that a detailed history is available and, in such cases, a review of medical records must, in fact, be an integral part of the screening process.

Although screening batteries may not do justice to the clinical needs of an individual patient, there are clearly situations where the goal is limited to identification of the possible presence of specific disabilities or disorders. Thus, school systems may wish to screen for poor reading abilities, and epidemiologists may wish to screen for dementia in an elderly population. The role of the neuropsychologist in designing screening protocols and in consulting with agencies, schools, hospitals, and health practitioners in the interpretation of such protocols is central if services are to meet and maintain the best interests of the patient and the consumer and result in true cost-effective practices.

For clinical purposes, the experienced neuropsychologist is best placed at the point of screening or triage. As argued earlier in this chapter, a process-oriented approach to assessment, by virtue of being hypothesis-driven has a built-in, implicit, screening procedure. Once the range of neuropsychological functions has been sampled, a more in-depth investigation of specific areas of concern is conducted. Follow-up evaluation can then be conducted with the assistance of supervisees as a more in-depth evaluation is undertaken.

The following guidelines are recommended in situations where screening evaluations are appropriate:

1. Specify the scope and purpose of the screening, which may range in scope from detecting specific deficits (e.g., a reading test in a school setting, or eye-hand coordination and developmental screening using the Beery Visual-Motor Integration Test [VMI; Beery, 1997] in a pediatrician's office) to a standardized protocol aimed at detecting cognitive dysfunction in individuals diagnosed with a neurological condition (e.g., a dementia screening in a geriatric care setting or an MS clinic), to a more open-ended exploratory assessment of basic functions. It is important to specify whether the purpose of the latter is for epidemiological reasons or is undertaken to determine whether further, in-depth assessment is required.
2. Describe the procedures utilized. The reader or consumer of the report will be better served if the following factors can be ascertained: the extent to which the person being assessed was monitored, what background information was gathered, and to what extent the history was integrated with the test results. These factors will affect the scope of any conclusions that can be reached.
3. In providing results, specify how cutoff scores were determined. If the instrument utilized affords the option (i.e., provides specificity or sensitivity ratios for different cutoff scores), give a rationale for having chosen one or the other. It is important to specify whether demographic corrections were employed and, if not, why not (e.g., the instrument has not been normed on such populations, etc.). The limitations of the instrument(s) being used should, as always, be indicated, highlighting those instances where the results are likely to be misleading (e.g., with linguistic or cultural minorities and specific age and education groups).
4. Whenever possible, go beyond cutoff scores. Although many instruments are constructed around statistical properties that favor the use of such global scores, observations and a qualitative analysis of responses may raise quite important and valid issues.
5. In giving your conclusions, it is essential to state any limitations inherent in the procedures utilized. This is not only ethically advisable, but it allows the consumer to have a more realistic understanding of the issues that require follow-up and monitoring. This may also provide the neuropsychologist with reasons to advocate for other procedures, should those be indicated.

Concluding Remarks

In this chapter, it has been argued that sensitivity and specificity are important criteria by which a test can be measured. Screening instruments are often used to identify individuals who are at risk for a problem or disorder, and this requires good sensitivity. Unfortunately, all too often, clinicians stop prematurely after a possible condition has been detected, rather than gathering further data for the purpose of a differential diagnosis.

It is argued that the function of a comprehensive assessment is in fact to elicit the information necessary to rule-out as well as rule-in competing hypotheses. Because many neuropsychologists are entrusted with the task of further evaluation *after* a screening has been performed, it is clear that screening instruments are unlikely to provide the information required and, therefore, are not an appropriate substitute for a comprehensive evaluation. Furthermore, screening instruments do not provide the necessary information required to formulate appropriate interventions.

Nonetheless, because screening instruments will continue to be used for a number of reasons, it is important to know their limitations and the demographic corrections necessary to enhance their sensitivity and specificity and, ultimately, their validity. In this regard, only experienced clinicians should be entrusted with the interpretation of results, in the context of supporting information. It is argued that the *expert* should be available from the outset to assist in deciding the need for follow-up and to make initial recommendations. In large settings, this may mean that neuropsychologists should conduct triages. Follow-up evaluation could be assisted by trained interns or technicians, but only under the supervision of the staff neuropsychologist. In smaller settings, the neuropsychologist can act as a consultant, supervising assistants, helping to determine which instruments or batteries are most appropriate for the population being served, and, if necessary, assisting in the development of such instruments.

There will be many occasions when the optimal conditions for a thorough assessment cannot be met (e.g., fatigue on the part of the patient, pressure to provide some immediate feedback, financial constraints, transportation difficulties, etc.). In such cases, several options can be explored. One important issue to remember is that serial assessments are often more appropriate than a one-time, lengthy comprehensive examination. Also, abbreviated assessments can be conducted. In either case, it is important that the nature of the procedure be disclosed to both the patient and the referral source, so they understand the extent and limitations of the assessments, what is hoped to be accomplished, and that further assessments may be necessary down the road. This approach will educate patients and referral sources about the many possible approaches to a neuropsychological evaluation.

Ultimately, neither the patient nor the health care budget can benefit from shortcuts (i.e., screenings). In the last analysis, careful determination of the kind of treatment required is bound to result in better resource allocation.

5

GATHERING BACKGROUND DATA

Lawrence G. Jasper and John T. Capuco

Only 5 months after a full neuropsychological assessment, the Case Manager for a rural brain injury rehabilitation program referred the patient for a second neuropsychological assessment. The Case Manager explained that the past evaluation had not helped staff members understand and deal with the client's angry outbursts, noncompliance, and suicidal threats that had evolved within weeks of placing him in a new residence and job setting. The evaluation had been done at a highly regarded urban tertiary care facility. The report showed that all the tests one might need for a good assessment had been administered. The scores indicated significant working memory and executive function deficits, which were clearly identified in the report.

What had gone wrong? Closer reading of the assessment revealed that although the report comprehensively and concisely reviewed medical and inpatient rehabilitation records, the program had relied upon the patient's mother to contact the neurologist to obtain a referral for the evaluation. Without input from the facility regarding behavioral functioning, and given a patient with a memory problem, the neuropsychologist obtained little specific knowledge of the daily issues that the patient and staff were struggling with in the patient's postacute rehabilitation program. Consequently, the report did not address these issues.

In response to the request for a second assessment, a brief evaluation was done at the facility, with collateral information from the hands-on residential and day program staff. They shared with the examiner the fact that the patient had taken a year to learn a very simple behavioral program in his prior setting. However, the patient had mastered his daily living skills so well that he was promoted from a structured group home to a less structured independent apartment. This was accomplished without the support of the structured behavior program. Once the examiner and staff could link the poor memory and compromised executive functions to the stress and symptoms that triggered the referral, the staff felt they could justify greatly simplifying the patient's program and adding supports.

Neuropsychological assessments often reflect neuropsychologists' training to use the best normed tests we can find, to follow standard administration procedures, and to gather some relevant history. However, those reports often suffer in their applicability because they have not captured the context that gave rise to the referral and into which the results and recommendations will flow. What is missing in these reports is an anchor in the reality of the patient's history and present struggles to adapt.

This chapter will deal with two goals of data gathering: (a) to provide objective verification of facts of past and current history, and (b) to supply information that will help identify who the consumers of the neuropsychological assessment really are, what their needs are, and what diagnostic and treatment information will be of most use to them.

Who Is the Consumer?

Too often the consumer is thought of as the referral source, who, in this case, was the neurologist (at the mother's request). In fact, the consumers who can have the greatest impact on the patient (for better or worse), are often those in the trenches who are dealing hands-on with the patient on a daily basis. Answering the question of who the real consumers may be will often point the way to individuals one should also consider as potential collateral informants. The examples presented in Table 5-1, though not exhaustive, may be illustrative.

Given the importance of collateral informants and the time constraints placed on the neuropsychologist by managed care, the question arises: "What are the most relevant traits to look for in a collateral informant?" In the authors' opinion, important factors include the following: longevity of the relationship with the patient, high frequency of contact with the patient, and with that, some personal quality to the contact.

The clinical value of an informant's information can also be influenced by a number of factors: whether the informant feels there is something for the informant to gain or to lose by candor (e.g., money or job security), the informant's degree of education, the informant's degree of supervisory

Table 5-1
Potential Collateral Informants

Nursing home patient	Nurse, aide, bus driver, janitorial worker, recreational staff, family members, and significant others
Student/child	Teacher, one-to-one aide, fellow students, friends, and family
Brain injury program patient	Direct Care staff, Case Manager, family, treating therapy staff, vocational planner, psychotherapist, housekeeping staff
Psychiatric inpatient unit	Admitting and treating physician, nurses, aides, psychologist, recreational staff, treating therapy staff, family
Personal injury case	Attorney, physician, family or significant other, employers, friends, coworkers

responsibility, and the informant having a personal record of success in dealing with the patient.

The latter three items require some discussion. Too often an advanced education provides the informant with a lens to unknowingly filter in and filter out data that may be meaningful. Well-educated informants sometimes mistakenly equate their conclusions with factual data or, in the least fortunate case, present the conclusions as if they were self-evident, without feeling the need to offer any factual data.

The presence of a supervisor in a team meeting may intimidate a front-line staff member and, if so, may interfere with candid discussion. Supervisors may not feel free to admit to lack of knowledge because of a need to present a certain role to the supervisee. Also, being in a supervisory role can distance the supervisor from the data. For example, in a nursing home evaluation, the head nurse who was assigned to talk with the neuropsychologist proceeded to give a coherent account of the patient's medical history and the current daily ward routine. However, it was the aide, who delivered and picked up breakfast trays and cleaned the room, who reported that the patient was occasionally found in the closet after breakfast, apparently hearing and talking to voices coming out of the ceiling.

Last of all, the staff person who has a special knack with the patient often has skills or personal qualities, or has devised interventions that others can learn from.

For economy of time, team meetings of three to six caregivers can usually be arranged in an institutional setting such as a school, nursing home, hospital, or brain injury program. This format helps avoid going over the somewhat overlapping material several times with different people. Team meetings also have the advantage of bringing out contrasts between, for example, behavior with the morning and the afternoon shift, or on weekends versus weekdays. The team structure also allows the neuropsychologist to evaluate the reliability of each informant by comparing his or her input with that of others in the group. The outcome of such a team meeting is often that the neuropsychologist learns the real context out of which the referral arose and is thus able to sharpen and appreciate the referral question the neuropsychologist has been asked to help answer.

Gathering the History

This section deals with the process of gathering the history, and the specific content of that history.

The Process

The process of gathering data often relies on what the patient, the readily available informants, and the documents can tell. Too often extra steps are not taken to obtain further collateral data in the form of interviews with significant others or by reviewing old records. For example, the attained educational level to estimate premorbid intellectual level is used, typically, without verification. However, a recent study (Johnson-Greene et al., 1997) demonstrated that at least half of all participants in a clinical veterans population inaccurately reported their high school grade-point average, mostly in the direction of overestimation. Patients with PTSD and alcoholism were significantly less accurate in recalling their educational history when compared with a group of control participants. Several patients claiming to have attended high school were found not to have attended at all.

Varney and Menefee (1993) have demonstrated that patients with damage to the orbitofrontal cortex can have relatively trivial medical findings and perform quite well on neuropsychological tests. However, interviews with collateral informants for some of these patients using a structured protocol (Iowa Collateral Head Injury Interview) demonstrate potentially catastrophic psychosocial and executive function deficits that often go undetected on neuropsychological testing.

Collateral information is critical in assessments of malingering (Faust, 1995), dementia, and depressed mood in Alzheimer's disease patients (Gilley et al., 1995), where the disorder impairs the patient's ability to report symptoms. Other cases where information from collateral informants is critical to accurate and relevant interpretation of test data involve patients who manifest *denial of illness* (i.e., anosognosia), or those with significant memory and attention deficit, including ADHD. By seeking out collateral sources of information, in the form of records and interviews with those who know the patient, neuropsychologists demonstrate to themselves and to the consumers that the history gathered is (or is not) valid and reliable.

In the clinical setting, whether institutional or private practice, most patients can understand the need for collateral informants. If asked for names, patients often willingly suggest them. All that has been said about selection of collateral sources of information in institutional settings also applies to those seen in private practice. Ideally, by the end of the first interview, the clinician has identified all relevant informants. The patient may be asked to speak to collateral informants, telling them to call or to expect a call from the clinician as part of the data gathering process. It is essential that the clinician obtain a signed release from the patient giving consent to contact those sources prior to approaching them.

The clinician needs to define the informant's role before gathering the information. Collateral informants should be asked what they were told about the evaluation (i.e., to verify their understanding that the patient has asked them to give information, and for what purpose). The informant needs to know that this information will likely be included in a report to which the patient will have access.

Informants often welcome the chance to help and do not seem put off by the fact that others may know what they have said. Reassurances that the information will be dealt with sensitively and diplomatically may occasionally be needed and should help diminish the reluctance of some informants. In the case of informants who want to give information but do not wish that information to be included in the report, it is better to try to resolve the matter before taking the information, or you may be in possession of critical information that potentially affects your conclusions but that otherwise cannot be independently validated. Some patients may suggest that an estranged spouse does not care, or is biased, and is not a good informant. However, sometimes the clinician is richly rewarded with critical information from such persons, and they should not be summarily written off.

Data gathering from collateral informants should be systematic. All informants should be asked how they know the patient, the length of their acquaintance, frequency and duration of contacts during the period in question; informants should then be asked for their observation of any changes in the patient, nature and time of onset of symptoms, impact on functioning, and so on, as well as a description of the patient's functioning and personality prior to the injury. In a forensic case, where verification is important, an effort should be made to contact more than one informant. In such cases, care should be taken to have prepared the questions in advance to allow for comparable responses from different informants. Structured interviews are often very helpful and include the Iowa Collateral Head Injury Interview (Varney & Menefee, 1993), the Head Injury Family Interview (Cavallo, Kay, & Ezrachi, 1992), or the Portland Adaptability Inventory (Lezak, 1995).

In-person interviews are preferable, but in the interest of time and cooperation, phone interviews can also yield valuable data. Checking to ensure that the informant is able to speak without being overheard and that the informant has enough time to talk is an elementary step, but it is often appreciated by the informant and necessary to the interview.

In addition to making phone calls, it is usually a good practice when setting up the first appointment to ask that any prior evaluations, medical reports (including neuroimaging), and other material conceivably relevant to the patient's history and complaints be provided either before or at that time. This gives patients a chance to request medical records from their physicians or hospital and to search for relevant documentation (e.g., school records) in advance.

The Content

Historical data form the framework within which neuropsychological assessment results are interpreted. This section will address what an adequate database consists of and suggest comprehensive and time-efficient ways to gather such data.

Primary Complaints and Their History

Establishing the primary complaints and the full range of associated symptoms may involve input from the patient; referral source, family members, friends, coworkers, staff members, or others involved with the patient. Before even interviewing the patient, the clinician may have been aided in this process by use of questionnaires that gather information concerning the onset, course, and present impact of the disorder, such as The Head

Injury Questionnaire, Head Injury Family Interview, or Reitan's Neuropsychology History Questionnaire (Wolfson, 1985). Neuropsychological Symptom checklists can save time and add detail. These include the following: Crook's MAC Memory Scale (Crook & Larrabee, 1992), Neuropsychological Symptom Checklist (Schinka, 1983), or various questionnaires for ratings of ADHD symptoms (Achenbach, 1991; Barkley, 1998; Conners, 1997).

For each of the major symptoms, one needs to know the time and nature of onset and subsequent progression. This is critical for the diagnosis of many conditions. For example, ADHD symptoms start in childhood, not adulthood. In contrast, postconcussion syndrome symptoms start after a head injury and should follow a course of gradual improvement over the following months, barring development of various medical complications such as seizure disorder, chronic pain, psychiatric disorders (e.g., PTSD, depression, etc.), or significant environmental changes (e.g., greater independence due to divorce, return to a stressful job, etc.).

Especially with traumatic brain injuries, it is often better to go through the exact details of all that the patient remembers or knows about the time prior to receiving the injury to establish onset of retrograde amnesia, and document the first memories following the injury to establish the time of anterograde amnesia. Inquiry for symptoms of PTSD could include questions about recurring nightmares, for example, or a brief questionnaire, such as the Impact of Event Scale (Horowitz, Wilner, & Alvarez, 1979; Zilberg, Weiss, & Horowitz, 1982) could be utilized. The patient's reply to such questions would be meaningless unless the clinician has understood the extreme event the patient has experienced.

It is important to differentiate what is recalled from what the individual has been told or read as well as to determine the immediate effects of the injury (i.e., altered levels of awareness or mental status). In this regard, utilization of emergency room (ER) reports, eyewitness accounts, and police reports can be invaluable. Often individuals' view of themselves and their functioning can be colored by what they have read or been told about the presumed disorder. Consequently, it is important to ascertain what information has been relayed to them by medical staff, family, friends, media, and lawyers, or what they have learned from research on the Internet. If the person had previously sought care for the neurological, medical, or psychological problems related to the injury, it is essential to know where the care took place, what treatment was attempted, and with what response.

The role of data-gatherer may include the need for intervention, as in discovering that manifestly unsafe driving or living situations are occurring in a case of dementia secondary to Alzheimer's or Lupus, for example. A case of depression with suicidal ideation following a postconcussion syndrome, or a reactive depression due to loss of function, may require immediate intervention in the form of referral for medications, counseling, or a period of inpatient care. At such times, the value of having involved collateral informants becomes apparent. These significant others are often the ones who can help make arrangements for hospitalizing the patient, or help with making alternate driving or living arrangements for a patient who cannot take care of these matters unassisted. In some instances of severe psychiatric disruption, it is often most beneficial to postpone any formal neuropsychological evaluation until after stabilization of the individual's psychiatric functioning.

An understanding of the present status of symptoms is necessary, along with a sense of their impact upon the patient's functional abilities in the areas of marital and family life, occupational performance, educational performance (of a student), hobbies and recreational activities, self-care, activities of daily living, social interactions, and religious activities, if any. In all of these, one needs to estimate the degree of disability and any decline from a previously higher level, using self-report, old educational and work records, and collateral informants.

Neuropsychological Social History

Neuropsychological social history deals with the older history, much of which may precede the episode that brought the patient to assessment. Any single neuropsychological test result can be of limited diagnostic meaning because so many variables can influence any given test behaviors. For example, a Major Depressive Disorder can act to reduce concentration and speed of performance. In an elderly person, depression can severely impact cognitive processing. A person may claim difficulties due to a current head injury, but exploration of old records may show that exactly the same kinds of disabilities preceded the injury. The history helps to establish a preinjury level of functioning. The history improves the accuracy of generalizing from samples of test behavior to making statements about the patient's functioning in real world situations and the ways these may differ from previous levels of functioning. As with the use of collateral informants, the history improves *ecological validity* of the interpretation of test results.

This historical material is obtained through an interview with the patient and collateral informants, and it is often supplemented through the use of questionnaires (given to patients and collaterals) and the use of old records.

Use of Questionnaires and the Interview

The advantage of using questionnaires is that they provide the examiner with a broad base of information in a cost-effective manner, allowing the examiner the opportunity to preview which areas are likely to need attention during the interview and which ones are unlikely to be an issue and require no follow-up questioning. Because patients do not necessarily give information in the same format that is convenient for the written report, such questionnaires help to place at least some of the information where it can be easily referenced for inclusion in the report and can also help in the organization of the information into a report. The questionnaire gives the patient a chance to warm up to the interview and serves as a preview of the knowledge that will be needed during the interview. During the interview, the examiner can go over the questionnaire material and clarify or expand on areas of ambiguity or diagnostic importance. Going over the questionnaire material provided by the patient can also help to add structure to the interview task and give both the patient and the examiner a defined common task and focus for the interview. Many questionnaires and formats for the interview process are available in published form or commercially (Siegal, 1996; Wolfson, 1995).

If the patient is an adult, the examiner needs a history that includes information regarding the present living arrangements; marital status; educational and work history; medical history; psychiatric and substance use history; history of trauma; past and present legal history, including pending litigation; and family and developmental history. This information is necessary in order to establish the level of premorbid functioning and to detect comorbid medical and psychiatric disorders, environmental conditions, or a combination, that may have contributed to, or be currently having, an impact on the primary problem with which the patient presented. There are several detailed neuropsychologically oriented developmental history forms available for children (e.g., Barkley, 1998; Levine, 1996).

The questionnaires are best filled out in the office for several reasons, including the advantage of the patient being able to ask questions about instructions and knowing how long it took the patient to complete the task.

If not done at the office, the examiner has no way of knowing if any kind of coaching took place. Additionally, some questionnaires are long and personal. If they are sent home to the patient, especially before the first interview and in the absence of a prior relationship with the examiner, it may be difficult for the patient to complete it. If this were to occur, it could jeopardize the patient's proceeding further with the evaluation.

Use of Old Records to Supplement History

To the degree that the information is needed, old records can greatly help to establish the premorbid level of functioning, the nature of the injury, and the impact of the injury upon current functioning, in a way that is independent of the patient's self-report. In the case of a motor vehicle accident resulting in a head injury, old records that would support an estimate of preinjury cognitive functioning may include high school and college transcripts and results of prior group achievement testing or individual testing. Pre- and post-injury job performance evaluations can also help to establish the level of functioning both before and after the accident. Previous IQ, personality, and neuropsychological assessments, where available, will help track and independently document the premorbid level and course since the injury and can provide a direct comparison between past and current levels of functioning. If the patient was on disability prior to the accident, then prior evaluations that helped to establish the existence of disability should also be sought.

With a motor vehicle or other type of accident, it is often possible to obtain records from the police and the emergency medical technicians who treated the patient at the scene and who transported the patient to the hospital. Emergency room and inpatient admission and discharge summaries are also helpful, along with postdischarge rehabilitation and medical care records. These all help to establish and document the existence and severity of the initial injury and the course and degree of the recovery. Records about preexisting conditions (e.g., MS, a seizure disorder, lead poisoning, etc.) should also be obtained because symptoms from the prior condition can potentially contribute to the present cognitive problems.

In the case of a child or adolescent evaluation, a detailed developmental history is important, and an interview with one or more parent is essential. Birth records can also be of help and will frequently contain Apgar scores or other information concerning potential complications associated with delivery (e.g., fetal distress, development of jaundice, etc.). The importance of medical records around perinatal events can be illustrated in one instance where a parent reported great fetal distress in a child for whom she was seeking disability benefits. However, the child's birth records were contradictory, showing excellent Apgar scores of 9 and 10. Other facts of perinatal life, such as birth weight, can also be very telling.

Use of Collateral Informants to Supplement History

If the patient is a child or adolescent, and the parents are the informants, ask them to bring records, including a baby book, if there is one. A baby book sometimes greatly aids in documenting old history, for example, by giving the date of an attack of meningitis or head injury.

A body of research has developed on potential cognitive impacts of varied mental illnesses and psychoactive medications (Puente & McCaffrey, 1992). In addition to inquiries for signs and symptoms of mental disorder, brief rating scales can supplement a patient's self-report regarding mood, family and marital problems, substance abuse, or a combination, all of which can potentially affect test performance. Examples of such scales are the Beck Depression Inventory-II (BDI-II; Beck, Steer, & Brown, 1996), the Beck Anxiety Inventory (BAI; Beck, 1993), the Michigan Alcoholism Screening Test (MAST; Selzer, 1971; Rumpf, Hapke, Hill, & John, 1997), and the Locke Marital Satisfaction Inventory (Locke & Wallace, 1959).

Sometimes, a simple inquiry around the presence or absence of major signs of mental disorder rules them out. But, if any such signs are present, a mental status examination (MSE) is in order to evaluate type and severity of the disorder and the impact of the disorder upon daily living, and, therefore, upon neuropsychological test performance. Examples of such neuropsychologically oriented MSEs can be found in Lezak (1995) and Siegal (1996).

Medications prescribed for physical and mental illnesses affect neurotransmitters and, in turn, affect cognitive functioning. The examiner may need to research these cognitive effects in order to consider them as potential contributors or causes for impaired neuropsychological performance. For example, a patient with an apparent loss of cognitive function on repeated neuropsychological testing over the preceding 5 years had also been receiving increasing doses of Clozaril. This, together with the fact that he appeared to be sedated, suggested that the medication increases might be responsible. Reduction of the Clozaril confirmed the diagnosis that sedation was the problem as the previously apparent decline in cognitive functioning was reversed. Specific inquiry should be made for the date and time (if recent) of the last use of any potentially mind-altering substance (whether prescription or nonprescription, legal or illegal) that the patient, collateral informants, or records have indicated the patient may have taken.

In sum, it is the process of gathering historical data that allows the clinician to go into the evaluation with hypotheses about what may be going on with the client, to select tests that will allow for the support or disconfirmation of those hypotheses, and to interpret the results. The data-gathering process also allows the neuropsychologist to identify who the real consumer(s) of the assessment will be and which issues they are struggling with. In gaining knowledge about the concerns, problems, resources, skills, and solutions the consumer has already attempted, the neuropsychologist has the best chance to develop a truly consumer-oriented assessment. Recommendations emanating from such an assessment would more readily be able to incorporate the use of resources that the consumer actually has. Gathering the historical data, although requiring some time and effort, is essential to the creation of the consumer-oriented neuropsychological report.

6

Reporting the Results of the Neuropsychological Evaluation

John Mendoza

The normal culmination of a neuropsychological assessment is to provide feedback to the referral source. This is typically done by means of a written report. In the process of developing this report, the neuropsychologist (a) reviews and analyzes the patient's personal and medical background; (b) makes clinical observations; (c) examines the patient and collects any necessary psychometric data; (d) considers the probable reliability, validity, and relevance or significance of each; and (e) condenses this information into a concise narrative that details the patient's condition and offers diagnostic impressions and recommendations for treatment. Although this process can be relatively informal (e.g., a brief chart note), it is the more formal, detailed written report that will be the focus of this chapter.

Although the written report has obvious importance for both the patient and the referral source, one should not ignore its relevance for the neuropsychologist. When writing a formal, detailed neuropsychological report, one is obliged to analyze and integrate all available information and data at a much deeper level than would ordinarily be necessary when only oral feedback or a brief written summary is required. The written report generally demands more rigorous attention to the subtle nuances and intercorrelations of the data. There is also a greater pull to resolve seemingly discrepant *pieces of the puzzle*. Thus, when composing the written report, the neuropsychologist is obliged to take a more penetrating look at the process by which hypotheses are formulated and defended. When approached in this manner, report writing can be a strong educational tool, even for the advanced clinician.

Additionally, each time a clinician arrives at a diagnostic conclusion, that clinician's professional reputation is placed on the line. The report is not only written documentation of the writer's diagnostic accuracy, but also a reflection of the clinician's professional knowledge and judgment. Even if the diagnoses, interpretations, and clinical logic are accurate, poorly organized reports filled with apparent inconsistencies and grammatical errors can be perceived as weak, confused, or conceptually deficient and, hence, diminish the credibility of their author. Thus, both content and style become important considerations in report writing.

Just as this book is not intended to teach the practice of neuropsychology, this chapter is not designed to teach report writing. The purpose is to suggest some general guidelines that might be considered when writing neuropsychological reports. Given the variety of training experiences, as well as the range of philosophical and psychometric approaches to neuropsychology, diverse styles of report writing are also common. However, whether the data were derived from fixed or flexible batteries, standardized instruments, or semistructured mental status examinations (MSEs), or whether they reflect a statistical versus a process-oriented approach, the resulting reports are likely to share many common features. Individual reports are most likely to vary along three primary dimensions: length, form, and style. Each of these will be discussed in turn.

Length of the Report

A neuropsychological report may vary from what can be handwritten on the front and back of a consult sheet to multiple typewritten pages. There are a variety of factors that may dictate the length of the report:

1. ***Nature of the Exam*:** Even a fairly comprehensive mental status exam is not going to generate the same amount of data as a 4- to 8-hour battery of tests and, therefore, the resulting report of an MSE is likely to be briefer than that of a test battery.
2. ***Efficiency*:** Report writing can be, and often is, a very time-consuming enterprise. The busy clinician who may be asked to see several consults a day, or who has other major responsibilities, simply may not always have the time to devote to writing multipage reports.

(Actually, in some respects, writing a good brief report can be a greater challenge, and it is a skill well worth mastering.) A more detailed, lengthy report, however, may be preferable for some consumers (e.g., forensic reports; see chapters 2 and 12).

3. ***Expectations or Purpose*:** A request for baseline data on a chronic dementia or presurgical tumor patient may be very different from a request involving a young, closed-head trauma patient who is being referred for vocational rehabilitation. All that may be needed or expected by the referral source in a chronic dementia case is a relatively brief summary of current findings along with a diagnostic impression against which future data might be compared. In a young, head injury case, a much more detailed report may be required to describe the pattern of behavioral and cognitive changes, along with their implications for education, training, and independent living (see chapter 3).

Form of the Report

Although they may not be totally independent of one another, it is useful to differentiate between what might be described as the form versus the style of the report. In presenting the results of a neuropsychological examination, the author, after determining the meaning of the findings, must decide the following: (a) in what order, or according to what schema, the data might be presented, and then (b) how to describe or discuss the actual data. The first is a question of form, and the second is a matter of style. For present purposes, form may be viewed as the general outline or format for organizing the data in a meaningful and logical manner. For example, the data might be arranged according to (a) the sources from which the data are derived; (b) the specific tests or categories of tests administered; (c) salient theoretical models of brain organization, or function, or both; (d) the patient's performance on the examination itself (e.g., strengths vs. weaknesses); or (e) some combination of these.

Despite their potential diversity, many neuropsychological reports are characterized by relatively similar formats. Divergence is most likely to occur in terms of how the test results themselves are reported or explained (see chapter 7). This difference in style will also be discussed in greater detail under the section on Style of the Report. Although the length of the report may impact its form, the brief and the more extensive report may often be somewhat comparable, especially if written by the same author. The main difference may be simply the amount of detail that is included. On other occasions, brief reports may take on a very different format, resembling the Summary and Conclusions section of a more detailed, formal report. The following sections represent a common, though not invariate, outline for a detailed neuropsychological report. This format is presented for illustrative purposes and is not meant to reflect the only way of organizing a report.

1. Referral Question—There are several benefits to including a separate section in the formal report that states the referral question. This may not only help the writer in structuring the content or focus of the report, but may also provide structure for its readers, preparing them for what is to follow. This may consist of a brief statement of the known or suspected problems and why the evaluation was requested (e.g., "40-year-old male who sustained a closed-head injury and complained of memory loss. He was referred to define possible cognitive or behavioral sequelae, or both, and to make recommendations for vocational rehabilitation"). Often the referral question as found on the consult is either only implied (e.g., "Patient is S/P CVA, please evaluate"), unclear, or improperly defined by the referral source. In such instances, it may fall to the neuropsychologist in collaboration with referral source(s) to refine the question (see chapter 3).

2. History and Background Information—Gathering history and background information typically begins by providing basic demographic information: age; gender; personal and familial handedness; educational, vocational, ethnic, or linguistic background; personal and familial psychiatric history; medical and neurological history; and laboratory findings. Medications and possible physical limitations are also included in this section. A more in-depth review of this material is presented in chapter 5.

If not previously addressed under the Referral Question section, any relevant behavioral, emotional, cognitive, or physical changes and the history of their onset and development as reported either by the patient or other outside sources (e.g., family members) are frequently reviewed or expanded upon at this time. This information is often crucial in establishing the diagnosis, once the validity of the presenting complaints has been established, along with any other associated symptoms or findings. This section may also provide details regarding the patient's current living situation, extraordinary stresses or demands the patient may be facing, and available support systems. This information can provide the reader with a framework in which to view and understand the potential impact of any behavioral or cognitive impairments that might be discussed in the report. Such information also serves as a basis for judging the external consistency of the findings outlined in the report.

3. Behavioral Observations—The writer may choose to incorporate behavioral observations under a combined History and Behavioral Observations section of the report. Regardless of where the behavioral observations are placed, as is the case with historical information, behavioral data are often more important than the actual test scores and may be critical to the interpretation of overall test performance as well as providing valuable insights into the patient's adaptive capacities. In addition, a sampling of how the patient functions in a social situation where varying demands are being placed on attention, interpersonal and communication skills, memory, and problem-solving abilities, provide the examiner with a real-time glimpse into the patient's insight, cognitive strategies or response style, and coping mechanisms.

Finally, behavioral observations can also be critical in assessing the internal or external consistency of the report. Factors to which one might routinely attend generally fall into two categories:

- Factors that may compromise the validity or reliability of the test results—for example, diminished attention, effort, or motivation; capacity to understand and remember test instructions (e.g., cultural, linguistic, academic, or intellectual limitations); physical limitations; affective or anxiety disorders; personality problems (e.g., hostility, paranoia), or other distracting conditions (e.g., pain, sleep deprivation, illnesses); and any suspicions of malingering, exaggeration of deficits, or other deliberate or subconscious attempts by the patient to manipulate the results of the examination.
- Factors that themselves may be symptomatic of brain disease or may be important in differential psychiatric diagnoses—for example, emotional lability; impaired judgment or behavioral disinhibition; impulsivity or excessively long response latencies; psychomotor slowing; distractibility; disturbed or unusual thought processes; confusion, disorientation, lack of insight, a breakdown in one's self-monitoring capacity, or a combination; perceptual anomalies (e.g., hallucinations); sensory, motor, speech, and language deficits, or a combination; perseveration, confabulation, or other anomalous behaviors.

4. Assessment Procedures—This may include chart reviews and clinical interviews with patient and/or family, but typically the focus is on the various instruments employed in the formal examination of the patient. This outline of tests administered is likely to be of interest not only to third party payors (e.g., HMOs and insurance companies, who will not be receiving the bulk of the report, but only the procedures and diagnoses), but to another neuropsychologist who might eventually receive or review the report as well.

5. Test Results—There are multiple ways one may choose to organize the results of formal testing and/or other examination procedures. The same general principles that apply to the report as a whole apply here: namely, to arrange the information in a manner that facilitates both ease of presentation for the author and increased meaningfulness and comprehensibility for the reader. Where and how these individual test results will be reported may vary depending upon the personal preference of the writer or the specific nature of the patient's performance. As suggested earlier, one may elect to structure this section according to the specific tests used, the strengths versus weaknesses in the patient's performance, a structural and/or functional model of the brain, or some variation of these.

Regardless of which approach or strategy is chosen, one would do well to remember that most, if not all, neuropsychological tests are multifactorial in nature, and deficits may result from any of a number of basic deficiencies other than those purported to be measured by the individual tests.

It is also important to remember that what ultimately matters is not how poorly a patient performs on "Block Design" or "Picture Arrangement" (chances are they will never be asked to tackle these tasks outside the testing situation), but rather the insights their performance on these measures offers regarding the integrity of basic brain functions. Hopefully then, such insights can be generalized to real-world situations. This identification, integration, and translation of cognitive, affective, perceptual, and sensorimotor deficits into behaviorally meaningful terms is the underlying goal of most neuropsychological reports.

Reports that are organized on a test-by-test basis, although easier to construct, may be cumbersome for the reader, who should neither be placed in the position of trying to integrate and interpret their interrelationships, nor put at risk of getting lost in a morass of minutiae. Most critically, such reports not only often fail to integrate the overall test results into meaningful neurobehavioral terms, they frequently either fail to resolve apparent inconsistencies within the data,[1] or they end up unnecessarily multiplying suspected sites of lesions. Likewise, computerized reports are generally notorious for being heavily reliant on statistical analysis, although lacking any analysis of the specific behavioral deficits in the individual patient that resulted in the observed scores.

For example, a given patient may have difficulties on the Block Design test for various reasons, including limited intelligence; specific visual-spatial, visual-perceptual, or constructional deficits; poor planning or problem solving strategies; or impulsivity and deficient self-monitoring capacity (cf. Kaplan, 1988). Tests of learning and memory provide another good example. Is the patient's performance a result of problems with attention, intention, the registration or encoding of specific types of information or through particular modalities, or a more general storage or retrieval problem?

The following demonstrates one approach to organizing the Test Results section of a report. It is presented for illustrative purposes and is certainly not intended to represent the only, nor even the most optimal possibility. Personal preferences or circumstances may demand something quite different (see chapter 11 for another example).

> ***5.1 Orientation***—If one chooses to make orientation a separate section within the Test Results section, then information relating to the patient's awareness of (a) person (e.g., age, date of birth, address, employment, or marital status), (b) place (e.g., city, building, type of institution), (c) time (e.g., year, season, month, day, date, time of day, passages of time), or (d) situation (e.g., awareness of problems, why the patient is being tested, the role of the examiner or others in the immediate vicinity), would likely be included here. However, these data could also be included under the Behavioral Observations section.
>
> ***5.2 Attention and Concentration***—In an Attention and Concentration section, one may choose to include those tests or behavioral measures that are thought to be particularly sensitive to the patient's ability to attend or concentrate (i.e., to focus his or her attention more intensely, or for a longer period of time, or both) on relatively rote or cognitively simple tasks such as those involving signal detection, freedom from distractibility, or even immediate recall of limited bits of

[1]For example, discrepancies between performance levels on different tests of memory, or on other tests which may have a strong memory component may go unexplained.

information (e.g., digit or spatial span).[2] At the same time, one should remain cognizant that most, if not all, neuropsychological tasks require and depend on a certain optimal capacity to attend and concentrate, and that this capacity may vary from test to test or from moment to moment. This can have a profound influence on the predicted validity, reliability, or both, of any test, and any such potential influence should be noted.

Measures of alertness such as response latencies and overall processing speed, may also be discussed in this section. Other measures of attentional functioning, such as divided or distributed attention, can be included in this section (cf. Prather & Kaplan, 1991; Cohen, 1993); discussions of hemi-inattention or hemi-neglect may also be placed in this section. Finally, one may want to compare or contrast behavioral evidence of the patient's capacity to attend and concentrate as witnessed coincidentally during the clinical interview or testing in general as opposed to the patient's performance on *specific tests* of attention and concentration.

5.3 Mental Flexibility/Executive Functions—Included in the Mental Flexibility and Executive Functions section might be any of a large number of cognitively complex tasks (verbal or spatial-perceptual, or both) that tap abstract or reasoning capacity, concept formation, ability to plan and organize, capacity to shift mental or perceptual sets, or ability to utilize feedback in making cognitive judgments or in problem-solving (see Delis-Kaplan Executive Function System; Delis, Kaplan, & Kramer, 2001). In addition to more formal tests designed to tap these functions, *executive deficits* can often be observed in any of a large variety of tasks. Some caution is urged in terms of how such groupings are used. Many of the descriptors used here are often associated with disruptions of frontal systems, not simply with *frontal lobe lesions*.

5.4 Primary Sensory and Perceptual Abilities—Many neuropsychological examinations include various measures of basic sensation and perception. The Primary Sensory and Perceptual Abilities section might encompass indications of primary auditory, visual, somesthetic,

[2]Although measured more formally through the use of such psychometric techniques, attention and concentration, along with general arousal, are also noted as part of behavioral observations.

and olfactory sensory deficits (e.g., visual field cuts, anosmia); secondary (but unimodal) perceptual disturbances (e.g., agnosias); or other higher order sensory or perceptual disturbances (e.g., unilateral neglect, suppression on bilateral simultaneous stimulation, autotopagnosia, and anosognosia).

5.5 Psychomotor Functions—Motor deficits covered in the Psychomotor Functions section of the report may range from gross behavioral observations (e.g., generalized psychomotor slowing, tremors, gait disturbances, or a unilateral decrease in spontaneous movement) to direct examination of specific motor functions. Such a direct examination might include assessments of change or asymmetries in strength, speed, or dexterity in manipulating objects, or a combination (e.g., coin rotation, finger tapping), or in free movements (i.e., dysdiadochokinesia). Postural drift, reaching for objects in space, as well as many manipulative tasks, combine sensory and motor components and, hence, may reflect deficits in either system.

In any motor (or sensory) exam, it is important to differentiate peripheral versus central and, in the case of a motor exam, cerebral versus cerebellar deficits. Although neuropsychologists naturally think of pyramidal, basal ganglia, and cerebellar systems when assessing motor functions, it is important to recall that disturbances in other systems may also result in complex motor symptoms. Thus, one may choose to include in this section disconnection syndromes with primary motor manifestations, such as deficits in reciprocal coordination or ideomotor praxis, or disruptions in complex motor programming, such as *go/no-go*, conflicting, or complex motor sequencing tasks (see Luria, 1980).

5.6 Speech and Language—As is the case with attention and concentration, there are generally at least two independent sources of information about speech and language areas of functioning: behavioral observations during the course of contact with the patient and the results of formal examinations or test measures. Any major discrepancies between these sources should be documented and explained. Typically included in this section are assessments of (a) spontaneous and elicited speech and language (e.g., initiation, articulation, volume, fluency, repetition, word-finding and naming ability; evidence of paraphasias; informational content and grammar), (b) auditory comprehension (for both informal conversational speech and test instructions, as well as for formal commands that range in complexity), (c) writing (e.g., composition, spatial organization, graphomotor skills, grammar, and spelling), and (d) reading (both aloud and for comprehension). Paralinguistic aspects of communication usually associated with right-hemisphere dysfunction (e.g., affective and linguistic aprosodias) might also be included in this section. Table 6-1 summarizes these paralinguistic aspects.

5.7 Visual Spatial Skills—Tests or functions subsumed under the Visual Spatial Skills section heading are less well defined than is the case with the areas listed earlier. Tasks involving graphomotor copying or free drawing of complex figures or geometric designs and two- or three-dimensional object assembly tasks such as Block Design (Wechsler, 1991), Benton's Test of Three-dimensional Block

Table 6-1
Right-Hemisphere Contributions to Communication

Expressive affective prosody—verbal
Imparting the desired emotional valence to one's speech through appropriate affective intonations (e.g., *sounding angry* when you are indeed upset)

Expressive linguistic prosody—verbal
Ability to vary the meaning of spoken expression through the use of appropriate tonal inflection to key words or phrases (e.g., "YOU (the perennial cheapskate) bought us two tickets to the football game?" vs. "You BOUGHT (when I could have gotten them free at the office) us two tickets to the football game?" vs. "You bought us two tickets to the FOOTBALL (when you know I don't like football) game?")

Expressive prosody—nonverbal
Expression of mood or emotional state through nonverbal means (e.g., facial expression, body posture)

Receptive affective prosody—verbal
Deciphering the meaning of oral verbal communication or mood of the speaker by accurately interpreting tonal inflections

Receptive linguistic prosody—verbal
Appreciation of humor, sarcasm, or emphasis in the speech of others

Receptive prosody—nonverbal
Ability to accurately decipher the mood of others, or the *message* others are sending by accurately interpreting facial expressions or body postures

Meta-aspects of oral or written communication
Organization of oral or written discourse—*staying on course, or keeping to the point*

Responsiveness to social cues (e.g., turn-taking, awareness of the impact one's discourse is having on others—via verbal and nonverbal receptive prosody)

Discerning the *point* or *theme* in the discourse of others

Interpreting the *message* in light of the overall context or circumstances in which it was delivered

Construction (Benton & Hamsher, 1989), as well as tests that simply involve the perceptual analysis of complex geometric patterns are typically included in this section. Echoing the warning in the introduction to this section on Test Results, tasks that normally might be labeled as *visual-spatial* or *visual-perceptual* are multifactorial and may involve considerable planning, self-monitoring, verbal-analytic, reasoning, or general intellectual abilities. These would include not only those tests that more clearly involve higher level problem-solving, such as the WAIS-III (Wechsler, 1997a) Object Assembly, Block Design, Picture Arrangement, or Raven's Progressive Matrices (1938/1996), but may extend to tasks such as the Rey-Osterrieth Complex Figure (Meyers & Meyers, 1995) and clock drawing (Freedman et al., 1994). On the other hand, some verbal tasks require varying degrees of visual-spatial abilities (e.g., arithmetic computations). One also has to be cautious in separating what is generally assumed to be a disorder which ostensibly reflects a higher order integrative ability from simple motor, primary sensory, or secondary, unimodal perceptual disturbances.

5.8 Intellectual And Academic Abilities—Although Intellectual and Academic Abilities is a relatively straightforward section that typically includes the results of formal intelligence tests and formal measures of academic achievement, one may choose to list these separately. Additionally, all or parts of some of these measures may be incorporated under other headings. For example, digit span may be reported as a measure of attention and concentration, whereas block constructions may be included with other tests of visual-spatial abilities.

Some authors may choose to include the results of formal intelligence tests under the Mental Flexibility and Cognitive Efficiency section as representing a broad measure of cognitive abilities in general. A word of caution about intelligence tests may be appropriate here. Although they can be very informative and useful in many cases, they are often found to be poorly correlated with either brain injury (especially if isolated to the frontal association cortices) or day-to-day adaptive functioning.

5.9 Learning and Memory—Again, formal psychometric data should be compared with information derived from the history and clinical interview. For example, questions should be raised if a patient can provide a fairly rich, detailed personal history, but "falls apart" on formal tests of learning and retention. Some of the more critical aspects of learning and memory that might be considered in the psychometric assessment of memory include: (a) capacity to learn new information across various input modalities (visual-auditory) as well as content areas (verbal, spatial, and procedural, or a combination); (b) capacity to retain new information over time or in the face of interference, using free and cued delayed recall, recognition memory, or implicit memory paradigms; and (c) anterograde or new learning versus retrograde or remote memory (defined, in part, depending on whether one has a fixed reference point in time for a suspected neurological event). Finally, as with other functional domains, one needs to consider other potential contributions of performance deficiencies on tests of memory (e.g., distractibility, poor motivation, sensory-perceptual deficits, or other cognitive or behavioral impairments).

5.10 Personality (Psychological) Assessment—Indices of psychosocial, emotional, and psychiatric difficulties as well as basic personality profiles typically constitute an integral part of neuropsychological examinations. Although the clinical interview provides information in this regard, it is frequently supplemented by more formal psychological tests and self-report measures. Questionnaires that are completed by family members can be included in the Personality (Psychological) Assessment section as well. At some point in the report, one commonly makes reference to the possibility or likelihood that a patient is malingering, exaggerating, or otherwise not performing in an optimal capacity, as well as an explanation of the possible dynamics behind such behavior. Depending upon the circumstances surrounding the individual case, measures specifically designed to assess these phenomena (e.g., symptom validity tests) may be either routinely or selectively incorporated into the formal assessment protocol. There may be an advantage in revealing any perceived tendency on the part of the patient to respond in a less than straightforward manner early in the report (e.g., in the Behavioral Observations section), as this will caution the reader to keep an open mind when reviewing any subsequent data.

6. Summary and Conclusions—It is generally within the Summary and Conclusions section that the author attempts to analyze, integrate, and interpret the most salient features of the data as derived from the history, clinical interviews, behavioral observations, clinical examination, and formal test data. Through this process, one hopefully arrives at a meaningful and comprehensive description of the pattern of the patient's neurobehavioral strengths and weaknesses (or deficits) and formulates a response to the referral question. This may include formal diagnostic impression(s) and recommendations for psychological, behavioral, educational, or vocational intervention. Although some preliminary statements regarding the level or qualitative descriptions of performance for individual tests or tasks can be provided under the Test Results section of the report, there are clear advantages to delaying final test interpretations until this section of the report when all clinical data, including any common elementary deficits, can be fully integrated.[3] Also, care should be taken not to introduce new data in the Summary that have not been previously mentioned in the body of the report.

Although there may be some variation from case to case, one will typically want to address the extent to which the patient's current level of functioning is suspected to reflect a change from baseline, along with a description of the fundamental nature, severity, and extent of these changes. More often than not, there may be real or apparent inconsistencies either within the psychometric data themselves or between the psychometric data and other sources of information (e.g., history or behavioral observations). If these inconsistencies have not been previously addressed, this would be a good place to discuss and, if possible, explain them. It is of particular importance to note and discuss any inconsistencies between the neuropsychological findings and the known or suspected neurological diagnoses.

Finally, in this section one can review the anticipated impact of perceived cognitive, behavioral, or perceptual-motor changes on the patient's adaptive capacity in that patient's environment. The possible interaction of personality, emotional, psychiatric, or environmental variables on the patient's overall psychological adjustment and any related potential management difficulties may also be discussed here. Specific recommendations, however, are best presented in a separate section of the report (see later discussion here and in chapter 8).

7. Recommendations—The recommendations may be very brief and general or quite extensive and very detailed. At their simplest level, these recommendations might suggest that the patient is not likely to be competent

[3]Test-by-test interpretation approaches tend to unnecessarily multiply reported deficits and are less likely to identify common, underlying factors that might better account for the observed behaviors.

to manage personal affairs, or they might advise reevaluation after a certain period to track further changes in mental status. In other situations, elaborate behavioral or environmental management suggestions may be included (but see the discussion in chapter 8 for the difference between recommendations and treatment plans). These suggestions may entail advising the patient (or the family) to consider alternate or compensatory strategies to more effectively circumvent functional deficits along with specific recommendations concerning the patient's current or proposed academic or vocational endeavors. Specialized remediation or therapeutic goals and treatment plans may be discussed in the context of identified follow-up plans and resources. Referrals for other services or specialty evaluations indicate an awareness that the patient's needs or problems may extend beyond the neuropsychologist's area of expertise or practice. Although the nature of the referral often dictates the nature and extent of the recommendations provided, as a general rule, some concrete suggestions are routinely included as an integral part of most formal reports.

It is normally ill-advised for a neuropsychologist to make a specific recommendation for cognitive rehabilitation in any program in which the neuropsychologist has a financial investment because this may be viewed as a direct conflict of interests. Although legitimate exceptions may occur, erring on the side of caution is advisable.

8. Diagnostic Impressions—Although the issue of differential diagnosis may be discussed in detail in the Summary and Conclusions section, some authors prefer to provide a brief statement of the probable diagnostic possibilities under a separate heading at the conclusion of the report. Although these may follow the form and content outlined in the *DSM-IV* nomenclature, this format may not always be necessary or practical.

The psychiatric manual (*DSM-IV*) is designed to discuss syndromes that are likely to be confused with or to have symptoms similar to those seen in functional psychiatric disorders. The manual does not provide the latitude or the depth for adequately classifying the myriad of syndromes common to many brain-injured patients, especially those with focal lesions. It is important to keep in mind that it is not always possible to arrive at a definitive diagnosis for each and every patient. Often, one may simply want to discuss the more likely alternatives, deferring the formal diagnosis until additional data have been obtained (e.g., follow-up testing in the case of suspected early dementia) or until other possibilities (e.g., depression) have been ruled out.

By way of summary, these last three sections of the report (i.e., Summary and Conclusions, Recommendations, and Diagnostic Impressions) generally attempt to answer the following questions:

1. Is there any evidence of behavioral or functional deficits or impairments?
2. What is the nature, extent, or degree of these deficits or impairments?
3. Do these deficits or impairments appear to reflect a significant change from the individual's baseline and, if so, over what period of time?
4. Do these changes appear to be the result of acquired brain dysfunction or impairment?
5. Does the pattern of deficits suggest any particular syndrome or disease entity?
6. Are there inconsistencies within the data that need to be addressed?
7. Are there inconsistencies with the presumptive diagnosis and, if so, what are the alternative hypotheses?
8. What other possible explanations (e.g., medical, behavioral, demographic, psychological) might account for the findings?
9. Are there independent psychological (or psychiatric) issues or diagnoses present?
10. What are the psychological or psychosocial effects of these impairments or this disease (or injury) process on the patient?
11. How will these impairments or this disease process affect the patient's ability to function on a day-to-day basis?
12. Are there any specific recommendations for treatment, management, or further diagnostic work-ups?
13. Are there any positive or negative prognostic indicators?

Style of the Report

If the form of the report describes the organization of the data, its style reflects the focus or approach that the author utilizes in presenting the data, including its interpretation and integration. As the two parts of the report that typically will be most affected by differences in style are Test Results and Summary and Conclusions, these are the main focus of this section.

Differences in style are often a function of the particular training and experiences of the writer. However, often the same individual may employ different styles depending upon the specific needs and circumstances of the case. In a broad sense, style may be said to vary along a continuum as a function of how the data (particularly the test data) are analyzed and presented. Although in practice they do not have to be and, in fact, are not always mutually exclusive, at one end of this continuum, tests may be presented in a highly quantitative style, almost as behavioral entities unto themselves. At the other end, test data may be represented by descriptions of what are thought to be more elementary or universal functions or factors that contribute to these individual tests or tasks, usually presented in a more qualitative style. Each of these two representative styles or approaches has its relative strengths and weaknesses and they are not necessarily mutually exclusive.

1. Quantitative Style—In the Quantitative style, the focus may be on presenting data in a more or less purely quantitative, objective fashion; in some ways this is not too dissimilar from the way medical laboratory results are reported (see chapter 7). Depending on the tests used, this usually translates into formal scores derived from normative data, such as IQ scores, *T* scores, percentile rank scores, standard scores, impairment indices, cutoff scores, grade equivalents, or raw scores (e.g., time, frequency, number or percentage correct, or errors) for each of the tests administered. The report of a survey by Finn, Moes, and Kaplan, presented in chapter 2 of this book, indicated that consumers largely favor percentiles as a mode of communicating quantitative data. This emphasizes the need for test developers to include percentile values in their tables so that they are readily available for neuropsychologists to include in their reports.

Independent of reevaluation, quantitative information can be highly informative to other neuropsychologists (or other professionals) who are familiar with both the tests and the meaning of the formal scores. For forensic purposes, one may feel more comfortable in citing the statistical references with regard to published research, normative, or standardization data. Another distinct, practical advantage is that reporting data in this manner is very efficient and generally less time consuming than other methods.

There are, however, some potential disadvantages in using a more quantitative, test-oriented approach, especially if it is used in relative isolation from other methods. Unless the consumer is intimately familiar with both the nature of the tests and the meaning of the particular statistic used to describe the results, scores (e.g., T scores or standard scores, or even means and standard deviations) may have little connotative value. This objection can be obviated, to some extent, by providing detailed descriptions of the tests and what they purportedly measure, using quantitative scores and ranges that are commonly understood. One example would be to convert all raw test scores into a common interpretive score such as a percentile rank.

Another problem is that, even if understood in terms of their statistical properties, quantitative scores by themselves can be either misleading or of limited value in certain situations (cf. Lezak, 1988). For example, an IQ score of 105 may reflect perfectly adequate performance in one individual, but reflect a substantial decline from premorbid capacity in a second patient. Another individual may be performing at the 5th percentile rank on a given test, but there may be no evidence that this result reflects a drop from this patient's normal baseline. Again, if adequate explanations accompany such scores, there is less likelihood of misinterpretation by the reader.

Possibly the most significant limitation to the quantitative approach, especially if used in isolation, is that what is being reported is a somewhat arbitrary test score derived from a test that is multifactorial in composition, that often has little known relevance or direct application to the patient's real life behavior, and that tells relatively little about the specific state of the patient's brain (cf. Kaplan, 1988; Caetano & Christensen, 1997). Most, if not all, tests consist of multiple, complex factors or require the convergence of many individual skills or abilities. By itself, a single test score cannot describe the individual factor(s) that seemed to have had the most significant impact on an individual's performance; that is, it cannot define the basic, underlying deficit(s). Also, unless clarified by the writer, the reader may have no way of knowing to what extent extraneous variables, such as educational background, culture, linguistic proficiency and background, premorbid intellectual limitations, attention to or cooperation with the examination, specific handicaps, or other situational factors, may have contributed to performance decrements.

2. Qualitative Style—Reporting the results of the neuropsychological examination in a more qualitative fashion can be accomplished in several ways. First, test results may be presented in general terms denoting the presence or absence of deficits, relative deficiencies or strengths, or a combination. For example, the patient's performance may be described as suggesting mild, moderate, or severe impairment, or as being borderline, superior, above or below average, or within normal limits. One advantage of such reporting is that it avoids the reification of a numerical score and takes into account a degree of error variance. Although such reporting lacks the degree of specificity of numerical scores, it may have more universal meaning to a wider range of individuals reading the report. Reporting in these terms is also more suitable to tests or procedures that do not readily lend themselves to such strict quantification. As has been recommended earlier, it is generally useful to independently indicate whether the patient's performance likely reflects a major change from estimated premorbid capacities, especially where nonpathognomonic signs or symptoms are involved.

On the other hand, because such descriptive terminology lacks the specificity afforded by standard scores, it is more subject to individual judgment or interpretive error by the examiner. Also, it may not always be safe to assume that these terms will have the same meaning to every reader. Unless reassessment is expected to be done by the same examiner, such terms can make test-retest comparisons more difficult. One compromise, as has been suggested in the literature (see chapter 7), would be for the examiner to report both formal test scores (where applicable) and descriptive statements regarding the perceived quality of the patient's performance. This might be particularly useful in situations where atypical (i.e., nonaverage) premorbid baselines are thought to exist or where other individual factors are considered relevant.

In addition to reporting level of performance in more qualitative terms, another method is simply to describe or define the specific behavior(s) generated by the test(s). Instead of reporting the data in terms of tests or subtests, this latter style generally focuses on either functional descriptions of the specific skills or abilities ostensibly being measured by the various tasks or, if possible, the more elementary factors that would appear to underlie the observed performance deficits. Such an approach might also involve detailing the type of errors made (e.g., segmentation in the Rey-Osterrieth Figure, or failure to use feedback effectively on the Wisconsin Card Sorting Test), the general strategy adopted in approaching the tasks, or any other variables that might have influenced either test performance or the way it is interpreted (e.g., premorbid limitations, mental or emotional set during the examination, or primary sensorimotor or cognitive deficits). This type of reporting can be particularly informative because it attempts to transcend the limits of the individual psychometric test and to define behaviors and factors that are more readily understandable to the nonpsychologist. It also, hopefully, more readily generalizes to *extratest* situations. A relative disadvantage of this approach is that such judgments may take more time and effort to report, are often subjective, and require considerable clinical expertise.

In summary, in writing any report, both the specific referral question and the interest and expertise of the referring source must be kept in mind. Such factors as the length of the report are not necessarily related to its usefulness or its relevance. Although a two-page report may be perfectly appropriate in some situations, it is not adequate for all. On the other hand, a 10-page, exquisitely detailed report may be deficient if it doesn't accurately capture the true nature of the patient's condition or if it fails to address what is important for the referral source. Similarly, despite what might be their inherent accuracy and relevance, unless the data are presented in such a manner that the referral source can translate or understand them in his or her own frame of reference, they fail to be optimally useful. In the Appendix to this chapter, common errors in report writing are described, in the hope that they will serve as warning posts to guide the writer to a successful, consumer-friendly neuropsychological report. There is no one commonly accepted style or approach to report writing, and each style is not without its benefits and limitations. Each neuropsychologist brings unique contributions to evaluation reports and must be fully mindful of the consumers and their needs.

Appendix 6-1

Common Errors in Report Writing

Clinical assessment and report writing involve multiple levels of subjective judgments on the part of the neuropsychologist. These include the following decisions: (a) what data to collect and report, (b) how the data should be interpreted, and (c) how the data should be organized and reported. Any time there is subjective judgment involved, there is always the possibility of error. Some errors may simply be due to carelessness, or may be relatively inconsequential (e.g., spelling or grammatical errors), whereas others may be much more egregious, potentially reflecting examiner bias, conceptual misunderstanding, or even basic incompetence. The latter usually have far more serious implications for the consumer as well as for the integrity of the profession. Because of this, both consumers (e.g., patients, referral sources, etc.) and practicing neuropsychologists should be aware of potential sources of error. The following is a brief, annotated list of what appear to be some of the more common errors found in reviewing both clinical and forensic neuropsychological reports over the years.[4]

I. Errors in Data Collection

1. Failure to provide adequate history.

Depending upon the referral question, a detailed clinical history that builds on an understanding and appreciation of neuropathology and neurobehavioral syndromes, can be as revealing, if not more so, than a 2- or 3-hour battery of tests. Additionally, a good history provides a context in which the psychometric data can be evaluated. Hence, it is important to answer the following questions:

1.1 Was the patient's premorbid level of functioning, including social and occupational performance, addressed and documented?

1.2. Was the nature, onset, and course of the presenting symptoms well established?

[4]This list was primarily based on the collective experiences of the author and Dr. Michael Howard, with additional input from other members of a Veterans Affairs (VA) Task Force charged with developing guidelines for the practice of neuropsychology within the VA system. A more complete review of this material was presented in a workshop by Dr. Mendoza and Dr. Howard at the October, 1996, annual meeting of the National Academy of Neuropsychology in New Orleans.

1.3. Was there a review of all pertinent medical, neurological, and other findings, both prior and subsequent to the onset of symptoms?

2. *Overreliance on self-reported symptoms.*

As noted earlier, a good clinical history is an invaluable diagnostic tool. However, on occasion, information provided by the patient (or family) can be misleading.

2.1. Is there evidence that the patient may be underreporting symptoms as a result of denial, lack of insight, or neglect such as might be found in dementia or certain focal brain lesions?

2.2. Is the patient overreporting current symptoms, or embellishing premorbid levels of functioning (as might be seen in forensic or compensation cases, or in certain psychiatric conditions such as depression)?

2.3. Is there an erroneous attribution of symptoms to the neuropathological condition in question (i.e., has the relative frequency with which the presenting complaints such as headaches or memory disturbances are reported in the general, forensic, or psychiatric populations, been taken into account)?

2.4. When appropriate, have adequate symptom validity measures been employed to assess the possibility of overreporting or underreporting symptoms?

3. *Inadequate behavioral observations.*

Along with the ability to conduct a meaningful interview, the power of observation is one of the clinician's more important diagnostic tools. Critical observations can either help establish or reinforce diagnostic impressions or, in some cases, reveal important discrepancies that should prompt the reevaluation of certain other data.

3.1 *During the clinical interview*, was attention paid to the patient's level of arousal, capacity for attention, recent and remote memory, language and organizational skills, social judgments and interactions, and general physical and emotional condition? As will be noted later, failure to contrast and compare such data with formal test results or in formulating diagnostic impressions can result in questionable conclusions.

3.2 *On formal assessment.* All neuropsychological tests are multifactorial, meaning that very different mechanisms or elementary behavioral deficits may result in performance deficits. Thus, during the administration of specific psychometric tests, was attention paid to the following:

3.2a. The specific difficulties experienced by the patient and the types of errors made?

3.2b. Whether the patient's approach to the task was random or systematic?

3.2c. The level and consistency of effort made by the patient?

3.2d. The patient's level of insight into errors made?

3.2e. The patient's capacity to readily shift strategies or response sets?

4. Inappropriate test selection.

Under certain conditions, many patients may be given similar batteries of tests. However, in most circumstances, tests are best selected based on the particular demands and circumstances of the case (e.g., the referral question, patient parameters, time available, and cost factors). Thus, in selecting the tests and examination procedures, the following questions must be addressed:

4.1. Was there adequate representation of all relevant functional areas?

4.2. Were the selected tests appropriate for the patient's age, cultural and educational background, physical limitations, and overall cognitive status?

4.3. Was the amount of testing justified given the patient's condition or the referral question?

4.4. Was there an attempt to employ direct assessments of neurobehavioral symptoms or syndromes for which formal psychometric tests were either unavailable or inappropriate (e.g., the aprosodias)?

4.5. Is *discrimination* sacrificed for *sensitivity*? (Tests that are most sensitive to brain injury are also generally very sensitive to a host of other factors. Although they should not be discarded, the examiner should be aware of the increased risk of false positive errors with the use of such tests discussed in chapter 4.)

4.6. Were tests designed to measure an aspect of behavior limited in number so as not to increase the risk of a false positive error (e.g., giving 10 malingering tests, each set at the .05 level of significance, thereby raising the chance of a false positive to 50% total)?

5. Errors in test administration and scoring.

The manner in which a test is administered will often significantly influence the quality and use of the information one derives from the test, including how the data may be interpreted. When utilizing standardized statistics, accurate scoring is obviously of critical importance. The following are frequent errors in administration and scoring:

5.1. Failing to adhere to standard administration procedures.

5.2. Adhering too rigidly to standard administration procedures. (Although this appears inherently contradictory, flexibility in test administration is occasionally necessary to (a) accommodate specific functional handicaps of the patient in order to better assess behaviors of primary interest, and (b) to better define the specific nature of the observed deficit(s). Adjustments obviously need to be made in the reporting of scores when nonstandard administration procedures are utilized.)

5.3. Unfortunately, formal scoring errors are not uncommonly found when raw data are independently reviewed. (Most errors result from simple carelessness, but at times they may result from a lack of familiarity with formal scoring criteria.)

II. Errors of Data Interpretation

1. Failure to appreciate the psychometric properties of tests and the normative sample from which the scores were derived.

One of the major advantages of standardized tests is the normative data they afford. However, if these statistics are misunderstood, misapplied, or are irrelevant to a particular patient population, then their use can be very misleading. The possible sources of error stem from failure to include the following:

1.1. Failure to differentiate between *statistical* and *clinical* significance (i.e., what is the frequency with which a particular score, range of scores, or difference between scores, can be expected to occur in the general population)?

1.2. Has the validity of a given test been established? If so, how, and for what?

1.3. Whether statistically or empirically, how well can one predict the performance on one test based on the score of another?

1.4. Has the standard error of measurement been considered (i.e., how reliable is this particular score)?

1.5. Is the patient representative of the population from which the standardization of the test was derived and, if not, how might this affect the interpretation of the results? Alternatively, what is the potential influence of covariables, such as cultural background, level of education, or premorbid IQ, on observed test scores (i.e., are individual differences being taken into account)?

2. Overemphasis on extreme scores.

Test scores that stand out, because they are either very poor or very good may be of great clinical significance. However, like all data, they need to be interpreted with caution, as individuals from nonneurological populations may also show considerable range and variation in their performances.

2.1. Is it routinely assumed that a low score(s) or poor performance on a particular task or measure is likely to reflect a neurological impairment?

2.2. Conversely, is there an assumption that a high score is likely to reflect the patient's premorbid baseline, against which all other scores might be compared? (Both of these positions fail to take into account variations in skills and abilities within individuals).

3. Reification of test scores.

Neuropsychological tests may, on occasion, inappropriately be viewed as being a direct measure of the functional integrity of the brain, rather than a sample of behavior that is subject to interpretation. Another way of saying this is that similar scores may not have the same behavioral meaning (i.e., diagnostic implications) for different individuals.

Is *brain damage* automatically predicted if a particular score or pattern of scores is obtained? (The potential problem here is related to one described earlier, namely, failing to take into account individual differences or the multiplicity of psychological (e.g., depression), physiological (e.g., pain), and situational (e.g., forensic evaluation) variables that might affect performance at any given point in time.) For example, a cutoff score of 23 on the Folstein Mini-Mental State Examination that fails to adjust for age and education is incorrectly taken as evidence of dementia (see chapter 4).

4. Excluding brain damage because of normal range scores.

This type of error represents the opposite side of the coin from the sources of error thus far listed in this section. Patients with clearly demonstrable brain pathology (e.g., from radiographic studies) may, on occasion, be found to perform well within the normal range on most, if not all, formal neuropsychological tests. This may result from one of the following causes:

4.1. Failure to ask the right questions (i.e., give the right tests).

4.2. Failure to adequately assess behavioral changes, other than those tapped by formal psychometric measures.

4.3. Slowly progressive, or old, static noninvasive lesions.

4.4. A regression toward the mean in a previously highly functioning individual.

5. Failure to consider the multifactorial nature of tests (the unnecessary multiplication of deficits).

As noted earlier, neuropsychological tests, no matter how simple they may appear, typically tap a wide range of brain-behavioral functions. Not only may different individuals fail a particular task for different reasons, but a given individual may evidence difficulties on a variety of tasks due to one or more common behavioral factors.

5.1. Is the functional deficit ascribed to an impaired test performance routinely the one that is suggested by the test publisher, rather than that resulting from a behavioral analysis of the patient's errors, along with comparisons involving both similar and diverse psychometric measures (tests)?

5.2. Are tests individually "interpreted" (as opposed to simply being reported), thus magnifying the possibility of an unnecessary multiplication of deficits by failing to take into account common variables which might account for deficits across a variety of tests? For example, failure to maintain set on memory, problem-solving, and constructional tasks does not mean that the patient suffers primary deficits in each of those areas.

6. *Reporting "test impairment" rather than "behavioral impairment".*

Neuropsychological tests are not meant to be ends unto themselves; rather, they are tools to help neuropsychologists gain insight into the patient's behavior and, by inference, into the integrity of the brain.

6.1. Does the report attempt to discuss examination findings in the form of meaningful brain-behavioral relationships?

6.2. Is there an attempt to discuss the test results in such a manner that the findings may easily be translated into real-world activities, rather than to merely report general test descriptions and test scores?

III. Errors in Data Integration

1. *Inconsistencies within the neuropsychological report.*

A neuropsychologist is not unlike a detective who gathers evidence and then attempts to piece together the facts into a cohesive explanation. Occasionally, some facts may appear irrelevant and some may defy explanation, but one attempts to account for as many as possible. Probably one of the more frequent and troublesome errors involves inconsistencies within the neuropsychological report. These inconsistencies may be either internal or external.

1.1. *Internal inconsistency*—are there statements within the different parts of the report which are (or appear to be) contradictory?

Example: A patient is described as well oriented and able to provide a detailed history during the clinical interview, but is also described in the discussion of test results as having severe learning and memory problems.

1.2. *External inconsistency*—are the judgments or conclusions reached justified or supported by the evidence (i.e., data) presented (including medical and social history, behavioral observations, and test data)?

Example: Diagnosis of severe declarative memory deficits (based on the Wechsler Memory Scale [3rd edition] and California Verbal Learning Test results) in a bilingual individual with limited mastery of English.

2. Failure to appreciate the hierarchical and complex functional organization of the CNS.

Neuropsychologists are expected to have a good working knowledge of the nervous system, its behavioral correlates, and functional organization.

2.1. Are motor or sensory deficits attributed to the cerebral cortex, when they might more parsimoniously be explained by lesions elsewhere in the neural axis?

2.2. Are *lesions* assigned to specific regions of the brain based on individual test performance (e.g., "poor performance on test *X* means frontal lobe damage")?

2.3. Is there any consideration of distributed systems, disconnection syndromes, or the multifactorial nature of tests?

3. Failure to consider base rates for specific disorders and their related behavioral signs and symptoms.

Neuropsychologists are likewise expected to have a good working knowledge of neuropathology and neurobehavioral syndromes.

3.1. Is the diagnosis consistent with the history and clinical presentation (i.e., similar to "external consistency")?

Example: What is the likelihood that a patient, given the degree of exposure to this particular chemical, should be experiencing these symptoms?

3.2. Is the clinical presentation (i.e., history and pattern of symptoms) consistent with this particular pathological entity?

4. Failure to consider comorbidity or preexisting conditions.

It is not uncommon for patients to suffer from multiple neurological conditions. Adults may have preexisting conditions from childhood, or they may suffer from degenerative dementia, as well as from the effects of COPD, a closed head injury, or both. It may be important, especially in forensic cases, to differentiate the probable contributions of each.

4.1. Are preexisting or comorbid pathologies discussed in the report, and is there some attempt to acknowledge the possible contributions of each to the current clinical picture?

4.2. Has an attempt been made to identify possible psychiatric or personality factors that may help explain the current symptoms?

5. Failure to acknowledge the limitations inherent in the practice of neuropsychology.

Neuropsychologists are routinely asked to draw conclusions about the nature, extent, and cause of brain damage and to make predictions regarding the long-range consequences of those injuries. Unfortunately, neuropsychology is still not an exact science.

5.1. Is there an acknowledgment of the limits of the instruments and of a neuropsychologist's ability to make definitive diagnoses, especially in questionable cases?

5.2. Is there an acknowledgment of the limited predictive validity of neuropsychological tests, specifically with regard to their ability to predict either future behavior or the long-range consequences of brain injury?

5.3. Is there an acknowledgment of the frequent difficulty in differentiating causal from casual relationships with regard to behavioral symptoms and specific brain pathology?

5.4. Is there an acknowledgment of the current limitations in the field of cognitive rehabilitation (and an acknowledgment of any possible conflict of interests with regard to recommendations to specific programs in which the psychologist might have a financial interest)?

5.5. Where relevant, is there an acknowledgment of the limitations of one's own competencies or scope of practice?

7

Reporting Scores in Neuropsychological Assessments: Ethicality, Validity, Practicality, and More

Jean Pieniadz and Donna Z. Kelland

There has been an ongoing debate in the clinical neuropsychological literature (cf. Freides, 1993, 1995; Naugle & McSweeney, 1995, 1996) about whether and how test scores should routinely be included in neuropsychological reports. Different aspects of the issue are reviewed with respect to score validity and generalizability, theoretical orientation of the examiner, and practicality or utility of reporting such scores vis-a-vis the referral question and source. In addition, the results are reported from a survey that was conducted in order to elicit information from directors of neuropsychological training programs regarding the actual practice and training of students on this issue.

Reporting Test Scores

It has generally been assumed that the reporting of test scores in neuropsychological reports should parallel the ethical guidelines created for data in all psychological test reports; that is, that such data need to be protected by a qualified examiner and revealed only as absolutely necessary. Indeed, the American Psychological Association's Committee on Psychological Tests and Assessment (1996) reiterated these guidelines and stressed the many issues that need to be considered in the examiner's decision to report test results. These included, but were not limited to, disagreements about the limits of confidentiality and consent of the examinee, test security, the release of data to unqualified persons, and the protection of test copyrights. Other issues that have been highlighted include whether the report is complete without all the test results presented and whether professionals are being honest or accountable in their presentation of results and interpretations.

Freides (1993) initiated a debate in the literature regarding the reporting of scores by asserting that all quantitative data from neuropsychological evaluations should be included in every report (e.g., in the form of a summary appended to each report). This would constitute a new standard for neuropsychological assessment practices. Freides' position was partly based on the notion that inclusion of all data maintains the integrity of the referral and consultation process in two ways. First, integrity may be more ensured when the neuropsychologist-consultant presents not only the data that support the case formulation and conclusions, but the nonsupporting data as well. Second, inclusion of all scores might minimize improper or incomplete scoring of test protocols, presumably because inconsistencies in scores are highlighted for the examiner in the process of completing a data summary. Current professional standards, on the other hand, allow examiners to submit data-free reports that may not be based on completely scored test protocols (Freides, 1995).

With regard to more practical concerns, Freides (1993) conjectured that, in forensic cases, the practice of appending all scores might eliminate the need for discovery (i.e., requests by one legal party to another for additional information), thereby decreasing deposition time and litigation expense. Another practical advantage to appending all scores would be the facilitation of ipsative longitudinal (i.e., follow-up) comparisons. Separately appending all scores might enhance the report writer's and reader's ability to focus more efficiently on qualitative findings in the *body* of the report.

In response to Freides' (1993) proposal, Naugle and McSweeney (1995) have presented several concerns. They discuss two ethical standards (American Psychological Association, 1992) that have some bearing on the suggestion of routinely appending neuropsychological test data to reports. Standard 2.02 (b), for example, states that "Psychologists...take reasonable steps to prevent others from misusing the information...(and this) includes refraining from releasing test results or raw data to persons, other than patients or clients as appropriate, who are not qualified to use such information" (p. 1603). The *qualified* person in this case was interpreted to mean only another psychologist (Canter, Bennett, Jones, & Nagy, 1994). Freides' proposal would be in direct contradiction to the current ethical code, according to Naugle and McSweeney (1996).

These authors also cite APA (1992) ethical standards 5.03 (a) and 5.06 that state that psychologists include in their reports "only information germane to the purpose for which the communication is made" (p. 1606), and that psychologists..."share information only to the extent necessary to achieve the consultation" (p. 1606). The purpose of this standard is to minimize intrusions on the patient's privacy. Naugle and McSweeney (1995) state that "...providing all test data because it might prove useful to another psychologist at a later date extends beyond the spirit of that guideline and might also be regarded as unnecessary disclosure." (p. 247)

These authors suggest that neuropsychological test data need to be the most protected aspect of the report with respect to any use beyond the originators. Matarazzo (1995) has disagreed, stating that one advantage of reporting scores is that it provides for the minimization or clarification of the writer's interpretation bias or idiosyncrasies. Sources of such bias include neuropsychological training, preferences for test (and norms) use, or criteria for labeling the extent and location of brain damage. Matarazzo also states the following:

> In regard to patient privacy, it seems unlikely that test scores, per se, are more 'intimate' than their interpretations. Also, the personal information...included in the report regarding social, medical, and psychological history is arguably at least as susceptible to misuse by an unqualified person as are the neuropsychological test scores. (p. 250)

Faced with the conflict between the Ethical Principles of Psychologists and the arguments in favor of test score inclusion (i.e., integrity, practicality, expediency), Freides (1995) has proposed that the ethical code be altered to allow for his original proposal, asserting that "Existing (ethical) practices have a ludicrous aspect" (p. 248). He, like Matarazzo (1995), suggests that interpretations of scores without the scores themselves are of much greater potential harm to patients and the public than the scores without interpretations.

An Expansion of the Controversy

Although the debate about reporting scores may represent an advance in the neuropsychological assessment literature, this debate cannot proceed without expanding into the question of exactly what is meant by (raw) data or test results. In at least one study of neuropsychologists' current practices regarding score reporting (Kelland & Pieniadz, 1996), the results suggested that most clinicians use some scores in their reports, albeit only in their standard forms. Generally, this refers to scores that have been converted to percentiles, T or z scores, or age-corrected scores.

The term standard, however, is not synonymous with more valid, as some might conclude. Any debate regarding the reporting of neuropsychological test data should be rendered moot if the data themselves, or their normative references, are invalid. Axelrod and Goldman (1996) raise questions about this issue by pointing out that the so-called norms for many standardized neuropsychological tests are based on data from (sometimes widely) differing demographic groups. They caution examiners to closely scrutinize the information regarding the normative data from which their particular test score was derived, or against which the score in question will be compared. Certainly, this issue arises most clearly when intercultural comparisons in test results are either being made (spuriously or not) or being ignored (Dana, 1993; Geisinger, 1992a; Mitrushina, Boone, & D'Elia, 1999; Sedlacek & Kim, 1995).

Some data presented as raw are actually interpreted as well. The examiner must make interpretive decisions at many junctures and levels in the evaluation process, from scoring (e.g., whether a response is a 1- or 2-point response) to deciding which norms are most applicable to or appropriate for the particular data set (e.g., age-corrected). Many neuropsychological reports do not specify how *far* from the raw data the presented score has been converted.

The fields of clinical psychology and clinical neuropsychology also contend with some factors unique to our participants and examinees that other fields (e.g., medicine) may confront perhaps only to a lesser extent. In the particular case of reporting psychological and neuropsychological test results, greater protection is required of data that are more prone to subjective interpretation than, for example, EEG readings or blood levels. The former are also arguably more susceptible to factors of an intentional (e.g., malingering) as well as unintentional (e.g., motivation, interest, fatigue, etc.) nature that may significantly affect their interpretation.

Perhaps the least controversial point regarding the inclusion of data in the neuropsychological test report is the fact that the report needs to be useful to the reader, consumer, and referral source. There are probably only rare, if any, instances in which the test data are *not* useful in some fashion to the reader—these instances that may have more to do with the manner or style of presentation (e.g., stanines vs. percentiles) than the presence of the scores themselves. Relatively poor test score utility may also be associated with a perceived lack of connection between scores and recommendations, or between scores and rehabilitation possibilities. This perceived want of ecological validity may contribute to neuropsychologists' and consumers' collusion in a general dismissal of test scores when they are presented without interpretation as well (cf. Sbordone & Long, 1996). The latter issues relate more to the critical role of the neuropsychologist as the purveyor and translator or interpreter of evaluation information. As interpreter of neuropsychological test data, the examiner must retain a certain authority over the evaluation process, even as the report passes into the domain of the report's readers. Neuropsychologists must be the protectors of the relationships between themselves, the examinees, the testing process and results, and the referral sources or report reader(s). This working principle supports an argument for presenting test scores along with an interpretation that could be construed as meaningful or useful to the reader. The extent to which this optimal (in the authors' opinion) convention is presently employed requires further research, a part of which has been conducted by the authors. The findings will be addressed in the section on Current Training Trends in Neuropsychological Assessment.

Theoretical Orientation and Score Reporting: A Brief Historical Note

Clearly, the reporting of neuropsychological assessment scores and data has borne a direct relationship to the type of assessments being conducted that, in turn, have been a product of the theoretical and empirical advances and sophistication in the field. To the authors' knowledge, it has only been fairly recently that substantive questions about the relative merits and disadvantages of reporting scores in neuropsychological assessments have been more pointedly raised (Freides, 1993).

What has been the relationship between assessment theories and scoring procedures in neuropsychological assessments, more generally? During the first half of the 20th century in the U.S., for example, neurological thinking was characterized by mass action concepts of brain function, and brain damage was studied as a unitary phenomenon. Hartlage (1987) notes that neuropsychological assessment utilized single tests that yielded single scores, indices, or descriptors, reduced to one class of cognitive functions, such as the Bender-Gestalt (Bender, 1938) and the Memory-for-Designs Test (Graham & Kendall, 1960). Such scores were intended to simply identify the presence or absence of brain damage.

During and after World War II, two trends contributed to the proliferation and elaboration of the field of neuropsychological assessment: (a) the much greater number of patients with head injuries resulting from military action and (b) the ascendance of clinical psychology as a profession, which resulted in more qualified trainees equipped to evaluate such head-injured patients. Halstead (1952) published his research on several hundred patients with brain damage, which asserted that he was able to identify differences between individuals with brain lesions (subsequently verified) and normal controls, with an extremely high degree of confidence. He used a combination of scores from 10 tests to derive an Impairment Index. The Impairment Index (II), which was documented in the results sections of neuropsychological assessment reports, represented an advance over previous assessment data in that it not only suggested the presence or absence of brain damage, but it quantified the degree of damage as well.

Although Halstead's (1952) index also effectively discriminated between those brain injured patients with cortical versus subcortical or noncortical lesions, his student and colleague, Ralph Reitan (1955, 1959, 1960), conducted research that correlated neuropsychological test findings to lateralization, and further localization of, cerebral damage (Reitan & Fitzhugh, 1971). His approach was based on assumptions and empirical research about which brain functions facilitated the individual's performance on each subtest of the Halstead-Reitan Battery (HRB). He derived a variety of formulae that combined different aspects of these subtest scores (e.g., differences between dominant and nondominant hand in Finger Tapping and Grip Strength), to suggest a lesion site. Reporting of the subtest scores and the products of these formulae came to be conventional in test result sections within (or appendices to) neuropsychological assessment reports.

The Halstead-Reitan Neuropsychological Battery and others like it (e.g., Golden, 1981) came to be associated with the fixed battery approach to neuropsychological assessment. This involves a standard battery of tests, routinely administered in the same manner to all examinees being evaluated. The scores derived from such evaluations are compared with some empirically derived cutoff score(s) that represent(s) a separation between brain-damaged and non-brain-damaged groups.

During the 1960s and 1970s in the U.S., alternatives to the battery approach gained momentum. Two trends may have contributed to such alternatives. Geschwind's work (see Geschwind, 1965; Geschwind & Kaplan, 1962) used a behavioral neurology case study approach and drew heavily upon European literature. The case study model of science had been devalued in U.S. psychology for several decades, but Geschwind's papers and other similar works (e.g., Hécaen & Albert, 1978; Heilman & Valenstein, 1979; Luria, 1966) served to renew interest in close, careful observations and descriptive methods as legitimate scientific endeavor. An approximately concurrent trend, which has come to be known as the process approach (Kaplan, 1983, 1988), values the evaluation of the brain-damaged individual on standardized tests and normative data, where available and appropriate, and emphasizes the manner in which a problem is solved or failed. (See Werner, 1937, for a further explication of the process vs. achievement distinction.) The examiner records, as part of the assessment procedure, the approaches—including types of errors—the respondent uses en route to achieving a final solution on each item. Certain aspects of the respondent's problem-solving process are often included in narrative form in the Results section of the process-oriented neuropsychological report. The quantification of process data has been increasingly mainstreamed as modifications to frequently used psychometric instruments (e.g., WAIS-RNI; Kaplan, Fein, Morris, & Delis, 1991, and the newly published WISC-III PI; Kaplan, Fein, Kramer, Delis, & Morris, 1999) have been made available.

Everyone Uses Only Valid Scores—Don't They?

As previously mentioned, a debate about the reporting of test scores in assessment reports becomes useless in our professional educational process if the scores are invalid. It may be argued that test scores presented without (a) their empirically derived normative references, (b) the sociocultural contexts in which they were attained (e.g., race, education), or (c) their possible process variables are virtually meaningless to the referral source. These issues converge most pointedly when examinees are people with disabilities, are members of a minority, or are illiterate. Internal and external validity and utility intersect in the domain of ecological validity. Upholding the ecological validity principle has probably always been an aspirational goal of psychological assessments (cf. Anastasi, 1988).

The three test score validity issues noted above will be addressed presently. One of the most important decisions an examiner must make about score reporting is whether the score is valid (using content and criterion validity methods). As Geisinger (1992b) states, "Threats to test validation threaten proper test interpretation" (p. 24). Along with the previously mentioned issues expressed by Axelrod and Goldman (1996), multicultural assessment researchers have expressed their concerns about the ethnocentrism inherent in the process of gathering most norms. Often, for example, measures normed on Caucasian participants are used to assess people of color. Interpretation of the resulting scores, thus, becomes questionable (Sedlacek & Kim, 1995). One common practice is to obtain norms for minorities or people with disabilities, post facto, to see how these test results compare with those of the (usually dominant culture) population on which the test was normed (Helms, 1992). This also creates a risk of drawing spurious conclusions about neuropsychological test results. Wherever possible, tests that have included a *culturalist perspective* from the earliest stages of test development and validation will yield the most culturally relevant and the most valid scores for interpretation (Dana, 1993; Geisinger, 1992b; Helms, 1992). Researchers have more recently begun to address this problem by developing instruments and norms for minorities.

Researchers in the area of multicultural assessment have noted the inaccuracies and unfairness of using test scores without citing their broader sociocultural context, or without citing their possible idiosyncratic meanings. According to Dana (1993), this *emic* perspective results in test scores and interpretations that cause people to be unduly pathologized, ignored, denied needed services, or underestimated in their abilities (Adebimpe, 1981; Dunn, 1987; Lesser, Fifer, & Clark, 1965; Padilla & Ruiz, 1973).

Knowing the process underlying a respondent's performance on neuropsychological tests increases the utility and validity of test scores as well. As Kaplan (1983, 1988) points out, respondents can achieve the same *score* for very different reasons. These reasons have important neuropsychological implications and, thus, interpretive power. On the WAIS-RNI Block Design subtest, Kaplan (1988) offers the following examples:

> Incorrect responses that all receive a score of zero may run the gamut from eating the blocks (in a confusional state), all the way to a flawless, systematic but slow construction (completed in 65 s, or 5 s over the time limit) of a nondemented patient with Parkinson's Disease. (p. 134)

Kaplan (1988) goes on to cite right-hemisphere lesioned patients who violate the 2 x 2 matrix of the block design en route to their final solutions, whereas left-hemisphere lesioned patients preserve the matrix (i.e., they do not *break configuration*) and commit many more errors on the right side of the design than on the left. The test score alone is clearly inadequate in capturing the essence of each of these examinees' performances. Ignoring a respondent's approach to tasks during the assessment is a missed opportunity to enhance the ecological validity of one's recommendations. Kaplan calls this "the needless loss of relevant diagnostic information" (p. 136).

Thus far, the ethicality and validity of various score reporting practices as well as the impact of the neuropsychological report writer's theoretical orientation on those practices have been considered. Clearly, these issues must be addressed in the graduate and postgraduate training process in order for trainees to adopt ethical, high-quality standards for their report writing. How are neuropsychological assessment training centers in the U.S. actually approaching these matters in their training of neuropsychology interns? There was special interest in self-reported scoring practices throughout these programs.

Current Training Trends in Neuropsychological Assessment: Focus on Score Reporting Practices

In an attempt to gather information regarding the actual practice and training of neuropsychologists with respect to including and appending neuropsychological test scores in reports, a brief survey of 137 directors of neuropsychology training programs was conducted (Kelland & Pieniadz, 1996) and a 59% return rate (n = 81) was achieved. Two respondents did not provide demographic information. The respondents averaged 14.3 years (SD = 6.3 years) of practice in neuropsychology and were, as a group, responsible for the supervision of 217 interns (M = 2.7) and 136 postdoctoral fellows (M = 1.7) and for weekly completion of approximately 456 reports

(M = 6.0). Respondents were asked whether or not they routinely append or include neuropsychological test scores in reports.

Respondents were also asked to indicate which of the following preferred approaches to neuropsychological assessment they identified with:

1. The Fixed Battery Approach, defined as a standard battery of tests, routinely administered in the same manner to all examinees evaluated. The scores derived from such evaluations are compared to empirically derived cutoff scores that represent a separation between brain damaged and non-brain damaged groups.
2. The Process Approach defined as an evaluation of the individual on standardized tests, using normative data, where available and appropriate, emphasizing the manner in which the problem/task is solved or failed. The examiner records, as part of the assessment procedure, the approaches–including types of errors the individual uses en route to achieving a final solution on each item.
3. The Flexible Battery Approach, in which the selection of tests may vary depending on various factors (e.g., referral question, successive performances, progressive hypotheses), but typically includes a core set of commonly used tests designed to survey functioning across a range of cognitive domains.
4. Finally, approaches other than the three mentioned above.

Regarding the practice of whether they routinely appended (or included) neuropsychological test scores to (in) reports, 35% responded *Yes* and 63% responded *No*. For every theoretical orientation, the *No* responders outnumbered the *Yes* responders. If individuals endorsed the practice of routinely appending test scores, they were more likely to adhere to a flexible battery approach to neuropsychological assessment. Those who did not routinely append data (i.e., *No* responders) were somewhat more likely to use a process or fixed battery approach than those who routinely appended data (i.e., *Yes* responders).

The *Yes* and *No* respondents did not differ with respect to years of neuropsychological experience or average number of reports generated weekly. Furthermore, there were no significant differences between those who did and did not routinely append test data with respect to either region of graduate education (or current program setting) or region of neuropsychological training (see Table 7-1). Nevertheless, with respect to the latter, an interesting trend emerged. Whereas neuropsychologists who were trained

Table 7-1
Number and Percentage of Survey Respondents Who Do and Do Not Routinely Append Test Data to Neuropsychological Reports by Current Program Setting and Region of Training

	Survey responses			
	Routinely append data (Yes)[a]		Do not routinely append data (No)[b]	
Respondent characteristics	Number	%	Number	%
Current program setting				
General hospital/Medical center	21	75	35	69
Rehabilitation center	1	4	7	14
Outpatient clinic			1	2
Other	6	21	8	16
Region of graduate education				
Northeast	6	21	16	31
Midwest/North Central	12	43	15	29
South	5	18	7	14
West	4	14	6	12
Other	1	4	7	14
Region of neuropsychological training				
Northeast	10	36	17	33
Midwest/North Central	12	43	12	23
South	4	14	8	16
West	2	7	7	14
Other	0	0	7	14

[a]n = 28. [b]n = 50.

in the Midwest were evenly divided regarding the inclusion of quantitative findings, neuropsychologists trained in most other regions responded approximately 2 to 1 against the routine inclusion of test scores. This is most likely related to the significant differences in responses due to neuropsychological approach presented in Table 7-2 (χ^2 = 12.75, p = .002). Given the small sample sizes, caution is necessary regarding the significance of these findings. A large majority of respondents who received their neuropsychological training in the midwestern or north central regions endorsed a flexible battery approach to assessment (see Table 7-3).

Table 7-2
Number of Survey Responders Who Append ("Yes") or Do Not Append ("No") Test Scores by Theoretical Orientation

Theoretical orientation of respondent	*Yes* response	*No* response	% of total *N*
Process (n = 9)	2	7	11.845
Fixed (n = 16)	5	12	22.360
Flexible (n = 48)	20	28	63.160
Other (n = 2)	0	2	2.635
Total (n = 75)	27 (35.53%)	49 (64.47%)	100%

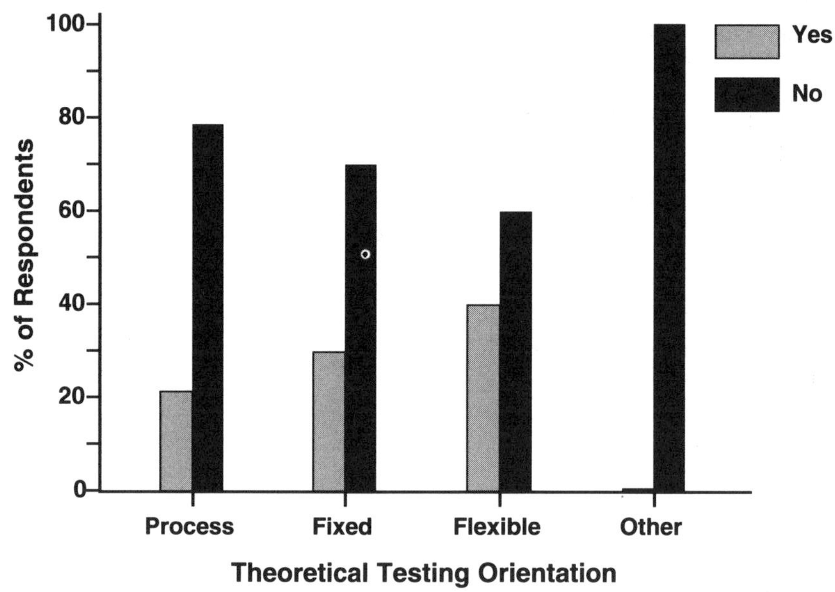

Figure 7-1. Percentage of *Yes* versus *No* respondents per testing orientation.

Participants were also asked to indicate which of the listed reasons were applicable to their decision about whether or not to include data (see Table 7-4) for rationales. As shown in Figure 7-2, of those respondents who do routinely include data, the most frequently endorsed reasons for doing so were thoroughness (100%) and facilitation of comparison (96%). Several of these respondents remarked that they include the scores in the body of the report. These scores are reported in age-corrected, or standard forms (or as percentiles). The respondents felt it was important for parents and schools, for example, to have the scores.

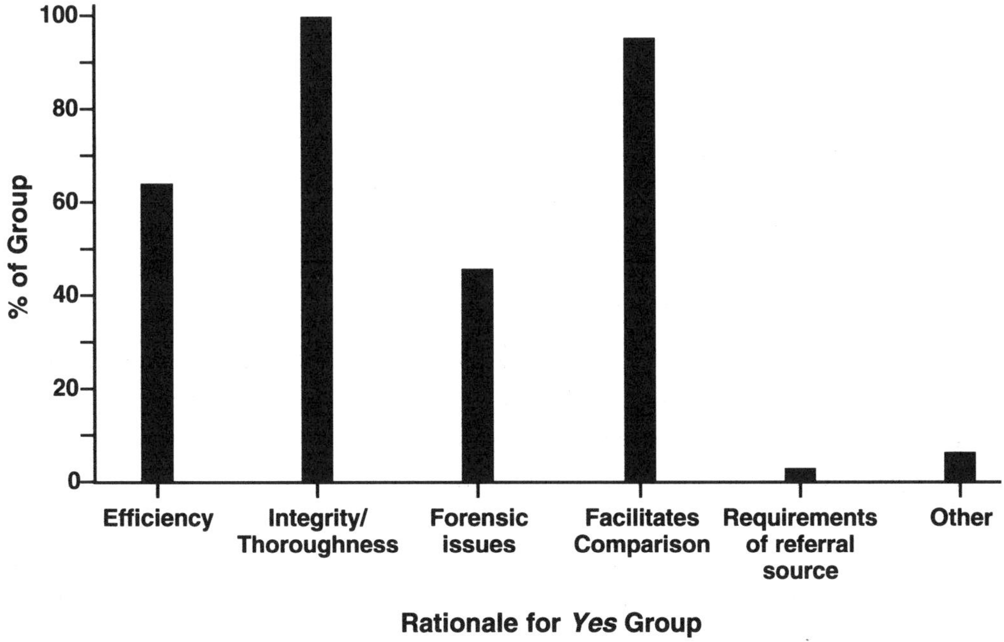

Figure 7-2. Percentage of *Yes* respondents' different rationales for routinely appending data to their reports (see Table 7-1 for further description of categories on X axis).

Table 7-3
Survey Respondents' Primary Approach to Neuropsychological Assessment by Region of Training

	Respondents' primary approach			
Region of training	Process (*n*)	Fixed (*n*)	Flexible (*n*)	Other (*n*)
Northeast	7	4	14	0
Midwest/North Central	0	3	20	1
Southern	1	3	8	0
Western	0	4	2	1
Other	1	3	2	0
Total	9	17	46	2

Of those who do not routinely append scores (see Figure 7-3), the most commonly endorsed explanation (80%) was that of data protection to avoid misinterpretation by unqualified persons. One respondent commented,

> Scores are a misplaced emphasis. The consultation is for my professional opinion—my interpretation of the scores in light of all other information available. Administering and scoring tests is not a professional-level activity. (When I request an EEG, I expect an interpretation, not reams of paper with squiggly lines.)

Those who routinely append or include test scores also endorsed routinely requesting the same type of data from others. In addition, just over half of the respondents who themselves do not routinely include such data, still expressed a preference that scores be reported by others. This may also be related to the issue of data protection; neuropsychologists generally feel more comfortable receiving data, and, thus, ensuring its protection, than sending data and inevitably relinquishing control over it, even when the recipient is a qualified professional colleague.

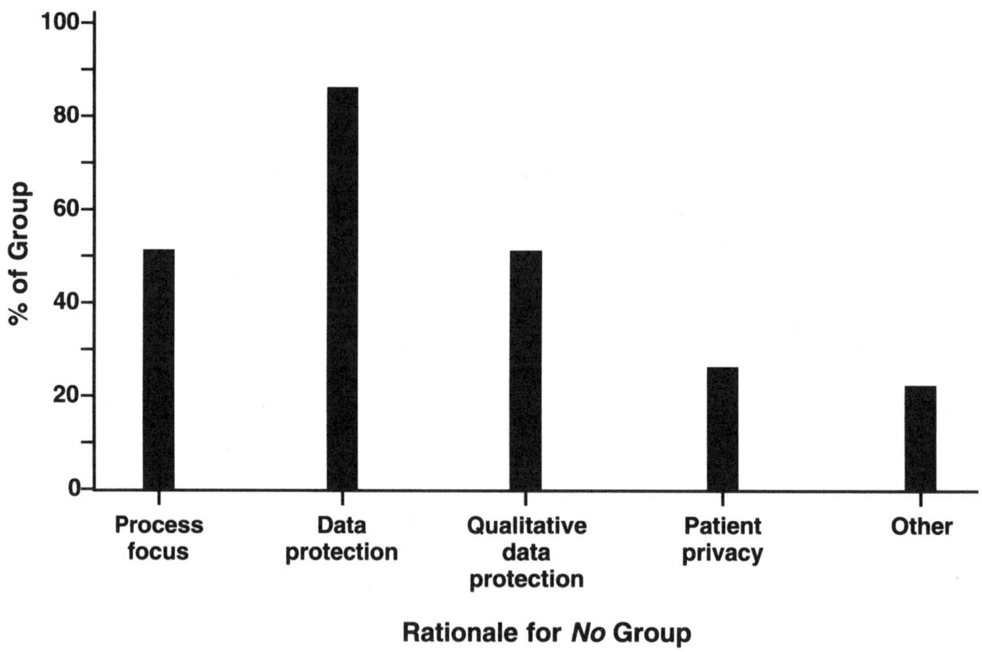

Figure 7-3. Percentage of *No* respondents' different rationales for not routinely appending data to their reports (see Table 7-1 for further description of categories on X axis).

Table 7-4
Endorsement Rationales for Survey Respondents Who Do or Do Not Append Test Data to Reports

Respondent category	Reasons provided
Append data (*Yes* response)	
Efficiency	Listing all test scores allows us to concentrate on qualitative observations in the body of the report
Integrity/ Thoroughness	Ensure that all data are presented, not only the data that support our conclusion
Forensic issues	Minimize or eliminate the need for discovery
Comparison	Facilitates comparison with previous or future testing, or both
Referral	Meet the requirements of the referral source
Other	Various
Do not append data (*No* response)	
Process	Prefer to focus on process or qualitative data, not scores
Protect professional data	Minimize the possibility that uninformed or unqualified persons might misinterpret data
Protect qualitative data	Minimize the possibility that even qualified professionals might overlook other potentially mediating factors that might compromise the reliability or validity of the data
Protect patient privacy	Minimize intrusions on patient privacy
Other	Various

Options for Addressing the Controversy About Score Reporting

What can be done, in practice, to address the debate as it has been described? The ethical and professional dilemma can be framed as follows: Does the need to protect the integrity of the assessment and test interpretation by withholding test scores outweigh the need to "double-check" our own and our colleagues' work? This is the essence of Freides' (1993, 1995) insistence on the inclusion of test scores. However, as discussed in this chapter, the issue appears (to us) to be more complex than the simple reporting of scores. It extends to concerns regarding appropriate selection of tests, depending on the normative population for which they were developed. It also includes assumptions of standard administration (not always a possibility when testing individuals with handicaps and/or when testing to clinical limits). It concerns the specific scoring procedures and normative study used to interpret the data (for further comments, see, for example, the Foreword by Dr. Satz to the *Handbook of Normative Data for Neuropsychological Assessment* by Mitrushina, Boone, & D'Elia, 1999). (Particularly in litigation settings, the danger of "norm shopping" cannot be ignored.) Even in the face of competently administered, scored, and interpreted neuropsychological testing, there will be instances of legitimate mitigating or disqualifying factors. The latter may include the phenomenon of testing an examinee's limits, for example.

When test scores are valid, norm-referenced data, additional practical issues arise. These practical matters with regard to reporting test scores are associated with the style or format of the report itself. A general stylistic preference among the respondents in our study was to report scores in the body of the report, as opposed to a special appendix or summary sheet. However, some neuropsychologists prefer to provide scores in a list or summary format, or in a figure/graph that plots the "standard" scores. The latter format may imply to the reader that the intertest comparisons between standard scores are indeed based on the same demographic variables or the same standardization sample. Although, practically speaking, the graph may be a helpful aid in reading the report, the issue of intertest comparability must be either controlled for or caveats provided (either in the report itself, or in a footnote included with the figure).

One's "philosophy" and theoretical base for neuropsychological assessment also has several clear implications with regard to test score reporting. For instance, a process approach toward neuropsychological assessment allows for qualitative analyses and a description of abilities that may avert reliance upon standard scores alone, or simple labels or typologies (e.g., "Average," "within normal limits," etc.) based on normative data. In such an approach, as is true of the flexible battery approach, the examiner uses multiple gates (or decision trees) the various skills or difficulties warrant "passing the examinee through" more specialized testing. These approaches often result in more tailor-made assessment processes/procedures, as well as neuropsychological reports that are highly individualized. This does not exempt the neuropsychologist from the use of normative scores (as it does not exempt those using a fixed battery approach from tailoring their reports), but such scores are not the central focus of a process-oriented assessment. Thus, philosophical and theoretical differences between colleagues may render comparisons between their reports (and the scores they report) inappropriate at times. Whether this poses insurmountable difficulties for evaluators attempting to use/interpret normative, as well as ipsative (if the examinee is tested by different evaluators over time) comparisons remains to be studied.

Finally, the importance of the referral source and the referral question have critical implications for the reporting of test scores in neuropsychological reports. The format of the report must meet the needs of the referral source, and this may mean that test scores should be included in as much detail as is ethical, or that no test scores be included at all. The scores can be made available to professionals, who may later become involved in the case, upon request. Some neuropsychologists feel that the referral question should be the most important indicator of whether and how scores are reported (see chapter 3).

One ethical and practical approach is to present scores for all tests administered, embedded in a narrative discussion of any caveats regarding nonstandard administration, limitations in extrapolating to ethnic or other minorities, behavioral and/or process-related observations, and so forth. To return to the example described earlier, a person might achieve a very low score on the Block Design subtest of the WAIS-III. The narrative would give the score, but would also indicate that it resulted from slowed processing because the person was able to assemble all items correctly. Scores that are invalid for whatever reason should be so indicated. An effort should be made to consciously reconcile all the data, including apparent contradictions. This provides the reader with both the empirical basis from which conclusions are derived (which goes beyond mere scores) and an explanation for the final interpretation. The need to reconcile in writing apparently contradictory aspects of the data forces the writer of the report to guard against confirmatory biases in interpretation as discussed earlier.

The decision about whether and how to report scores should be based on the complex interaction of several factors. These include examinee-referral variables (referral question, referral source, purported use for the report, etc.), examiner variables (e.g., theoretical bias), and instrument-related variables (e.g., types of validation, available norms, amount of informational "yield"). We feel this would be one of the best applications of the current ethics code, in conjunction with the professional expertise of the neuropsychologist.

We have attempted to highlight some of the issues to consider in deciding whether to include test data by presenting the inclinations of one sample of neuropsychologists who train others in the field. The ranges of responses and the issues to keep in mind are a reflection of the field's scientific limitations, its professional conscience, its diversity, and its evolution.

8

WRITING CLIENT-CENTERED RECOMMENDATIONS

Carmen G. Armengol, Elisabeth J. Moes, Dana L. Penney, and M. Melanie Sapienza

Introduction and Overview

A vast amount of information is gathered during a neuropsychological evaluation. How this information is imparted will, in many cases, determine the way in which the client will be perceived by self and others and the kind of help that will be sought or made available. For these reasons, the entire report must be approached with the realization that what is either written or conveyed orally will have immediate consequences for clients and their significant others.

Ideally, the report will be the culmination of a process of discovery, and the client, the significant others, and the referring sources will, as a consequence, have a clearer understanding of a pattern of functioning that reflects the client's personal and *system* strengths and weaknesses. Conversely, the neuropsychological assessment endeavor will be considered a waste if its relevance is not made clear to the client and other interested parties in the form of a cohesive and useful summary of findings and pertinent recommendations.

However lengthy or complex the report is, it must have internal consistency and clarity and it must be driven by the referral concerns. Thus, the mandate and organizing principle is to offer clarification and understanding regarding areas of concern and, where difficulties are identified, to offer solutions that are consistent with the client's areas of strength.

Laying the Foundation for Recommendations

It is helpful to the reader to start the Summary and Recommendations section with a brief overview, or summary, of the evaluation. The summary is especially important to the time-constrained reader who may not have read the entire report. The summary should consist of the relevant referral information, including the referral source and the referral questions. The salient findings of the evaluation should be organized and clearly stated and should include the client's strengths and weaknesses. One option is to organize the salient findings in the order in which they were presented in the body of the report to make it easier for the reader to refer back for more detailed information. Alternatively, it may be useful to organize findings in order of importance to the referral situation.

For example, an intake rehabilitation evaluation report might be organized with weaknesses or deficits stated first, followed by the client's strengths, in order to emphasize the need for rehabilitation (deficits) and the suitability of rehabilitation services (i.e., strengths upon which to capitalize in the rehabilitation setting). In contrast, a discharge evaluation might state the client's strengths first (along with improvements resulting from rehabilitation), followed by a description of any persistent weaknesses (leading into recommendations for postrehabilitation interventions).

Finally, the summary should clearly state the diagnostic impressions. It is helpful to the reader to organize the diagnostic impressions in order of importance. It is also essential that the diagnostic impressions be separated from the recommendations. Occasionally, lack of clarity on these issues may result in a disorganized discussion in the Summary and Recommendations section, which could be confusing and difficult to read. When recommendations are intermingled with diagnostic impressions, their impact is lost or diluted.

In fact, it is very easy to miss the recommendations completely as one focuses on the merits of the ideas being discussed. An example of how this can happen follows:

> Mrs. X reports anxiety and depression, and results of the MMPI are suggestive of moderate depression. She also exhibits considerable deficits in higher level attention, initiation, and slowness in responding. A psychiatric referral should be considered. Psychotropic medications could be helpful; however, they may have

> negative effects on cognition. Also, Mrs. X may not be able to follow a medication routine that requires her to remember to take medications two or three times per day. On the other hand, some medications can actually improve some aspects of attentional functioning and may be worthwhile to consider.

This could have been more successfully formulated as follows:

> Mrs. X reports anxiety and depression, and results of the MMPI-2 are suggestive of moderate depression. She also exhibits considerable deficits in higher level attention, initiation, and slowness in responding, which are consistent with a diagnosis of depression.
>
> Mrs. X would benefit from referral to a psychiatrist for consideration of antidepressant medication. Medication compliance will need to be addressed to ensure that she remembers to take medications as prescribed. Her husband may be helpful in ensuring that the routine is followed; we can schedule a follow-up session to review other techniques and devices that may be helpful in this regard.

From Psychometrics and Diagnosis to Intervention

In the past, neuropsychologists have been asked to provide differential diagnosis along the lines of the functional or organic distinction using a psychometric approach that resulted in a score along the continuum of an impairment index. Developments within the discipline have significantly broadened the scope of the neuropsychological evaluation (e.g., chapters 1 and 4; Trexler, Webb, & Zappala, 1994). Neuropsychologists worldwide have become increasingly involved in treatment planning, consultation, and rehabilitation (Lezak, 1995; Walsh, 1991). As the process-oriented approach to neuropsychological assessment (Kaplan, 1983, 1988) has gained momentum in the U.S. and its role as a tool in treatment planning has been highlighted (Cohen & Mapou, 1988), the connection between assessment results and recommendations has been made more relevant. The recent emphasis on ecologically valid assessment and intervention (cf. Sbordone & Long, 1996; Wilson, 1993) has contributed to an awareness of the various factors that must be incorporated into a neuropsychological formulation of a person's profile of strengths and weaknesses and intervention strategies.

With increasingly sophisticated assessment tools, neuropsychologists have developed a more refined understanding of the intricacies of cognitive functions and their relationship to each other. It is now common to think in terms of primary and secondary deficits (e.g., attentional deficits undermining memory). Cognitive functions have been broken down into numerous subcomponents (e.g., attention into divided, sustained, focused and span, or memory into visual vs. verbal information, retention vs. retrieval, or organization of information). With this increased understanding has come the ability to propose more focused recommendations and interventions. This, in turn, provides necessary tools for addressing the needs of the patient or client, based on the information obtained from the neuropsychological assessment.

The focus on rehabilitation was fueled in the 1980s by the increase in the number of head-injury rehabilitation centers and the expectation that early interventions would result in major benefits at all levels of analysis. Although this early optimism has somewhat faded, advances continue to be made in our knowledge base regarding interventions that do or don't work and directions for future work. In Europe and in other countries where the case-study, qualitative, hypothesis-testing approach to assessment has been in the mainstream, assessment and intervention have been more readily integrated (cf. Caetano & Christensen, 1997; Luria, 1963).

Despite the gains made by the field in the area of intervention, formulating and writing good recommendations is, arguably, often the hardest part of composing a report. Unlike reporting the history or the results, where outlines and formulae can be more readily followed, both integrating findings and providing recommendations can be challenging. Knowledge of rehabilitation approaches, integration of the person's milieu and resources, as well as the person's profile of strengths and weaknesses are all necessary in order to write recommendations that are practical and useful to the consumer.

General Guidelines to Writing Recommendations

Keep Sight of the Forest

In deciding *what* areas need to be targeted, it is recommended that the neuropsychologist approach this task at several different levels of specificity. The dictum *first and foremost a clinician* is central to offering helpful and meaningful recommendations. Neuropsychologists are trained academically to engage in detailed analytic work in the course of teasing apart elements of neurocognitive functioning such as memory, language, and so forth. Areas of functioning are minutely analyzed (particularly by those who adhere to the process models of neuropsychology) in an attempt to provide a description of how functioning in one area impacts on others and to link the clinical presentation to a specific etiology or neurologic event. This analytic focus on the trees may lead the neuropsychologist into a mindset that overlooks the forest, where the trees are the specific aspects of neuropsychological functioning and the forest is the patient functioning as a whole person within the contexts indicated in the following paragraph.

The most important directive is to see the person as a whole, functioning in a given psychological, family, economic, social, political, religious, ethnic, sexual orientation, cultural, and physical environment. This is where the *psychologist* supersedes the *neuro*psychologist.

Address the Referral Question

It cannot be sufficiently emphasized how important it is to *address the specific questions that prompted the referral*. If the referral question is poorly formulated, or misses an important aspect of the patient's functioning, it is incumbent on the neuropsychologist to explain to the referral source how the findings are relevant to the patient's care and to make a connection to the specific referral question(s) being asked (see also chapter 3 on The Referral Process). As the neuropsychologist proceeds to identify findings that emerged in the course of the evaluation, specific referral questions are sometimes neglected or ignored. Ideally, the referral question should guide the focus of the assessment: Every effort should be made to select tests that will best elicit answers to the questions being asked. For example, using only the WRAT-3 and WAIS-III Arithmetic subtests to evaluate a possible math disability is unlikely to provide the kind of information necessary to fully assess the individual's underlying math skills, even though they may be adequate to screen for math disabilities in other assessments. To respond more adequately to the referral question, the examiner would probably wish to administer various subtests from the Woodcock-Johnson, Key Math, or some other battery that provides more in-depth examination of math functions.

As another example, suppose that an older lady is referred with a question regarding her ability to manage her own finances. If an enumeration of her strengths and weaknesses is provided, without explaining how they impact on her fiscal management abilities, the neuropsychologist will ultimately have failed to provide an answer to the question that was asked. Noting that the woman's sleep/wake cycle is seriously disrupted, and that she scores at the 15th percentile on the WRAT-3 Arithmetic subtest with significant fluctuations in attention, does not automatically or easily translate into either an understanding of her functional abilities or a clear recommendation regarding her needs. The reader is left to bridge the gap between findings and their practical implications. Although it is true that neuropsychologists may, at times, be reluctant to generalize beyond their data, it is certainly unfair to expect the reader to do so instead.

If the implication is that improved sleep and arousal will also improve her math and mental control abilities and, thereby, her fiscal management, then this needs to be explicitly stated. Furthermore, the recommendation should then be made that she be retested specifically with regard to her ability to manage her money once the sleep/wake issue has been addressed. Importantly, in the interim, she cannot manage her money, and this needs to be stated, perhaps with the recommendation that she obtain assistance in balancing her checkbook and overseeing her accounts.

State the (Not So) Obvious

If there are changes in neurovegetative functions (e.g., sleep, appetite, libido, and mood) recommendations addressing these areas are important. There is little point in suggesting that a client attend a daily cognitive retraining program to work on attention and memory when inadequate or disturbed sleep patterns that affect attention and memory are not addressed. Patients with neurological or psychiatric deficits, or both, frequently report disturbances in these functions.

Three cases illustrate the importance of these issues for neuropsychologists. The first is a young professional who was referred with issues of ADHD. He was scheduled for a day of testing, and took a lunch break at midday. He returned approximately an hour later, but later that afternoon mentioned, almost parenthetically, that he was hungry, but had not had lunch because he had taken the opportunity to have some work done on his car. His hunger was distracting him from the task at hand. Furthermore, it transpired that he was chronically sleep deprived. Because he was a very slow reader, it took him many more hours to complete his work. He then insisted on relaxing in front of the television for 2 hours; allowing himself only 5 to 6 hours of sleep (which was clearly inadequate for him). His food and sleep deprivation had an impact not only on his cognitive abilities during testing, but also on his day-to-day ability to function.

Another client with significant organizational deficits and poor judgment appeared for her second session after having spent the entire night sorting papers in her garage. As a consequence, it was hard to determine which aspects of her performance resulted from her lack of sleep, and which from the chronic organizational and attentional problems. As one might imagine, her life was erratic and characterized by extremely poor self-care habits.

A third example is a young boy who was referred with a history of lead poisoning, and who presented as unruly, agitated, and attentionally impaired. In this case, his mother admitted that he typically stayed up until midnight or 1:00 in the morning, but then was drowsy the next day in school. The interview with his mother and behavioral observations in the waiting room clearly indicated that his mother did not set limits or have a good grasp of how to perform her parental responsibilities.

An important recommendation in each of the above cases was to address the lack of sleep; however, in each case the specific intervention(s) had to be individually tailored. The neuropsychologist must be attuned to the person's *unique* circumstances, in order to develop recommendations that are acceptable, practical, and have a reasonably good chance of being successfully implemented.

Test Results Are Not Recommendations

In formulating a diagnosis, one concern might be "What is the significance of a decreased level of alertness for this child's performance on the CVLT?" This question is appropriate in sorting out the factors influencing the test results. It is important to identify primary versus secondary deficits (e.g., memory deficits resulting from impaired attention). One would expect areas of secondary deficit to improve when the targeted primary areas are successfully addressed. The goal in formulating recommendations is to target the primary deficits for intervention, and to ameliorate the secondary deficits as best as possible. In order to successfully address the primary deficit, however, the questions become broader: "What factors undermine the child's ability to stay focused, and what would help? Is the sleep/wake cycle disrupted? Why? How might it be improved? Is a pharmacological intervention one that the family will feel comfortable with? How can it best be presented? Who will monitor adherence to a medication regime and the child's response to it on a day-to-day basis (e.g., in school)? Furthermore, how does this child construe presenting difficulties? What should the child be told? Who should tell the child? How will this be arranged?" These are all issues that need to be considered and anticipated in formulating useful recommendations that will be implemented.

Be as Concrete and Specific as Possible

In the previous section, the need to place recommendations within the broader scope of the person's life was discussed. A second level of analysis concerns interventions geared toward specific aspects of cognitive functioning. Recommendations are sometimes overly general. For example, one might read that the client should "write information down in a memory notebook." This recommendation is often made under the assumption that this strategy will benefit all persons with compromised memory, *regardless of the nature of their deficits*. Information regarding the type of memory dysfunction that a given individual manifests is not mentioned or incorporated when the proposed intervention is introduced. Furthermore, this is an example of a recommendation that is both too generic and too nonspecific with regard to implementation (i.e., it is not adapted to the specific needs of the individual).

Failure to be more specific may end up sounding more like an identification of a deficit than a constructive suggestion for remediation. It is rather like insisting that a person with ADHD or executive function disorder get organized by means of a daily planner. One can adopt strategies in the implementation of these tools (i.e., memory book and daily planner) that are more or less likely to be successful. It is quite likely (and in the authors' experience, almost inevitable) that without further instruction and in-person follow-up, these nonspecific recommendations will fail. In fact, as Sohlberg and Mateer (1989) have pointed out, teaching a brain-injured individual with prospective memory difficulties to utilize a diary as a compensatory device requires very intensive and systematic training to be successful. If a person remembers to use a memory book or knows how to use a planner, that person would not need those interventions in the first place. It is not entirely surprising that in the survey of referral sources described by Finn, Moes, and Kaplan in chapter 2, 74% of respondents felt that "recommendations are often too general to be useful"; 27% felt this was *frequently* or *always* the case.

Referral sources may be equally frustrated by the generality of some recommendations. For example, when it is stated that a person needs *"extra time on examinations,"* one should specify how much extra time is appropriate. Furthermore, it is important that recommendations follow logically from the findings presented in the history and test results sections of the report. This should help the reader understand the necessity for the intervention rather than obliging the reader to make the necessary connection. So, for example, it is more persuasive to say; "Given the significant difficulty in expressive language, particularly with organization of ideas when writing, double time will be necessary when this student is required to participate in essay-type examinations," or, "Based on the slow reading speed documented by the Nelson-Denny and the Stroop test, this student will need at least twice the amount of time given to other students to complete reading assignments and to have time to formulate answers on examinations that require comprehension of written text."

An employer is more likely to agree to provide reasonable accommodations mandated by the Americans with Disabilities Act, when the connection between the recommendation and enhanced performance is made explicit. For example, a vague recommendation such as, "Mr. Smith has significant difficulty with divided attention and mental tracking of information and will require accommodations at work" would leave the employer to come up with creative solutions that take into account these cognitive limitations. The employer may not feel (or be) up to this task and will need more specific guidance. A good alternative recommendation might read, "Mr. Smith has significant difficulty with divided attention and mental tracking of information. His current job as a switchboard operator taxes his abilities in these areas. On the other hand, his capacity to remain focused and attend to detail, and his mathematical abilities are significant strengths. Consideration must be given to his being assigned to tasks that emphasize those strengths. He has expressed interest in tasks such as bookkeeping and data entry, which would seem to more adequately maximize his strengths at this time."

A poignant example of giving directions that are too general involves a 9-year-old girl whose father, frustrated by her (well meaning but intrusive) attempts to help others, instructed her to "Mind your own business." During the session, the girl tearfully asked, "How do you mind your own business?" Her confusion stemmed from both the lack of feedback about specific behaviors that she engaged in that were unwelcome and a failure to instruct her in alternative behaviors more appropriate to the circumstances.

Recommendations Do Not Have to Be Treatment Plans

Having addressed recommendations that are too broad, this section will discuss recommendations that are too lengthy and detailed. Occasionally, one sees reports listing three pages of highly specific interventions (sometimes taking the form of a checklist where specific items are simply ticked off). One gets the feeling that recommendations are being mistaken for a treatment plan. In this situation, the neuropsychologist is being both too ambitious and, yet, is too limited in scope to ensure successful implementation of the recommendations. There are at least three problems with this approach. One is that if the client is going to be referred to another professional (e.g., an educational specialist or speech and language pathologist), then it may be inappropriate to dictate what the specific interventions should consist of. A telephone conversation to share ideas would be a more appropriate means of communication, or further detailed written suggestions can be added in an appendix, if that would be useful and expected. (Some school systems prefer this level of direction.)

Second, if the expectation is that the client will be implementing the recommendations, then trying to provide a cookbook of interventions is likely to fall woefully short of its goal. Typically (as reviewed earlier in the case of memory notebooks), follow-up sessions that provide didactic structure as well as the opportunity to monitor outcomes and make appropriate modifications will be more successful. The interactive nature of the follow-up is also more likely to ensure compliance and follow-through, rather than leaving clients to their own devices. Arguments against a follow-up session (or sessions) on the basis of cost should be counter-balanced with the understanding that if the recommendations are not successful, then the evaluation upon which they were based will have made little difference and may, in itself, have been a waste of time and money.

Third, more is not always better. Humans have limitations regarding the number of items they can juggle. Part of the daily struggle, particularly in modern life, is what information to filter out. Thoroughness can be a liability when providing recommendations, especially when they are not categorized or prioritized. Although it may be appropriate to suggest recommendations that would be applicable after more immediate concerns have been addressed, there should be no doubt as to what the priorities are. A follow-up session or sessions may be scheduled after recommended actions have been undertaken (in time periods varying from days to months) in order to provide consultation and further recommendations at that time. What is being argued, essentially, is that it is important to distinguish between treatment, supervision or consultation to treatment providers, and the report itself.

The Feedback Session

In the authors' experience, when clear and meaningful feedback is provided to clients, the large majority respond positively, with a sense of fulfillment and empowerment. Similar arguments are reviewed by Tallent (1993) regarding the therapeutic value of providing testing feedback to clients, which in the context of an examiner acting as an assessor or therapist becomes "a means of setting the stage for therapy" (p. 218). Persons providing feedback are urged to use everyday language and a direct style in order to maximize the positive impact of this process. Tallent, citing the work of John G. Allen and collaborators, also warns against the dangers of using language that would result in a person feeling "assaulted by references to 'brain damage,' 'brain lesions,' and 'cognitive deficits' " (p. 219).

By and large, neuropsychologists do an extensive job of summarizing testing results. Most also provide a good description of a person's functioning across the assessed areas and place their findings in the context of known brain-behavior relations. Unfortunately, these aspects of the neuropsychological report generally overshadow the discussion on how to utilize the data in the form of functional recommendations.

The overall goal of intervention might be stated as "helping the person to maximize his or her highest level of functioning." In the majority of situations, it will be appropriate for the client to receive direct feedback about the results of the evaluation. In this sense, the client becomes a central consumer. If a client is confused about his or her own behavior, or cognitive problems, or both, then one critical intervention (that applies almost universally) is to provide that client with an explanation or an account of factors impacting on these functions (cf. Prigatano, 1986). This information is obviously also relevant for the referral source.

There are very few situations where the client should not, at some point, have access to results from the testing. (The most obvious exception would be the significantly impaired head-injured or demented person who cannot understand or cope with the loss in function.)

Although there are a number of modalities in which to deliver feedback, feedback is most often delivered in a written (report or letter) or discussion (feedback session) format, or both. It is important to structure the delivery of feedback to the needs and capacities of the audience. For example, the severely head-injured or demented client could be overwhelmed by a lengthy report or feedback session. Face-to-face discussion of a single finding (e.g., strength, weakness, diagnosis, or planned intervention) may be the maximum amount of feedback from which the client may benefit.

In the written format, a single page, briefly highlighting in bullet form the most significant strengths and weaknesses along with three or four specific recommendations, provides the client with concrete feedback and simultaneously minimizes the possibility of information overload. In the authors' experience, it is not only the patient who benefits from the reduction in information but other attendees as well (i.e., family members, case managers, or health care professionals). A face-to-face feedback session is an invaluable adjunct to the written summary page and will ensure that the written recommendations have been clearly understood. Providing information in a format that enables the client to understand the results is not only in accordance with ethical principles of psychologists (APA, 1992) and respects the dignity of the patient, but also serves the important function of engaging the client in the treatment process by helping the client to understand the basis for the recommended interventions. Thus, the client's participation and cooperation is engaged at the outset. If objections are raised to recommendations during the feedback session, then clearly these objections need to be addressed in an open-minded, collaborative, problem-solving manner.

Implementing Recommendations

Neuropsychologists will differ in terms of their perception of what their level of involvement in the follow-up care of the patient should be. This is influenced by such variables as work setting (e.g., in a rehabilitation center with a treatment team vs. outpatient private practice), the extent to which the extra time spent is reimbursable, other resources available to the patient, and whether there is a designated case manager (e.g., a referring physician, social worker, rehabilitation nurse, etc.). In addition, individual practitioners will differ in terms of assigning responsibility for ensuring that appropriate recommendations are made and implemented. In the words of Rempel (1994) "very few families have the will, time, strength, or corporate decision-making skills necessary to ensure that what is relevant, rather than what is available, becomes the rehabilitation opportunity of choice" (p. 380). Responsible practitioners will feel it incumbent upon themselves to ensure that relevant, and not just expedient, recommendations are made. These factors, affecting the neuropsychologist's role in the follow-up care of the patient, will influence the types of recommendations made.

The client's ability to understand and accept the consequences of injury or illness and the cognitive limitations clarified by the assessment will be a significant factor in how recommendations are formulated and implemented. In some cases, anosognosia (neurologically based denial of deficits) may preclude acknowledgment of deficits. In other cases, emotional factors may limit the client's ability to accept the scope of the problem. Diller (1994) discusses the need to deal with the psychological sequelae of a diminished sense of self-efficacy.

Safety issues will dictate to what extent recommendations need to be immediately implemented (e.g., not driving) and to what extent it is possible to provide the client with psychological space to come to terms with the issues before attempting to engage his or her cooperation. In dealing with denial or anosognosia, or both, it is important to remember that recommendations will primarily be directed toward significant others and providers, but where possible, every attempt should be made to establish agreement with the client regarding the areas that can be worked on. In the broader context, dealing with denial or anosognosia becomes one of the first rehabilitation priorities (Prigatano, 1997; Prigatano & Schachter, 1991).

Recommendations that result in the client appearing obviously brain-damaged to peers, coworkers, or family, seriously affect posttraumatic self-image. Most clients would prefer not to have any visible signs of posttraumatic compensation or adjustment. In such cases, recommendations that are highly visible and make the client appear disabled will not be followed through. For instance, one client complained of organizational deficits, which led to her being fired from a series of high level jobs. When it was recommended that she start using a daily planner and take the planner with her at all times (from the gym to the business meeting), she expressed some consternation at the thought of bringing it to a professional meeting and wondered if this wouldn't "look strange" and "make people wonder." It was important to reassure her that many high level executives and professionals (including the neuropsychologist) rely on these organizational tools, and that, in fact, this was more likely to convey an organized and businesslike image. Once the image issue had been addressed, it was possible to proceed successfully.

Yet, the implementation of some recommendations can cause adjustment difficulties above and beyond those brought about by the brain impairment. In situations where necessary interventions cannot be readily implemented, it may be important to provide the client with a face-saving rationale. This offers a way to justify what is being done without necessarily having to acknowledge significant and embarrassing cognitive difficulties. Alternatively, helping the client to feel comfortable explaining a problem to others (e.g., through role-playing) may also be useful. This may be particularly important when dealing with children. Helping classmates to understand why a child with refractory seizures may need to wear a helmet, or may have difficulty with speech due to a head injury, may be helpful in normalizing the experience. Although the recommendations should deal with the need to address these issues and also provide an explicit format for doing so, it is inappropriate to provide the specifics of the intervention, particularly when the client is being referred to other professionals. For example, if the client requires a behavioral program, the report need not contain a detailed intervention plan when the person writing the report will be the one implementing such a program. On the other hand, an explicit statement relating the client's cognitive profile specific to modifications that would be needed for a successful behavioral plan should certainly be included (see Armengol, 1998). Further consultation with the behavioral psychologist may be necessary.

Even when clients do acknowledge that they have some cognitive deficits and are willing to utilize compensatory strategies, they and their significant others or caregivers will have their own views about brain trauma and what strategies would be effective in dealing with the deficits. At times, within a family or a support system, or among rehabilitation professionals involved in a client's care, views do not necessarily coincide (Prigatano, Altman, & O'Brien, 1990). Incorporating divergent views in the discussion of recommendations and, when necessary, offering education and corrective feedback is important (Commissaris, Verhey, & Jolles, 1996; Halper, 1997).

Differing views can be the result of limited understanding of brain-behavior relationships. In addition, lack of clarity regarding identified deficits and strengths and the recommended interventions can add to the lack of consensus in the direction of rehabilitative efforts.

Clients and families may also have their own ideas regarding recovery and treatment strategies based on their personal and cultural belief systems or their own or others' experiences with therapy. It is often a good idea to explore the client's feelings and attitudes toward medication and other medically based interventions. This can be done either during the assessment (e.g., while reviewing medication history), or during the feedback session itself once the recommendations have already been made. It is not necessary to provide an extensive justification in the report. Explaining the benefits of an essential medication should only occur in a nonthreatening fashion after acknowledging any reluctance or objections from the client. Phrases such as "It is essential that the client be referred for pharmacological consultation..." run the risk of precipitating a confrontational response, rather than negotiating a compromise position. In many cases, one might simply tell the person, "I understand your concerns, but I feel that I would not be doing my job if I didn't at least tell you that there are medications that may effectively treat some of your problems. I mention them also because they could make a significant difference in your ability to function. However, I recognize that you have some concerns and perhaps you would like to think this over and discuss it with Dr. X."

Clients may favor alternative approaches to a medical model or may hold cultural or religious beliefs that preclude participation in such treatment. It is not uncommon for individuals to ask about *natural remedies* and other alternatives to traditional medicine. Familiarity on the part of the neuropsychologist with some of these alternatives (e.g., acupuncture and herbal medicines) reassures the client that his or her concerns have been taken seriously and that treatment will be coordinated from the perspective of overlapping world views.

Armengol (1999) provides the example of a Central American man whose cultural world view made the heart the principal organ of behavioral regulation, a belief that impacted his acceptance of anticonvulsant medication and other proposed rehabilitation strategies. Arguing from within his cultural paradigm, it was possible to bring his understanding into alignment with current views. In another case, a Jehovah's Witness had been referred to a behavioral psychologist for treatment of an anxiety disorder. Unfortunately, the psychologist had a chart based on evolution of animals that he used to explain the fight/flight response. This so offended the client (whose beliefs are incompatible with the theory of evolution) that he withdrew from treatment. It was subsequently explained to him that it is not necessary that he accept evolution in order to benefit from deep muscle relaxation and desensitization techniques. These real-life examples are offered simply to reinforce the clinical dictum that it is imperative to respect the client's world view, if there is to be any hope of success in treatment.

Practicalities

The pragmatics of implementing recommendations are often neglected. For example, it may be recommended that a person undergo outpatient cognitive therapy. If the patient is no longer able to drive and has no easily accessible means of transportation, this suggestion might just as well not have been made as it will most probably not be followed. A more useful recommendation will point out the transportation problem and suggest that treatments be provided at home (e.g., on-line), or that alternative arrangements be made to transport the person to therapy.

A person with good insurance coverage or a personal injury settlement could potentially afford in-house services or special transportation arrangements (e.g., a cab). For instance, one client was able to attend a support group for traumatically head-injured Hispanic survivors, when, on the recommendation of the neuropsychologist, the insurance company's rehabilitation nurse and case manager approved the use of taxis for transportation.

Cost may also refer to time, mental effort, and persistence requirements. Some interventions do not require a monetary expenditure but are likely to be ignored because of the effort required (e.g., some forms of cognitive remediation). Although theoretically justified, their implementation may be difficult for a given client. A case in point is the use of mental imagery (e.g., bizarre images) to enhance the encoding process, which in turn is expected to lead to better retention of information and ease of retrieval (Cermak, 1975; Paivio, 1969). This procedure is, however, demanding, and its success with people with amnestic disorders is limited at best, as is its applicability to daily functioning (Wilson, 1987). Even for people without known brain impairment, this mnemonic technique requires mental effort and good divided attention skills, along with initiation and perseverance. The cost (i.e., effort required) to individuals with brain dysfunction is too great, and the benefits are questionable. It is, thus, imperative that before making a recommendation, the neuropsychologist be mindful and cognizant of the literature regarding the applicability and benefits of interventions to be recommended.

At times, recommendations fail to consider the weaknesses in a person's support system. Not everyone returns home to a supportive family and friends who are available and willing to be involved in the client's rehabilitation. Family, neighborhoods, and workplaces may prove to be quite dysfunctional and lack the resources to deal with the emotional investment, time, effort, and financial demands that are placed on them (Brooks, 1984; Voogt, 1997). Families, in particular, tend to be quite stretched by these demands.

When specific information regarding follow-up recommendations is provided, there is a much higher chance that they will be successfully implemented. Even recommendations that appear to be *do-able* from the perspective of a well educated neuropsychologist may overwhelm the client or support system, or both. Knowing how to access services, whom to call, or even where to find telephone numbers can be a daunting and, therefore, overwhelming task to some clients (especially when cognitive deficits are present).

Know Your Resources

Recommendations should address not only *what* areas need to be worked on, but also *where*, *when*, *how*, and by *whom*. This again brings up the problem of recommendations that provide a general statement identifying a need to intervene in one area (e.g., "memory remediation techniques need to be acquired to assist the patient in coping with everyday demands") without specifying how this is to be done. In the previous example it would be helpful to specify: "Dr. X, in the Memory Disorders Clinic at 555-1212, ext. 123, can be contacted for assistance in memory retraining."

In terms of addressing the "whom," we have found it extremely helpful to maintain a *resource list* of professionals and providers of a broad range of services. Particularly in the case of the private practitioner, it is important to be aware of individuals with expertise in such areas as behavioral interventions or cognitive rehabilitation, medical specialists (e.g., behavioral neurologists, neuroendocrinologists, psychiatrists, psychopharmacologists), social workers and specialists in identifying residential and nursing home care, attorneys, reputable financial advisors, credit consolidation companies, and so forth. Not only does awareness of resources available in the area promote good patient care, but an additional benefit is the potential for reciprocal referrals and networking opportunities. Sitting in one's office as an ivory tower specialist does not do justice to the client or enhance one's clinical work or the profession as a whole.

In addition to local resources, directories of professionals in other locations and national organizations are valuable. Currently, Internet resources provide another venue by which clients can obtain access to information about neuropsychological conditions (through advocacy and support organizations) and join chat groups and online support groups. For example, a teenager living in Puerto Rico, diagnosed with Obsessive-Compulsive Disorder, was able to utilize an online support group that was helpful, especially because no appropriate support groups were available to her locally. Kerns, Matteer, and Brousseau (1998) provide a categorized compilation of over 150 World Wide Web resources of relevance to neuropsychologists. Grohol (1997) was a pioneer in developing online mental health resources and has provided an excellent guide to listserves, web sites, search engines, databases, and ways to find or locate much useful information (including the web addresses of colleagues and friends). Kittleson (1997) also provides a listing of web sites for health professionals.

For the neuropsychologist who is new to an area or who wishes to expand resources, it may be valuable to contact schools that deal with special populations as well as state educational and vocational agencies to obtain names of tutors, special educators, job programs and coaches, and other resources. Professional organizations often have information and referral lines (e.g., the state bar association can indicate which attorneys specialize in head injury). Professionals in disciplines other than neuropsychology often have useful information regarding specialists and other referral options. State agencies (e.g., Department of Mental Retardation, Department of Social Services, Department of Youth and Family Services, etc.) can also provide information.

Having a good resource network can sometimes generate helpful recommendations that might otherwise not have been considered. One is more likely to target employment-related issues with recommendations if one knows of a good job coach who will work with employers to successfully place a client who has cognitive or behavioral difficulties. In the same vein, a neuropsychologist is probably more likely to recommend group therapy for someone if there is already an awareness of an ongoing group for individuals with similar issues. In conclusion, knowledge of available resources provides a specific and practical means of obtaining help for clients and is a cornerstone of good clinical practice. Taking the time to explore resources (especially because so much information is now available online) is a worthwhile investment for any neuropsychologist.

Summary

Recommendations should be stated after the diagnoses and test results have been clearly formulated. They should always explicitly address questions raised in the referral. From a clinical point of view, recommendations should consider the person broadly and take into account the need to address changes in neurovegetative functioning (e.g., sleep, mood, etc.), as well as more specifically delineated cognitive and behavioral deficits. Where possible, the client's strengths should be used to compensate for weaknesses. Environmental supports (e.g., family, finances, insurance, and other providers) should be realistically assessed, gaps in the support network identified, and practical solutions proposed. A thorough knowledge of external resources (locally, nationally, or even internationally) is essential. Recommendations should not be so general and so nonspecific that it is difficult to know how to follow up on them, nor should they be so narrow as to either turn into an extended treatment plan, or be overly prescriptive of how other professionals should provide services. Lists of detailed recommendations can only overwhelm the reader and may result in paralysis. It is always important to ensure that all relevant parties (client, family, and other providers) have a clear understanding of the neuropsychological results and how they logically relate to the suggested recommendations. It is important that an opportunity to engage the patient, family, and providers in a discussion of recommendations be made available, preferably face-to-face, during a feedback session. Follow-up sessions and consultations should be offered whenever possible in order to monitor and assist in implementation of the recommendations and to modify or expand them, as needed, over time.

As someone who has gained significant information about the client and an understanding of his or her neuropsychological profile, the neuropsychologist is an important resource for the clients and other people involved in their day-to-day activities. The skills and knowledge of the neuropsychologist will not be used to full advantage if follow-up and ongoing consultation are not an integral part of the assessment services.

9

Computerization of Neuropsychology Services: A Consumer Viewpoint

Tina M. Trudel and James E. Taylor

Introduction

Judging from commercial catalogs and advertisements in various psychology-related publications, there has been a dramatic increase in the development and availability of computer-based products for use by neuropsychologists. At the same time, today's desktop and portable computers are less expensive, yet more powerful and versatile than their predecessors. Despite evidence that psychologists are slow to adopt computer-based technology (Rosenn & Weil, 1996), these changes may persuade more neuropsychologists to include some form of computerized assessment in their neuropsychological evaluation. In fact, some neuropsychologists predict that in the future "...many, if not most neuropsychological tests and cognitive rehabilitation will be computer-based." (Johnstone et al., 1995, p. 6).

Unfortunately, computer-based technology does not come without its problems, not the least of which may be the gap between potential versus actual practical benefits (Kane & Kay, 1992, 1997). A number of factors will likely influence a neuropsychologist's decision to incorporate computerized components into their assessment of neurobehavioral disorders. This chapter focuses on practical issues related to the use of computer-assisted administration, scoring, interpretation and report-writing programs in the neuropsychological evaluation.

Administration and Scoring Accuracy

There seems to be little disagreement that computer programs can reduce errors in administration, scoring, and data manipulation. Computerized test programs can be very efficient at administering instruments, such as the WCST (Heaton & PAR Staff, 1993), that require "...intense effort on the part of the examiner in order to ascertain that recording of responses is accurate" (Artiola i Fortuny & Heaton, 1996, p. 420). Unlike most examiners, a computer program can easily manage the multiple administration tasks of the WCST, such as recording responses, providing "correct" and "incorrect" feedback to the client, and determining the appropriate time to change the sorting category based on the number of correct responses. Paolo, Axelrod, Ryan, and Goldman (1994) examined the recording errors of 14 examiners who manually administered the WCST. In that study, about 70% of the administrations contained errors. The authors concluded that computerization of the test would readily eliminate these types of errors.

Automated scoring systems are highly accurate in situations requiring tallying and grouping and regrouping of numerous responses, multiple or complex calculations, decision branching, and conversion of data using multiple tables. Allard, Butler, Faust, and Shea (1995) examined the accuracy of hand scoring by trained clinical personnel on the revised edition of the Personality Diagnostic Questionnaire (Hyler, 1996). They found that 53% of the inventories contained at least one error, with 19% having errors that would alter the clinical diagnosis. In addition, the authors found an average of 2.5 errors per protocol on a random sample of Symptom Checklist-90–Revised (SCL-90-R; Derogatis, 1975) protocols, with 83% of the sample having errors that would alter *T*-score profiles. In the latter case, a computer scoring program was used to tally subscale totals. Errors occurred when *T*-score profiles were calculated manually using a look-up table.

Computerized test programs also have the potential to reduce errors by test takers. Current versions of personality inventories such as the MMPI-2 and Millon Clinical Multiaxial Inventory (MCMI) administered by National Computer System's MICROTEST Q software present only one test question at a time. This method of presentation would seem to keep the client focused on the question at hand and reduce such errors as skipping an item or mistakenly recording the response to one item in another item's response column. At the end of the administration, the computer program can easily identify and regroup omitted items for almost instantaneous review by the examiner, who can then present them to the test taker for completion.

Time Savings

Because of the computer's capacity to efficiently process large amounts of data, one would expect that computerization of neuropsychological tests would result in a clear and substantial saving in time for the examiner and the test taker. This presumed advantage would be particularly attractive to clinical neuropsychologists, given the time pressures imposed by many managed care organizations. From a practical viewpoint, time saving resulting from computerization may be restricted to certain types of instruments (i.e., personality inventories) and highly dependent upon the complexity of administration and scoring.

In their study assessing microcomputer administration of the MMPI, Russell, Peace, and Mellsop (1986) noted a time savings of 30% in comparison with standard paper-and-pencil administration for a group of psychiatric inpatients. Another study by Watson et al. (1990) showed a significant, although lower, time savings of 18% (about 12 minutes) when they compared computer-assisted with pencil-and-paper administrations of the MMPI. To date, the authors are unaware of published studies comparing time savings on computerized adaptations of pencil-and-paper or manually administered tests used to assess cognitive functions. Although it would seem that tests designed specifically for computer administration, such as the MicroCog: Assessment of Cognitive Functioning (Powell et al., 1993), would save time by eliminating examiner tasks (e.g., the need to change stimulus books and record sheets), the actual time savings is unclear and, perhaps, irrelevant because there are no comparable manually administered formats for direct comparison.

Perhaps more meaningful time savings may be realized on computer-assisted programs that perform complex data analysis and eliminate housekeeping tasks. Computerized scoring of tests, such as the MMPI, eliminates the necessity of using multiple individual templates to tally and group numerous responses and then transfer those scores to profile sheets. On cognitive tests such as the CVLT-II (Delis, Kramer, Kaplan, & Ober, 2000) and the children's version (CVLT-C; Delis, Kramer, Kaplan, & Ober, 1994), computer programs can save time by eliminating manual conversion of multiple scores using look-up tables and by performing complex calculations. It is also assumed that most clinicians would gladly give up time-consuming tasks such as reordering the stimulus cards from the WCST after an administration. Although there seems to be a lack of studies detailing the actual time savings from the perspective of data analysis and routine housekeeping tasks, it seems clear that significant benefits could be realized on instruments requiring more complex data analysis and administration procedures.

Stimulus Presentation and Response Recording

In general, there is little disagreement over the issue of whether computerized programs are superior to human examiners in terms of their ability to consistently and reliably present test stimuli and their capacity to record complex response parameters. As noted by Kane and Kay (1997), one significant advantage is that computers allow for precise control over stimulus presentation. Unlike human examiners, computers are able to present test stimuli (e.g., questions, figures, words, letters) with the same resolution, frequency, and format, time after time without deviation. Thus, stimuli such as word-lists can be easily and reliably presented with the same tone of voice or at a consistent pace (e.g., one word per second). Although audio tape presentations offer the same advantages, computer programs allow for presentation of both auditory and visual stimuli.

However, neuropsychologists need to be aware of timing problems secondary to technical issues related to hardware and software limitations. These problems have been reviewed in detail by Kane and Kay (1992, 1997). In part, they note that the assessment of reaction time based on stimulus presentation and response latency can be problematic given variations in microprocessor speeds and the internal means by which computers control timing. Another source of variability is related to differences in transmission rates for input devices such as keyboards, mice, and joysticks. Hardware-related problems can also interfere with software performance. For example, the authors recently experienced problems with a neurofeedback unit when a new sound card disrupted the program, causing everyone to appear to have aberrant brainwaves. At present, there is no universal solution to this problem, and the burden of ensuring accuracy seems to rest on the software developers and neuropsychologists who use those programs.

Despite issues of timing accuracy, computerization may be the only means for neuropsychologists to evaluate more complex aspects of cognitive and neurobehavioral functioning. A striking example of this need for automation is evident in the objective measurement of attentional disorders. The randomization, rate, precise timing and consistency of stimulus presentation, precise recording of response parameters, and calculation of complex index scores would not be possible with traditional or paper-and-pencil tests (Grant, Ilai, Nussbaum, & Bigler, 1990). Today, a neuropsychological evaluation of an individual with a suspected attentional disorder that did not include some computerized attentional or continuous performance test would seem to be incomplete.

The detection of malingering or response bias is another area in which computerized assessment is showing promise. Slick, Hopp, Strauss, and Spellacy (1996) evaluated the ability of the Victoria Symptom Validity Test (VSVT; Slick, Hopp, Strauss, & Thompson, 1997) to detect cases of feigned or exaggerated cognitive dysfunction. Their findings showed that the two-choice recognition test accurately identified biased responding for only extreme scores (i.e., those falling well below the 50% chance level). The authors suggested that analysis of response times might help classify cases where scores were close to the cutoff score (i.e., in the questionable range). Consistent with this perspective, several symptom validity tests with sophisticated response measurement and data analysis are commercially available. The Word Memory Test (WMT; Green, Allen, & Aster, 1996) and the Computerized Assessment of Response Bias (CARB; Conder, Allen, & Cox, 1992) can be used together to assess response bias on several parameters including chance scores, implausibly low scores, unexplained variability, and inconsistency in the test profiles (Green, Allen, & Aster, 1996). The Validity Indicator Profile (VIP; Frederick, 1997) uses a multimodal approach to detect invalid test performance (i.e., verbal and nonverbal subtests) with classifications of valid or invalid being based on six measures and use of a graphical presentation of the individual's performance based on item difficulty. All of these instruments rely on computer-assisted analysis of complex data.

Test Equivalence

Computerized neuropsychological assessment has evolved from two distinct branches of clinical and experimental neuropsychology. The clinical approach is primarily focused on diagnosis, prognosis, and intervention. This is accomplished by automating traditional neuropsychological tests.

Cognitive status and degree of impairment are determined by comparing the individual's performance against established norms. In contrast, the experimental tradition in neuropsychology has focused on the measurement of human performance, typically, through serial testing and repeated measures designs. Much of the published research on computerization in neuropsychology emanates from this experimental perspective, with tests being developed in research settings, and then later being integrated into clinical neuropsychology practice. Computerized tests developed from both of these perspectives pose problems for neuropsychologists who wish to utilize them in their evaluations.

Many computerized neuropsychological tests are presented to practicing clinicians for use as alternative or equivalent forms to their traditional counterparts. Neuropsychologists need to be aware of the fact that computer-generated testing does not merely involve the automation and computerized presentation of a test. Computerization may change task demands (Devivo, Rothland, Price, & Fein, 1997; Ozonoff, 1995), modify instructions, or both, so as to render the existing normative data unusable for meaningful interpretation (León-Carrión et al., 1991).

The issue of equivalence of forms predates the advent of computerized testing. It has fostered much research and debate as demonstrated by the history of the Category Test (Reitan & Wolfson, 1993) when it was converted from the cumbersome traditional testing apparatus (slides) to booklet format years ago (Choca, Laatsch, Wetzel, & Agresti, 1997). The equivalence of computerized versions of the Category Test has been questioned, due in part to significantly lower scores on the computerized form (Berger, Chibnall, & Gfeller, 1994). In a further review of the computerization of the Category Test, Berger, Chibnall, and Gfeller (1997) supported the construct validity of the automated form, demonstrated the same factor loadings (i.e., primarily spatial abilities) as the traditional form, and indicated that equivalence had been established. In their overall review of various methods of administering the Category Test, Choca et al. (1997) stated that "...it would seem that the issue of whether the examinee can perform the task is predominant enough that the effects of variation in administration, or in the manner of presentation, are minor or irrelevant" (p. 62).

Less reassuring results concerning equivalency come from a study of the WCST by Ozonoff (1995). He examined the performance of autistic and learning disabled children on a computerized version of the WCST and concluded that the computerized version was "...not equivalent to the standard administration and may measure somewhat different constructs" (p. 9). One finding was that autistic individuals tended to perform better on the computerized format in comparison with manual administration. The author hypothesized that this might reflect a reduction in social and verbal demands on the computerized version that would be beneficial to individuals who had difficulty responding to human interaction. It was also suggested that normative data and impairment thresholds based on human-administered tests not be used to interpret performances on computerized tests until equivalency between the two had been demonstrated.

Based on their experience with the MicroCog battery, Devivo et al. (1997) noted that the Computational subtest of that battery was not a valid measure of arithmetic computational skills because of the method of response entry. MicroCog users must enter their solutions using a keyboard with solutions being entered in left-to-right order (i.e., contrary to written solutions, which are entered right-to-left). Devivo et al. found that this method of data entry reduced accuracy due to an added burden on working memory. This is a good example of how neuropsychologists must be vigilant and monitor proper use and interpretation of computerized tests.

As previously noted, computerization in experimental neuropsychology emphasizes comparisons of individual or group baseline data with change measured over time after the occurrence of some intervening event, such as an environmental modification or exposure to a substance. Many studies of normal populations have been done using this methodology. Experimental studies examining the gross and subtle effects of sleep deprivation on pilots, drugs and alcohol on reaction time, and toxins on speed and accuracy of processing are examples of the effective use of computerized neuropsychological tests in human performance literature that have carry-over into clinical neuropsychology (Allen, Ellinwood, Everett, & Logue, 1993; Kane & Kay, 1992; Kennedy, Baltzley, Wilkes, & Kuntz, 1989; Kennedy, Wilkes, Dunlap, & Kuntz, 1987).

Although performance assessment may involve automated versions of traditional neuropsychological tests, there have also been efforts to develop specific batteries for this purpose. A number of such batteries have been developed by the U.S. Armed Services in an effort to assess factors influencing military personnel, with special emphasis on neurotoxins (Kane & Kay, 1992). Although some of the military-derived tests have been cross-fertilized into everyday clinical neuropsychology, they pose a special challenge in terms of application because of their use of military recruits in the normative samples. Therefore, when using such computerized neuropsychological batteries, it is strongly recommended that the normative reference group be identified in the report, as its applicability to the individual being evaluated may be questionable. The issue of appropriateness and comparability of the normative reference group may be of particular concern in forensic evaluations.

Human-Computer Interface

Several studies report test takers' preference for, or neutrality toward, computerized administration in comparison with manually administered or paper-and-pencil formats (French & Beaumont, 1987, 1990; Spinhoven, Labbe, & Rombouts, 1993). Computerized testing was favorably received by clinical populations in psychiatric settings, although researchers recommended a preassessment interview to evaluate computer comfort levels to ensure the appropriateness of that method of administration. Spinhoven et al. found that computer-person interaction was enhanced by education, previous experience with computers, and positive attitudes toward computers. Of the 452 patients who were offered the opportunity to engage in computerized testing, it is noteworthy that the 54% who declined were older and less educated than those who volunteered for the computer tests. Interestingly, neither the nature, nor the extent, of psychopathology were significant predictors of willingness to participate in computerized testing (Spinhoven et al.).

Ivnik, Malec, Tangalos, and Crook (1996) assessed the reactions of older normal adults (mean age = 70 years, mean educational level = 13 years) on traditional versus computerized cognitive assessment. Traditional tests such as the revised edition of the WAIS (WAIS-R; Wechsler, 1981) were given in one session with computerized tests of everyday memory skills being given in the second session. The human-computer interface was a touch screen. Although there were minor differences in ratings, with a slight preference for human administration, computer testing was well received by the group.

Researchers have generally found that test takers respond more openly and honestly to the impersonal nature of computerized questions and interviews (Russell et al., 1996). However, in a noncognitive scenario involving selected measures, Potosky and Bobko (1997) noted that a computerized form resulted in greater response distortion consistent with social desirability. Differences in clarity and complexity of displays and instructions may also adversely influence accurate data collection (French & Beaumont, 1987), and these factors may be of particular concern for the neurologically impaired populations commonly seen in clinical neuropsychology practice.

From the examiner's perspective, some computerized tests do not allow for analysis of spoiled protocols or correction of test-taker input errors. One computerized version of the WCST, for example, will only generate a printout of responses if all 128 items have been administered or the criterion of six correct sorts has been reached. Thus, results for individuals who are unable to complete the full administration are lost. In addition, errors due to impulsive responding, inattention, or difficulties with keyboard entry cannot be overridden. It has been a frustrating experience to have individuals press the enter key before positioning the selection arrow under their intended sorting card, due to incomplete depression of the arrow key or simple inattention or impulsivity. In those cases, the examiner must either note the error and reinterpret the data in the computer printout or consider the test to be invalid.

Most commercially available computerized tests require the test taker to input answers or responses using a limited number of keyboard keys, a mouse, or a joystick. Although not overly difficult for most people to use, these modes of input may be problematic for some individuals who are unfamiliar with these devices or whose neurologic condition imposes limitations on upper extremity movement or interferes with fine eye-hand coordination. Although newer input devices, such as the light pen, touch screen, and microphone with voice recognition software are commercially available, they have not yet gained widespread use in computerized neuropsychological tests.

Interpretation

In addition to software programs that administer and score tests and manipulate data, a growing number of programs provide interpretive narratives in a report-like format. Clinical interpretation of data obtained by computerized assessment programs or by traditional assessment methods should be based on the same principles of objectivity and knowledge about the condition under investigation and the characteristics of the measures being used. Unfortunately, there is a lack of information regarding interpretive programs. Snyder, Widiger, and Hoover (1990) reviewed the status of computer-based test interpretation (CBTI) and concluded that "...the development and application of CBTI systems has far exceeded careful attention to the validity of these techniques" (p. 10). They stressed the need to study the decision rules on which statements were based and to analyze statements in terms of their accuracy, relevance, exclusion and inclusion of important information, and usefulness in classification or treatment (p. 11). It is the current authors' opinion that neuropsychologists need to be extremely careful when using software programs that generate narrative interpretations. This is especially true with programs that present the narrative in an official looking report format or allow cutting and pasting of the narrative to standard word processing programs.

Computer analysis and interpretation of neuropsychological tests are primarily based on three approaches. The taxonomic key approach is modeled from biological classification procedures, wherein rules are established to sort test data, according to decision trees that reflect common characteristics of groups. This method is most common and reflects the current diagnostic systems used in health care professions (i.e., *DSM-IV*). Geometric approaches have attempted to match cases with computer-generated graphic standards, in some instances relying on mathematical conceptions of the brain. Less technologically intensive models have tried to reflect the clinical reasoning process of neuropsychologists by utilizing algorithms that reflect the clinical interpretive practice and lore (Horton, Vaeth, & Anilane, 1990).

Empirical evaluation of the three aforementioned interpretive frameworks indicates satisfactory ability to confirm the presence or absence of brain damage, with poorer results for matters of greater specificity. The efficacy of interpretive systems appears comparable with either the Halstead-Reitan Neuropsychological Test Battery, or the Luria-Nebraska Neuropsychological Battery as the source of clinical input data (Horton et al., 1990). The Horton et al. findings are consistent with Lezak's (1995) comments reflecting the limited accurate scope of analysis afforded by actuarial computerized interpretive systems as well as the earlier work of Adams and Heaton (1985) indicating that computer programs were not as diagnostically accurate as human clinicians.

Sole reliance on actuarial evaluation of scores is not suitable for the complex issues typically addressed in the clinical neuropsychological evaluation. Actuarial predictions are found to be more accurate than clinical analysis only in cases of simple decision-making meeting criteria such as the following: (a) that there be only a small number of probable outcomes (e.g., left- vs. right-cortical lesion, diffuse damage, no impairment), (b) that the prediction variables be known (which limits the amount of information on which the formula was based), and (c) that the data from which the formula was derived be relevant to the questions asked (Pankratz & Taylor, 1982).

Even in what appear to be simple, straightforward tests, automated interpretive results may be misleading. For example, Bornstein (1986) noted significant cross-cultural differences in finger tapping wherein 80% of his Canadian random sample was impaired based on available normative data. Automated application of normative data to specific cultures and subgroups, even on a seemingly straightforward parameter, such as finger tapping speed across the U.S. and Canadian border, poses risks for false positives and false negatives when viewed in actuarial isolation.

Automated interpretation of the MMPI was spurred by the discriminating power of actuarial prediction. Items and scales were developed to maximally discriminate normal control participants from those individuals with psychiatric diagnoses. However, even with this well-established and researched tool and its evolution to the MMPI-2 (Butcher, Dahlstrom, Graham, Tellegen, & Kaemmer, 1989), false positives and false negatives occur and result in inaccurate automated interpretive reports. Most relevant to clinical neuropsychologists are situations in which symptoms common to traumatic brain injury and other acquired brain disorders cause MMPI-2 scale elevations that mimic psychiatric syndromes. A study by Gass (1991), for example, found that 14 MMPI-2 items related to physical and cognitive sequelae of brain injury could produce significant *T*-score elevations on the Hypochondriasis (*Hs*), Depression (*D*), Hysteria (*Hg*), Psychasthenia (*Pt*), and Schizophrenic (*Sc*) scales. To compensate for this, Gass recommended use of a correction factor. Cases such as these require individualized analysis in order to effectively determine which items were endorsed related to neurologic symptoms versus those items that reflect preexisting or emerging psychopathology (Lezak, 1995). Although the MMPI-2 provides the most substantial research foundation and actuarial data, it may not be the optimal personality assessment tool for individuals with neurologic impairment. In general, the clinical neuropsychologist may be assisted by automated interpretation, but this information is grist for the mill of clinical judgment, not a replacement thereof. Computerized test reports are, by and large, highly psychometric, emphasizing means and standard deviations, and their suitability to the average consumer is highly questionable. Under no circumstances should the language and format of a neuropsychological report consist of such highly technical, dry language that is devoid of context.

Another area of concern regarding computer interpretation is the potential for the neuropsychologist to become isolated from the individual who is being evaluated, with interpretation being done remotely. Wedding (1991) points out that the confluence of enhanced technology, proliferation of software, and widespread adoption of technician assistants has reduced the total amount of time that direct professional involvement occurs in the evaluation process. The clinical neuropsychologist may review data long after the test taker has departed, and yet must determine from the available data whether (a) directions were understood, (b) scores are acceptable, (c) reaction times are of reasonable length, (d) response patterns are non-random, and (e) a host of other test-taking factors. These problems seem more likely to occur in situations where computer-based tests are unobserved by the neuropsychologist, or when technicians are used to monitor computerized assessments. Qualifications, skills levels, procedural standardization, and documentation are all problems inherent in the widespread use of testing technicians. The scope of technicians' assistance should not exceed their training and competence and should be limited to administration, observation, and scoring of tests, not interpretation or drafting the actual reports. It is recommended that technician use be documented within the neuropsychological report in a manner that identifies the technician's role in the evaluation process.

A final area of concern involves the neuropsychologist's ability to process and integrate the amount and detail of analysis provided by computerized testing. Wedding (1991) has commented on the concomitant increase in the amount of data collected through more extensive evaluation protocols. His review of the data on judgmental accuracy suggests that neuropsychologists are far more likely to collect too much data rather than too little, and that this may tend to decrease judgmental accuracy, a view supported by Faust (1991).

Faust (1991) has suggested that forensic neuropsychological evaluations might benefit from computerized assessment, scoring, and interpretation to minimize the impact of salient data provided by attorneys as well as any confirmatory bias that might be present. The tendency to find what one is seeking, which often occurs when two opposing prominent neuropsychologists present differing conclusions based on the same data set, may be reduced by increased utilization of computerized clinical interpretive algorithms and reference to actuarial standards. The use of computerized tests and interpretation is in keeping with the Daubert Rule, wherein the legal testimony by expert witnesses must be based on scientific underpinnings, rather than individual opinion.

Faust (1991) stated that it is possible to develop algorithms or formulae that replicate clinical decision making with great accuracy. He pointed out the advantage of actuarial versus automatic judgment, with actuarial judgment involving not only the formulae of automated procedures, but also deriving conclusions based on empirically established frequencies, thus enhancing accuracy. From Faust's perspective, actuarial procedures are preferable based on his overview of research on the limited capacity of humans to manage or use complex data. This actuarial approach conflicts with the orientation and perspective of process-approach and hypothesis-testing neuropsychologists, for whom the aspect of how a task is completed weighs heavily in diagnostic, treatment, and prognostic formulations (Lezak, 1995). As discussed later in this chapter, the clinical neuropsychologist incorporating computerized actuarial judgments within a report is well served to use this tool in the context of supporting interview, observational, and other test data.

APA Professional Standards

In a 1986 report, the APA Committees on Professional Standards and Psychological Tests and Assessment outlined responsibilities associated with the use and development of computer-based tests and interpretations. This report identified four involved parties: test taker, test user, test administrator, and test developer. In neuropsychology, rarely is the test taker also the test user, as may be the case in self-directed guidance systems and interest inventories. The clinical neuropsychologist is most often the test user, utilizing test results in order to diagnose, advise, or predict. Neuropsychologists may also serve as test administrators, delegating the proctoring of computerized test administration to another person, as discussed previously. More and more often, neuropsychologists are serving in the roles of test developers and test authors, placing them in the position of working with software programmers and marketing their products with test or software publishers. As both test developers and test authors, neuropsychologists retain the responsibility for adherence to sound professional practice and ethical guidelines for those computerized tests and interpretive tools with which they are engaged.

Conclusions

Computerization of neuropsychological services appears inevitable, given the technological advances and the demands for more sophisticated and efficient evaluation of neuropsychological disorders. At present, practical benefits of computer-based assessment can be seen in the administration of lengthy personality inventories and tests requiring precise or complex stimulus presentation and response recording, or both, and in the processing of complex data to generate various scores and indices. In addition, computers have the capacity to store a number of tests in a convenient and, in the case of laptops, portable format. Nevertheless, restrictions in range of observation, flexibility and probing, difficulty assessing the *how* of performance, and actuarial limitations highlight the fact that, at present, computerized tests are only another tool for clinical neuropsychologists and not a replacement for observations, adaptations, modifications, judgments, and analyses brought to bear by the skilled clinician.

Computerization is likely to place increased responsibility on neuropsychologists who utilize this technology. They must be willing to review computerized manuals and published research in detail to be certain that the administration procedures used are comparable with the standardization sample procedures and to ensure that computerization has not changed task demands. They must exercise caution when applying standardized test norms to computerized forms and should review available research supporting equivalence of forms and norms for the test being used. The quality of new normative data should be scrutinized prior to application, as tests from the experimental branch of neuropsychology have often relied upon college students and military personnel for standardization and development of new computerized neuropsychological tests.

Although test developers and publishers typically provide much of this information for software tests (as they do for traditional tests), they should also be encouraged to provide information on hardware and software compatibility as well as defining the appropriate operating system and hardware configurations needed to properly run the software program. If the California survey by Rosenn and Weil (1996) can be generalized to other sections of the country, only a small population of psychologists are using computers for anything other than simple word processing. This suggests that psychologists are not well prepared to critique the complex and sometimes subtle problems or aspects of computerization previously discussed. Although software review articles (e.g., Kane, 1996; Kane & Kay, 1992), are quite informative, there is a need for greater emphasis on validity studies and head-to-head comparisons of computerized tests measuring similar domains or disorders (e.g., Attention-Deficit Disorder, response bias).

At present, it is difficult to see the significant time savings that is often assumed to be gained by computerization. Any time savings generated by computer-based testing will likely be used up in tasks such as orienting the test taker to the computer interface and program, researching and becoming proficient with computer hardware and software, and processing the amount of added information generated by the program. In addition, hypothesis-testing and process-approach neuropsychologists will likely be observing the test taker during computer administration of a test to obtain important details regarding demeanor and problem-solving behaviors. The latter responsibility may be of particular concern in terms of reimbursement if managed care companies assume that such work should be paid at a lower rate or not at all (i.e., payment for interpretation and not for administration).

Perhaps the biggest danger stems from changes brought about by managed care. Although managed care companies are not solely responsible, there may be added pressure and incentives for neuropsychologists to more fully automate the assessment process to maximize client flow and fit the evaluation into narrower allowable time frames. Test automation, use of technicians, and reliance on computer-generated interpretations and reports all have the potential to be misused by neuropsychologists and non-neuropsychologists, especially if pressures for cost containment outweigh optimal service quality. Thus, neuropsychologists will not only need to become knowledgeable consumers of computerized services, but they will also have the added responsibility of informing others of the benefits and problems associated with computerization.

Finally, the neuropsychological report should not consist of a reiteration of the typical, highly psychometric findings that comprise the computerized report. The computerized report does not and cannot take into account the individual patient's background and context, nor does it incorporate the consumer's referral question and primary need for interpretation and integration of the data within the client's specific circumstances and needs. Although the goal is for computerized reports to have fully incorporated the expert (i.e., neuropsychologist) into the system, this ideal of incorporating the patient into the machine is far from a reality.

10

NEUROPSYCHOLOGICAL REPORTS IN MANAGED HEALTH CARE

Joan P. Scanlon and James A. Grubman

Introduction

The neuropsychological report is the written interface between the neuropsychologist's assessment and other behavioral and medical health care providers. As such, it provides not only a description of the patient's status and treatment needs, but also a snapshot of the service performed. Through the neuropsychologist's report, treatment staff and case managers can evaluate the medical necessity for the service, the quality of the assessment, and the extent to which the service contributes to the patient's overall care. The report needs to be timely, concise, and useful. Through its ability to clarify diagnoses, it points to the most appropriate treatment plan, and steers providers away from costly, ineffective, redundant, or misleading procedures.

This chapter will address past and emerging trends in managed health care and will describe options for the neuropsychological report in various managed care settings.

History

The evolution of health care dynamics in recent years is well known to most clinicians, especially in the private sector. The escalating proportion of health care costs in the Gross National Product during the 1980s led to pressures for increased monitoring of health care expenditures. Mental health was a particular area of concern, especially the ever-increasing costs of inpatient care for adolescents and substance abusers. Unfortunately, neuropsychology fell into this mix, given that the only available codes within the American Medical Association (AMA) Current Procedure Codes Terminology (CPT) designation were embraced under mental health.

It was about this time that Antonio Puente (1994) spearheaded efforts to relocate the CPT codes for neuropsychology within the medical and neurology codes, apart from the psychiatric procedure codes. This, thereby, allowed differentiation of neuropsychological from psychological services, but a great deal of effort was required on the part of the provider to educate insurance company reviewers and other third-party payers as to the distinct nature of neuropsychological services. Since that time, the CPT codes have undergone further permutations under Dr. Puente's efforts, and both neuropsychological and psychology testing codes have a separate heading in the AMA 1999 CPT handbook.

Neuropsychological services remain, unfortunately, funded primarily under mental health, as opposed to medical health, benefits. Insurance companies ultimately may decide which benefit (medical or mental health) to access based on the referral question. In general, experience has shown that managed care companies have sought to restrict traditional psychological testing as a benefit, and one company noted that such testing was not only overused, but that the recommendations were typically not integrated into the overall care of the patient (see also chapters 2 and 8). From a cost standpoint, it appeared simply cheaper and more cost-effective to conduct a diagnostic interview and to limit psychological testing to instances of needed differential diagnosis. Hours of testing were typically limited as they were for psychotherapy. Neuropsychological testing was subject to the same limitations and biases as well, wherein batteries often had to be abbreviated. Regulatory changes by Medicare have also reflected this trend, with limitations being imposed on total hours of testing based on what appear to be flawed data, in the service of containing costs (Daniels & Deters, 1996).

Other companies have proven more enlightened, recognizing that the application of mental health benefits for neuropsychological procedures unduly misidentifies the patient as having psychiatric difficulties; these companies have created a separate procedure and provider listing for neuropsychological referrals. A managed care company for mental health benefits took a more unusual approach with one of the authors (JPS), in which the determination of whether medical or mental health benefits would be accessed depends upon the psychiatric history of the patient, despite the nature of the referral question (e.g., r/o Organic Brain Syndrome).

Sweet et al. (1995) conducted a survey of ABPP and non-ABPP neuropsychologists, the majority of whom described negative impacts of managed care on their practice. Issues included increased administrative time and paperwork, diminished patient care time, and declining incomes. Denials of service have appeared arbitrary in some instances and are made by individuals who may lack sufficient training to produce informed decisions. Several neuropsychologists reported the need to increase the volume of patients to maintain income levels; others adapted by joining an HMO or another managed care system.

The managed care systems continue to mature as well and to gain market penetration; that is, the proportion of health care consumers enrolled in some type of managed care is increasing. Hence, the viability of clinical neuropsychology will ultimately depend upon successful integration within various health care systems. Thus, the neuropsychological report must now address the needs of the system.

The following is an overview of an array of health care systems and ways in which neuropsychological reports are, or can be, attuned to the needs of the health care delivery system.

Traditional Payment Systems

In the past, traditional neuropsychological reports often focused either on test results or on functional descriptions. Test-oriented reports typically provide a brief history, behavioral descriptions, and a lengthy test results section listing performance results on each test administered. It is not uncommon to find such a report describing, for example, under Executive Functions, that "on Trail Making Test A, John Doe completed the sequencing of numbers within 27 seconds, whereas, on the more difficult task of Trail Making Test B, involving both numbers and letters, Mr. Doe took 107 seconds, which was within the severely deficient range." In the function-oriented report, similar results might be described as follows: "Performance was adequate on a task that requires sequencing of an automatized number series and visual scanning (Trails A = 27 seconds), but on a task that demands serially alternating between two automatized series (numbers and letters), performance was markedly deficient (Trails B = 107 seconds)." These methods of describing results are cumbersome and not very intelligible to non-neuropsychologists. Unfortunately, such reports may have largely served to create a sense of impatience in the reader who awaited the summary section in order to understand what it all meant with regard to the referral question.

Under traditional fee-for-service health care payment in which the preparation of extensive reports was reimbursed, such a report may have been regarded as acceptable. As the major audience was assumed to be other health care providers, a tome may have been allowed and expected. However, non-health-care professionals have long been complaining about the unintelligibility of many neuropsychological reports. For example, school systems and vocational rehabilitation counselors have pointed out that the minutiae of neuropsychological test findings and the professional jargon used do not readily translate into a description of behavior and ability in a way that the referral question is addressed. For example, should this person be placed in a special education program? Can this individual function in a competitive work environment? Is this person competent to execute a will? Neuropsychologists writing for these audiences in response to real-world referral questions must clearly summarize their findings in such a way that their relevance to the question is emphasized and must provide recommendations that are practical and useful, and that can be readily implemented.

Case Management Systems

The advent of managed care has raised the question of ecological (Heinrichs, 1990) and predictive validity (Lezak, 1995) of neuropsychological reports. When paying for an expensive service, primary care physicians (PCPs), behavioral health case managers, or utilization case reviewers expect and demand a usable final product.

Currently, there are several basic models of case management that comprise managed care, largely distinguished by who is doing the utilization or case management. Neuropsychological services and the resulting report may be handled somewhat differently in each model as reviewed below.

No Case Management

No case management is essentially the traditional fee-for-service model like an indemnity insurance plan, with the exception that providers agree to a contractual rate for services. Referrals can be made by anyone within or outside the health care system, including the patient, and there is no oversight of the process as long as the service is reimbursable under the insurance plan benefit guidelines. Although clinicians may long for the preservation of this type of system, marketplace forces in health care appear to point to its gradual extinction for all but the wealthiest of citizens.

Third-party Administrators Performing Utilization Management From a Distance

Third-party administrators are companies that contract with insurance plan payers or employer-based plans to manage utilization, patient referral pathways, insurance benefit utilization, and treatment reviews. Such participants are bound by the terms of their contract with the payer or the employer as well as the terms of the insurance plan that subscribers access. Requests for psychological testing are high-visibility referral requests because of their expense and the belief (mistaken or accurate as the case may be) that there is often a limited payoff in patient care relative to the costs involved in the testing. Many third party administrators (TPAs) automatically require more intensive review of requests for psychological testing, with neuropsychological testing getting an even finer-grained scrutiny. Case reviewers are often at a distant site, contacted by telephone or via written treatment plan forms. When case management functions are split off from the local clinicians in this manner, there is often a tendency to view the process of case management as adversarial. Clinicians seeking authorization frequently feel as if they are *dialing for dollars*, finding themselves persuading or begging in order to obtain authorization from utilization management (UM) reviewers.

Under the case management system, neuropsychological testing is usually considered a *boutique service*, authorized in special circumstances for clear referral questions with a likelihood of obvious payoff for the patient's clinical care. Service has often been authorized according to a two-tiered system: cognitive screenings of up to 3 hours, and full assessments of around 6 to 9 hours. Cognitive screenings are more frequently authorized, with the expectation that the resulting report reflects a focused, targeted assessment that was not intended to cover all possible bases. Addressing the specific referral question is paramount, both in terms of the evaluation procedures and the final report.

Case management has and will increasingly call upon providers to demonstrate the efficacy of neuropsychological services that are delivered in a cost-effective manner. In fact, failure to fully utilize neuropsychological services when appropriate can well lead to inappropriate and more expensive care. For example, Ruthven (1996) illustrates how identification of subtle organic issues can circumvent the delivery of ineffective services. Psychotherapy for depression without sufficient attention to the attendant effects of a head injury is not as effective as the provision of more targeted rehabilitation efforts. Neuropsychology has been and can continue to be useful in discriminating between organic versus psychological conditions or, more likely, delineating the contributions of both to a patient's presentation, thereby developing an appropriate treatment plan for complex cases.

A full assessment would, thus, be appropriate in the following examples:

1. A 57-year-old Chief Executive Officer (CEO) with a superior premorbid IQ and a moderate head injury along with a prior history of moderate alcohol use shows irritability, emotional reactivity, and moderately impulsive decision-making upon return to work.
2. A 45-year-old accountant, recovering from a ruptured anterior communicating artery aneurysm with secondary hydrocephalus, shows depression over loss of job and diminished cognitive capacities.
3. A 28-year-old woman with chronic-progressive MS of 8 years is downplaying her deficits while neglecting her household tasks and her care of her family.
4. A 7-year-old child with early history of head injury is experiencing increasing academic and behavioral difficulties, including distractibility and impaired reading.

For these evaluations, a full assessment would help clarify important diagnostic issues leading to coordination of care among many providers. By purchasing the comprehensive, well defined service that a clinical neuropsychologist can deliver, the case reviewer saves money through avoidance of unnecessary procedures on both the mental health side and the medical side. In addition, it promotes clinical integration, which facilitates appropriate management of the case as a whole. The report also serves as a template for guiding subsequent psychological or medical authorizations, because future requests for services by other providers can be evaluated in light of the neuropsychological recommendations.

Case Management Integrated With Clinical Care

Integrated systems may actually allow for more sophisticated use of the clinical neuropsychologist. Here, the middle man of behavioral managed care companies gives way to direct contracting between insurance companies, employers, and so forth with a comprehensive delivery system that is either vertically or horizontally integrated (or both). Vertical integration is the degree to which linkages are established with providers within a core health system such as a hospital; horizontal integration is the provision of the same array of services over a defined geographic area (American Psychological Association Practice Directorate, 1996). Such systems seek to offer lower cost structures by ensuring quality of services with a capability of serving a spectrum of diagnoses along a continuum of care. Guidelines are developed by multispecialty teams to gauge quality of care from diagnosis to discharge. The measurement of outcomes, thus, becomes critically important.

Various forms of integrated models have emerged. The gatekeeper system, a model with which most clinical neuropsychologists are likely to be familiar, is comprised of PCPs. Within an HMO or preferred provider organization (PPO) the PCP is the front-line clinician who makes decisions about allocating resources and efficiently managing an individual patient's care. Although, historically, clinical neuropsychologists have related to neurologists and psychiatrists, it is now necessary to establish a working relationship with the PCP, bringing into focus the relevance of the contribution that the clinical neuropsychologist can make to the care of patients. In addition, there have been recent shifts in financial relationships among employers, insurers, clinicians, and health care systems, whereby groups of clinicians or multispecialty systems have been willing to contract in various ways. Under *capitation*, clinicians assume the risks and benefits of managing care for a patient population without the necessity for a third-party administrator. The physician-hospital organization (PHO), a large multispecialty medical group, or behavioral health service, receives a set amount of money to care for a given number of patients per contract year.

The neuropsychologist is, thus, confronted with a choice of whether to be on the inside or the outside of this type of arrangement. The clinical neuropsychologist who chooses to remain an outside provider maintains greater independence and diversification of referral sources. However, being perpetually an outside provider to the capitated system potentially diminishes the number of referrals, as those services are perceived as an added expense to the system. There is always the additional risk that systems will find a lower cost alternative through an inside provider at some point in the future.

Of course, the prime advantage for being part of the clinical staff on the inside of the system is the freedom that comes from being able to make clinical decisions without the often heavy-handed oversight of a third-party administrator or a separate utilization manager. Clinicians are most typically salaried under this arrangement, with some type of variable compensation linked in varying degrees to individual or departmental performance. As with any freedom, there are concomitant responsibilities to manage the care effectively.

Acceptance by and close collaboration with the medical side may seem like the Holy Grail of neuropsychology practice, coming after years of having to fight for credibility within the medical system. Ironically, many neuropsychologists may find that they are welcome to take their place at a table that is fast becoming laden with leaner meals. Nevertheless, neuropsychological service providers under this type of system tend to have more options than in the segregated utilization management or clinical care system. The neuropsychologist may provide a brief consultation or case review on an outpatient or inpatient basis, resulting in a brief consultation report. A cognitive screening may be selected for an individual patient, or a fuller evaluation may be performed up to a complete, traditional neuropsychological assessment.

Under a capitated system there is a tendency to allocate the responsibility for certain parts of the neuropsychological evaluation to other team members (e.g., speech pathologists, occupational therapists, physical therapists, etc.) In addition, under the purview of the clinical neuropsychologist, neuropsychology technicians provide assistance in the administration of selected standardized tests. Such a delegation of responsibilities would be difficult under a traditional fee-for-service arrangement, but it becomes much more time- and cost-efficient in a salaried, capitated system.

Neuropsychological service delivery can be enhanced with the ready availability of the neuropsychologist in program planning and delivery not only in the traditional areas of neurology and psychiatry, but also in geriatrics (i.e., development of a dementia clinic), rehabilitation, and so forth. The product may not be the testing report in all instances; rather, it may be the design of a full array of services at the least amount of cost and the provision of needed consultation to other disciplines to sharpen treatment focus, thereby making the most of limited resources. At a minimum, the neuropsychologist working outside the system will be expected to provide access to patients in a timely manner, to think flexibly about the most efficient procedure needed to address a diagnostic or treatment question, and to respond clearly and rapidly with a written report comprehensible to other providers in the system when required.

Managed Medicare/Medicaid

Until recently, government-sponsored insurance programs such as Medicare and Medicaid, were notable exceptions to the movement toward managed care. Neuropsychologists serving Medicare and Medicaid populations were able to practice without case management oversight, although the downside was low reimbursement rates, barely comprehensible coding systems, and delayed payment. Government-sponsored plans have begun to enter the managed-care fold with state-administered managed Medicaid plans and the advent of Medicare HMOs.

Neuropsychologists have had to deal with government-sponsored programs in a few areas, some of which have been the mainstay of clinical neuropsychology. Medicare has supported assessment of the elderly for dementia, deficits related to cerebrovascular accidents (CVAs), and medical disorders such as chronic obstructive pulmonary disease, brain cancer, and Parkinson's disease. Medicaid and Medicaid/Medicare coinsurance plans are the largest payers for patients under 65 years of age who qualify for disability under Social Security Administration guidelines. These patients include individuals with MS, AIDS dementia, head injury, and developmental deficits. The movement toward capitated and case-managed Medicare and Medicaid systems means that neuropsychologists will see a greater number of patients with utilization management for populations heretofore unmanaged.

The Report as a Viable Product

In the primary care system, the neuropsychological report becomes more like the radiologist's MRI report. In all likelihood, a report solely focused upon diagnosis or a profile of cognitive abilities will offer little assistance to meet a PCP's need for managing the patient on a functional basis; that is, how can this patient's memory problems be best managed in terms of cognitive rehabilitation to improve daily functioning, family issues, pharmacological interventions, and so forth? How much structure does the patient need? Does another family member need to be engaged in the treatment? Hence, the neuropsychological report may well have a heavier focus on remediation than on diagnosis.

Another issue is the efficiency of the assessment. By refining the referral question (see chapter 3) and efficiently gathering the relevant history and background evaluation (see chapter 5), the clinical neuropsychologist is in a position to conduct a more focused, less redundant, and more relevant assessment as opposed to a comprehensive fixed battery of procedures that may or may not be relevant to the specific questions posed.

In the end, the recommendation section may be viewed by managed care as the most crucial within the report. Needless to say, the clinical neuropsychologist is expected to provide access to patients in a timely manner, to think flexibly about the most efficient procedure needed to address a diagnostic or treatment question, and to respond clearly and rapidly with a written report that is comprehensible to other providers in the system. The report must have sections clearly and succinctly delineating history, behavior, procedures, results, summary, and recommendations (see chapter 6). It is obvious from the previous discussion that the neuropsychological report takes on new and varied roles and responsibilities in the era of managed health care. Increasingly reserved for the unusual, the difficult, or the potentially costly patient, a neuropsychological assessment is becoming a specialty service that is expected to provide a good return for the money spent, namely a series of well thought out diagnostic impressions and treatment recommendations. Here, then, are a series of recommendations to assist the neuropsychologist in generating reports that are consonant with the needs of providers functioning in a managed care climate.

General Recommendations

These recommendations are mandated by the constraints imposed by managed care administrators.

1. Given that there may be more than one reader of the report, even though there may be only one referral source (see chapter 3), medical, neurological, and neuropsychological jargon should be avoided. The use of technical terms should be parenthetically explained. For example: "...there were no deficits in ideomotor praxis (motor planning ability)."

2. Reports should be as brief as possible (five to seven pages). Whereas five closely typewritten pages might be considered a short psychological report, they would be considered a long medical report. Using a larger font to make the report longer or more visually readable simply appears to be wasting valuable space in the medical record.
3. Use clearly readable headings, with at least a 1 inch margin on the left to accommodate hole punching for inclusion in the chart.
4. Needless to say, the report should be produced within 1 to 2 weeks. If this is not practical, a short note or summary letter should be sent within 5 business days, followed by the report no more than 3 weeks later.

Specific Recommendations for Sections of the Report

Reason for Referral:

A brief categorical description will suffice. For example: "Assessment of dementia," "Differential diagnosis of noncompliance behaviors," or "Recommendations for treatment of postconcussive syndrome."

History:

1. Summarize rather than detail the patient's psychodynamics, family dysfunctions, or complex personal stresses. There are two reasons for this. First, by contrast with detailed mental health records, the neuropsychological report may be kept in the patient's medical record and will be available to be seen by multiple providers over time, most of whom will not be psychologists. Because the report is intended to be seen as a medical document, it needs to follow the level of personal detail typically seen in medical office notes rather than in mental health records. Second, most readers will not see the relevance of a fine-grained analysis of intrapsychic factors.
2. Detail important medical factors including current medications (listed with dosages and schedules) and recent relevant medical test results. Note the importance of any psychoactive medications as possible influences in the patient's current symptoms or test performance.

3. Given that most readers will skim the report, the use of the terms such as normal, noncontributory, unremarkable, and within normal limits, is acceptable. If there was nothing unusual in the family or patient's personal history, say so. For example, "Family and childhood history are unremarkable."
4. Include references to the assessments or interventions of other providers, including the impact on the patient's status or diagnosis. Note which procedures seemed to be at least partially effective. For example, "A previous history of behavior management training was unsuccessful, possibly due to the patient's drinking at the time and sabotaging by the patient's wife."

Behavior:

Descriptions of the patient's appearance, interview behavior, and test-taking behavior should be succinct. Detailed descriptors and behavioral anecdotes that show the fine nuances of a patient's behavior are unnecessary unless they significantly contribute to the diagnosis or recommendations. Observations of interview or test-taking behavior that add materially to the ultimate diagnosis or formulations should be included. Of particular interest are behaviors that either clearly support or contrast with the test results. Note the following examples: "Mr. Miller was poorly oriented, could not recall what he had for breakfast that morning, and had to think for over a minute to remember the name of his primary care physician; " "Mrs. Jones joked easily with the receptionist about the long detour she had to take on the way to the office, in contrast to her slow, depressive, and hesitant behavior later during the memory testing."

List of Tests and Procedures:

1. To conserve space, tests administered should be listed in paragraph format using a smaller font than the rest of the report.
2. Test listing may be deferred to the end of the report as an addendum.

Test Results:

1. There are currently different opinions about whether to include raw test data as part of the report (Naugle & McSweeney, 1996; also see chapter 7 in this book). In a managed care environment, it is useful to compare data across time in different evaluations. Having the raw data facilitates utilization review by another neuropsychologist, although the risk exists that they will be misinterpreted by

nonqualified professionals. It also serves as a record of performance for possible future comparisons without later having to go through the often prolonged process of obtaining data via release of information.

2. Raw test scores are routinely available to individuals in educational settings and are helpful in the managed care arena. Ideally, raw data should be presented in an addendum to the report or in graphic format. Provide, if possible, a graphic format for viewing test results.
3. For brevity purposes, test descriptions in the body of the report should be avoided. Similarly, rather than providing a test-by-test discussion with attached data in the report, a function-centered discussion is preferable. Highlight the person's strengths and weaknesses, focusing especially on the referral question.

Summary and Recommendations:

1. State the referral question, relevant medical history, and personal history concisely, highlighting only the most important areas for the reader to remember. Due to time constraints, many readers of neuropsychological reports look only at the summary and recommendations sections. Use the summary section wisely, and focus on practical recommendations.
2. Summarize the patient's abilities as illuminated by the test findings, highlighting the most important results. Avoid recapitulating all the test results in detail again in the summary section.
3. List at least one *DSM-IV* or *ICD* diagnosis with numerical codes, along with other diagnoses as relevant. Include rule out diagnoses, noting whether further information is needed or recommended to be obtained. If the evaluation is even partly designed to clarify level of functioning, include a current *DSM-IV* Global Assessment of Functioning (GAF) score (American Psychiatric Association, 1994).
4. Provide clear, practical, and detailed recommendations including further workups to clarify diagnoses, academic or workplace recommendations, counseling recommendations, or suggestions for medical treatment.
5. Evaluate the appropriateness of any prior recommendations in the light of the current evaluation. For example: "...Individual, insight-oriented psychotherapy is unlikely to be of benefit in Mr. Miller's head-injury adjustment because of Mr. Miller's limited abstraction

and poor short-term verbal memory. His memory impairment alone would limit the carryover from session to session of what was discussed in therapy. Counseling is much more likely to be effective using the following guidelines: (a) his wife attends each session with him; (b) he writes down notes during each session of what is most important; (c) at the end of each session he and the therapist agree on one or two main points and choose one homework assignment for him; and, (d) at the start of the next session, the therapist and the Millers go over what happened in the previous session and the assigned homework."

Conclusion

For the purpose of reimbursement, the specialty of neuropsychology is increasingly viewed as a medical subspecialty. Consequently, the neuropsychologist's work is being judged along the same lines as other medical procedures and office records. The role of a neuropsychologist in various managed care settings can be either that of a consultant specialist, or a part of the treatment team managing the care of a population of patients. Increasingly reserved for the complex, difficult, or high-utilization patient, the neuropsychological evaluation has, in fact, a strong role for clarifying issues crucial to treatment planning in managed care. However, this means bypassing extensive evaluations for relatively routine treatment planning questions.

The neuropsychological report is one of the most useful documents in managed health care if, and only if, it assists primary and specialty providers in the delivery of efficient and effective care to the patient. Neuropsychologists who produce a readable and usable report will find themselves in high demand as the health care environment continues to evolve.

11

Neuropsychological Assessment in the Schools

Richard Guare and Margaret Dawson

As an increasing number of children with CNS insults are integrated into the regular school setting, schools provide an important arena for neuropsychological assessment. The neuropsychologist is in an ideal position to help teachers and parents understand the relationship between neurologic factors, cognition, and behavior (cf. Gaddes & Edgell, 1994; Hooper, Willis & Stone, 1996). In fact, the need for this type of information often leads parents or schools to seek out a neuropsychological assessment. Although establishing a relationship between neurologic status, cognition, and behavior or outlining cognitive profiles is an important first step in the evaluation process, it is not an end in itself. If the evaluation stops there, without detailed and relevant intervention strategies keyed to the child's needs, then the needs of the child, the parent, and the school have not been met. In this case, the evaluation, rather than providing an important service, may become a source of frustration because considerable time and expense failed to produce a practical intervention plan.

In the schools, intervention is crucial and is most often the primary and, perhaps, sole purpose for an assessment. Although schools make use of diagnostic information, it is typically in the service of determining intervention strategies. Historically, much of neuropsychology has concerned itself with diagnosis, delineation of brain-behavior relationships, and even localization. Less attention has been paid to the specific strategies, instructional methods, and materials that rehabilitation specialists and teachers might employ to help children or adults capitalize most effectively on their strengths and overcome or compensate for their weaknesses (Uzzell, 1997).

There are a number of reasons for this lack of attention to intervention. Training of neuropsychologists traditionally has placed more emphasis on formal evaluation and diagnosis and less on intervention. Training programs in the past have not routinely included or attempted to integrate cognitive, instructional, and behavioral psychology with neuropsychology. Such integrated training would allow for more informed interventions and strategies that could be matched with behaviors and characteristics known to occur in certain neuropsychological profiles.

A second issue has to do with ecological validity, or the lack thereof, in regard to assessment instruments typically employed by neuropsychologists or, for that matter, by school psychologists (cf. Sbordone & Long, 1996; Teeter & Semrud-Clikeman, 1997). Intelligence tests have reasonable predictive value for academic achievement, and achievement tests generally correlate well with actual academic achievement (Salvia & Ysseldyke, 1998). Beyond this, there are no well established relationships between what various tests purport to test and the relevance of those skills to a child's classroom performance. For example, although memory tests are used fairly routinely in neuropsychological assessment, the implications of strong or weak performance on a particular subtest or set of subtests is not clear. Thus, if intervention is in fact the goal, then achieving this goal is made harder by the fact that some neuropsychological tests, although useful for diagnosis or elucidation of problems, do not have good predictive validity for the classroom situation. As an example, executive skills have recently been recognized as important to classroom performance (cf. Barkley, 1998), yet we are only at the beginning stages of developing good measures to assess those skills (see the Delis-Kaplan Executive Function System). Moreover, we are only beginning to determine the relationship between performance on these measures and behavior observed in the classroom.

If the neuropsychologist hopes to make relevant contributions to the development of classroom interventions, a shift is required in assessment. Ideally, this refocusing would include more reliance on parent and teacher interviews, observations through checklists, and formal observation of the child engaged in various instructional settings and academic tasks.

For example, asking parents and teachers to provide specific descriptions that reflect a child's cognitive and behavioral strengths and weaknesses can readily lead to formulation of hypotheses about neuropsychological issues. Such information can be integrated into the picture that the neuropsychologist will paint of the child in the Impressions section of the report. Such information helps parents and teachers realize the evaluator has an accurate sense of the child and is responsive to their concerns.

Moreover, such information helps to identify where interventions need to be directed and often what they need to be.

We are not proposing that formal assessment be eliminated. Rather, we should critically examine the purposes for which evaluations are conducted, and the degree to which formal assessment data can address those purposes, other modes of assessment that may complement and enhance the goal of developing appropriate interventions. Although this may seem a radical notion, in fact, it returns neuropsychology to its roots in the observation of behavior. It goes beyond this foundation, however, by incorporating the systematic and, in some cases, norm-based observations that are possible through formal assessment with ecologically valid observational data. Lest we forget, schools generate large amounts of data about children on a daily basis, and teachers are less in need of formal assessment information than perhaps other populations that neuropsychologists serve. Moreover, when teachers are in need of formal assessment, school psychologists are often available to assess cognitive and academic skills. Sattler (1992) provides school psychologists with specific guidelines for report writing, many of which generalize nicely to neuropsychological report writing.

Role of the Neuropsychologist

The neuropsychologist performs a number of important roles in the assessment of children. These roles may range from conducting full, detailed evaluations of a broad range of neuropsychological functions to reviewing records, or providing consultation. Evaluations must address the specific referral questions in a manner that accurately delineates the problem and leads to potential solutions.

Neuropsychologists are frequently called upon to evaluate children with various neurological and neurodevelopmental disorders who have had little or no previous testing. For example, children with a range of acquired brain injuries, such as strokes, tumors, head injuries, toxic exposures including drugs, and AIDS, are all potential candidates for comprehensive neuropsychological evaluations. In addition, a variety of systemic illnesses have potential impact on neurologic functions; these include, but are not limited to, heart disease, diabetes, and kidney diseases, as well as other neurologic disorders including hydrocephalus, seizures, and Tourette's syndrome that may warrant evaluation. Various genetic disorders such as Fragile X syndrome, Turner syndrome, Down syndrome, and Williams syndrome may also warrant evaluation. Finally, a range of degenerative diseases that impact on neurologic functioning should be referred for evaluation.

In all such cases, neuropsychologists can make significant contributions to the family and school personnel because they understand the neurologic implications of these various injuries and disorders and the impact they are likely to have on learning and behavior. The neuropsychologist's input in this area can be especially critical both for the development of interventions and for the enhancement of the psychological well-being of the child or adolescent.

As an example, the authors have seen situations where, subsequent to a traumatic brain injury with an apparent good recovery, an adolescent's difficulty with task initiation or follow through has been interpreted as a motivational problem and labeled as laziness. They have also seen situations where special education services were instituted but then discontinued when the child began to perform well, only to require reinstitution at a subsequent date. In these situations, the neuropsychologist will consider both the short- and long-term implications of a particular disorder. The neuropsychologist can explicitly state, or at least hypothesize about, the potential behavioral and instructional implications likely to be encountered over the progression of the disorder or the course of recovery.

A second area of assessment for the neuropsychologist involves the child who evidences complex or multifaceted learning problems that have not responded to current intervention efforts. In such cases, a review of the data and instructional techniques as well as additional relevant assessment may shed light on neuropsychological variables impeding the child's progress. For example, in some situations, there may be a task by child interaction such that the child's skills and abilities are mismatched with performance demands. The neuropsychologist can provide an explanation and examples of the child's thinking in relation to a specific task and how variables such as attention, working memory, and spatial reasoning affect performance of specific tasks. A more detailed understanding of the child's thinking accompanied by suggestions to modify tasks to better match these skills can be helpful.

A third circumstance in which a more detailed evaluation may be warranted involves second opinions. Outside of the school system, neuropsychologists, with their specialized training and specialized assessment skills, are arguably in the best position to conduct an evaluation when the emphasis is on cognitive factors or a combination of cognitive and emotional factors. Parents and schools are becoming increasingly cognizant of this service, especially as the availability of child neuropsychologists grows. Thus, it is not unusual for parents or school districts to request another opinion from these professionals regarding a child's diagnosis and intervention strategies. So long as neuropsychologists can offer credible information and present it in a format that can be used effectively by schools and parents, this area is likely to constitute a source of growth for pediatric neuropsychology.

Minimum Competencies

As noted earlier, although most neuropsychologists receive extensive training in assessment, intervention is often underemphasized. Furthermore, the area of child neuropsychology, as a specific area of study, is only now beginning to be recognized (Teeter & Semrud-Clikeman, 1997). The context of school performance presents with its own unique demands and challenges. The authors believe that to operate successfully in this arena and to enhance the reputation of the field, neuropsychologists must possess certain skills.

Ideally, beyond formal training in child neuropsychology and developmental psychology, the practitioner would have either direct training or experience working in a school setting. In the absence of such experience, ongoing contact with schools through discussions with teachers, attendance at school meetings, and classroom observations of children is essential. Schools are unique social systems and classrooms are structured in unique ways. Without some appreciation of these contexts, the likelihood that interventions will miss the mark is greatly increased.

Neuropsychologists, particularly those who do not have extensive experience in schools, should acknowledge at the outset of any school-based consultative relationship that the expertise of school personnel is as important as their own skills. The neuropsychologist should view teachers and other school personnel as equal partners in the consultation process and should communicate this understanding clearly. In addition, regardless of the type of experience the neuropsychologist has or the nature of the consultative relationship, neuropsychologists should possess a good working knowledge of the literature in cognitive and educational psychology as well as specific learning disabilities.

The Neuropsychological Report

Simply stated, the neuropsychological report is the most critical element of the assessment process. The report translates and communicates evaluation data and, more importantly, the impressions and recommendations that arise from those data. Although, as will be argued later, the report should not be the sole source of communication, in reality, for reasons of time and expense, this will often be the case. Thus, this may be the only opportunity for the neuropsychologist to communicate the results of a time consuming and costly evaluation that is often anxiously awaited and that may have significant implications for the child's treatment. Regardless of the significance of the results, they will be of no benefit if the writer is unsuccessful in the effort to communicate them clearly to the referring party.

In the case of the child neuropsychological evaluation, the report is particularly critical. Results may help determine the need for additional medical evaluation, the nature of rehabilitation services, the outcome of litigation, and eligibility for and determination of the type of educational services that a child is to receive. In addition, the report may influence decisions about medical intervention, including medication.

Given the range of reasons for which children may be referred for a neuropsychological evaluation, a *one size fits all* mentality should not govern the neuropsychological report. Particularly in today's fiscal environment, the desire for a thorough and comprehensive detailing of history, findings, and recommendations must be balanced against factors of efficiency and cost-effectiveness. As noted earlier, it would be argued that in children, the primary reason for neuropsychological assessment is intervention. With constraints imposed by managed care companies in terms of time allowed and by school districts in terms of dollars budgeted for assessment, it is difficult to justify pages and pages devoted to extremely detailed reviews of history, previous assessment information, and results unless that degree of detail is germane to the recommendations.

Unfortunately, the authors have reviewed a variety of psychological and neuropsychological evaluations that are long on reviews of background information and test results and short on recommendations. This leads the reader to question whether the person writing the report was able to write appropriate recommendations. The individuals receiving the report should not be responsible for synthesis of the results into recommendations. Further, the strengths and weaknesses discovered in the course of the evaluation should be related to the child's presenting problem(s), and recommendations should specifically address those presenting problems (see chapter 8). If weaknesses are detailed but are unrelated to presenting problems, then the receiving parties may not know how to assess either the importance of the weaknesses or the value of the recommendations.

The objective of the report is to consider the child's current functioning from the perspective of parents, teachers, and perhaps therapists and physicians, and to integrate those observations with the evaluation results. The goal is to present a picture of the child that is coherent and that is accepted by parents and teachers because their own perspectives have been integrated and perhaps validated. When there are conflicting or contradictory views of the child, it is important for the neuropsychologist to provide some explanation and perhaps some resolution of these contrasting perspectives.

It was suggested previously that the primary purpose of the neuropsychological evaluation is intervention and, for the most part, there is a belief that this is true. There are, however, a few situations (e.g., forensic evaluations) where diagnosis and explanation of the problems rather than intervention strategies may be called for (see chapter 12). Thus, it is true that some neuropsychological evaluations do not necessitate recommendations for intervention strategies. However, all neuropsychological evaluations must respond to the implicit or explicit questions of the referral source. As noted earlier, there are concerns about cost-effectiveness and the clinical importance of consumer satisfaction when resources are limited. Given these concerns, a thorough response to the questions from the referral source is important both to preserve the reputation of the individual neuropsychologist and for the field of neuropsychology as a whole and to ensure respect and an appreciation for the type of services that can be rendered.

In light of this, it is recommended that the neuropsychologist actively solicit questions from the referral source or from the individuals who will have the specific responsibility for intervening with the child. For example, solicitation from teachers of questions and appropriate clarifying information makes the referring party an active participant in the evaluation and helps ensure that the results will provide relevant information. Solicitation of questions also helps the consumer (i.e., referral source) clarify the reason for the referral, determine whether the referral is appropriate, and decide whether evaluation information is sufficient to respond to the questions. Periodically, individuals have been referred to the authors who, with clarification of the referral question, are determined to be more appropriately referred to other specialists such as neurologists, speech and language pathologists, or vocational specialists.

The body of most reports should incorporate the following main headings: Reason for Referral, Background Information (to include pertinent histories), Behavioral Observations, Tests Administered, Results (listed by various functions), Impressions, and Recommendations (see chapter 6).

In terms of the actual construction of the report, the Reason for Referral section should clearly and succinctly state the overriding question(s) or concern(s). The consensus is that it need not be extensively detailed because more detailed information will be provided in the Impressions and Recommendations sections. The Background Information section, however, requires more detailed treatment, including a review of prenatal, birth, development, medical, education, and psychosocial histories. If there are factors in any aspect of the history that contribute to or help to explain the presenting problem, then this information should be reviewed in sufficient detail for the reader to understand its importance. In addition, past evaluation results should be highlighted for their relevance to the current problem. This also allows for a comparison of past results with findings from the current evaluation so that both consistencies and discrepancies can be noted.

The Behavioral Observations section should present an overview of basic physical and mental status (e.g., appearance and grooming, language and motor functions, affective state, and coherence of thought). In addition, the child's reaction to and behavior during testing should be described with regard to tasks to which the child responds positively or negatively, along with features such as anxiety, frustration, humor, and so forth. Perhaps most important will be the examiner's effort to paint a picture of the child in a performance situation that captures the task approach and the style of interaction. The credibility of the report can be influenced by the degree to which the examiner's observations are felt to accurately portray the child as that child is known to parents and teachers.

Mindful of the need to be concise, the Background Information and Behavioral Observations sections of the report deserve at least the same degree of attention and thoroughness as the data sections. It is believed that the neuropsychological assessment is a multiaxial process, and the report should provide sufficient review and consideration of extra-test information to validly consider the factors that play an important role in the integration of the constellation of findings.

There are a number of different options for the presentation of data and results. Most neuropsychologists prefer to present results by cognitive functions using from 4 to as many as 10 different categories, depending on the degree of specificity required. The authors prefer the following categories, usually presented in the order reported here: General Cognitive Abilities; Language/Verbal Reasoning; Visuo-Spatial/Constructional Skills; Memory; Attention/Executive Skills; Academic Achievement; Motor Sequencing/Motor Speed; and Behavioral/Psychological Factors. This last section does not include behavioral observations, but rather various personality tests, symptom checklists, and self-report forms.

The final sections of the report include Impressions and Recommendations. There is a preference to provide specific test data in the body of the report because this allows for integration of specific performance information with more qualitative statements regarding cognitive factors and the processes that the child used to arrive at the solution. However, the authors are not unequivocally wedded to this approach and understand that some individuals would prefer to limit the body of the report to qualitative statements about performance in different cognitive functions and to provide a data sheet at the end. There is no noticeable disadvantage to this and, in fact, in the case of longer reports, it may decrease the amount of information contained in the body and, thus, be helpful to the reader. It is recommended that if a summary of data is to be appended, the results be organized to match the sequence of presentation in the body of the report (see chapter 7).

When reporting data in the body of the report, relevant scores by subtest can be listed at the beginning of each section. Within the body of the paragraph, providing a single-sentence explanation of what the task involves, a description of the process by which the child addressed the problem, and any interesting or unusual features that would help to explain the child's underlying cognitive process is useful. If there is an unusual or atypical result, an explanation for why this may have occurred should also be provided.

The Impressions section is meant to serve a number of functions. The first is to briefly summarize the presenting problem, history, and data obtained in the report. A second function is to weave together the various psychosocial, emotional, behavioral, cognitive, and medical factors. This aims to provide both an accurate picture of the child's current functioning as well as an explanation for why that picture is as it is. Third, and perhaps most importantly, the Impressions section explains, at least in a hypothetical way, the cognitive and emotional processes that underlie the child's behavior so that parents and teachers can understand why the child adopts a particular problem-solving approach to a task. This explanation should inform the direction of the intervention strategies to be discussed in the Recommendations section.

The importance of this element in the evaluation report cannot be overemphasized. Often, the Impressions section merely restates and summarizes earlier information and refers to strengths and weaknesses in an obvious or a surface manner, but does not help parents or teachers to understand how the child's thinking and emotional processes relate to the current behavior. It is in this area, more than any other, that the neuropsychologist can bring to bear specific skills to provide explanations that are typically not found in other psychological or psychoeducational evaluations. When properly written, the Impressions section will flow naturally into the Recommendations section. More importantly, it will also allow people who are working with the child in an educational or rehabilitation setting to understand the types of interventions that will most likely be effective.

As noted earlier, the Recommendations section is the most critical part of the report because it most often makes the specific recommendations for which the evaluation was requested in the first place. Well stated, effective recommendations give the report its ultimate value and give true meaning to the notion of assessment for the purpose of intervention.

As with the Impressions section, certain fundamental questions must be answered in the Recommendations section if the report is to have credibility. Chief among these is the reason for which the child was referred. In most evaluations, there is an implicit or explicit question regarding how best to provide for the needs of the child. At the very least, the report must address specific, concrete recommendations that will help to ameliorate the presenting problem. In many cases, the report will have detailed other issues (i.e., beyond the referring questions) that require recommendations.

The authors favor a system that breaks down recommendations along a few different dimensions. One dimension involves whether the intervention is aimed at the child or at the environment. Intervention at the level of the child involves those techniques or actions that are meant to directly modify the child's behavior or cognition in a way that results in the child adapting to the demands of the environment. Behavioral strategies designed to increase on-task behavior or cognitive-behavioral strategies designed to enhance error monitoring are examples of interventions at this level. Medication also is an intervention at the level of the child. Interventions at the level of the environment involve changes in the environment itself or changes in task demands that result in an accommodation to the child's cognitive and behavioral capacities. Changing the complexity or rate of information presented, the child's seat in the classroom, or the methods by which a math concept is presented are examples of environmental types of intervention. Modifications at the level of the environment conceivably could provide most or all of the strategies needed to help the child. However, modifications at the level of the child typically also involve modifications at the environment level.

In terms of content of the recommendations for the school setting, at least three areas should be addressed: behavioral and cognitive-behavioral strategies, instructional techniques, and curriculum. Behavioral and cognitive-behavioral strategies may address specific management issues (e.g., noncompliance, aggression) as well as more cognitively based problems (e.g., executive skills, memory). Interventions may range from reinforcement programs to self-instructional strategies. Instructional techniques may address the pacing of instruction, preparatory strategies (e.g., pre-teaching), or specific teaching techniques such as the vanishing cues method. Curriculum involves the use of specific materials that, in light of the child's neuropsychological strengths and weaknesses, are likely to facilitate learning. With respect to curricular materials, it is unlikely that neuropsychologists will be conversant with the latest offerings. However, it would be helpful for them to be familiar with the broad approaches and principles underlying instructional materials in the basic subject areas (i.e., reading, written language, math) in order to be able to comment on an appropriate direction for the child. If the neuropsychologist lacks experience at this level, then the previously noted partnership with school personnel is critical. The role of the neuropsychologist will be to explain cognitive processes in sufficient detail for teachers and other specialists to translate this information into appropriate instructional strategies and materials.

As a general rule for recommendations, it is helpful to provide examples of where the child succeeds and where the child breaks down in the classroom and to key recommendations to these specific situations and tasks. This will help to ensure that referral concerns have been recognized and that suggested interventions are ecologically valid.

12

Writing the Forensic Neuropsychological Report

Wilfrid N. Derby

Introduction

Forensic neuropsychology deals with neuropsychological issues related to the law and legal proceedings. Most clinical neuropsychologists will become involved in forensic issues at some point in their careers. Some will choose to specialize in this area. Most, however, will encounter legal cases in the course of their clinical work. Although many will wish to avoid facing the stress of cross-examination, the law does not offer a choice! The purpose of this chapter is to introduce the clinical neuropsychologist to the realm of forensic neuropsychology.

For whatever reason a neuropsychologist becomes involved in a legal case, the written report will become a principal focus of attention for several reasons. The Federal Rules of Civil Procedure require attorneys to disclose the persons whom they may call to testify as experts at trial and also that the expert provide a signed written report (*Expert Disclosure*, 1997). This may also be a requirement in many state courts. But of probably greater importance to the neuropsychologist is the fact that the report will provide the basis for the clinical testimony. Consequently, not only does the report serve to inform others, but it also becomes the important vehicle for organizing both the data on which the neuropsychologist will rely and the reasoning involved in arriving at conclusions. The time to organize and formulate thoughts about the evaluation is in the relaxed atmosphere of one's office and not under the stress of cross examination at deposition, arbitration, or on the witness stand at trial. Consequently, writing a well organized, thorough report is probably the most important thing that the neuropsychologist can do to prepare for the adversarial atmosphere of the legal arena. The purpose of this chapter is not only to discuss certain technical issues of writing the report itself, but to provide the clinician with an understanding of the central role the report will play with regard to legal issues, as well as to describe a number of practical issues that the neuropsychologist will encounter in the legal forum.

Neuropsychology and Neurolaw

The participation of neuropsychologists in legal proceedings has increased dramatically over the past 2 decades. A recent survey found that the word *neuropsychologist* appeared in more than 400 legal opinions. Ninety-eight percent of these appeared since 1980 (Taylor, 1998). This has been the result of several significant factors. The increasing sophistication and complexity of scientific knowledge, the creation of new and complex theories of legal liability, and the liberalized modern rules of evidence have combined to enhance the relevance, acceptance, and demand for expert consultation and testimony (Rossi, 1991). Today, the outcomes of both criminal and civil trials often turn on the testimony of expert witnesses.

The Scope of Forensic Neuropsychology

Forensic neuropsychological evidence and testimony are required in a wide range of civil and criminal cases. Personal injury cases are, by far, the most frequent ones. These become the subject of personal injury lawsuits or Workers' Compensation, Social Security, or insurance claims. When the nature or extent of the injuries is in dispute, there is litigation. With the increasing frequency of these types of litigation, a new field in law, called *neurolaw* (Taylor, 1998), is evolving as more and more attorneys are acquiring special expertise in dealing with these cases. Nevertheless, the growth in the number of lawyers specializing in these cases has been slow because of the failure of many attorneys to recognize that their clients have brain dysfunction, especially in cases involving mild brain injury.[1] One of the reasons for this has been the absence of sensitive diagnostic tools of neurology and neuropsychology capable of detecting dysfunction in mild brain injury.

---

[1]Both the terms *mild* and *minor* traumatic brain injury (MTBI) have been used interchangeably in the literature. However, as *mild* is the preferred term (Mild Traumatic Brain Injury Committee of the Head Injury Interdisciplinary Special Interest Group of the American Congress of Rehabilitation Medicine, 1993), this term will be used throughout this chapter.

With the development of more sensitive diagnostic instruments in neurology, neuroradiology, and neuropsychology, however, lawyers are increasingly able to provide the evidence necessary to substantiate the existence of dysfunction in mild brain injury patients that they were previously unable to do.

Some civil cases involve competency. These include a range of issues, such as competency to make a will, competency to make decisions about one's medical treatment, or competency to control one's financial resources (Melton, Petrila, Poythress, & Slobogin, 1997).

Neuropsychological evaluation and testimony will most often be requested in cases of mild brain injury, and these will generally be the most difficult ones in which to establish the nature and extent of the impairment and disability as well as the causal connection between an accident and the dysfunction suffered by the patient. For this reason, the examples in this chapter will focus on mild brain injury.[2] In the majority of these cases, there will be little evidence from neuroimaging techniques to support the claims of brain dysfunction. Most often, the only evidence to support or refute the claims of the plaintiff or the defendant in civil or criminal cases will be the findings of the neuropsychologist (Silver & McAllister, 1997a, 1997b). Regardless of the nature of the brain dysfunction, the report-writing principles described in this chapter are generally applicable in any forensic case.

With recent advances in surgical treatment and medical care, there has been a dramatic increase in the survival rate from traumatic brain injury (TBI) sustained in motor vehicle accidents, industrial accidents, sports and recreational accidents, and falls. Of some 500,000 people who are hospitalized each year with TBI, about one half to three quarters are classified as mild TBI. But for each person hospitalized for TBI, it has been estimated that about four or five others sustain mild brain injury but receive treatment as outpatients or receive no treatment at all. Somewhere between 1 and 2 million people suffer a mild TBI each year (Silver & McAllister, 1997a, 1997b). The National Brain Injury Association has characterized the dramatic increase in the number of these cases in recent years as a *silent epidemic*.

Criminal cases are much less frequent. Most often they involve the question of competency to stand trial. Much less often the question involves the

[2]About 90% of the 2 million traumatic brain injury cases each year comprise the *mild* category based on the Glasgow Coma score of 13-15 (Ommaya & Ommaya, 1997).

mental state of a defendant at the time of a crime. These are the *criminal responsibility* or *not guilty by reason of insanity (NGI)* cases. As both competency to stand trial and criminal responsibility cases require considerable knowledge of legal issues, these cases should be either referred to an experienced forensic neuropsychologist or conducted under the supervision of an experienced forensic psychologist.

The Nature of the Forensic Neuropsychological Report

Writing a neuropsychological report for a forensic, or legal, purpose involves a number of considerations that do not concern the neuropsychologist working in the clinical setting. One of the principal objectives of this chapter is to discuss these differences. Because the *forensic neuropsychological report* is intended for different consumers and for a different purpose than most clinicians are familiar with, this chapter describes many of the conditions that the clinician working in the legal field should understand when conducting a forensic neuropsychological evaluation and preparing a report. In discussing the forensic report, the term *forensic* applies to the situation in which the neuropsychologist is specifically engaged to conduct a neuropsychological evaluation to serve a legal purpose (Committee on Ethical Guidelines for Forensic Psychologists, 1991). This occurs most often in personal injury litigation but may also occur in criminal cases involving competency to stand trial or criminal responsibility (i.e., the insanity plea). Some referrals are made for administrative purposes such as Social Security disability or Worker's Compensation claims, or for Medicaid or Medicare applications. Occasionally, an evaluation will be requested for the purpose of determining the competency of a person to make decisions about personal finances, medical care, or a will (Taylor, 1996).

A neuropsychologist who has conducted a clinical evaluation and prepared a clinical report may be called upon to testify regarding the evaluation or assessment of the patient. This type of report is *not* a forensic report as discussed in this chapter and the clinician is *not* considered to be a forensic neuropsychologist. A forensic neuropsychologist is one who offers professional services specifically to serve a legal purpose (Committee on Ethical Guidelines for Forensic Psychologists, 1991).

The nature of the forensic neuropsychological report is related to the different role that the neuropsychologist plays when working within the legal system. In the clinical role, the neuropsychologist interacts primarily with other medical, psychological, social work, or rehabilitation colleagues. They all share a common background and language related to the clinical activities in which they jointly engage. It is quite different for the neuropsychologist in the forensic area who works with lay persons at several levels who have varying degrees of education and knowledge, or often a lack of knowledge, about the vocabulary and content of neuropsychology and the neurosciences.

The forensic neuropsychologist may serve as either a *litigation consultant* or an *expert witness*. The litigation consultant serves as a mentor of the attorney. The expert witness serves as a teacher of the finder of fact (i.e., a jury or judge). The written report is the framework for all that must be communicated to these consumers. The forensic report serves a much different purpose than the clinical report, and it must even be written in a different language.

Format of the Forensic Neuropsychological Report

The format of the report will differ depending upon whether the neuropsychologist conducts a clinical evaluation of the client, a forensic evaluation for a legal purpose, or an Independent Medical Evaluation (IME). For a litigation consultant, the report may consist of anything from a set of notes that will be discussed with the attorney to a formal letter. In some cases, an IME may consist only of a records review and the report of a neuropsychologist engaged by the opposing attorney, as well as a written critique. As a litigation consultant, one of the neuropsychologist's roles is usually to analyze the neuropsychological evaluation of the opposing side and to review (with the attorney) the neuropsychological factors involved in the case so that the attorney can understand the issues and adequately prepare to examine or cross-examine witnesses. In other cases, the neuropsychologist will conduct a complete clinical evaluation and will then be called upon to testify as an expert witness. In either instance, the neuropsychologist may assist the attorney to frame appropriate questions for examination or cross-examination of witnesses. As already noted, in federal courts a formal written report is required if the neuropsychologist is to serve as an expert witness.[3] In state courts, depending upon the jurisdiction, a formal report, or at least an informal written statement, of the opinions that the expert will be expected to offer and the basis for them will be required.

The Forensic Neuropsychologist as Expert Witness or Consultant

With the increasing number of TBI cases now reaching far more than 1 million each year (Silver & McAllister, 1997a), and with the increasing frequency of toxic tort cases, the number of attorneys specializing in brain injury has increased dramatically. With this, of course, has come an increasing demand for the specialized assistance of neuropsychologists, not only for evaluations, but also as expert witnesses or as litigation consultants. Any neuropsychologist can be called upon to testify regarding a patient that he or she has seen for clinical evaluation. However, in this role the clinical neuropsychologist can testify as either a fact witness or an expert witness. In the former instance, the neuropsychologist can testify only as to *facts* about the patient. If the attorney intends to go beyond facts and ask questions involving an *opinion*, then the neuropsychologist is considered an expert witness. In almost all cases, the neuropsychologist will be called to testify as an expert witness.

The neuropsychologist may also be engaged as a litigation consultant to assist the attorney in understanding the nature of brain dysfunction and the neuropsychological evaluation process, to analyze the neuropsychological report of the opposing side, and to assist in preparing the legal rebuttal. In most jurisdictions, the litigation consultant does not have to be disclosed.

When the forensic neuropsychologist serves as an expert witness, the role is different from that of a litigation consultant. The role of the expert witness is to assist the finder of fact: a jury, an arbitration panel, or a judge.

---

[3]The Federal Rules of Civil Procedure (Rule 26(a)(2)) were amended to require the disclosure of the identity of persons who may testify as experts at trial and, except as otherwise stipulated by the court, must provide a report prepared and signed by the expert containing a complete statement of all opinions to be expressed by the expert and the basis and reasons for them; the data or other information considered by the expert in forming the opinions; exhibits to be used to summarize or support the opinions; qualifications of the expert; and a list of cases in which the expert has testified as an expert, at trial or by deposition, in the last 4 years.

Testimony of the expert may range from presenting the findings of the evaluation of the plaintiff or defendant (depending on whether the case is civil or criminal), presenting testimony regarding an IME records review, or to simply presenting scientific information. The expert witness may testify not only to his or her personal observations, as is the case with the *fact* witness, but may present *hearsay* evidence (if it is of the type that he or she ordinarily relies on in the course of regular professional activities) and may also offer an *opinion*.

The neuropsychologist should be careful to clarify, when asked by an attorney, usually by phone, to conduct a neuropsychological evaluation, whether the attorney is asking for a forensic evaluation and report or is simply referring the patient for clinical diagnosis and treatment. Often, the attorney may not be aware of the distinction. The neuropsychologist should make clear that there is a difference in both the role of the neuropsychologist and the nature of the evaluation in a forensic case versus a clinical case; both the report and the cost should be discussed. If the referral is for diagnosis with the primary purpose being treatment, then health insurance can properly be charged. However, if the referral is primarily for legal purposes, usually to support a personal injury lawsuit or a claim for insurance, Workers' Compensation, or Social Security, then the costs are not properly chargeable to health insurance. Sometimes there is a narrow dividing line and often, there is a gray area. For example, an attorney may be seeing the patient for a personal injury lawsuit not involving a TBI. However, in the course of interviewing the client, the attorney may become aware of an apparent mental dysfunction exhibited by the client that the attorney thinks may need treatment. It is for this reason, rather than for litigation, that the attorney refers the client. The referral is for diagnosis and treatment, but the attorney would like to have a copy of the patient's records to use for legal purposes. If a clinical report will be written for use by another health professional (e.g., a neurologist or other physician), then a clinical report would normally be written and a copy of that report would be furnished to the attorney.

If the neuropsychologist is approached by the attorney specifically for the purpose of conducting a neuropsychological evaluation with a report designed for use in legal proceedings, then the neuropsychologist is practicing forensic neuropsychology and is bound by the *Ethical Principles of Psychologists and Code of Conduct* of the American Psychological Association (1992) regarding the practice of psychology outside the limits of one's specialty, as well as by the additional *Specialty Guidelines for Forensic Psychologists* jointly promulgated by APA Division 41, the Psychology–Law Division, and the American Board of Forensic Psychology. Although any neuropsychologist may be called as a witness to testify regarding a neuropsychological evaluation that he or she has conducted, the neuropsychologist is not considered to be a forensic psychologist and is bound only by the APA ethical guidelines. However, if a neuropsychologist offers services for forensic purposes, then the additional, more stringent ethical guidelines for forensic psychology apply. Consequently, the neuropsychologist who offers his or her services to the legal community should be aware of the additional guidelines.

Many neuropsychological evaluations that begin for the purpose of medical or psychological diagnosis, treatment, or rehabilitation, subsequently are also used for forensic purposes. If it appears from circumstances surrounding the injuries that litigation may be involved, the neuropsychologist should communicate with the patient's attorney. If litigation will be involved, the neuropsychologist should clarify with the attorney the differences between a clinical evaluation and a forensic evaluation and determine whether the attorney wants the lengthier forensic evaluation. As discussed earlier, it is also important to clarify with the attorney how the fees are to be paid.

Focus of the Forensic Neuropsychological Evaluation

It is critically important, in conducting the evaluation as well as in writing a report, that the neuropsychologist ensure that the evaluation and report answer both the implicit and the explicit purposes of the evaluation. Many attorneys are not familiar with either the nature of a neuropsychological evaluation or exactly what the important questions are that should be addressed by the evaluation. It is often necessary for the neuropsychologist to clarify the exact purposes for which the evaluation is intended and to elicit from the attorney the specific legal questions the evaluation is intended to answer. In order to avoid any misunderstanding, the neuropsychologist should ask that these questions be specified in a letter from the attorney. If the neuropsychologist is not familiar with the law that is applicable in the particular case, the attorney should be asked to provide a copy of the relevant statute or case law. From a legal perspective, the precise wording of the conclusions will be important. The purpose of the evaluation should be clearly stated in the beginning of the report, usually under the Referral heading (see chapter 6).

When the referral is for a forensic evaluation, the findings and opinions should be discussed with the attorney before committing the evaluation to a written report. Once a report is written, it is discoverable. That is, the opposing attorney is entitled to have a copy of the report and of all clinical notes and records (with the exception of restricted psychological test data discussed below). These documents are often subpoenaed by the opposing attorney. Sometimes the initial thoughts of the neuropsychologist may not represent his or her later thoughts. Committing them to writing too soon can come back to haunt the neuropsychologist. In some cases, if the anticipated report will not be favorable to the client's position, the attorney may choose not to have a report written and may choose not to use the results of the evaluation. The attorney's role in the legal process is different from the psychologist's role. The role of the attorney is to win the case for the client. The neuropsychologist's role is to conduct an unbiased, scientific evaluation. The attorney is an advocate for the client; the neuropsychologist is not. The neuropsychologist is an advocate only for the best scientific opinion. In the forensic setting, it is the responsibility of the finder of fact (i.e., the jury or judge, or sometimes an arbitration panel) to determine the truth.

Confidentiality, Privilege, and Records

In nearly all cases, the neuropsychologist will receive either an information release or a subpoena for all records regarding a patient or client, including all notes and test results. Compliance should not be automatic. Several issues should be considered. If the request comes in the form of an information release signed by the patient or client, the neuropsychologist must first determine whether the evaluation was conducted as a clinical evaluation or a forensic evaluation initiated by the patient's attorney. If the purpose was clinical, then the requested information (except for the restricted test data) should be provided. However, if the purpose was a forensic evaluation conducted for the patient's attorney, then the records should not be provided unless authorized by that attorney. If the attorney requested the evaluation, then the data may be considered *work product*.[4]

[4]Work product refers to materials that are prepared by an attorney in preparation for litigation and are privileged from discovery by the attorney of the opposing party.

As noted earlier, the attorney may choose not to use the evaluation and, therefore, not to release the neuropsychological results to the opposing attorney. *The Psychologist's Legal Handbook* (Stromberg et al., 1988) provides a ready reference for the neuropsychologist confronted with the questions of privacy, confidentiality, and privilege.

If the records are subpoenaed, then the same procedure should be followed. The attorney should be notified. If the attorney considers that the records are protected under the attorney-client privilege or the records are considered to be a work product, then the attorney may so inform the opposing attorney or enter a motion to quash the subpoena.

The neuropsychologist must avoid sending either test data that require interpretation by a clinical psychologist or neuropsychologist, or data that could be misinterpreted (e.g., MMPI scores or computer-generated interpretation). The Committee on Psychological Tests and Assessment (1996) has described the policy of the APA regarding the release of information to persons not qualified to interpret the data. The neuropsychologist should respond to the request, or subpoena, by saying that the test data will be sent to whatever clinical neuropsychologist the attorney designates. If challenged in such an instance and the attorney insists on receiving the test data, then the possibility that the patient's attorney request a motion to the court for a protective order should be considered.

Although the neuropsychologist can make editorial changes at the suggestion of the attorney in order to clarify the meaning of the report, it is unethical to omit essential facts that may not be favorable to the attorney's position. If there are findings that are unfavorable to the attorney, it is usually preferable to face such issues and provide a reasonable explanation to the attorney.

The opposing counsel will usually have engaged a clinical neuropsychologist to conduct an IME. Thus, the clinical notes, test data, and report will receive not only a review but also a critical examination. The neuropsychologist will check every detail of your data (e.g., the accuracy of calculations, score conversions, etc.) as well as the basis for your conclusions and opinion. Sometimes a neurologist or neuropsychiatrist as well as the neuropsychologist will review and critically comment on the report.

The opposing attorney may choose to have an IME of the records and report conducted either by a litigation consultant, who will not be called to testify, or by a neuropsychologist, who will conduct an additional neuropsychological evaluation. The critical evaluation of the original report as well as cross-examination questions prepared by the opposing council's neuropsychologist can be used by the opposing counsel in the deposition and at the trial.

The critical assessment of your report and the way in which you testify at the deposition may often be the deciding factor in the litigation. The opposing attorney will size up the quality of your work and your ability to present competent and convincing testimony during the deposition. In the vast majority of cases, this will lead to settlement of the case by negotiation. When the attorneys do not settle, some cases go on to arbitration and a few to trial.

Writing for the Consumer

In writing the report, the neuropsychologist must keep in mind the consumer of the forensic report. The readers often will be lay persons (e.g., attorneys, judges, or insurance adjusters), not medical or psychological specialists. The writer must also keep in mind that the report will serve as the focal point in organizing the presentation to the finder(s) of fact (i.e., usually a jury but, in some cases, a judge or an arbitration panel of lawyers). As an expert witness, your presentation to the finder(s) of fact will be an oral description of all of the significant elements of the report. The role of the expert witness is to help the finder(s) of fact to understand the evidence in order to determine the truth. The expert must *teach* the finder(s) of fact about brain functioning and the effects of the injurious agent (e.g., trauma, toxin, or disease) on the individual's premorbid level of brain functioning. The task is like teaching a semester graduate course to a class that has no outline of the subject matter and no textbook, and in most jurisdictions is not permitted to take notes or ask questions. And this must all be done within a few hours on the witness stand in an adversarial environment.

In drafting the report, the neuropsychologist must remember that many of the readers of the report will have limited knowledge about the functioning of the brain. Although most attorneys and insurance adjusters who deal with brain injury will have a certain amount of knowledge, others (e.g., judge and jury) will not. The usual neuropsychological test data must be included so that the neuropsychologist engaged as the consultant or expert by the opposing side can fully understand your evaluation. Certain terms (e.g., executive functions, working memory, intellectual processes, etc.) should be explained in nontechnical language. Although your expert testimony will be presented orally at deposition and at trial to the finder(s) of fact (usually a jury), it is helpful to include these definitions in the written report. Description of tests and details of the patient's or client's specific test performance should be very much abridged compared with the usual clinical report. Such information can often be included in a "for example" statement. It is much more meaningful to the consumer of the forensic report to provide a summary statement of your findings and interpretation than to give a detailed description of test performance.

Diagnoses and technical terms must be translated into understandable lay terminology. When citing scores in the report, it is desirable to include the percentile score in parentheses in the body of the text or in a table of scores. A percentile score is a quantitative value and is more easily understood by the lay person than equal interval or standard scores.

It is important always to keep in mind the adversarial nature of the civil and criminal justice systems: "You Are Not Among Friends!" This often comes as a shock to those who work in the collegial atmosphere of the clinical setting. In clinical practice, the neuropsychologist works in a social environment of colleagues and patients, where everyone is focusing on the common goal of helping the designated patient and often the family as well. In the forensic arena, the other parties involved are focused on one objective: *winning*. There usually are winners and losers. And the stakes can be high, usually in terms of money or individual freedom. Every statement and all the data in your report will be carefully scrutinized by both the opposing attorney and the consulting neuropsychologist. You must be prepared to counter challenges to the accuracy, relevancy, and validity of your findings.

Special Issues in Forensic Evaluations

As forensic evaluations are conducted to meet the needs of the civil, criminal, or administrative law systems, a basic orientation to forensic psychology will assist the clinical neuropsychologist in understanding the different demands and issues that can be expected when working with these legal systems (Hess & Weiner, 1999).

The increasing number and sophistication of neuropsychological diagnostic instruments to detect and measure the deficits of mild brain injury has been one factor in the increasing demand for forensic neuropsychologists (Lezak, 1995; Silver & McAllister, 1997a, 1997b). Although neurologists, neurosurgeons, and neuroradiologists may also be of importance in legal cases, the central role of the neuropsychologist cannot be emphasized enough. Particularly important are the ability of neuropsychological procedures to measure functional impairments as well as to diagnose and document the concomitant emotional and social effects of TBI (Reitan & Wolfson 1997). This is especially critical in cases of mild brain injury, where the neuroimaging procedures of the neuroradiologist are not capable of detecting the functional effects of these injuries, and because many neurologists are not especially skilled in diagnosing mental disorders and social impairments. Furthermore, forensic neuropsychologists have been especially innovative in developing procedures for detecting exaggeration of symptoms and malingering. Because this is a very significant consideration in most forensic cases, there has been an exponential increase in empirical studies for detecting malingering of cognitive dysfunctions and the development of tests for this purpose (e.g., Franzen, Iverson, & McCracken, 1990; Haines & Norris, 1995; Rogers, 1997).

Exaggeration of Symptoms and Malingering

Exaggeration of symptoms, malingering, and deception (or factitious disorders) are not a major concern in usual clinical neuropsychological evaluations, but they are of particular concern in forensic evaluations (Franzen et al., 1990; Greiffenstein, Baker, & Gola, 1994; Haines & Norris, 1995; Millis, Putnam, Adams, & Ricker, 1995; Reynolds, 1997; Youngjohn, 1995). The neuropsychologist must anticipate that questions will be asked in the course of a deposition or trial as to whether the patient could be exaggerating, or even falsifying, the claimed neuropsychological impairments. The neuropsychologist must then be prepared to defend the position that the impairments that have been identified in the course of the evaluation are *bona fide* and not the result of exaggeration or malingering. For example, you must be ready to respond to the opposing attorney's question, "Well, doctor, couldn't the plaintiff be exaggerating or faking his memory problems?" It is probably best to recognize and admit that when the patient has something to gain in either a personal injury or a criminal case some degree of exaggeration may be expected. You should be prepared to say that the question was considered and to explain the procedures that led to your conclusion that the patient was or was not endeavoring to exaggerate or falsify responses on the examination (Berry et al., 1995; Palmer, Boone, Allman, & Castro, 1995; Youngjohn, Burrows, & Erdal, 1995). In forensic cases, the neuropsychologist must continually be alert for evidence of exaggeration or elaboration of symptoms, or for outright malingering. This requires both knowing the signs of malingering on the neuropsychological tests that were administered as well as administering several of the tests specifically designed for detecting malingering (Frederick, 1997; Slick et al., 1997; Tombaugh, 1996). If the opposing attorney asks for an explanation of the specific items you look for as evidence of malingering or asks about the specifics of the tests employed, you should refuse on the same basis as a refusal to release test data, saying that this information will be furnished to the neuropsychologist that the attorney has engaged as a consultant. There is evidence that unethical attorneys have coached their clients on how to manipulate test responses to achieve the outcome they desire (Lees-Haley, 1997). A specific section in the forensic neuropsychological report should be devoted to the issue of exaggeration of symptoms and malingering.

The Nature of Expert Testimony

The greater acceptance of expert testimony by the courts is another major factor that has fostered the demand by attorneys for neuropsychological services. The long-standing rule for the admissibility of expert testimony had involved whether the subject matter was *beyond the ken of the ordinary juror*. This rule severely limited the role that the expert could play. In fact, the courts often refused to admit the testimony of expert witnesses. However, the 1975 enactment of the Federal Rules of Evidence 702 through 705 (Legal Information Institute, 2000) brought a major change in the acceptance of expert testimony. These new rules expanded and welcomed the admissibility of expert testimony. Rule 702 provided the following:

> If scientific, technical, or other specialized knowledge *will assist* the trier of fact to understand the evidence or to determine a fact in issue, a witness qualified as an expert by knowledge, skill, experience, training, or education may testify thereto in the form of an opinion or otherwise.

Since the enactment of the new Federal Rules of Evidence, most states have followed with almost duplicate rules. Many changes in litigation have resulted as the new rules have been tried and tested. The most important of these concern the qualifications for an expert witness and facts and opinions on which the expert may testify. Rule 702 states that a witness can qualify as an expert by "knowledge, skill, experience, training or education." The qualifications must be in accordance with the matter of the testimony (Rossi, 1991). This decision, together with the question of whether the testimony will be helpful to the finder of fact, is left to the broad discretion of the trial court.

Another major change in the law relates to the appropriate subject matter for expert testimony. This is especially important with respect to scientific evidence. From 1923 until the enactment of the new Rules of Federal Evidence, the recognized standard had been the *Frye* rule. This rule imposed limitations on what evidence would be admissible as scientific. The standard for the admissibility of scientific evidence was that the theory or methodology about which the expert was to testify was "generally acceptable to the scientific community." Unfortunately, the *Frye* rule often resulted in *junk science* being admitted in testimony. The new federal rules and the states' counterparts were silent on the subject of general acceptance. The courts were left to wrestle with the issue of whether the *Frye* rule survived the new rules. The question was finally resolved by the U.S. Supreme Court in *Daubert v. Merrell-Dow Pharmaceuticals, Inc.* (1993). Justice Blackmun, in writing the decision, defined in legal terms the criteria for an assertion or statement to be considered scientific and, therefore, admissible. The basic criterion is that of testability. That is, the assertion must be capable of being tested, it must be capable of being falsified, and it must have been tested. The U.S. Supreme Court ruled that falsifiability rather than verification is the essential characteristic that defines a scientific statement. This, of course, is the basic research principle of defining the null hypothesis and then presenting evidence to falsify it. This is also exemplified in the criminal law by the null hypothesis that the defendant is "innocent until proven guilty." The defendant enters court under the legal presumption of innocence. The role of the prosecutor is to introduce evidence to falsify this presumption.

In some ways, the *Daubert v. Merrell-Dow Pharmaceuticals* decision resulted in a much more liberal rule than its predecessor. It does not require general acceptance by the scientific community. However, general acceptance may be admissible as a factor to be considered. On the other hand, the criteria set forth by the U.S. Supreme Court for testimony to meet the standard of scientific acceptability is considerably more stringent than the prior *Frye* rule. Psychologists, having been educated in scientific methodology, should feel quite at ease in formulating their own expert testimony as well as in assisting attorneys in analyzing opposing expert testimony for scientific acceptability.

Most states have adopted the Federal Rules of Evidence or very similar standards. The critical change that has greatly increased the presence of the expert in the courtroom is the new standard: "assist the trier of fact." Thus, the principal criterion for the admission of expert testimony is that it will be helpful to the jury. This hurdle is much easier to overcome than the older criterion, the "beyond the ken" standard.

The Question of Causality

Many forensic neuropsychological evaluations are intended to show change in the patient's functioning from some previous level following brain injury or disease. In nearly all personal injury cases, the lawsuit will involve a demonstration that the patient suffered some impairment of premorbid functioning as a result of the injury. These data form the basis for determining the severity of the impairment and the extent of monetary damages to be claimed. In other civil cases (e.g., determining the competency of a decedent to have changed a will), the level of functioning at some earlier time may be the critical question. In criminal cases, the state of mind of a defendant at an earlier time when a crime was committed (i.e., the insanity defense) may be the critical question. In all such cases involving either large sums of money or deprivation of personal freedom, the mental state or mental capacity of the person at an earlier period of time becomes the critical question.

Unfortunately, neither experimental nor clinical neuropsychology has developed accurate methods for estimating premorbid functioning. Nevertheless, psychology and neuropsychology are better prepared than psychiatry or neurology to perform this task. The importance of this matter is highlighted by the special issue of the *Archives of Clinical Neuropsychology: Estimation of Premorbid Neuropsychological Ability* (Reynolds, 1997).

Therefore, it is critically important when conducting a forensic evaluation that you obtain, whenever possible, independent verification for all statements made by the patient about prior level of academic and occupational accomplishments and performance. Oral history from relatives and friends about the premorbid personality and behavior of the patient is important, but in a forensic case, you must endeavor to obtain the most reliable, impartial, objective, and quantified data that you can. Transcripts of educational history are most important. Not only do they give the actual grades of the patient, but they often indicate class standing and group IQ test scores. If information about medical history (e.g., prior head injury, seizures, etc.) are important, do not just take the patient's word for it, but obtain the earlier medical records (see chapter 5). This task can be much simplified by asking the attorney to obtain these records. Their staff members are quite experienced in obtaining background information. They also have the power of the subpoena, which can be effectively used on those occasions when difficulty is encountered in obtaining needed records. Be prepared to have every assertion in your report challenged!

In personal injury cases, the *proximate* cause of deficits or impairments will be one of the most important conclusions in your report. Proximate cause refers to the direct and immediate cause of an injury. For this reason, the choice of words in your report or testimony can be of critical importance. The language should be clear and unambiguous. Avoid the term "consistent with," as this term implies that a conclusion is not inconsistent with, that it is not contradictory. The term cannot be used to imply a causal relationship. For example, a high fever is consistent with encephalitis, but it is also consistent with scarlet fever, pneumonia, measles, and many other diseases. It certainly is not diagnostic of any one of these diseases.

In most cases, a prognosis is an important part of the report. In personal injury cases, the significant question concerns how disabling the injury is and what degree of recovery is expected. Is the impairment permanent, or what will be the likely recovery period? How will the impairment affect the individual's ability to earn a living? What will be the effect of the injury on the quality of the person's life? These are questions that the neuropsychologist has usually had little experience in ascertaining and writing about.

Discovery and Deposition

Discovery is the process by which attorneys obtain the information that will be used by opposing counsel. Each attorney is required to deliver to the opposing side a list of all witnesses that side intends to call; the nature of the testimony that each witness is expected to provide, including opinions of experts; copies of all written material including clinical notes; and a list of all other evidence. As part of the discovery process, each counsel has the right to depose all persons that the opposing attorney intends to call as witnesses in civil cases and, in most but not all jurisdictions, in criminal cases. In a deposition, the witness is examined under oath and a record is kept of the testimony by a court reporter. A neuropsychologist may be called simply as a fact witness or as an expert. Even if your initial involvement with the patient was as a treating or examining neuropsychologist, the attorney for the patient will usually want to call you as an expert witness. As an expert witness, you will testify regarding the observations that you made during the evaluation and you will also be permitted to testify regarding certain hearsay evidence. You may testify about information that you typically receive from others and rely upon in the course of your professional activities. This would include, for example, medical and other records on which you relied, reports from other professionals, statements about the patient's behavior (or observations of the patient) from family, friends, coworkers, police, and so forth. And, finally, you will also be expected to give opinions.

The opposing counsel will have already obtained a copy of your report and *all* of the records and data in the files except the restricted test data described earlier. Restricted data will have been sent to the neuropsychologist that the opposing counsel will usually have engaged to critically review your report.

The attorney may choose to have the records and report reviewed by a litigation consultant who will not be called to testify, or by a neuropsychologist, who may also conduct a neuropsychological evaluation—an IME. In the former instance, and in most jurisdictions, the name of the litigation consultant need not be disclosed. However, the critical evaluation of your report, as well as cross-examination questions prepared by the consultant can be used by the opposing counsel in the deposition, arbitration, or trial.

Although all clinical psychologists must be familiar with the rules and law regarding confidentiality and privilege, the psychologist working in the forensic arena must be acutely aware of the potential for compromise. Someday, a sheriff's deputy will appear at the door, ask for you by name, and hand you a legal document. When you read the document demanding that all documents be produced, you shouldn't panic! Although the subpoena may demand that certain records be produced, there are circumstances when you do not have to do so and should not do so. When the records are protected under the doctor-patient/client privilege, a clinician probably does not have to provide the records without a written information release from the patient. In other cases, as discussed previously, the information may be protected by attorney-client privilege. However, you should never simply disregard the subpoena. You must respond or you will be subject to legal penalties. If you consider that the information is privileged, you should respond with a refusal which states your reasons for refusing. The appropriate action is to inform the patient. If the patient is involved in a legal matter and has an attorney, you should, after consulting the patient, contact the patient's attorney. However, there are some circumstances when you should feel competent to make the decision without consultation. The situation that is most frequently encountered is a demand for all the test data. This can be handled quite adequately without counsel, as discussed earlier.

Challenges to The Evaluation

You should anticipate that the evaluation and report will be challenged on a number of grounds. First, it may be challenged on the selection of the specific tests. There has long been discussion and controversy in the literature regarding fixed versus flexible batteries. The issue is often raised that the fixed batteries, for example, the HRB (Reitan & Wolfson, 1998a, 1998b; Williams, 1997) or the Luria-Nebraska Battery (Golden, Hammeke, & Purisch, 1980), have undergone extensive and rigorous standardization. The HRB is generally administered by technicians. The neuropsychologist makes interpretations on the basis of the quantitative data (i.e., the scores), regardless of the processes by which the scores were attained. A neuropsychologist following the process approach (Kaplan, 1988; Kaplan et al., 1991; Milberg, Hebben, & Kaplan, 1996) is equally concerned with obtaining quantitative data from strict adherence to the test administration procedures as well as information on how the patient responds to the test stimuli or tasks.

A neuropsychologist who utilizes a process-oriented approach with a flexible battery of tests must be prepared to defend the choice of tests employed, both on the basis of their comprehensive coverage of the neuropsychological functions that could be impaired and the adequacy of their reliability and validity. A very useful tool for this purpose is to have available at the deposition or trial a cue book (Blau, 1988, 1992), which contains relevant information on the tests used as well as other information to which one may want to make quick reference. The cue book should be continually updated with any new test information as well as summaries of significant new reports in the literature. If the process-oriented neuropsychologist keeps up-to-date with the latest validated tests and norms, then he or she can defend the protocol against the arguments supporting the use of fixed batteries. The process-oriented neuropsychologist must also be prepared to discuss the comprehensive coverage of the tests chosen.

As the opposing attorney may call a neurologist as an expert witness to testify about the absence of any neuroimaging evidence of brain injury, the neuropsychologist must be prepared to cite research findings to support the opinion that the patient did indeed suffer brain injury which, although not detectable by neuroimaging or other neurological diagnostic procedures, is neuropsychologically documented.

Updating the Forensic Data

If a long time has elapsed between the evaluation and deposition, arbitration, or trial (which is usually the case), then the patient should be reevaluated. The question necessarily arises about the extent of the patient's recovery from the head injury and what, if any, residual impairments can be expected to be permanent. Although most neuropsychological tests do not have alternate forms for repeated measurement, there are instruments such as the Automated Neuropsychological Assessment Metrics (ANAM; Reeves, Kane, Winter, & Goldstone, 1995) that consists of tests that were specifically designed for repeated measures with normal to mildly impaired individuals (Blieberg, personal communication, November, 1998). Other tests that are resilient to practice effects or have alternate forms are also available (e.g., the CVLT).

In the context of conducting repeated assessments, the neuropsychologist must also be prepared to discuss the data and statistics on recovery from TBI. Ideally, the patient was examined shortly after the injury, and the recovery was monitored during the following year or two as the case approached settlement. One important benefit from this type of observation is that it facilitates the delineation of dysfunction resulting from the injury. In many cases that are involved in protracted litigation, however, the dysfunction is mild brain injury, and the neuropsychologist will not have had the opportunity to examine the patient until a year or more after the accident. This has two significant consequences. One is that the patient has probably reached a maximum level of recovery. An unfortunate result of this is that the benefits of early rehabilitation interventions are missed. Also, if the neuropsychologist is unable to monitor changes from the time of the injury, it is somewhat more difficult to establish that the patient's current state of functioning is the proximate result of the injury.

Another issue that the neuropsychologist must be mindful of is the fact that results from tests and office examinations may often not reveal real-life difficulties of patients at work or at home (cf. Prigatano, Altman, & O'Brien, 1990; Sbordone & Long, 1996). Caution must be used, as defense attorneys will grasp at every opportunity to demonstrate that the plaintiff is not as severely impaired as claimed.

Of special concern is the paucity of instruments that adequately assess prefrontal dysfunction, a frequent consequence of injuries sustained secondary to motor vehicle accidents. Determination of deficits in this area may not be as pressing in treatment facilities where the person's activities are highly structured, the person is being closely monitored, and there is an opportunity for ongoing observation. Adjustments to treatment and rehabilitation activities can, thus, be more readily effected. The need to ascertain the patient's capacity for self-direction and self-regulation is, however, paramount in determining long-term vocational and community reintegration. It is encouraging, given the need to properly assess these functions, that progress is being made in the development of more sensitive tools to evaluate such impairments (e.g., Delis, Kaplan, & Kramer, 2001).

Summary

Most neuropsychologists will, at some time in their careers, become involved in the legal aspects of neuropsychology. Some will choose to specialize in forensic work; others will become involved incidental to their clinical work. In either case, the neuropsychologist must be aware of the differences between the demands of clinical work and forensic work. The writer of a neuropsychological report must be sensitive to the needs and interests of the consumer of the report in each of these circumstances. There are differences in the mental set of the neuropsychologist depending on whether the purpose of the evaluation is clinical or forensic. The style, content, and language of the report must be appropriate to the purpose of the evaluation and the needs of the consumer (Melton, Petrila, Poythress, & Slobogin, 1997). As the author of the report, you must also be aware of the subsequent participation in legal proceedings. The report is the important means of organizing your data, analyzing those data, and formulating your conclusions. It will be the means of presenting the results of your neuropsychological evaluation in a format and language that will be meaningful to the recipient of the report as well as represent the core of the testimony and expert opinion that you will be called upon to give.

13

Sample Reports

Introduction

The sample reports provided in this chapter serve to illustrate some of the suggestions provided in the main text. These reports were generated for real patients and referral sources in a variety of clinical and educational settings. To preserve confidentiality, names and specific identifying features have been altered; however, to preserve the original style and a sense of "readability," we (the editors) decided to provide fictional names for the individuals, places, and organizations involved. In agreement with the recommendations provided in chapter 7, the example reports tend to provide specific scores expressed, by and large, in percentiles. (Respondents to the survey, described in chapter 2, generally felt that reporting percentiles was the most "user friendly" method of presenting test scores.)

There are a total of 10 sample reports and one sample client feedback summary. The reports vary considerably in length; thus, for example, the longest report (13 pages of text plus 6 pages of test scores) was written for a residential rehabilitation facility, whereas the shortest report (results of a Wada procedure) was written for inpatient surgical purposes.

Prior to each report, the editors have written a brief introduction, highlighting specific characteristics with regard to issues discussed in the relevant preceding chapters along with feedback from consumers elicited via the survey of professionals described in chapter 2.

Medical Setting Reports

The first four reports were generated by the same neuropsychologist who provides both in- and outpatient services in a hospital setting. These reports involve a young woman (Mrs. James) with long-standing temporal lobe seizures, who was seen for a pre-surgical evaluation, a Wada test, and two follow-up evaluations, one performed shortly after the surgery and one approximately one year later. Consistent with the data obtained in the survey of neurosurgeons (see chapter 2), the evaluations were less focused on differential diagnosis than on providing an assessment of cognitive functioning pre- and post-surgical intervention. As is typical of reports generated in these settings, extensive summaries of assessments by other providers are not included because this information is typically available in the patient's chart. The results of the Wada procedure are provided in a brief, two-page report. The follow-up evaluations include impressions of the woman's functioning at home, derived from an interview with her husband. Survey data indicated that surgeons are more likely to value interviews with family members than other referral sources, perhaps emphasizing their interest in real-life functional outcomes, rather than subtle changes in neuropsychological test scores alone. In addition to evaluating changes in cognition and mood over time, recommendations to assist in the patient's recovery were also provided. Note that one resource is specifically identified by name to facilitate follow-through (see chapter 8).

Medical Setting Report 1
Pre-Surgical Neuropsychological Evaluation

Name: Mrs. P. James
Hospital ID: SR56789
D.O.E.: 9/29 and 10/13/1997
D.O.B.: 11/25/1966

REFERRAL & BACKGROUND INFORMATION:

Mrs. James is a 30-year-old, right-handed, former travel agent, with 16 years of education and complex partial seizures, who is referred by Drs. Smith and Roberts for presurgical neuropsychological evaluation for intractable epilepsy. Comprehensive medical and neurological histories are contained in the hospital records and will not be detailed here.

In brief, Mrs. James experienced a febrile seizure at age nine months, and was medicated with Phenobarbital until age six years. She was seizure free until age ten or eleven, at which time she began to experience partial seizures. At age thirteen years, she had her first grand mal seizure. She experiences a prodrome of being "jittery" and a sense that she is going to have a seizure. Her seizure consists of epigastric symptoms, déjà-vu for approximately five to ten seconds, followed by lip smacking, moving of hands, and losing contact with her environment. More recently, Mrs. James has noted a tendency to fall towards the left side. There is some postictal confusion of approximately five minutes duration. She experiences ten to fifteen seizures per month with increased frequency around the time of her menses.

Mrs. James reports some long-standing memory problems. For example, she reports "always" having trouble recalling the particular restaurant where she went to eat. She describes increased short-term memory problems over the past few years, which she attributes to medication changes. More specifically, she has difficulty recalling movies and retaining the content of what she reads. There are times when she has difficulty recalling what her husband said to her. She denies any problems managing her daughter, recalling what her daughter does during the day, or any progressive memory decline per se. She describes an excellent memory for remote events, particularly those involving "trauma." For example, she clearly recalls sustaining a cut with a nail on her leg, "breaking bones," and a long-standing fear of water. Mrs. James reports occasional depression and a sense of "confinement" secondary to her seizures. She describes some problems falling asleep and a 25-30 pound weight gain over the past two years.

The neurological history is significant for a half-brother who is left-handed, a maternal grandmother with brain cancer, and a paternal cousin with mental retardation. Mrs. James's neurological history is significant for a closed head injury at age ten or eleven sustained in a fall while ice-skating, with several minutes' loss of consciousness. In 1986, when she was twenty, she sustained a head injury with brief loss of consciousness after hitting her head on the corner of a table. Mrs. James received psychological counseling in college for approximately one year.

An EEG conducted on September 29, 1997 revealed brief sharp transients in the right temporal lobe. Inpatient telemetry suggested right temporal focus. MRI conducted May 18, 1997 was read as within normal limits.

Current medications:
Tegretol, Depakote, Klonopin, and Tylenol.

BEHAVIORAL OBSERVATIONS:

Mrs. James reported on time to the neurosurgical evaluation, was fully oriented, well dressed and well groomed. She demonstrated a full range of appropriate affect, was hard working, and appeared to work to the best of her capacities, with good frustration tolerance. Mrs. James demonstrated a thumb wrap pen grip.

NEUROPSYCHOLOGICAL PROCEDURES:

Clinical interview, WAIS-R, Spatial Pointing Span, Auditory Continuous Performance, Weintraub-Mesulam Unstructured Letter Cancellation Test, Trail Making Tests A & B, Comalli-Kaplan Stroop Test (as reviewed in Mitrushina et al., 1999), Wisconsin Card Sorting Test, Boston Naming Test, Controlled Oral Word Association Test (FAS), Aphasia Screening and Cookie Theft Narrative Writing from the BDAE, WRAT-3, Gates-McGinitie Reading Test Level F-Form 1, Right/Left Orientation, Praxis Screening, Hooper Visual Organization Test, Clock Drawing Test, Rey-Osterrieth Complex Figure, Benton Judgment of Line Orientation Test, Benton Facial Recognition Test, Wechsler Memory Scale-R/Boston Adaptation, Verbal Selective Reminding Test, Dynamometer, Grooved Pegboard, Finger Tapping Test, Luria Three Step Hand Sequences, Double simultaneous stimulation, Reciprocal Motor Programs, Repeated Graphomotor Patterns, Visual Selective Reminding Test, Peabody Individual Achievement Test-Revised (PIAT-R, Spelling), Woodcock Reading Mastery Test-Revised (Word Attack), Tactile Performance Test, MMPI.

RESULTS:

Motor:

Upper extremity motor evaluation reveals rapid finger oscillation to be within normal limits for the right dominant and average for the left non-dominant hand, with the expected right hand superiority. Grip strength is within normal limits for the right and mildly impaired for the left nondominant hand. Performance on the Grooved Pegboard is mildly impaired bilaterally, with the expected right hand superiority. Praxis evaluation is unremarkable. Performance on Luria Three Step Hand Sequences and double simultaneous stimulation is within normal limits bilaterally. Performance on repetitive graphomotor patterns and reciprocal motor programs are within normal limits.

	Right Hand			Left Hand		
	RS	*T*	%ile	RS	*T*	%ile
Finger Tapping (taps/10 sec)	51.3	53	62	47.5	57	76
Grip Strength (kg)	26.5	46	34	20		8
Grooved Pegboard (sec)	66	38	11	74	38	11

Attention, Concentration, and Executive Functions:

Auditory attention span is within normal limits with a digit span of 6 digits forward and 7 digits backward. Visual attention span is within normal limits with a position pointing span of 6 positions forward and 5 positions backward. There are no problems on a task of sustained auditory attention. Sustained visual attention as measured by Trail Making Test A is moderately impaired. There are no problems with shifting of attention as measured by Trail Making Test B. Performance on the Wisconsin Card Sorting Test is somewhat below expectation with 6 categories obtained in 96 cards. Mrs. James had no difficulty initially shifting between the three sorting categories, but had trouble reestablishing the initial category on the fourth shift. Performance on the Stroop is within normal limits, demonstrating normal reading speed and the ability to inhibit responses.

Speech and Language:

Spontaneous speech is fluent, well articulated, prosodic, and without word finding difficulties or paraphasic errors. Confrontation naming (53/60, Boston Naming Test), sentence repetition, the comprehension of complex auditory ideational material, controlled word production (80-84th percentile, FAS), auditory discrimination, oral paragraph reading and right/left identification are all within normal limits. Spelling to dictation (87th percentile, WRAT-3), spelling recognition (12.9 grade equivalent, PIAT-R), oral single word reading (81st percentile, WRAT-3), silent reading vocabulary (70th percentile, Gates-McGinitie Reading Test), and silent reading comprehension (52nd percentile, Gates-McGinitie Reading Test) are all within normal limits. Spontaneous writing to the Cookie Theft Picture is within normal limits. Calculations were slightly below expectation (32nd percentile, WRAT-3). Reading of nonsense syllables is within normal limits (12.9 grade equivalent, Word Attack).

Visuospatial:
The scanning of visual space is symmetric, rapid, and accurate across a scattered Letter Cancellation Test. Visuospatial perception is within normal limits. There are no problems with the identification of graphically depicted objects presented in a disjointed array (Hooper Visual Organization Test), facial recognition, or the estimation of angular displacement (Judgment of Line Orientation). The copy of the Rey-Osterrieth Complex Figure is performed with a very slightly fragmented approach, but is otherwise within normal limits. Block Design constructions are within normal limits. The drawing of a clock to command is unremarkable.

Memory:
Immediate recall of auditory verbal prose passages is moderately impaired. Recall following a long delay filled with interpolated tasks remains moderately impaired with 65% of initially recalled material freely recalled on the delay. Long delay recognition is somewhat improved over long delay free recall. Performance on the Verbal Selective Reminding Test is within normal limits for long-term storage and long term retrieval, but is mildly impaired for consistent long term retrieval. Recall following a long delay filled with interpolated tasks is within normal limits, with 11 of 12 items correctly recalled.

Immediate recall of elementary graphic designs following a brief "study" presentation is mildly impaired (RS=22, 6th percentile). Recall following a long delay filled with interpolated tasks remains mildly impaired, with 100% of initially recalled material freely recalled after the delay. Performance on the Visual Selective Reminding Test is within normal limits for long term storage, long term retrieval, and consistent long-term retrieval. Recall following a long delay filled with interpolated tasks is within normal limits with 12 of 12 items correctly recalled.

Intellectual:
WAIS-R indices are nominally in the Average range, with a Verbal IQ=95 (Average), Performance IQ=94 (average), and Full Scale IQ=94 (Average).

	SS	%ile		SS	%ile
Information	8	25	Picture Completion	10	50
Digit Span	11	65	Picture Arrangement	8	25
Vocabulary	8	25	Block Design	11	65
Arithmetic	11	65	Object Assembly	8	25
Comprehension	12	75	Digit Symbol	9	37
Similarities	8	25			

MMPI:
The validity profile on the MMPI was within normal limits, suggesting that the responses were likely to reflect Mrs. James's current status. Persons with similar profiles (6802) have been described as shy and withdrawn, with some social introversion. There may be some unusual thinking with suspiciousness, and there is likely impairment in memory and concentration. There appears to be a significant level of clinical depression.

IMPRESSION & RECOMMENDATIONS:

Mrs. James is a 30-year-old, right-handed, former travel agent with sixteen years of education and complex partial seizures, who is referred by Drs. Smith and Roberts, for presurgical neuropsychological evaluation for intractable epilepsy. Current evaluation reveals mild bilateral motor findings, left greater than right, and very mild impairments in visuospatial organization. There are mild to moderate impairments in new learning. The pattern suggests retrieval difficulties, rather than encoding problems per se. Visuospatial perception and language capacities are within normal limits. IQ indices are in the Average range, with a Verbal IQ=95, Performance IQ=94, and Full Scale IQ=94. Performance on the MMPI suggested a significant level of depression. Overall evaluation results are consistent with generally well-preserved cognitive capacities with bilateral temporal and a suggestion of right frontal involvement.

The results of this evaluation will be discussed with the Epilepsy Surgical Team.

______________________________, PhD
Clinical Neuropsychology

Medical Setting Report 2
Amytal Evaluation

Name: Mrs. P. James
Hospital ID: SR56789
D.O.E.: 12/9/1997
D.O.B.: 11/25/1966

REFERRAL AND BACKGROUND INFORMATION:

Mrs. James is a 31-year-old, right-handed, former travel agent with 16 years of education, who is referred by Drs. Smith and Roberts for a pre-surgery Amytal evaluation for intractable epilepsy.

Mrs. James experienced a febrile seizure at age six months, was medicated with Phenobarbital until age six years, and was seizure-free until age 10 or 11, at which time she developed partial seizures. She had a grand mal seizure at age 13. Current seizures consist of a prodrome of being "jittery," epigastric symptoms, déjà-vu, followed by lip smacking, moving of hands, and losing contact with her environment. There is a tendency to fall to the left side, with postictal confusion of approximately five minutes' duration. Seizure frequency is approximately 10-15 seizures per month with increased frequency around the time of her menses. An EEG conducted on September 29, 1997 revealed brief sharp transients in the right temporal lobe. In-patient telemetry suggested a right temporal focus. MRI conducted 5/18/97 was read as within normal limits. Current medications consist of Tegretol, Depakote, Klonopin, and Tylenol.

EVALUATION PROCEDURE:

The patient underwent standard right hemisphere angiography, and pre-injection stimuli were presented. 110 mg. of Amobarbitol was injected. Following the onset of hemiparesis, Amytal stimuli were presented for approximately two minutes. Ten minutes following presentation of the Amytal stimuli, recall of the stimuli was conducted. Left-sided angiography was then performed, and the procedure was repeated.

<u>Right Injection</u>:
110 mg. of Amytal was injected. Mrs. James demonstrated left-sided grip loss, left facial weakness, pupil dilation, and EEG changes for approximately three minutes. There was no loss of speech, eyes remained open,

and Mrs. James was able to track and name stimuli appropriately. Mood was calm.

On delayed recall, Mrs. James spontaneously recalled pre-injection stimuli. She spontaneously identified 4 of the 10 stimulus items. Ten of 10 targets were correctly identified with multiple-choice format.

Left Injection:
110 mg. of Amytal was injected. Mrs. James demonstrated right-sided grip loss, right facial weakness for 3 minutes and 45 seconds. EEG changes were noted for approximately four minutes. Amytal stimuli were then presented. As speech returned, there were impairments in naming, the comprehension of complex ideational material, repetition, and spontaneous speech. Mood remained calm.

On delayed recall, Mrs. James spontaneously recalled the pre-injection stimuli. She was unable to spontaneously recall any post-injection stimuli. Mrs. James correctly identified 1 of the 10 stimuli with multiple-choice format.

IMPRESSION:

Results suggest left hemisphere dominance for speech.
Right hemisphere memory is demonstrated, with 10 of 10 stimuli correctly identified.
Left hemisphere memory was not demonstrated, with 1 of 10 stimuli correctly recognized.

______________________________, PhD
Clinical Neuropsychology

Medical Setting Report 3
Post-Surgical Neuropsychological Evaluation

Name: Mrs. James
Hospital ID: SR56789
D.O.E.: 3/10/1998
D.O.B.: 11/25/1966

REFERRAL & BACKGROUND INFORMATION:

Mrs. James is a 31-year-old, right-handed, former travel agent with sixteen years of education, who is referred by Drs. Smith and Roberts for neuropsychological reevaluation status post-right temporal craniotomy with temporal lobectomy and amygdalohippocampectomy on January 24, 1998, for intractable right temporal lobe epilepsy with right mesial temporal sclerosis. Comprehensive medical, neurological and neurosurgical evaluations are contained in the Hospital records and will not be detailed here. The history is reviewed in the initial neuropsychological evaluation dated September 29 and October 13, 1997, and will not be repeated here.

Mrs. James has been seizure and aura free since her surgery. She denies any cognitive problems in the areas of attention and concentration, memory, visuospatial, or language. She denies any problems immediately following her surgery, but reports the onset of depression in mid- to late February. She describes depressed mood with depressed appetite and tearfulness. She reports negative thoughts and feelings, and fears regarding the uncertainties of her future. She denies suicidal ideation per se. She reports a similar episode of depression as a senior in college, when faced with the uncertainties of an unstructured future following graduation. She describes successful treatment through counseling and the development of a "goal." Mrs. James has recently been withdrawing from childcare activities but has initiated social activities with a craft organization, and has pursued outpatient counseling through the Community Network Clinic in her town. She is being followed by Robert Adams, M.S., on a biweekly basis. She is being followed on an intermittent basis by Alex Martin, MSW, through the St. Rocco's Hospital Clinic.

BEHAVIORAL OBSERVATIONS:

Mrs. James presented on time to the neuropsychological evaluation, was alert, fully oriented, well dressed, and well groomed. She initially appeared dysphoric, but mood improved to within normal limits as the structured evaluation session progressed. She demonstrated good frustration tolerance and responsiveness to humor, and appeared to work to the best of her abilities. She continued to demonstrate a thumb wrap grip. Current evaluation results may underestimate Mrs. James's actual capacities given her significant level of self-reported depression.

NEUROPSYCHOLOGICAL PROCEDURES:

Clinical interview, WAIS-R, Spatial Pointing Span, Auditory Continuous Performance, Weintraub-Mesulam Unstructured Letter Cancellation Test, Trail Making Tests A & B, Stroop Test, Wisconsin Card Sorting Test, Boston Naming Test, Controlled Oral Word Association Test (FAS), Aphasia Screening and Cookie Theft Narrative Writing from the BDAE, WRAT-3, Gates-McGinitie Reading Test Level F-Form 1, Right/Left Orientation, Praxis Screening, Hooper Visual Organization Test, Clock Drawing Test, Rey-Osterrieth Complex Figure, Benton Judgment of Line Orientation Test, Wechsler Memory Scale Form 2, Verbal Selective Reminding Test, Dynamometer, Grooved Pegboard, Finger Tapping Test, Luria Three Step Hand Sequences, Repeated Graphomotor Patterns, Reciprocal Motor Programs, Visual Selective Reminding Test-Form 2.

RESULTS:

Motor:

Upper extremity motor evaluation reveals rapid finger oscillation to be high normal bilaterally. Grip strength remains within normal limits for the right and mildly impaired for the left nondominant hand. Performance on the Grooved Pegboard has improved to high normal with the right dominant hand and has declined to moderately impaired with the left nondominant hand. Praxis evaluation and performance on Luria Three Step Hand Sequences is within normal limits. Performance on repetitive graphomotor patterns and reciprocal motor programs is within normal limits.

	Right Hand			Left Hand		
	RS	*T*	%ile	RS	*T*	%ile
Finger Tapping (taps/10 sec)	52.8	56	73	48.5	57	76
Grip Strength (kg)	29	46	34	20.5	36	8
Grooved Pegboard (sec)	53	56	73	78	33	4

Attention, Concentration, and Executive Functions:
Auditory attention span is high normal with a digit span of 9 digits forward and 7 digits backward. Visual attention span is high normal, with a position pointing span of 6 positions forward and 6 positions backward. There are no problems on tasks of sustained auditory attention. There are no problems with the speed of shifting attention as measured by Trail Making Test B. Performance on the Wisconsin Card Sorting Test is improved from the baseline obtained in October 1997, but remains slightly below expectations with 6 categories completed in 87 cards. Her performance on the Stroop continues to be within the expected range.

Speech and Language:
Spontaneous speech is fluent, well articulated, prosodic, and without word finding difficulties or paraphasic errors. Controlled word production (65th to 69th percentile) is very slightly reduced from October 1997, but is well within normal limits. There are slight improvements in arithmetic calculations with performance now at the 42nd percentile (WRAT-3). Confrontation naming (53/60, Boston Naming Test), sentence repetition, the comprehension of complex auditory ideational material, oral paragraph reading, spelling to dictation (90th percentile, WRAT-3), silent reading vocabulary and reading comprehension (73rd and 52nd percentiles, Gates-McGinitie Reading Test), spontaneous writing, and right/left identification are all within normal limits.

Visuospatial:
The scanning of visual space is symmetric, rapid, and accurate across a scattered Letter Cancellation Test. The copy of the Rey-Osterrieth Complex Figure continues to be performed with a slightly fragmented approach, and is now remarkable for a single detail omission on the left side of space. Block Design constructions and the drawing of a clock to command are within normal limits and unchanged from presurgical levels.

Memory:
Immediate recall of auditory prose passages is moderately impaired (RS=13, 4th percentile). Recall following a long delay filled with interpolated tasks remains moderately impaired with 70% of initially recalled material freely recalled on delay (RS=9, 8th %ile). Performance on the Verbal Selective Reminding Test is mildly impaired for long term storage, long term retrieval, and consistent long-term retrieval. Recall following a long delay filled with interpolated tasks remains within normal limits, with 11 of 12 items correctly recalled. Overall performance on verbal memory tasks appears comparable to presurgical levels.

The immediate recall of elementary graphic designs following a brief "study" presentation showed improvement from mildly impaired (RS=22, 6th percentile) prior to surgery, to a performance in the average range (RS=34, 56th %ile). Recall following a long delay filled with interpolated tasks remains average, with 80% of initially recalled material freely recalled on the delay. Performance on the Visual Selective Reminding Test is high average for long term storage, and consistent long-term retrieval. Recall following a long delay filled with interpolated tasks remains well within normal limits with 12 of 12 items correctly recalled. Overall performance on tasks of visual memory appears improved when compared to presurgical levels.

Intellectual:
WAIS-R indices are nominally in the Average range, with a Verbal IQ=97 (Average), Performance IQ=98 (average), and Full Scale IQ=98 (Average). Overall indices may underestimate Mrs. James's actual capacities given her reported level of depression.

	SS	%ile		SS	%ile
Information	8	25	Picture Completion	10	50
Digit Span	13	84	Picture Arrangement	10	50
Vocabulary	9	38	Block Design	11	65
Arithmetic	12	75	Object Assembly	7	16
Comprehension	11	65	Digit Symbol	11	65
Similarities	7	16			

WAIS-R indices are essentially unchanged from presurgical levels. There appear to be mild fluctuations across subscales with slight improvements in auditory attention span, and in Mrs. James's capacity to attend to pictorial nuances as necessary to arrange pictures into logical sequences. Overall performance is otherwise essentially unchanged.

IMPRESSION & RECOMMENDATIONS:

Mrs. James is a 31-year-old, right-handed, former travel agent with sixteen years of education referred by Drs. Smith and Roberts for neuropsychological reevaluation status post right temporal craniotomy with temporal lobectomy and amygdalohippocampectomy for intractable epilepsy. Current evaluation results reveal IQ indices to be within the average range, with a Verbal IQ=97 (Average), Performance IQ=98 (Average), and Full Scale IQ=98 (Average) and unchanged from presurgical levels. There are mild improvements in attention and cognitive flexibility. There are improvements in the learning and recall of nonverbal graphic material, with overall performance now in the average range.

The remainder of the neuropsychological evaluation is essentially stable from the initial presurgical evaluation level. Current evaluation results may underestimate Mrs. James's capacities given her significant level of self-reported depression.

Mrs. James reports the onset of depression several weeks following surgery, associated with her "loss" of seizures, loss of identity, and uncertainties about the future. She reports "negative thoughts and feelings," but denies suicidal ideation. She describes a comparable episode of depression during her senior year of college when faced with the uncertainties of graduation. She reports good resolution of her college depression with counseling and the development of some direction in her life. She is being followed through the Community Network Clinic for psychological services. She will continue to be followed by Alex Martin at St. Rocco's Hospital.

The results of this evaluation were discussed with Mrs. James following the formal evaluation session. She was reassured that her feelings of loss of self, fears about uncertainties in the future, and anxieties about forging a new identity were not unexpected adjustment issues associated with a successful surgery outcome. She was reassured that there did not appear to be any neuropsychological basis for her depression and that her current depressive episode was very similar to her response to graduating from college and being faced with choosing a new identity and future uncertainties. Given the success of psychotherapy in resolving adjustment issues associated with leaving college, it was strongly recommended to Mrs. James that she continue to actively pursue counseling to assist with her current adjustment issues. It is anticipated that Mrs. James will continue to experience improvements in cognitive functioning over the course of the next two years, and neuropsychological evaluation in approximately one year is recommended.

______________________________, PhD
Clinical Neuropsychology

Medical Setting Report 4
Neuropsychological Reevaluation

Name: Mrs. James
Hospital ID: SR56789
D.O.E.: 3/13/1999
D.O.B.: 12/25/1966

REFERRAL & BACKGROUND INFORMATION:

Mrs. James is a 32-year-old, right-handed, former travel agent with sixteen years of education, who is referred by Drs. Roberts and Smith for neuropsychological reevaluation status post right temporal craniotomy with temporal lobectomy and amygdalohippocampectomy on January 24, 1998, for intractable right temporal lobe epilepsy. Comprehensive medical, neurological and neurosurgical evaluations are contained in the Hospital records and are reviewed in the previous neuropsychological evaluation reports dated September 29, 1997 and March 10, 1998, and will not be repeated here.

Mrs. James continues to be aura and seizure free since her surgery. She now works part time as a hospital volunteer, and was employed as a temporary sales clerk during the holidays. She has begun to drive an automobile without mishap. She has been involved in ongoing counseling for panic attacks and adjustment issues, and is currently deciding whether to return to school. She continues to experience fluctuation in her emotional state with some episodic mild depression, but describes her overall mood as improved. Mrs. James, in general, believes she is functioning quite well, but does experience some persistent mild memory problems. More specifically, she occasionally has momentary difficulty recalling "what to do next" after completing a task. Otherwise, Mrs. James is unaware of any cognitive difficulties.

Current medications consist of Klonopin 0.5 mg ¼ tablet, Tegretol 200 mg, 1½ tabs. b.i.d., and Depakote, 250 mg., b.i.d.

BEHAVIORAL OBSERVATIONS:

Mrs. James presented promptly for the neuropsychological evaluation, and was alert, fully oriented, neatly dressed, and well groomed. She demonstrated a full range of appropriate affect and a nice sense of humor. She was unaccompanied, having driven independently to her doctor's appointment. She was invested in evaluation procedures, appeared to work to the best of her capacities, and demonstrated excellent frustration tolerance. Evaluation may be considered a good estimate of Mrs. James's actual capacities.

NEUROPSYCHOLOGICAL PROCEDURES:

Clinical interview, WAIS-R, Spatial Pointing Span, Auditory Continuous Performance, Weintraub-Mesulam Unstructured Letter Cancellation Test, Trail Making Tests A & B, Stroop Test, Wisconsin Card Sorting Test, Boston Naming Test, Controlled Oral Word Association Test (FAS), Aphasia Screening and Cookie Theft Narrative Writing from the BDAE, WRAT-3, Gates-McGinitie Reading Test Level F-Form 1, Right/Left Orientation, Praxis Screening, Hooper Visual Organization Test (HVOT), Clock Drawing Test, Rey-Osterrieth Complex Figure, Benton Judgment of Line Orientation Test (JLO), Wechsler Memory Scale (Boston Revision), Verbal Selective Reminding Test, Dynamometer, Grooved Pegboard, Finger Tapping Test, Luria Three Step Hand Sequences, Reciprocal Motor Programs, Repeated Graphomotor Patterns, Facial Recognition Test, Beck Depression Inventory.

RESULTS:

Motor:
Upper extremity motor evaluation continues to reveal high average bilateral finger oscillation. Fine motor control as measured by the Grooved Pegboard is improved to high average bilaterally. Grip strength remains within normal limits for the right and mildly impaired for the left non-dominant hand. Gait, praxis evaluation, and performance on Luria Three Step Hand Sequences remains within normal limits. Performance on repetitive graphomotor patterns and reciprocal motor programs is within normal limits.

	Right Hand			Left Hand		
	RS	*T*	%ile	RS	*T*	%ile
Finger Tapping (taps/10 sec)	52.5	56	73	48.2	56	76
Grip Strength (kg)	28	46	34	19.5	36	8
Grooved Pegboard (sec)	53	56	73	59	54	66

Attention, Concentration, and Executive Functions:
Auditory attention span remains high average with a digit span of 8 digits forward and 5 digits backward. Visual attention span remains unchanged and is high average with a position pointing span of 6 positions forward and 6 positions backward. Sustained auditory attention as measured by an auditory continuous performance task is within normal limits, with a

single error of both omission and commission. There are no difficulties with speed of establishing, shifting, and maintaining cognitive set as measured by Trail Making Test B (high average) and the Wisconsin Card Sorting Test. Performance on the WCST is improved and is now within normal limits, with six categories successfully completed within seventy-eight cards. Performance on the Stroop remains unchanged and within normal limits.

Speech and Language:
Spontaneous speech is within normal limits. Controlled word production (FAS) remains high average (75th to 79th percentile). Confrontation naming (53/60, Boston Naming Test), the comprehension of complex auditory ideational material, sentence repetition, oral paragraph reading, spelling to dictation (87th percentile, WRAT-3), and silent reading vocabulary (78th percentile, Gates-McGinitie Reading Test) all remain within normal limits. Spontaneous writing to the Cookie Theft prompt is improved for content and remains within normal limits. Mrs. James was able to accurately identify her right from her left, but was inconsistent with reversal commands on the examiner. There appears to be a very slight decline in silent reading comprehension (32nd percentile, Gates-McGinitie Reading Test). Calculations remain low average.

Visuospatial:
The scanning of visual space remains within normal limits. Visuospatial perception and non-motoric visuospatial integration (Hooper Visual Organization Test) remain within normal limits. The copy of the Rey-Osterrieth Complex Figure remains slightly fragmented but is essentially stable. Block Design constructions are somewhat improved from March 1998 (going from the 63rd to the 75th percentile). The drawing of a clock to command is significant for a hand reversal error.

Memory:
Immediate recall of auditory prose passages is only slightly improved (RS=15, 8th percentile). Recall following a long delay filled with interpolated tasks is improved and is mildly impaired with 75% of initially recalled material freely recalled on the delay (RS=11, 13th percentile). There is a good learning curve across the Verbal Selective Reminding Test, which is improved to within normal limits for the long term storage, long term retrieval, and consistent long term retrieval. Recall following a long delay filled with interpolated tasks remains within normal limits, with 10 of 12 words correctly recalled. Overall performance on verbal memory tasks appears comparable to pre- and post-surgical levels.

Immediate recall of elementary graphic designs following a 10 sec. presentation remains average. Recall following a long delay filled with interpolated tasks is within normal limits with 90% of initially recalled material freely recalled on the delay. Performance on the Visual Selective Reminding Test is high average for long term storage, long term retrieval, and delayed long term retrieval. Recall following a long delay filled with interpolated tasks remains intact with 12 of 12 items correctly recalled. Overall performance on tasks of visuospatial new learning appears consistent with performance obtained in March 1998, and is improved from presurgical levels.

Intellectual:

WAIS-R indices are again in the average range, with Verbal IQ=99 (Average), Performance IQ=110 (High Average), and Full Scale IQ=103 (Average). There is a significant 16-point improvement in Performance IQ when compared to her pre-surgical (9/97) level and a 12-point improvement compared to her (2/98) post-surgical level. Even with this improvement the current IQ indices may slightly underestimate Mrs. James's actual capacities given her mild level of self-reported depression.

Mrs. James demonstrates improvement from presurgical levels, primarily across Performance subscales (see scores on individual subtests below). Performance across the Verbal subscales is essentially stable.

	1997	1998	1999
Information	8	8	10
Digit Span	11	13	11
Vocabulary	8	9	10
Arithmetic	11	12	12
Comprehension	12	11	11
Similarities	8	7	8
Picture Completion	10	10	11
Picture Arrangement	8	10	10
Block Design	11	11	12
Object Assembly	8	7	12
Digit Symbol	9	11	12
Verbal IQ	95	97	99
Performance IQ	94	98	110
Full Scale IQ	94	98	103

Beck Depression Inventory:

Mrs. James was administered the Beck Depression Inventory and received a score of 10 out of a maximum total score of 63. Scores of 10 to 16 are suggestive of mild depression.

IMPRESSIONS & RECOMMENDATIONS:

Mrs. James is a 32-year-old, right-handed, former travel agent (now a hospital volunteer) with sixteen years of education, who is referred by Drs. Smith and Roberts for neuropsychological reevaluation status post right temporal craniotomy with temporal lobectomy and amygdalohippocampectomy on January 24, 1998 for intractable temporal lobe epilepsy. Current evaluation results reveal mild improvements in upper extremity motor functioning, cognitive flexibility, and executive functions. Speech and language capacities appear qualitatively improved but essentially stable from pre- and post-surgical levels. There are improvements in visuospatial capacities, including visuospatial organization and object assembly. There are mild improvements in new learning for both verbal and nonverbal material when compared to both pre- and post-surgical levels, with very mild learning difficulties for verbal material and a high average capacity to learn nonverbal material. IQ indices are in the average range with a Verbal IQ=99 (Average), Performance IQ=110 (High Average), and a Full Scale IQ=103 (Average). There is a 12- to 16-point Performance IQ index improvement when compared to presurgical (10/97) and post-surgical (3/98) levels. Mrs. James continues to report a mild level of depression. Nonetheless, she has experienced interim improvements in quality of life. More specifically, she has begun to drive, volunteers part time at a hospital, has worked as a temporary sales clerk, is more able to provide childcare duties for her daughter, and is considering returning to school.

Mrs. James continues to report panic attacks and mild depression, with benefit from ongoing counseling. She may wish to discuss with her counselor the option of seeking cognitive-behavioral treatment for her panic attacks, particularly in the event that these should become worse. CBT Associates of Melville are recommended for their expertise in this area.

It is expected that Mrs. James will continue to experience some improvements in her cognitive functioning over the next year, and neuropsychological reevaluation in approximately one year is recommended. The results of this evaluation were briefly reviewed with Mrs. James following the formal evaluation session.

________________________________, PhD
Clinical Neuropsychology

Wechsler Adult Intelligence Scale-Revised (WAIS-R):

	1997		1998		1999	
	SS	%ile	SS	%ile	SS	%ile
Information	8	25	8	25	10	50
Digit Span	11	63	13	84	11	63
Vocabulary	8	25	9	37	10	50
Arithmetic	11	63	12	75	12	75
Comprehension	12	75	11	63	11	63
Similarities	8	25	7	16	8	25
Picture Completion	10	50	10	50	11	63
Picture Arrangement	8	25	10	50	10	50
Block Design	11	63	11	63	12	75
Object Assembly	8	25	7	16	12	75
Digit Symbol	9	37	11	63	12	75
Verbal IQ	95	37	97	42	99	47
Performance IQ	94	34	98	45	110	75
Full Scale IQ	94	34	98	45	103	58

Wechsler Memory Scales:

	1997[a]		1998[b]		1999[a]	
	RS	%ile	RS	%ile	RS	%ile
Logical Memory I	13	4	13	4	15	8
Logical Memory II	8	7	9	8	11	13
Visual Reproduction I	22	6	34	56	35	65
Visual Reproduction II	22	13	27	25	32	61

[a]Wechsler Memory Scale-Revised, Boston Revision. [b]WMS-Form 2.

Dementia Screening Report

An older man (Albert O'Malley) suspected of cognitive decline and possible dementia was referred by his primary care physician. He was assessed with a widely used instrument, the Dementia Rating Scale, which was specifically developed for this purpose. Lezak (1995) cites Lau et al. (1988) as indicating a high degree of sensitivity (93%) and specificity (96%) in individuals ages 65 years or older with the DRS. The examiner has added normative data from later studies that take into account important demographic corrections (see chapter 4), in order to appropriately interpret the results. Importantly, the report emphasizes the need for a more in-depth assessment to better characterize the patient's neuropsychological status and provide specific recommendations.

Dementia Screening Report

Name: Albert O'Malley
Date of Birth: April 20, 1935
Date of Evaluation: December 24, 2000
Referred by: H. D. Walsh, M.D.

PROCEDURES:

Dementia Rating Scale (DRS)
Geriatric Depression Scale

REFERRAL QUESTION:

Albert O'Malley is a 65-year-old, Caucasian, married, right-handed man with a 12th grade education. Mr. O'Malley is retired, lives at home with his wife and mother, and volunteers in church activities. This screening was requested by his primary care physician, Dr. Walsh, following his wife's reports of significant memory difficulties, which raised concerns about a dementing process.

RELEVANT HISTORY:

A referral note by Dr. Walsh indicated that Mr. O'Malley has a history of diabetes, hypertension, and high cholesterol. Current medications include Procardia XL, 30 mg., and Lipitor, 10 mg.

BEHAVIORAL OBSERVATIONS:

Mr. O'Malley came to his appointment promptly, and accompanied by his wife. He was well groomed, and while effort and motivation were good, he needed encouragement on some tasks, as he anticipated failure.

TEST RESULTS:

In reviewing results of this evaluation, it is important to underscore that the DRS is a screening tool, and that while the global score has good convergent and predictive validity, interpretation of individual scales is affected by varying degrees of reliability and validity.

Mr. O'Malley obtained a global score of 118, over six standard deviations below the mean for individuals between the ages of 60-69 with 12 years of education (*M*=144, *SD*=3; Schmidt et al., 1994).[1]

His score was at the 86th percentile for a sample of individuals with probable Alzheimer's Disease. Based on recently published age and education corrected norms for unimpaired individuals (Lucas et al., 1998), this score is quite compromised. Subtest scores are presented below, together with relevant normative comparisons.

Scale	Raw Score	62-79 yr. old norm[1] *M*	*SD*	MOANS Sample (<69 yr.)[2] SS	%ile	SDAT Sample[3] %ile	*T* Score	Cutoff
Attention	36	35.5	1.6	11	60-71	90.3	63	32
Initiation/ Perseveration	34	35.5	3.0	7	11-18	90.3	63	29
Construction	6	5.8	.6	10	41-59	97.1	69	4
Conceptualization	29	37.2	2.6	5	3-5	75.8	57	32
Memory	13	23.3	2.1	2	<1	61.8	53	19
TOTAL SCORE	118	144	3	3	1	86.4	61	123

On the Geriatric Depression Scale, Mr. O'Malley obtained a score of 10, indicating that he is not currently depressed.

IMPRESSIONS & RECOMMENDATIONS:

Mr. O'Malley shows severe compromise in memory and reasoning. A complete neuropsychological assessment is highly recommended to determine more precisely the nature of those difficulties, help clarify their etiology, and provide recommendations to help deal with those deficits. In addition, referral to a behavioral neurologist is advised, particularly in light of a history of cardiovascular risk factors.

______________________________, PsyD

Licensed Psychologist
Director of Neuropsychology

[1]Schmidt, R., Freidl, W., Fazekas, F., Reinhart, B., Grieshofer, P., Koch, M., Eber, B., Schumacher, M., Polmin, K., & Lechner, H. (1994). The Mattis Dementia Rating Scale: Normative data from 1,001 healthy volunteers. *Neurology*, *44*, 964-966.

[2]Lucas, J. A., Ivnik, R. J., Smith, G. E., Bohac, D. L., Tangalos, E. G., Kokmen, E., Graff-Radford, N. R., & Petersen, R. C. (1998). Normative data for the Mattis Dementia Rating Scale. *Journal of Clinical and Experimental Neuropsychology*, *20*, 536-547.

[3]Mattis, S. (1988). *Dementia Rating Scale*: Professional manual. Odessa, FL: Psychological Assessment Resources.

Residential Rehabilitation Report

The following report is quite different from the preceding dementia screening. It was generated by the Clinical Director of a long-term residential rehabilitation facility. Her role is to provide consultation and direction to the interdisciplinary (or, in the words of the author, *transdisciplinary*) treatment team, and also to provide direct neuropsychological assessment and to develop and supervise behavioral interventions. As such, the report provides a thorough review of prior and current records (see chapter 5), as well as the results of the neuropsychological testing. In contrast to the previous reports, the recommendations of this report are both more detailed (in providing specific cognitive and behavioral interventions) and more comprehensive (integrating and directing the roles of different disciplines). The Recommendations section is also more comprehensive and detailed than is required by most neuropsychological evaluations.

Residential Rehabilitation Report

Client:	Robert ("Rob") D.	**DOB:**	12/5/84
Program:	Child & Adolescent	**DOA:**	2/10/98
School:	Sunrise Learning Center	**DOE:**	Feb., 1999

REASON FOR REFERRAL:

Rob is a 13-year-old boy who has been participating in the Sunrise residential program for one year. Rob was admitted from the Atlantic Psychiatric Institute Acute Psychiatric Program where he had been diagnosed with Attention-Deficit Disorder-Hyperactive Type, Oppositional Defiant Disorder, Impulse Control Disorder and Mild Mental Retardation. He has demonstrated improvement in behavioral self-management and functional skills acquisition. Additional information for treatment and discharge/long term planning is requested. Previous testing was not completed due to Rob's severe maladaptive behavior and refusal to participate.

INFORMATION SOURCES:

Family:
Rose Richards (aunt/custodial parent).

Records:
Sunrise Medical Record (including those from referral source, Atlantic Psychiatric Institute), Behavioral and pharmacological databases.

Treatment Team Members:
Tanya Fish, PhD,Clinical Manager, Psychologist; Jack Broom, M.Ed. (Behavior Analyst/Psychotherapist); Helen Haus, B.A. (Case Manager); Richard Spiegel., M.Sc., SLP (Speech Language Pathologist); Donna Martin., M.A., OTR/L (Occupational Therapist); Gregory May, P.T. (Physical Therapist); Kim Li, B.SpEd. (Special Education Teacher); William Young, M.SpEd. (Vocational Supervisor, woodshop); Teresa Ortiz, M.A. (Team Leader); Grace Lane, M.D. (Psychiatrist-consult); Gilbert Zachary, M.D. (Neurologist-consult).

BACKGROUND:

Rob has been participating in the Sunrise Children and Adolescents Program for the past year, where he also receives educational services through the on-site special education program. He resides in a unit with seven other adolescent boys. He has frequent contact with his aunt, who is very involved in his care and is the identified discharge caregiver. Interdisciplinary Team evaluation at the time of admission to Sunrise indicated that Rob was oriented to person and place; cranial nerves were intact and auditory screening within normal limits. Rob's processing was delayed and he was noted to check his answers two to three times. His conversation was limited by both weak breath support and impaired language/communication abilities. He was able to read and write simple one-syllable words, and could follow up to three step commands. His physical functioning was not impaired, with negative Romberg and good heel-toe gait. He performed at the first percentile on a standardized test of visual motor integration, and was later referred for optometric consult by the occupational therapist involved due to concerns about visual acuity. Mild hyperopia and astigmatism were diagnosed, with glasses fitted for correction, which Rob rarely wears.

Rob is the product of a full-term pregnancy with difficult delivery. According to his aunt (custodial parent), his mother was 17 or 18 at the time of Rob's birth. His mother smoked during pregnancy, but was not reported to be actively using drugs or alcohol during that time. Rob's Aunt recalls suction being used for the delivery, his mother requiring many stitches following his birth; there was also concern at the time about a "conehead" appearance in Rob, which persisted for months. His aunt reports that Rob was always very difficult to manage. His walking developed normally, but language commenced around age three, and was unintelligible until after seven or so. Toilet training was also delayed, with nighttime enuresis persisting to this day.

Rob's father has a long and chronic history of substance abuse, criminal conduct, violence, unpredictable behavior, and multiple incarcerations. Rob was physically and emotionally abused within the home, although the specific nature and extent of abuse are unclear. Rob's mother also reportedly has a history of substance abuse. She had difficulty managing Rob throughout his childhood, and transferred custody to her older sister in 1992. By that time (age 7), Rob had already had one inpatient psychiatric admission for "acting out" (records unavailable). His aunt reports that he broke his toys, fought with peers, tortured his younger sister and attacked his mother with a knife. He had also been transferred out of public school in first grade for multiple episodes of aggression, restraints, and need for escorts by the police. His records note difficulty with verbal self-expression, and that intellectual testing was completed at this time (FSIQ=69, VIQ=72, PIQ=69). Rob has a younger sister who appears to be developing uneventfully, and a younger brother who has also had psychiatric admissions and was diagnosed with a seizure disorder. Both younger siblings reside with their mother, who lives near Rob and his aunt.

Rob did not receive any intervention services until he entered the school system. He was referred to the SABC Program for educational services, and also received outpatient supports while residing with his aunt and older cousin from 1992-1997. He was positively participating in school, with most difficulty in the areas of reading and writing. He also had been attending Baptist Sunday school. He was sexually inactive and did not abuse drugs or alcohol. Although Rob had good peer relations in school, he had few friends in the neighborhood. Rob's aunt reports that he could not be left alone as he would get into fights and break windows. Over time he became increasingly uncontrollable, his assaults became more serious (knocking out four teeth of a peer before an adult intervened), and he no longer showed remorse.

In the summer of 1997, Rob did not return home after a visit to his mother. His aunt found him "on the streets" where he was attempting to run away from the limits and structure she had imposed for him. Rob then became violent and assaulted (bit) a police officer. He was sent to the State Youth Center, but charges were reduced to disorderly conduct and Rob was remanded to treatment at the Atlantic Psychiatric Institute, where he was admitted on 8/25/97. Rob's guardianship was transferred to the Department of Human Services during this chain of events. He has a new guardian who is currently familiarizing herself with his case.

At the time of Rob's 8/25/97 admission to API, records indicate that he was violent, had destroyed his aunt's apartment, and was threatening suicide. He was also engaging in self-injury, biting and head butting staff, and demonstrating poor safety awareness. He was reported to have a history of fire setting and cruelty to animals, which his aunt explicitly denies. During his stay at API, Rob did attempt suicide by hanging. His discharge note indicates that he remained violent throughout his stay, requiring locked seclusion and frequent restraints. Some improvement was noted prior to discharge. Records reference psychological testing, including the WISC-III (FSIQ=55), Children's Memory Scale (CMS) and possibly the Bender-Gestalt; however, these records have not been obtained as of yet. An addendum to this report will be filed if data are received.

Rob has been on Ritalin (methylphenidate) since 1996, which he and his aunt report as helpful. Attempts to discontinue Ritalin at API were reported as unsuccessful. Attempts to discontinue Mellaril and introduce Depakote resulted in vomiting and were also unsuccessful. Rob did not tolerate Clonidine, which caused hypotension. On a positive note, Pamelor improved mood and spontaneity, while also reducing enuresis. Tenex was also noted to be beneficial by reducing irritability. An EEG study was mildly abnormal. Recommendations had been made for sleep deprived EEG and genetic studies.

BEHAVIORAL OBSERVATIONS:

Rob is a right-hand dominant young man who appears smaller than his age (10th percentile for height and weight). He agrees to meet with me in the NeuroLab as a means of earning his way out of restriction time. He is very reluctant to participate in any evaluation, and his cooperation is secured through utilization of reinforcers, including earned privileges, edibles (soda pop) and small items (key chain, penlight). He presents as younger than his chronological age and is noted to have subtle craniofacial anomalies (bridge of nose, nose to upper lip, dentition) often associated with neurodevelopmental anomalies. He wears sneakers, jeans and a denim jacket that is buttoned to the top. After rapport is established in the well-heated NeuroLab, he finally removes his jacket and adopts a noticeably more relaxed posture. Rob also wears a baseball cap, which when removed reveals a recently shaved head with multiple scars evident. He cannot account for the scars with the exception of a left parietal laceration sustained during horseplay with peers in early November 1998 (no loss of consciousness). He tells me that his aunt will let him shave his head here, but that she doesn't like it, and he will not be able to do this when he goes home. Follow up reveals that head shaving, although popular with peers, was prompted by a recent episode of gum-in-the-hair.

Rob speaks softly and can be difficult to understand. His response delays are variable, ranging from near typical to extremely slow in comparison to his peers. He frequently expresses his desire to return to his unit, but continues the evaluation with encouragement. Even after being reminded he chooses not to bring his eyeglasses to the assessment. Prior to our sessions, he has completed a personality inventory (done by interview) and some computerized attention and problem solving tasks. Given his history of resistance and severe maladaptive behavior, I engage him by allowing each of us to pick out some of the tests that we will do together. He first selects motor tasks and then a visual integration task. I select test batteries consistent with his past records. We shake hands and make a contract outlining each of our commitments. Although he has previously refused many attempts at test administration, Rob engages and is able to complete 8 hours of testing (with breaks) over the 2/27-28/99 weekend, during which time he would have been otherwise restricted.

Rob listens well and follows 2-3 step instructions during our afternoon and evening sessions. Our morning meeting is marked by inattentiveness and hyperactivity. Rob tells me he is not a morning person. He settles over time, but requires more structure and frequent breaks in our pre-lunch meeting. Rob demonstrates good manners and a desire to please once he engages. He is embarrassed by his self-perceived poor performance, and often wants to quit. He is very reluctant to guess and typically assumes that he is wrong. During test administration, I at times inserted bogus easy items between tests, in order to facilitate Rob's willingness to continue. He responds positively and warmly to praise and encouragement. He smiles and makes good eye contact when he feels he has done something well.

Rob's affect is blunted but appropriate to content. His mood appears depressed and his verbalizations support this, along with low self-esteem and little confidence in his abilities. He does not want to talk with me about his past or his feelings, but does share that he is angry at his father for being in jail and for hurting him when he was little. He endorses angry feelings more than sadness when speaking of his childhood. When asked if he has anyone that he feels comfortable talking with, he speaks positively of Jack (psychotherapist) and Helen (Clinical Manager). He also expresses warm feelings for his mother, aunt, siblings and cousin. He speaks highly of his uncle, who although separated from his aunt, would still bring him out on carpentry jobs now and then on weekends. Rob says he would like to be a carpenter, and that he really liked working on his truck with Bill in the woodshop. This is his most animated conversation. There is no evidence of hallucinations or delusions. Rob acknowledges that he is working on his anger and aggression, and that at times he wants to hurt other people or himself. When asked how often, he indicates that this has improved, and that he doesn't have those bad feelings every day any more. He is looking forward to eventually returning home and is very happy about his therapeutic leaves of absence that he has earned of late.

Current Medications:

Nortriptyline (Pamelor)	25 mg 3 caps QHS
Zyprexa	10 mg HS
Mellaril	50 q 4-6 hrs prn agitation (rarely accessed by client)
Mellaril	50 mg bid 8am 4pm
Tenex	1 mg tid 8am noon 5pm
Ritalin	200 mg tid 8am noon 5pm
Tegretol	400 mg bid 8am & HS; 200 mg at 5pm

TESTS & QUESTIONNAIRES ADMINISTERED:

Wechsler Intelligence Scale for Children-III (WISC-III),Children's Memory Scale (CMS), California Verbal Learning Test for Children (CVLT-C) – refused, Woodcock-Johnson Scale of Independent Behavior (SIB), Wide Range Achievement Test-III (WRAT-III), Finger Tapping, Grooved Pegboard, Conner's Teacher's Rating Scales (completed by teacher), Conner's Continuous Performance Test (CPT), Controlled Oral Word Association Test (COWAT F-A-S), Animal Word List Generation, Children's Category Test – refused, see next item, Wisconsin Card Sorting Test – computerized, Peabody Picture Vocabulary Test (PPVT) – refused, Boston Naming Test – refused, Bender Gestalt – refused, Hooper Visual Organization Test (Visual Organization Test), Trail Making A (B and C not applicable), Children's Apperception Test-Human (CAT-H) – refused, Millon Adolescent Personality Inventory (MAPI).

EVALUATION FINDINGS:

Orientation:
Rob is oriented to person and place but not to time. He is able to use a watch and calendar as a reference.

Attention:
Rob is alert and aroused. He has been receiving Ritalin since 1996 for the treatment of ADHD. Both he and his aunt report that this has been very helpful. It has been observed that Rob's ability to attend and concentrate changes over the course of the day. This is evident in our AM versus PM testing sessions and is supported over multiple administrations of the CPT. This variation may be due to Rob's bedtime medication dosing schedule, and is also consistent with his difficulty getting up and getting focused for his morning routine. When he demonstrates impaired attention, his performance is characterized by inattentiveness, difficulty sustaining his focus, slow responding, and inconsistent arousal. Rob's CPT performance and teacher ratings reflect more inattentive rather than hyperactive symptoms, though consideration must be given to the effect of his medication regimen in depressing hyperactivity symptoms.

Intellectual Functioning:
On the WISC-III Rob achieved a Full Scale IQ of 54, which places him in the intellectually deficient range and is consistent with his previous diagnosis of mild mental retardation and a chart note indicating a previous Full Scale IQ Score of 55. His Verbal IQ of 66 is intellectually deficient, with his Performance IQ of 49 as far more impaired. Although records are unavailable at this time, it does appear that current results are consistent

with findings from 1997, and that both of these measures represent a decline from the borderline scores noted in reference to a 1992 report. This apparent decline in IQ scores is due in large part to Rob's inability to keep pace intellectually with his peer reference group, and his behavioral difficulties negatively affecting his actual time in school.

Rob's lower Performance IQ (17 points below his Verbal IQ) is significant, and is only explained in part by his slow processing, as he had difficulty with many test items even when offered extra time for completion. Rob's Perceptual Organization Index is 50 (below the 0.1 percentile), consistent with prior visual integration tests (1998 VMI >1st percentile), and also accounting in large part for his lower Performance IQ.

With regard to WISC-III subtests (see appended scores), Rob demonstrates strength in his ability to understand social judgments: he gives evidence of good common sense and an appreciation of positive social values such as honesty and fairness. This is consistent with my observations and interactions with him, where he demonstrates these skills in action when able to self-manage his behavioral dyscontrol. Weaknesses include Rob's fund of general information and his visual-perceptual skills. He is most frustrated by visually based tasks that require simultaneous processing, such as arranging a sequence of picture cards to make a sensible story, and analyzing a complex visual design. His processing delay is most evident when asked to define vocabulary words, and appears rooted in his embarrassment at knowing few words.

Linguistic and Academic:
Rob is sensitive to his language based difficulties, and declined a number of tests in this area. His vocabulary is limited and he has great difficulty generating words and sentences. Although not formally assessed, he appears to have adequate auditory/language comprehension, as he is able to follow multi-step instructions and complete arithmetic word problems without having items repeated. His apparent slowness in conversation is probably due to processing speed and confidence factors rather than a receptive language problem.

On the WRAT-3, Rob's academic difficulties are apparent, with his reading, spelling and arithmetic scores all below the 1st percentile. It is probable that his academic underachievement is both a product of, and contributor to, his behavioral problems in school settings, and that both of these problems are rooted in complex neuropsychological and psychosocial interactions. Rob is noted to check his math work and to understand the concepts of addition, subtraction and multiplication, even though he may not have the skill to complete the operation. For example, when presented with the problem of 6x3, he writes 12+6 on the page, and counting with his fingers, is able to produce the correct answer.

Rob has a longstanding history of language impairment evident in his attempts at reading and spelling. He has difficulty decoding, is phonetically inaccurate (primarily with non-short vowels) and is easily frustrated with language tasks. He is able to identify his letters by name and accurately articulates most consonant sounds. He has yet to master the alphabet beyond the letter "H." When asked to write a sentence, he chooses to write "I like soda." He is unsure about the spelling of "like," but when encouraged, spells it correctly, and then proceeds to copy the word soda from the label of the soda bottle on the desk. His printing is crude, and he is only able to print his name at this time.

Visual-Perceptual:
Rob demonstrates impaired visual perceptual functions. He has great difficulty both breaking apart (analyzing) and integrating together (synthesizing) visual perceptual information. These tasks are particularly frustrating for him. He is noted to make errors of design reversal and to lose his place on the page when working on tasks that are visually "busy" and complex. When given the opportunity to draw basic shapes, he was disinterested, but then did attempt to copy a complex figure. His complex figure drawing reflects visual planning and organization problems and is consistent with right hemisphere difficulties.

Motor:
Rob enjoys the motor tasks and puts forth a solid effort. His finger tapping speed is within normal limits bilaterally, and he does not display any dominant-nondominant hand discrepancy on this simpler, pure speed task. However, when performing a more complex motor task requiring coordination and dexterity (i.e., placing grooved pegs into slotted holes), Rob is able to manage with his dominant hand, but has great difficulty with his nondominant hand, suggesting right greater than left hemisphere involvement, consistent with his aforementioned pattern of greater relative difficulty in functions associated with the right hemisphere (visual spatial tasks), a pattern common to nonverbal learning disabilities.

Learning & Memory:
Rob achieved a General Memory Score of 63 on the CMS, which is consistent with his Full Scale IQ (below average). In examining the various aspects of memory assessed, Rob achieves higher scores on tasks such as remembering the themes and stories rather than word lists, and remembering visual information with a familiar context, such as depictions of a family having a barbecue, rather than the location of dots. His learning

curve for repeated exposure to a variety of types of information is inconsistent, but generally less than that expected for his age. Both Rob's visual immediate memory and most importantly, his attention and concentration (the underpinning of memory and learning), are significantly lower than predicted by his intellectual ability. Attention/concentration skills are at the 0.1 percentile and adversely impact Rob's entire learning and memory process. It should be noted that by virtue of scheduling needs, the CMS was administered in an AM testing session, the time when Rob's attention and concentration are lowest. Rob demonstrates average abilities to recognize (rather than recall) information that he has been exposed to, such as story content and people's faces. Although his delayed recognition scores evidence some inconsistency, it does appear that his difficulties are at times retrieval or access based.

Executive/Abstract Functions:
Rob demonstrates impairment in initiating and sustaining verbal output, regardless of the structure provided. His performance on tests of word fluency (FAS, Animals) is below the 1st percentile. These findings are consistent with his overall difficulty initiating and maintaining behavior. As previously mentioned, visual perceptual tasks are marked by disorganization, difficulty with abstract thinking, and poor planning. Strengths in this area include Rob's ability to engage in social reasoning, appreciate the perspective of others, and to a lesser degree, form abstract concepts and classes. When highly motivated on a computerized test of trial and error learning, mental flexibility and working memory, Rob performs much better than expected in comparison to age peers. His abilities to benefit from feedback, learn, shift sets, and maintain set range from average to the borderline range. However, given the degree to which card sorting is a difficult, complex task, Rob's performance is quite satisfactory given his difficulties in other areas.

Adaptive Behavior/Functional Skills:
Rob's functional living skills are well below average and are adversely impacted by his difficulty initiating and sustaining effort. It is difficult to determine what he actually can do, as his behavioral acting out episodes tend to bias those involved with Rob to underestimate his abilities. Staff ratings on a standardized adaptive behavior measure (SIB) appear lower than the repertoire that I have observed Rob performing. His maladaptive behavior clouds his potential in functional as well as academic areas. In general, Rob is functioning at the 10+ year old level of development. His strongest skills are in his own personal hygiene. At times, Rob is capable of taking care of most of his Activities of Daily Living with minimal external support and structure.

Behavioral/Psychosocial:
After an initial difficult period, Rob has made noteworthy progress over the past six months within the program. He has required intensive multi-modal treatment, and is still not at a point where discharge is imminent. He has serious episodes of aggression and self-injury, and although the number of episodes per month requiring physical intervention has decreased from 18/month in early 1998 to 8/month since October, 1998, these episodes often involve multiple restraints and pose serious risk of endangerment to self and others. Personality profile scores are consistent with acting out, impulsivity and noncompliant behaviors. Rob continues to grow in his adaptive skills, and is engaged in both skill acquisition and individual/group psychotherapy activities. He has demonstrated the capacity for change and responsiveness to treatment.

Rob's personality profile is consistent with his presentation in the program and during this evaluation. His self-concept is shaky, he has difficulty managing his emotions, and he at times feels hopeless. He is rather emotionally labile and may engage in periods of severe impulsive acting out. He often feels embarrassed, misunderstood and disappointed in himself. He is struggling to find a direction and to find a comfortable place within his family and peer group. His self-esteem and confidence are low, and he reports feeling little recognition from others. It is noteworthy how little positive feedback was required during testing to brighten his affect and successfully encourage him to continue.

SUMMARY AND RECOMMENDATIONS:

Rob presents with a complex interaction of neurodevelopmental impairment manifested as limited intellect, attention and self-regulation problems, and behavioral dyscontrol. Pre- and perinatal factors, family dysfunction, an early history of abuse and neglect, and educational low achievement are principally contributing to his clinical picture. Rob has shown a positive response to a well structured environment and stimulant medication. Of concern is that if he is not provided with intensive treatment for the plethora of difficulties that he exhibits, he has a high probability of falling into a chronic pattern of undercontrolled behavior. Behavioral dyscontrol is a major factor impacting on his level of independent functioning. Even though Rob has demonstrated benefit from treatment thus far, this has proceeded at a slow rate of progress and his prognosis is guarded.

DIAGNOSIS:

Axis I:
ADHD with positive response to Ritalin
Oppositional Defiant Disorder
Depression NOS

Axis II:
Mild Mental Retardation

Axis III:
Hypotensive reaction to Clonidine

Axis IV:
Severe. Chronic separation from parents, history of abuse

Axis V:
GAF 40

RECOMMENDATIONS:

1. Follow-up Evaluations

- Continue efforts to obtain prior neuropsychological test data. Once obtained, analyze in comparison to recent evaluation.
- Rob is a good candidate for EEG neurofeedback, complete QEEG and Brain Map. Compare with neuropsychological test findings and sleep deprived EEG results, and consider adding as adjunct treatment for attention deficit.
- Previous physician recommendations for genetic studies and sleep deprived EEG were never completed and may have significant diagnostic and prognostic implications. These studies must be followed up and results incorporated into treatment as appropriate.
- Reevaluate neuropsychologically 2/2000.

2. Psychopharmacological Review and Monitoring of Treatment Response

- Rob's pattern of AM/PM attention and learning variability may be related to his medications and/or sleep-wake cycle. Work in conjunction with team to review sleep log, doses, and schedule of medication administration to facilitate improved AM functioning. Some of Rob's medications may be slowing his cognitive processing. As his behavior continues to improve and stabilize, psychoactive medications should be periodically reviewed for their risks, side effects and benefits.

3. Vocational/Motivational Activities Development

- Rob is interested in and has the ability to do carpentry/construction. Increasing access to the woodshop and engaging in activities that teach functional work skills (such as painting and roofing the fire hydrant enclosures with a couple of other "guys") will help increase future life options and enhance self-esteem.
- Utilize carpentry for examples in classroom, particularly in mathematics.

4. Rehabilitative Therapies and Implementation of Compensatory Techniques

- Continue existing programs and services (Behavior Therapy, OT, SLP, PT, Psychology, Special Ed., and Vocational).
- Provide instruction, demonstration and motivation for improved articulation and breath support to improve efficacy of communication.
- Introduce and practice with compensatory devices such as calculators and voice-activated reminders to build skills, options and independence.
- Teach Rob to sign his name.
- Mastery of the alphabet and continued development of phonics (especially vowels) must be pursued but may be resisted by Rob. Using game formats, woodwork examples, and picture cards may help break up the monotony, but should not be infantilizing.

5. Behavioral Management Strategies and Socialization

- Intensify use of positive practice as a behavioral strategy to facilitate learning of conventional prosocial alternatives. Implement variable ratio distribution of "positive passes" for prosocial adaptive behavior.
- Minimize use of response cost-based behavioral techniques. Intensify use of differential reinforcement schedules. Consider variable ratio reinforcers as described above, with a simple point/level system wherein maladaptive responses only prevent earning points for a set interval, but do not have any penalty. Points/level would be the basis for accruing access to reinforcers through an earned privilege system that would be easily modified to more closely replicate the home discharge environment for ease of implementation and generalization.
- When Rob refuses tasks, consider attempting some of those after a period of time elapses.

- Undesirable behaviors will never be successfully extinguished unless alternative behaviors that attract naturally occurring reinforcement are available and developed. Since Rob has the foundation of some of these–good manners, religious beliefs, appreciation of moral values, work ethic–design programming to spotlight these aspects of Rob, increasing his self-esteem, recognition and leadership. This may be difficult to initiate within his current peer group and may better be broached in structured therapy settings.
- In all contexts, work with Rob on verbal mediation skills that are the foundation for successful self-regulation. Support, encourage and model dialogue. If problem-solving worksheets are introduced, this should be done through direct care staff providing a structured interaction.
- If therapeutically viable, assess availability of setting Rob up with a "Big Brother." His cousin (now 22) served in this capacity at home, and was a positive, stabilizing influence.

6. Independence Skills Development

- Rob has been relatively medication compliant and would benefit from controlled, repeated exposure to a medication education and self-management curriculum.
- Introduce repeated exposures through hands on learning of necessary adult living skills such as the food pyramid, money management, basic first aid, using the telephone, directional sense and household safety. Rob appears to retain this type of practical knowledge and is interested in learning more about how to take care of himself.

____

Clinical Director
Director, Neuropsychology, Neurofeedback & Behavior Services

Overview of Test Data for Robert "Rob" D., 14-Year-Old Male

NEUROPSYCHOLOGICAL TEST DATA:

WISC III:

Scale	Index*	Percentile
Full Scale	54	0.1
Verbal	66	1
Performance	49	<0.1
VC	68	2
PO	55	<0.1
FD	64	1
PS	61	0.5

**Note*. All indices and standard scores: M=100, SD=15 unless otherwise noted.

Verbal Subtest	Scaled Score (M=10; SD=3)	Performance Subtest	Scaled Score (M=10; SD=3)
Information	1	Picture Completion	1
Similarities	5	Coding	2
Arithmetic	4	Picture Arrangement	2
Vocabulary	3	Block Design	1
Comprehension	7	Object Assembly	2
Digit Span	3	Symbol Search	3

Memory:

CVLT-C – refused

CMS:

Scale	Index*	Percentile	
General Memory	63	1	
Visual Immediate	66	1	Significant ability-memory discrepancy, p = .05
Visual Delayed	85	16	
Verbal Immediate	75	5	
Verbal Delayed	69	2	
Attention/Concentration	51	0.1	Significant ability-memory discrepancy, p = .05
Learning	66	1	
Delayed Recognition	75	5	

Adaptive/Functional Status:

Woodcock Johnson Scales of Independent Behavior:
(interviewer Behavior Services staff–J. Broom, M.Ed.)

Domain	Age Score	Instructional Range	Percentile
Broad Independence	9-9	8-6 to 11-3	2
Motor Skills	8-4	7-1 to 9-8	1
Social/Communication	9-11	8-7 to 11-3	8
Personal Care	11-2	9-9 to 12-6	7
Community Living	10-8	9-7 to 12-0	6

Index of Maladaptive Behavior Types on W-J SIB
Internalized – Mildly Serious Problem
Asocial – Moderately Serious Problem
External – Serious Problem

General Index – Serious Behavior Problems

Academic:

WRAT-3

Subject Area	Standard Score*	Percentile	Grade
Reading	57	0.5	2
Spelling	60	0.8	1
Arithmetic	60	0.8	3

Motor:

Test	Score		Percentile
Finger Tapping	Dominant	40	16
	Non Dom	40	50
	Difference	0	WNL
Grooved Pegboard	Dominant	86 sec	9
	Non Dom	108 sec	<1
	Difference	22 sec (25%)	WNL – 10%

**Note*. All indices and standard scores: *M*=100, *SD*=15 unless otherwise noted.

Attention:

Conners' Teacher's Ratings: (completed by W. Young, B.Sp.Ed.)
(Low scores reflect clinical population skew and may be an underestimate when compared to the general public school population)

Area	*T* Score (*M*=50, *SD*=10)	
Conduct Problems	57	WNL
Hyperactivity	52	WNL
Inattentive-Passive	59	WNL
Hyperactivity Index	54	WNL

Conners' CPT:
(3 administrations to assess perceived AM/PM variability)
Methylphenidate dose schedule 20 mg TID 8 am, noon, 5 pm

Measure	AM Sample Day 1–9:30	AM Sample Day 2–10:00	PM Sample Day 3–1:15
# Hits	98.30[a]	98.30[a]	89.91[b]
# Omissions	98.30[a]	98.30[a]	89.91[b]
# Commissions	8.36 (Good)	19.42 (WNL)	26.84 (WNL)
Hit Rate	1.48[c]	1.0[c]	1.0[c]
Hit Rate Std Error	75.54 (WNL)	97.97[a]	76.69 (WNL)
Variability of SE	54.05 (WNL)	93.79[a]	52.08 (WNL)
Block Change:			
Hit Rate	97.97[a]	89.99[b]	29.98 (WNL)
Hit Rate Std. Error	53.20 (WNL)	8.84 (WNL)	43.59 (WNL)
ISI Change:			
Hit Rate	97.03[a]	99.00[a]	72.97 (WNL)
Hit Rate Std. Error	74.51 (WNL)	99.00[a]	25.71 (WNL)
Attentiveness	52.37 (WNL)	63.14 (WNL)	54.37 (WNL)
Risk Taking	99.00[a]	99.00[a]	87.02[b]
OVERALL INDEX	16.23[d]	15.11[d]	0.00 (does not suggest ADD)

[a]Markedly atypical, [b]Mildly atypical, [c]Atypically slow, [d]Strong evidence of ADHD.

Executive Abstract Functions:

COWAT:
F = 0
A = 2
S = 3
Animals = 2, 1st percentile, all impaired

Complex Figure – impaired

Children's Category Test – refused

WCST:
(cooperated with computerized administration by technician R. Downs)

Measure	Standard Score*	Percentile
Total Errors	80	9
Perseverative Responses	76	5
Perseverative Errors	75	5
Nonperseverative Errors	88	21
Conceptual Level Responses	82	12
Categories Completed	5	>16
Trials to Complete 1st Category	11	>16
Failure to Maintain Set	0	>16
Learning to Learn	WNL	>16

Other Verbal Tests:

PPVT – refused
Boston Naming Test – refused

Other Nonverbal Tests:

Bender Gestalt – refused
Hooper Visual Organization Test – <5th percentile
Trail Making A: 58 sec, 1 error <1st percentile
Trail Making B & C – N/A, does not know alphabet

**Note*. All indices and standard scores: *M*=100, *SD*=15 unless otherwise noted.

Behavioral Incident Database:
Frequency of episodes requiring physical management (may consist of multiple interventions per episode):

Admit 2/10/98 thru 1/31/99

Feb 98	5	August 98	14
March 98	23	September 98	17
April 98	14	October 98	9
May 98	21	November 98	8
June 98	14	December 98	8
July 98	15	January 99	4

Personality Testing:

Children's Apperceptive Test-Human (CAT-H) – refused

Millon Adolescent Personality Inventory (MAPI):
(administered by Behavior Services, J. Broom, M.Ed.)

Scale	Score (*M*=50, *SD*=10)
Personality Styles:	
Introversive	75
Inhibited	82
Cooperative	50
Sociable	35
Confident	35
Forceful	56
Respectful	12
Sensitive	83
Expressed Concerns:	
Self-concept	84
Personal Esteem	75
Body Comfort	67
Sexual Acceptance	65
Peer Security	75
Social Tolerance	68
Family Rapport	78
Academic Confidence	69
Behavior Correlates:	
Impulse Control	89
Social Conformity	65
Scholastic Achievement	71
Attendance Consistency	61

Outpatient Vocational Assessment Report and Feedback Summary Report

The next section provides a report and feedback summary describing the assessment of a woman (Anne Wilson) referred by her vocational counselor. Anne Wilson's report highlights the usefulness of collateral information, in this case a telephone interview with her mother, after the first session (see chapter 5). Ms. Wilson was well spoken and, despite her low score on Vocabulary, she occasionally used low frequency words appropriately and provided a good narrative writing sample. In addition, her apparently unremarkable educational history was surprising in the context of poor performance on measures of academic achievement, whereas her medical history was negative for head injuries or other illnesses that could account for her profile. Her mother was able to provide valuable information about her early development, as well as some early records of prior assessments. It was also interesting to note that the family had rejected the label of mental retardation early in Anne's development, while still providing her with an academically enriched and supportive environment at home. Finally, this report illustrates the usefulness of graphing the difference between her verbal and performance abilities. For the client, the visual representation of the results was particularly helpful.

In chapter 8, we discuss the importance of the feedback session. In the case of the residential rehabilitation report (Robert "Rob" D.) presented previously, feedback is likely to be most effective when communicated orally and behaviorally, given his significant difficulties with reading and memory. For individuals who are less severely handicapped, but who are easily overwhelmed and who may also have limitations in the areas of reading and recall, a summary of strengths, weaknesses, and recommendations is a useful, concrete reminder of the points discussed during the feedback session. The feedback took place at the office of the vocational counselor and was attended by the client, her husband, her vocational counselor, and the neuropsychologist. Copies of both the full report and the summary were made available to everyone present, with the consent of the client (obtained privately before the meeting). Providing the client with the full report in addition to the summary is critical, even if the client may never fully understand its content. It symbolizes the equality of all participants at the feedback session (with equal access to information) as team members engaged in collaborative problem solving, with the client in center stage.

It is important that the client can both relate to the findings at a personal level and feel comfortable agreeing or disagreeing with aspects of the report. If the person being evaluated understands that the "final report" is open to correction or revision (within limits), then there is a sense of empowerment, participation, and ownership of the results; this, in turn, enhances the likelihood that recommendations will be followed and that the assessment has served a useful purpose. This attitude can be fostered by simple comments in the beginning, when the report is handed out, to the effect that if, despite the examiner's best intentions, there are any inaccuracies in the history, such inaccuracies can be easily remedied using a word processor. Clients generally realize that the purpose of an evaluation is to gain a better understanding of their abilities in order to help them overcome setbacks or barriers to success. It is a truism that people are better able to acknowledge their limitations when their input is invited and taken seriously. In short, the results should generally "make sense" or "feel right" to the person they purport to describe.

Outpatient Vocational Assessment Report

Name: Anne M. Wilson
Date of Birth: 3/29/55
Date of Evaluation: 12/13/00 and 12/27/00
Age: 45 years
Referred by: Steven Amador, CRC
Examiner: ______________________________, PhD, ABPP

REASON FOR REFERRAL:

Anne is a 45-year-old, left-handed wife and mother of two children who was referred for an updated assessment of neuropsychological functioning. Anne has a long history of involvement with the State Rehabilitation Agency dating back to 1976. She is currently unemployed, having most recently been employed bagging at a grocery store from 11/99 to 5/00.

PROCEDURES:

Record review; telephone interview with Laura McDermott, Mrs. Wilson's mother; history and mental status exam; WAIS-III; Vigil (computerized continuous performance test); cancellation tests; Digit Span and Spatial Span subtests of Wechsler Memory Scale-III; Wisconsin Card Sorting Test (WCST); Stroop test; Trail Making A and B; Narrative Writing; WRAT-3; Nelson-Denny Reading Test (reading rate and comprehension); California Verbal Learning Test (CVLT); Logical Memory subtest of WMS-III; Rey-Osterrieth Complex Figure Test (copy, immediate and delayed recall, delayed recognition); finger tapping; Personality Assessment Inventory (PAI).

BEHAVIORAL OBSERVATIONS:

Anne Wilson is a middle-aged woman appearing her stated age, of average height, with medium length dark hair, and wearing casual clothes. She was friendly and cooperative throughout the assessment, even though she canceled the first session out of a sense of frustration and discouragement with the entire vocational rehabilitation process. She responded well to sympathy and encouragement and agreed to come in on another date. Speech was unremarkable. Results of the assessment are considered a valid indication of her current optimal ability.

HISTORY:

The following information was obtained from Anne, her mother, and previous reports. Anne is the youngest of four sisters. Her father, currently in his seventies and retired, is a physician. Her mother is a college graduate who administered her husband's office. Both parents currently live in Florida. Anne's siblings are all college graduates of good schools; her oldest sister is a plastic surgeon, and another switched from medicine to photography. They are all married with children, and live in adjacent states.

According to her mother, there were no complications surrounding her pregnancy with Anne, and delivery was normal. She walked at the usual time, and there were no early concussions or injuries. She did not learn to talk until she was three years old. Her mother felt that her comprehension was good but that she had difficulty expressing herself. Anne noted that she was slow to learn to talk and that at one point she was put on thyroid medication out of concerns that she was "slow." However, she attended public school and, according to her mother, there was no indication from the school until fifth grade that there might be any problem. Anne's pediatrician was her great aunt (her father was the school doctor). She was frequently teased because she struggled in school. In third grade, she was evaluated independently by a psychologist and found to score in the retarded range, but her mother added that, "we didn't see that at home." Her parents did paint a blackboard in her room, and her mother actively helped teach her to read and do math. Anne was not coded by the school until the 12th grade. A report from the school at that time (5/74) indicated that Anne's greatest strength was her reading vocabulary (9.2 grade level), but she was comprehending reading material at the 7.2 grade level. Word attack skills were at the 7.1 grade level. Arithmetic was her greatest weakness (3.9 grade level). On the Detroit Test of Language Ability, she did best on Verbal Opposites (12.6 year level) and Likenesses and Differences (15.3 year level).

After leaving school at age 19, Anne worked for several years assembling circuit boards at an electronics company. She then worked at another company in a similar position, where she met her husband Tom. Anne has held several positions as a file clerk and warehouse worker, and as an assembly worker. Anne and Tom married on March 3rd, 1988. He works as a custodian and is in his 50s. They have two children, a girl, Susan (10), and a boy, Tim (7). Anne indicated that she has seen many counselors over the years, although she denied that she has been diagnosed with any psychiatric illness. Instead, she said the counseling was helpful to "talk things through." Anne reports no history of legal problems.

Medical history is positive for high blood pressure. She has been on Synthroid for years for thyroid problems. She acknowledged that for a limited time, when they were dealing with high bills, she stopped her medication, in part to see if there was any difference (she noted slight mood increase, but "not much"). There is no history of head injuries. She is under the care of Dr. Harold Dunster at the Parsons Clinic.

Appetite is "so-so" and less than before. She reported a weight gain of several pounds in the last several months. She averages eight hours of sleep a night, and reports no nightmares. Libido is reportedly diminished. On a scale from 1 to 10, she rated her mood an 8 or 9 (10 is the positive end of the scale). She feels like a 1 or 2 when she worries about their financial situation. She reports occasional incontinence (urinary and fecal), in part because her stomach is upset so often. She denied any change in memory or thinking, or in language or motor functions. There are no sensory changes. She wears bifocal glasses.

Anne enjoys a social drink approximately once a week, and there is no history of blackouts or problem drinking. She has not smoked for the last ten years. She denied any experimentation with illicit substances.

Leisure interests include arts and crafts. She likes to knit. She also likes working with animals and has volunteered at an animal shelter in the past.

TEST RESULTS:

In the following section, test results are reported by area of functioning. A Summary and Recommendations section follows.

Activation and Attention:
On a computerized test of sustained attention (Vigil), Anne missed many of the uncued targets (63) and, due to slowed response times, she occasionally responded to incorrect targets (9). However, she improved steadily across the four trial blocks. On the cued trials, she missed fewer targets (16), and again improved across trials, but she had great difficulty initially establishing set. Thus, she responded to the cue instead of the target, but gradually got better. Response times on both conditions were significantly slower than expected. Mild perseveration was also apparent.

On visual scanning tasks, Anne was very systematic in her approach to the letter cancellation task and paused at the end to check her work. She made no errors. On the symbol scanning condition, she proceeded more randomly and did not check her work, but she completed both tasks in average time frames.

Working memory was assessed with span tasks and the Letter-Number Sequencing subtest of the WMS-III. On the Digit Span subtest, she recited 3 numbers forward (below 1st percentile) and 2 backward (also below 1st percentile). Spatial span was better, with a forward span of 4 and variably 5 (31st percentile), and the same backward (48th percentile). On the WAIS-III, she obtained a total Digit Span score at the 2nd percentile. Letter-Number Sequencing was below the 1st percentile. Arithmetic (another subtest that contributes to the Working Memory Index of the WAIS-III) was at the 1st percentile. It is clear that Anne has significant difficulties with respect to holding verbally based material in mind.

General Intellectual Ability:
On the WAIS-III, Anne obtained a Verbal IQ of 69 (below average) and a Performance IQ of 91 (average). This represents a significant difference. Based on this difference, a Full Scale IQ (in her case 77) would not be valid. Data for the IQ, Index, and subtest scores are presented at the end of the report.

Anne's best performance was on the Picture Arrangement subtest (50th percentile), which required her to place picture cards into a sequence to depict a story as quickly as possible. In general, she was able to understand and infer the motives of the characters and place them in a coherent sequence. Despite this relatively good performance on a task involving social understanding, she had great difficulty on the Comprehension subtest, which demands a more abstract, verbal understanding of social rules and laws (2nd percentile). Working memory, as described above, was another area of significant weakness. Processing speed was measured with a Symbol Search task (which required her to rapidly scan a row of symbols for targets presented on the left) and Digit Symbol-Coding (a speeded eye-hand coordination task that also relies on incidental learning and working memory). These subtests produced a Processing Speed Index score at the 21st percentile. The marked difference between her verbal and her visuospatial skills was also reflected in the (statistically significant) difference between her Perceptual Organization score at the 27th percentile and her Verbal Comprehension score at the 7th percentile.

Executive Functions:
On the Vigil CPT test, Anne took a while to firmly establish set on each condition, with demonstrated improvement over time. On the WCST, which required her to infer sorting rules for cards based on the examiner's yes/no feedback, she was able to complete only 4/6 sorts over 128 trials. She demonstrated inefficient use of feedback and perseverated on responses that were previously correct, even after the rules had changed.

She was able to describe the various dimensions the sorting rules were based on subsequently, but was not able to explain how the rules applied. Throughout the test, she was very quiet and thoughtful, hesitating and, at the last moment, occasionally moving her response to a different response pile. Thus, her difficulty appeared to lie in her ability to apply logic to the feedback she received and, thereby, correctly infer the appropriate response. She was not impulsive.

She scored at the 39th percentile on Trails A, where she had to connect numbers scattered on a page in sequence as rapidly as possible. She tended to be "pulled" to the nearest number, and made two (and almost three) errors this way. On the more challenging Trails B task, where she had to retain the set of alternating rapidly between numbers and letters in sequence, she scored in the below average range with respect to time (<1st percentile), and she had difficulty retaining set (she made three errors).

On the Stroop test, Anne was slow on both the Color Naming and Word Reading conditions (below average). On the Interference condition, she scored in the low average range for speed and made fewer errors than is typical. Since her word reading speed was barely faster (by 7 seconds) than her color naming, she may have experienced less interference on this task. Nonetheless, she was able to inhibit impulsively producing the word instead of the color when required to do so.

<u>Motor Functions</u>:
Anne is fully left-hand dominant. Family history is positive for only one other left-handed relative (a maternal uncle). On a screening for motor planning (praxis) she performed transitive and intransitive commands without difficulty, except for lack of extent bilaterally when demonstrating the use of a hammer. On a test of motor speed (Finger Tapping), she scored in the below average range bilaterally, with an average of 32 taps with the left hand and 28.5 with the right, thus demonstrating the expected 10% difference between dominant and nondominant hands.

<u>Visuospatial Functions</u>:
Based on the absence of perceptual errors on scanning and other tasks, gross visual acuity appears to be intact (eyes corrected with glasses). On the WAIS-III, the Perceptual Organization Index (27th percentile for her age) was her area of greatest strength, with her best performance on the Object Assembly subtest (a puzzle task). All performance subtest scores fell in the average range.

When asked to draw a clock, a daisy, and a house showing three-dimensional perspective, she set the time incorrectly on the clock (showing hands pointing to the 10 and 11 instead of the time of 11:10, as requested). Her daisy was unremarkable, and her house showed good three-dimensional perspective. She improved when provided with models by the examiner.

When asked to copy a complex geometric design, the Rey-Osterrieth Complex Figure (ROCF), she started (somewhat atypically) with the internal "star," bisecting horizontal, vertical, and diagonal lines; and proceeded to fill in the contour, and then the inner and outer details. Although she scored at the 63rd percentile (using the Denman [1984] norms), her copy contained several minor errors, usually involving duplication of features (e.g., drawing a separate line with cross-lines in addition to the bottom right diagonal). Placement and proportion were relatively good. Overall, her approach demonstrated planning and an appreciation of both global configuration and details.

Language and Academic Functions:
Speech was unremarkable. On a word fluency test (FAS), she produced fewer words in the time given than expected (F=6, A=4, S=8). Although she demonstrated the expected improvement with categories (animals =13, fruits and vegetables = 16), she had difficulty producing first names (7, where over 25 is typical). Her vocabulary was at the 2nd percentile on the WAIS-III. Her Verbal Comprehension Index was at the 7th percentile (low average), with her greatest strength (as years before) in identifying similarities between two words or concepts (Similarities, 25th percentile).

On the WRAT-3, Anne scored at the 3rd percentile on the Spelling subtest, with the first 13 words correctly spelled but with errors on almost all subsequent items. Errors often consisted of omitted syllables and phonologically unrecognizable neologisms. On a narrative writing sample, she produced fluent and grammatical sentences in beautiful script, with only periods missing. Content was descriptive of the picture she was given.

On the single word Reading subtest, she scored at the 25th percentile, with syllables omitted or added on the harder items. Her word attack strategy suggested that she has mastered certain (but not all) phonological decoding skills. On the Nelson-Denny test, she scored at the 37th percentile with respect to reading rate, but at the 6th percentile within standard time on the Comprehension subtest, and at the 7th percentile with an extra 12 minutes. She correctly responded to 11/20 questions in 20 minutes and 20/34 in 32 minutes (she did not have time to attempt the remaining 4 questions). Thus her scores appear to be a reflection of conceptual rather than speed of reading or phonological decoding difficulties.

On the Arithmetic subtest of the WRAT-3, Anne had great difficulty (< 1st percentile, which is consistent with previous testing). She can do simple addition and subtraction, but interprets multiplication signs as addition signs and she made errors on multi-digit subtraction. She did not attempt any division problems. This was consistent with her score on the aurally-presented math problems of the WAIS-III Arithmetic subtest.

Learning and Memory:
Incidental learning (Digit Symbol Incidental Learning from WAIS-III) was good (8/9 pairs retained without prior warning). Her recall of stories read aloud to her (WMS-III Logical Memory) fell in the average range (16th percentile on immediate recall and 25th percentile on delayed recall), with thematic scores at the 9th and 16th percentiles respectively. She demonstrated improvement on the second story (from a raw score of 9 to 12) when it was read twice. She misunderstood the first story as indicating that the woman was robbing the bank herself. She correctly answered 23/30 multiple choice questions.

On a word list learning task (CVLT), Anne recalled 7/16 words on the first trial (low average performance), but on subsequent trials her recall was variable, demonstrating inconsistent retrieval abilities. She went from 7 to 10, 9, 11, and 8 words, such that her performance on the fifth trial was in the seriously impaired range. She recalled 8/16 words on the interference list, and 10 and 13 of the words from the first list thereafter (spontaneously and then with cues), indicating that she did better after the interference than before! This again points to reasonably good encoding but variable retrieval of information. Anne is likely to appear better after hearing information just once than when she is expected to reproduce the information subsequently. Thus, she will do best in positions that do not rely on her memory. She retained 11 and 12 words on uncued and cued delayed recall and correctly recognized 14/16 words on recognition, with two false positives (one from the second list and one phonemically similar to a word on the first list).

Memory for visuospatial information was assessed with the ROCF. Both immediate and delayed recall were highly similar to her copy, and her scores fell in the above average range for her age (SS=15, 95th %ile, on each). Thus her memory for visual information, even fairly complex in nature, is quite good.

Personality Assessment:
Anne completed the 344-item Personality Assessment Inventory (PAI), with some inconsistencies in answers to similar questions. Thus caution

in interpreting the hypotheses and interpretations is warranted. Otherwise her protocol indicated that she answered in a forthright manner.

One clinical scale was significantly elevated, suggesting heightened activity and aspects of a manic episode. She may be somewhat over-committed to a large number of activities. Others may perceive her as demanding and impatient at times.

At the same time, she indicates that she is uncertain and indecisive about major life issues. She also acknowledges experiencing some degree of anxiety and stress, although this degree of worry falls in the normal range. Her interpersonal style seems friendly and extroverted, and she is able to communicate her interest in others in an open and straightforward manner. Nonetheless she experiences her level of social support as somewhat lower than that of the average adult. She may have relatively few close friends or be dissatisfied with the quality of some of her relationships.

Anger issues are important in treatment considerations, as aggressive behaviors appear to play a prominent role in the clinical picture. In general, she believes that she is in control of her anger and expresses angry feelings infrequently. When she does lose control of her anger, she is likely to respond with more extreme displays, including damage to property and threats to assault others. Some of these displays may be sudden and unexpected, as she may not display her anger readily when it is experienced.

SUMMARY AND RECOMMENDATIONS:

Anne Wilson is a 45-year-old Caucasian mother of two young children, who was referred for a neuropsychological assessment in order to obtain recommendations for vocational assistance. Anne comes from a family of high achievers, all of whom have college degrees and some of whom have advanced degrees. Anne's early history is remarkable for delays in language acquisition and early struggles in school. Her parents were active in providing extra tutoring, and Anne was not coded by the public school she attended until 12th grade. Since graduation Anne has successfully held a number of assembly jobs (e.g., assembling circuit boards and other electronic devices), which she enjoyed. Medical history is remarkable for thyroid difficulties (she has taken Synthroid for many years), and high blood pressure in the past. Mental status examination suggests recent stress (decreased appetite and libido, weight gain), probably related to her unemployment and strain on the family finances. Continued therapy to help her cope with these stresses is highly recommended.

Current testing indicates that there is a significant difference between Anne's verbal and performance abilities, with the former in the below average range and the latter in the average range. This difference extended to verbal working memory versus spatial working memory, and she had substantially greater difficulty on verbal memory tasks in general. Vocabulary, spelling, arithmetic, and understanding of verbally presented social situations (Comprehension subtest of WAIS-III) were below average. Motor speed is below average. In contrast, Anne drew very well and was able to produce a fluent and beautifully handwritten description of a picture. Her best performance was on the Object Assembly subtest of the WAIS-III, a puzzle task. Incidental learning was very good (her ability to retain information without being explicitly warned to do so). Retrieval of information after having heard and encoded it is less reliable.

Anne will do best in job situations similar to those involving assembly of component parts that she has already engaged in; she has also indicated an interest in working with animals. She will need extra learning trials in the beginning until she is able to establish consistent set, and will do best when the task is presented in chunks over time rather than in one detailed presentation. She learns with practice, and gets faster in the same way. She is also apt to do best on tasks where the expectations are made explicit in advance, and not left to be inferred.

DIAGNOSTIC IMPRESSION:

Axis I:
294.9 Cognitive Disorder NOS (verbal, executive, motor, and memory disorder)
315.1 Mathematics Disorder
315.2 Disorder of Written Expression (Spelling)

Axis II:
309.9 Adjustment Disorder

Axis III:
Thyroid disorder (treated with medication)

Axis IV:
Unemployment and financial stress

Axis V:
GAF = 70

____________________________________, PhD, ABPP
Board Certified in Clinical Neuropsychology

Summary of WAIS-III Scores

Verbal subtests	**Raw score**	**Scaled score**	**%ile**
Vocabulary	16	4	2
Similarities	19	8	25
Arithmetic	6	3	1
Digit Span	8	4	2
Information	9	6	9
Comprehension	10	4	2
Letter-Number Sequencing	2	2	<1
Performance subtests			
Picture Completion	20	9	37
Digit-Symbol Coding	63	8	25
Block Design	33	9	37
Matrix Reasoning	12	8	25
Picture Arrangement	14	10	50
Symbol Search	26	8	25
Object Assembly	37	11	63

	IQ	**%ile**	**CI* (95%ile)**	
Verbal	69	2	65-75	extreme low
Performance	91	27	85-98	low average
Full Scale	77	6	73-86	borderline
	Index	**%ile**	**CI (95%ile)**	
Verbal Comprehension	78	7	73-85	
Perceptual Organization	91	27	84-99	
Working Memory	57	<1	53-56	
Processing Speed	88	21	80-98	

*Confidence interval at the .05 chance level.

WAIS-III IQ and Index Scores

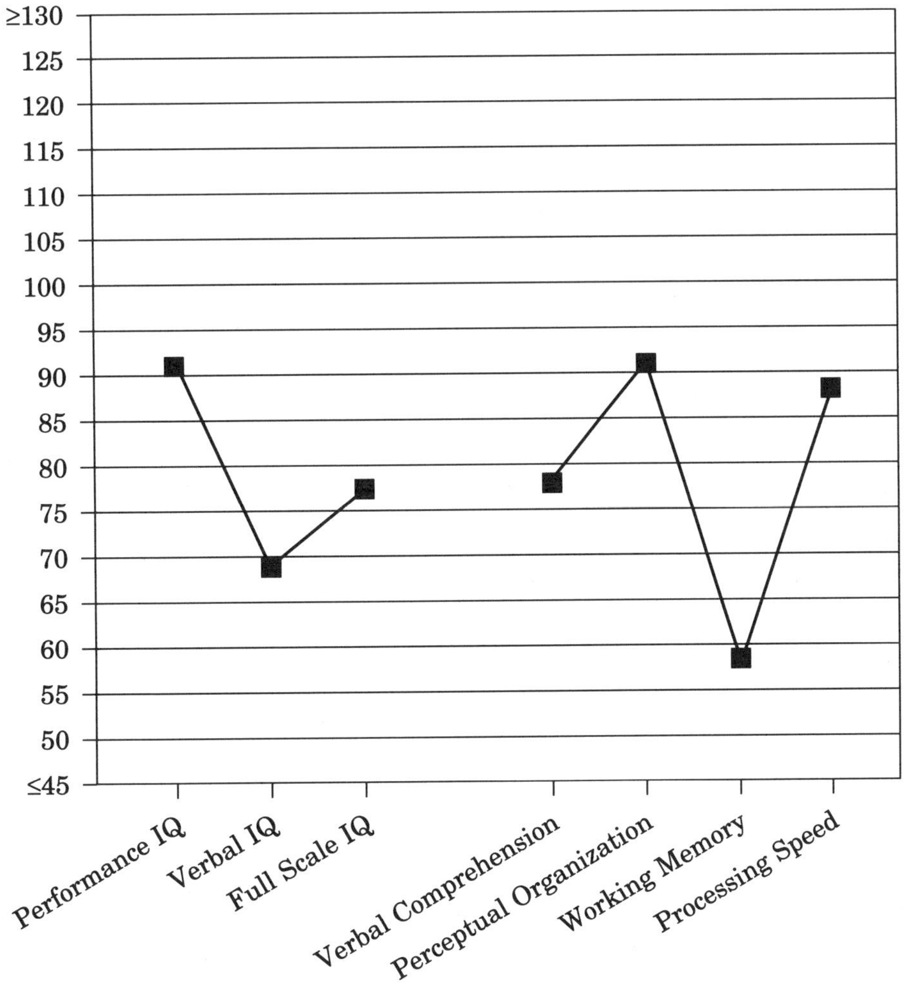

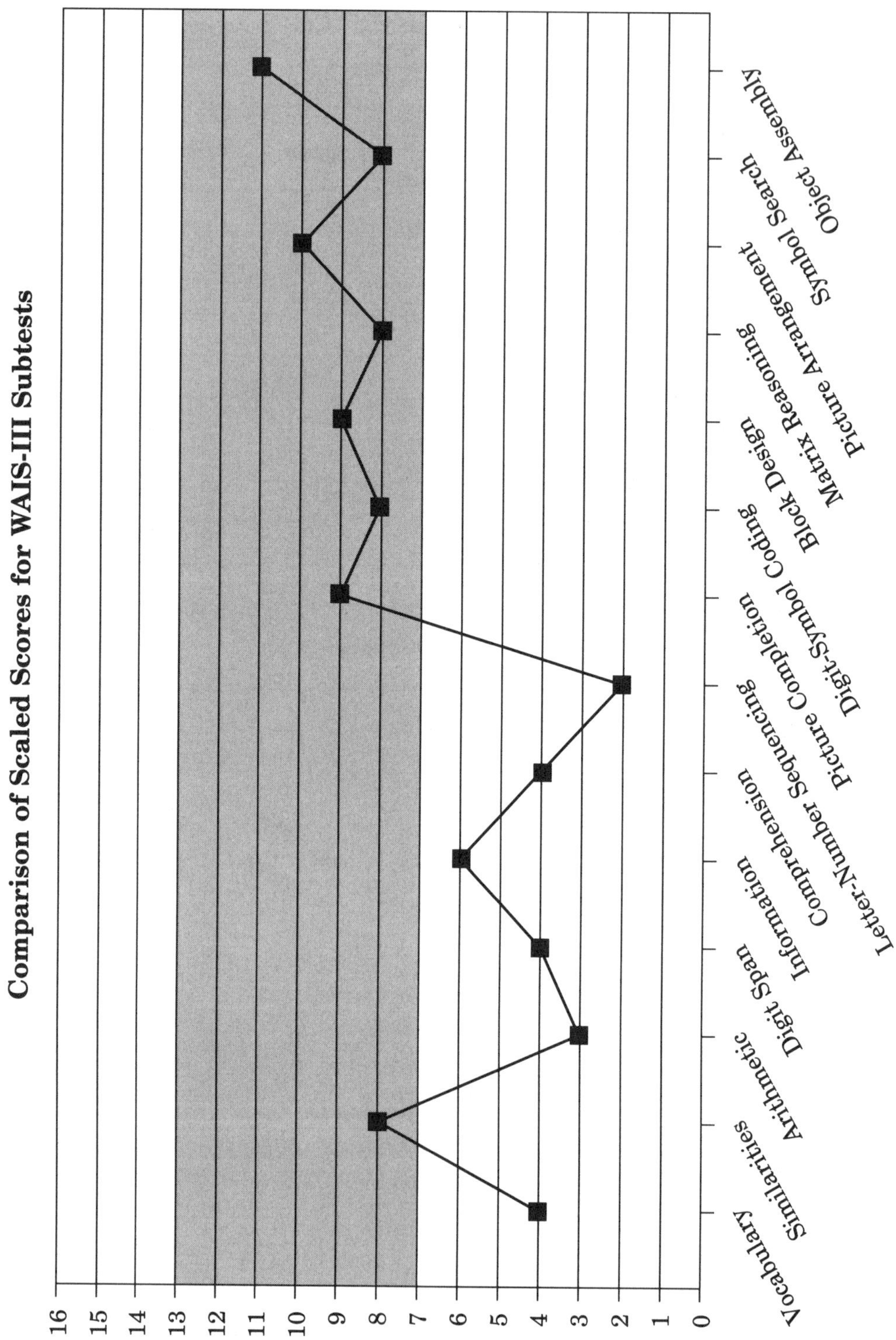
Comparison of Scaled Scores for WAIS-III Subtests
16
15
14
13
12
11
10
9
8
7
6
5
4
3
2
1
0
Vocabulary
Similarities
Arithmetic
Digit Span
Information
Comprehension
Letter-Number Sequencing
Picture Completion
Digit-Symbol Coding
Block Design
Matrix Reasoning
Picture Arrangement
Symbol Search
Object Assembly

Feedback Summary Report

Name: Anne M. Wilson
Date of Birth: 3/29/55
Date of Evaluation: 12/13/00 and 12/27/00
Age: 45 years
Referred by: Steven Amador, CRC
Examiner: ______________________, PhD, ABPP

Strengths

- Good performance ability – you are good at solving puzzles and putting things together.
- Good interpersonal ability

Weaknesses

- Poor verbal and math skills
- You need extra practice to learn new skills (that is, before you "get the hang of it")
- Memory is not great, especially for lists of things presented verbally

Recommendations

- You will do best in jobs where the expectations are clear and your supervisor knows that you may need extra help and practice in the beginning.
- A job coach would be helpful, especially in helping you to find a job and get started.
- Therapy should be continued as a means of talking through any difficulties you are experiencing at home or elsewhere.

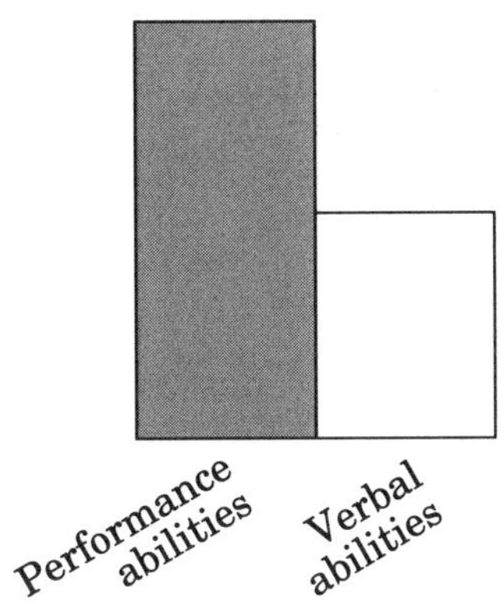

Comparison Reports: HMO Report Versus Comprehensive Outpatient Report

Two reports based on the same assessment illustrate the differences between a report prepared for an HMO environment and a more comprehensive version. The assessment concerns a young woman (Kim White) who was exposed to carbon monoxide fumes at the restaurant where she worked. In the HMO version, results are briefly summarized and scores are provided (in an appendix to the report) for comparison with other assessments as needed (see chapter 10). The emphasis is on brevity and on the immediate implications for future treatment.

A second, and more complete report of Ms. White's assessment is provided as a means of highlighting the strengths and weakness of each version. This second version has a longer narrative and provides significantly greater detail about test performance. The report spells out in narrative form a detailed description of test performance, and test scores are embedded in the body of the report. This is helpful in situations where the neuropsychologist needs to reconstruct the rationale or basis for the conclusions presented (in this case, in support of litigation). This is also important when retesting (either by oneself or by another neuropsychologist) is recommended, or for the benefit of other readers/consumers who wish to understand the process at that level of detail. For some non-neuropsychologists who need to make decisions about accommodations and/or compensation, this is considered critical information. In response to the debate about whether or not test scores should be included, we would argue that scores without explanation provide as high a risk for misinterpretation as conclusions without scores (see chapter 7 for an extensive discussion of this issue). For the reader of the report who does not wish to be immersed in this level of detail, a brief comment in the beginning of the Test Results section points the reader to the Summary and Recommendations section that follows.

HMO Report

Name: Kim White
Date of Birth: 7/16/63
Dates of Evaluation: 8/4, 8/14, and 8/24/00
Referred by: Dr. Jean Norman
Examiner: ______________________________, PhD, ABPP-CN

REASON FOR REFERRAL:
One year follow-up of the effects of carbon monoxide poisoning.

PROCEDURES:

Record review; history and mental status exam; visual cancellation tests; Paced Auditory Serial Addition Test (PASAT); auditory continuous performance tests (As and alphabet trails); verbal fluency (FAS and categories); Vigil (computerized continuous performance test); MicroCog (computerized test battery); Digit Span, Spatial Span, Faces, and Logical Memory subtests of the WMS-III; Shipley Hartford Institute of Living Scale; Block Design, Digit Symbol, and Matrix Reasoning subtests of the WAIS-III; Wisconsin Card Sorting Test (WCST); Stroop test; Trail Making A and B; Narrative Writing; Boston Naming Test (BNT); drawings to copy and command; California Verbal Learning Test (CVLT); Rey-Osterrieth Complex Figure Test (ROCF; copy, immediate and delayed recall, delayed recognition); Finger Tapping; Personality Assessment Inventory (PAI).

BEHAVIORAL OBSERVATIONS:

Ms. White is a 37-year-old, right-handed Japanese-American woman of slight build and stature who came in a timely fashion to her appointments. She has long dark hair and wore dark, casual and appropriate clothing. She was rather quiet in her demeanor, although she answered questions readily, choosing her words carefully and thoughtfully. She was unable to continue testing for sessions lasting longer than two hours, as she tended to fatigue. Prior to the second session she had had little sleep, having awakened during a seizure affecting her jaw, and shaking in half her body (she thought the left side, in contrast to the right, which is usually affected). She slept after this event, but came in feeling less refreshed. She requested and received a 45 minute break in the middle of the session, during which she had tea in a small room by herself while she relaxed. Overall she appeared serious and motivated to do her best on the tests, which are considered valid indices of her current optimal functioning.

HISTORY:

Ms. White is the youngest of four siblings who are all working professionals, married, with children. Birth and early childhood were unremarkable. She did well in school and completed a B.A. in English Literature. Following graduation she traveled in the South Pacific, eventually settling in Hawaii, marrying. She divorced after two and a half years, and on her return she spent several years working at a museum shop. Seeking to pursue a law degree, she quit her job and took part-time clerical jobs to support herself, but eventually left law school. Subsequently she worked for several years as a cataloguing assistant at a library. Finding herself bored and socially isolated, she eventually turned to waitressing and baking six mornings a week at a Japanese restaurant.

Two years into her job, she experienced headaches of increasing frequency and intensity (mostly left-sided), burning in her eyes, and visual hallucinations (consisting of bright stripes of color and, once, a "rat-like animal moved across the table"). She also had unpleasant episodes of being in a dream-like state, and began to have memory difficulties. Finally, it was discovered that carbon monoxide was leaking into the kitchen. She went to the ER the following day, and a carboxyhemoglobin level was done, but she was told it was too late for detection. An EEG (3/28/99) showed abnormalities in the temporal region similar to those observed in childhood petit mal, and an MRI done on the same day revealed "minimal white matter pathology in the periventricular and subcortical white matter and in the left external capsule region." She was referred for further assessment to Dr. Foley, who is currently following her for her seizures.

Family medical history is noncontributory. Past medical history is positive for mild hypothyroidism (for which she has taken Synthroid). In addition she had appendicitis at age 21, and was diagnosed with possible Crohn's Disease. Her X-rays are currently fine. She also sought help for mild depression in college, and off and on since then. She started seeing a new therapist, Dr. Naomi Wolf, last winter, following the carbon monoxide poisoning. Family history is positive for depression in her brother, requiring inpatient treatment for a year while he was in high school.

A neuropsychological assessment by Dr. Ris in June of 1999 revealed verbal problem-solving in the superior range, whereas she scored in the average range on several Performance tasks (in part because she dismissed certain correct responses as being too obvious). Difficulties in word fluency, naming, and in verbal as well as nonverbal learning and memory were found, consistent with left temporal involvement.

Ms. White reports that in the past year she has had spells up to five times a week, with the bad spells (occurring between once a month to once a week) resulting in significant fatigue. More frequently she experiences lighter spells with déjà vu and vibration of her jaw, and numbness to touch, again followed by fatigue. Since the spells started she has experienced fairly persistent left-sided headaches, which vary in severity, along with pain and stiffness in her hip and lower back. Appetite and weight are unchanged, despite occasional nausea episodes. While previously averaging eight hours, sleep now varies, with occasional nightmares. Mood is depressed (3 on a 10 point scale); she denies active suicidality but worries that she may get to that point. Difficulty articulating her emotional state was evident.

Ms. White noted that she is unable to multi-task effectively and that she currently burns things, whereas previously she was quite good at divided attention tasks and could track six different things baking at once. She has found it more difficult to concentrate on learning and complex issues, has noticed word-finding difficulties and, on the Phenobarbital, experienced increased clumsiness. She complains of being in a mental fog at times, and while having spells she also gets a sharp abdominal pain. She has experienced ringing in her right ear; a recent test indicated that she has a 20% conductive hearing loss in that ear. She has been told she may need a stapedectomy. No other sensory problems were reported; her sense of smell is unchanged, and vision is good.

Ms. White has been on several medications for her seizures. First she was on Phenobarbital from April '99 to November '99, then briefly on Tranzene, then Neurontin (which worsened her headaches). She will try a different version of Neurontin now that her assessment has been completed in the hope that it will have fewer side effects. At the time of assessment she was taking only Pepcid for her stomach and an occasional Tylenol.

SUMMARY OF FINDINGS:

Current testing was consistent with prior testing in documenting intact reasoning ability (she scored in the high average to superior range on the Shipley), although her speed of information processing is considerably slower than expected (MicroCog). At this time Ms. White continues to demonstrate the reduced endurance for sustained effort and the fatigue that was observed a year ago. Although she did not cancel any testing sessions, she did require significant breaks and the sessions had to be limited to two hours maximum in length.

Overall, Ms. White's activation level and ability to attend and respond to information over limited periods of time (approximately twenty to thirty minutes) is intact (Vigil CPT), although she approaches tasks carefully and slowly, and appears to be relatively better on auditory than visual tasks. Mental manipulation of visual information (spatial span; average range) was also less proficient than of verbal information (digit span; superior range). Errors on a visual scanning task occurred in the upper right quadrant, which is consistent with left temporal lobe involvement.

Mental control is good, as judged by above average performance on tasks of divided attention (PASAT; span backward). Executive functions, including the ability to inhibit responses, to establish, maintain, and shift set on tasks, and to use feedback to modify responses were all unremarkable (WCST; verbal fluency; Stroop; Trails A and B).

Motor speed (Finger Tapping) was significantly slower with the right hand, which is consistent with her scores a year ago. At that time she attributed her pattern to tendonitis and carpal tunnel problems. While these may be continuing problems, she did not complain of them at this time, and the persistence of the pattern of results, together with some difficulties in the ability to sequence and plan motor acts (praxis), suggests ongoing dysfunction of the left motor area.

Speech production and comprehension were normal. Reading and writing were unremarkable. Verbal fluency (25th percentile on letter tasks, and 5th percentile on semantic categories) continues to be an area of weakness, with relatively little improvement noted since last year. In the context of her strengths in the verbal area, her naming problems a year ago indicates that she could do better before her toxic exposure. While no errors of approximation (paraphasias) on a naming task were observed this time (as opposed to last year), her current lower score constitutes continued difficulty and possibly even a mild decrease in functioning.

Incidental learning was impaired for both verbal and nonverbal material (Digit Symbol Incidental Learning; ROCF). Memory for stories and for a word list was intact, and her working memory (digit span) was above average. Although her ability to recognize faces was average, difficulty in recalling a complex figure was observed (specifically, in her ability to recall details), indicating impairment in her ability to retrieve nonverbal information. This is consistent with her performance a year ago.

On the Personality Assessment Inventory, Ms. White responded consistently and somewhat defensively. The profile was remarkable for preoccupation with health issues, and reflected mild depression. More specifically, she reported experiencing occasional and transient thoughts of self-harm, and is undoubtedly unhappy and pessimistic about the future. Her responses revealed notable stress and she experiences her level of social support as somewhat lower than that of the average adult. Ms. White's self-concept appears to be reasonably stable and self-confident and her assertiveness, friendliness, and concern for others are typical for normal adults.

CONCLUSIONS:

Ms. White continues to demonstrate significantly reduced verbal fluency, incidental learning, retrieval of visual details, and generally slowed information processing. Errors on a scanning test indicate inattention to the right upper quadrant, which is consistent with left temporal involvement. Right motor speed continues to be significantly slower than expected, and she demonstrates difficulties with motor planning. Fatigue continues to be a major factor, limiting the amount of time she can perform effortful tasks to two or three hours, and her mood is depressed. This pattern of deficits suggests subcortical involvement in addition to specific left temporal lobe dysfunction.

RECOMMENDATIONS:

- Continued therapy with Dr. Wolf for emotional support and to address and monitor Ms. White's level of depression. Anti-depressant medication is recommended. Given her level of social isolation, group therapy may also be quite helpful. Dr. Hurlihey at City Hospital runs such a group, and I would be happy to make a referral.

- Fatigue and symptoms related to seizure disorder are the greatest barriers to Ms. White's current ability to work. Her cognitive profile reflects many strengths that would otherwise enable her to find meaningful and challenging work. While it is unlikely that she will be able to function successfully in a job setting at this time, she should be encouraged to participate in rewarding and mentally stimulating activities (e.g., acquiring computer skills, or enrolling in continuing education courses) that can be performed in short spurts of time lasting up to an hour or two on a daily basis, in order to provide a measure of structure and purpose to her day.

- Ms. White might find it helpful to work with a vocational counselor and/or her therapist to explore and clarify her future occupational goals and interests, and if possible to come up with a specific plan to pursue in this regard, while taking into account her current limitations. A referral to the State Rehabilitation Agency would enable her to obtain such counseling and put her in contact with other vocational services that they provide.

- Ms. White will continue to be followed by Dr. Foley for her neurological issues, in particular her seizure disorder.

- Repeat testing in nine months to a year will help to clarify her status and ability to re-engage in competitive employment at that time.

DIAGNOSTIC IMPRESSION:

Axis I:
300.4 Dysthymia
296.3 Major Depression, mild to moderate, without psychotic features
294.9 Cognitive Disorder due to toxic exposure

Axis II:
V71.09 No diagnosis or condition

Axis III:
Seizure disorder due to carbon monoxide exposure; mild hypothyroidism (per records); mild conductive hearing loss in the right ear; h/o possible Crohn's Disease.

Axis IV:
Stress related to medical problems, cognitive difficulties, social isolation, and unemployment.

Axis V:
GAF current = 50 (serious symptoms)

____
Board Certified in Clinical Neuropsychology

Summary of Scores

NAME: Kim White
DOB: 7/16/63
Age: 37 years
Education: 16 years
DOE: 8/4, 8/14, and 8/24/00

ACTIVATION AND ATTENTION:

Vigil Continuous Performance Task:

	Uncued (K) Scores	%ile
Time:	376.55 (*M*=416.64, *SD*=42.68)	63
Omissions:	0 (*M*= .58, *SD*=1.15)	63
Commissions:	1 (*M*=1.62, *SD*=1.9)	75

Microcog:

Information Processing Speed: SS=82, 12 %ile

Cancellation Test:

	Time	Omission Errors
Unstructured letters:	142 sec (*M*=81, *SD*=22)	3
Unstructured symbols:	95 sec (*M*=55.9, *SD*= 13.8)	0

Paced Auditory Serial Addition Test:

3 sec: 95% correct, WNL
2 sec: 91.5% correct, WNL

Span Tests:

Microcog Numbers Forward:	SS=8, 25 %ile
Microcog Numbers Backward:	SS=9, 38 %ile
Microcog Tic Tac:	SS=7, 16 %ile

WMS-III: Digit Span Forward:	7,	Raw Score=11, 94 %ile
WMS-III: Digit Span Backward:	5,	Raw Score=10, 92 %ile
WMS-III: Visual Span Forward:	6,	Raw Score=11, 94 %ile
WMS-III: Visual Span Backward:	4,	Raw Score= 7, 48 %ile

WAIS-III:

Digit Symbol: SS=12, 75 %ile

GENERAL INTELLECTUAL ABILITY:

Shipley Institute of Living Scale:
94 %ile (Estimated WAIS-R FSIQ = 118, 88 %ile)
Vocabulary: 92 %ile
Abstract Reasoning: 93 %ile

WAIS-III Matrix Reasoning: 95 %ile (SS=15)

Microcog:
General Cognitive Functioning: SS=91, 27 %ile
General Cognitive Proficiency: SS=91, 27 %ile

	Speed	Accuracy
Analogies	5 %ile (SS=5)	91 %ile (SS=14)
Object Match A	9 %ile (SS=6)	50 %ile (SS=10)
Object Match B	75 %ile (SS=12)	84 %ile (SS=13)

EXECUTIVE FUNCTIONS:

Trail Making Tests: A: 20 sec, 62 %ile; B: 67 sec, 38 %ile

WCST: Age and education corrected norms (R. Heaton & PAR Staff, 1990)

	Raw Score	SS	*T* Score	%ile
Trials administered	76			
Total Correct	69			
Total errors	7	106	54	66
Perseverative responses	4	104	53	61
Perseverative errors	4	104	53	61
Nonperseverative errors	3	106	54	66
Conceptual level responses	69	109	56	73
Categories completed	6			>16
Trials to complete 1st category	17			6-10
Failure to maintain set	1			>16
Learning to learn	-0.49			>16

Stroop:

	Time	Errors	Errors (self-corrected)
Color Naming:	54 sec (*M*=62.1, *SD*=12), 63 %ile	0 (*M*=0.5, *SD*=.8)	0
Word Reading:	38 sec (*M*=45, *SD*=6.7), 63 %ile	0 (*M*=1.4, *SD*=1.5)	0
Interference:	123 sec (*M*=109.4, *SD*=29.5), 25 %ile	0 (*M*=3.5, *SD*=2.9)	1

LANGUAGE FUNCTIONS:

Word Fluency:

FAS Total=45 (*M*=50.1, *SD*=6.4), 25 %ile
Animals=15 (*M*=23.4, *SD*=4.9), 5 %ile
F=19 (*M*=17.2, *SD*=5), A=11 (*M*=14.5, *SD*=4), S=15 (*M*=18.4, *SD*=4)
Fruits & Vegetables=23
First Names=24

Boston Naming Test:
57/60 (*M*=56.6, *SD*=2.84), 50 %ile

MOTOR FUNCTIONS:

Finger Tapping:
Right Hand: 40.6 taps/10 sec, SS=6, 11 %ile
Left Hand: 43.8 taps/10 sec, SS=9, 50 %ile

LEARNING AND MEMORY:

Digit Symbol Incidental Learning:
Raw Score= 4, 2 %ile

Rey-Osterrieth Complex Figure: (Denman [1984] norms)

Immediate Recall:	SS=5,	5 %ile
Delayed Recall:	SS=4,	2 %ile

California Verbal Learning Test:

	Raw Score	%ile
Trial 1	12	98
Trial 5	15	50
List B	11	84
Immediate Free Recall	11	16
Immediate Cued Recall	14	50
Delayed Free Recall	15	84
Delayed Cued Recall	15	50
Delayed Recognition	16	50
Delayed Recognition False Positives	0	50
WMS-III Memory for Faces:		
I	42	91
II	41	75

Comprehensive Outpatient Report

Name: Kim White
Date of Birth: 7/16/63
Dates of Evaluation: 8/4, 8/14, and 8/24/00
Referred by: Dr. Jean Norman
Examiner: ______________________, PhD, ABPP-CN

REASON FOR REFERRAL:

Kim White is a 37-year-old divorced, Japanese-American, right-handed woman who was exposed to carbon monoxide that was leaking into a restaurant over an undefined period of time while she was working there. She developed seizures and a variety of other symptoms as a result of her exposure and stopped working on March 25, 1999. This reevaluation was recommended when she was seen for a neuropsychological evaluation a year ago. She is currently off her seizure medication, and is about to restart with a different medication (a new form of gabapentin).

PROCEDURES:

Record review; history and mental status exam; visual cancellation tests; Paced Auditory Serial Addition Test (PASAT); auditory continuous performance tests (As and Alphabet Trails); verbal fluency (FAS and categories); Vigil (computerized continuous performance test); MicroCog (computerized test battery); Digit Span, Visual Span, Faces, and Logical Memory subtests of the Wechsler Memory Scale-III (WMS-III); Shipley Hartford Institute of Living Scale; Block Design, Digit Symbol, and Matrix Reasoning subtests of the Wechsler Adult Intelligence Scale-III (WAIS-III); Wisconsin Card Sorting Test (WCST); Stroop Test; Trail Making Tests A and B; Narrative Writing; Boston Naming Test (BNT); drawings to copy and command; California Verbal Learning Test (CVLT); Rey-Osterrieth Complex Figure Test (ROCF; copy, immediate and delayed recall, delayed recognition); Finger Tapping; Personality Assessment Inventory (PAI).

BEHAVIORAL OBSERVATIONS:

Ms. White is a woman of slight build and stature who came in a timely fashion to her appointments. She has long dark hair and wore dark, casual and appropriate clothing. She was rather quiet in her demeanor, although she answered questions readily, choosing her words carefully and thoughtfully. She was unable to continue testing for sessions lasting longer than two hours, as she tended to fatigue. Prior to the second session she had had little sleep, having awakened during a seizure affecting her jaw, and shaking in half her body (she thought the left side, in contrast to the right, which is usually affected). She slept after this event, but came in feeling less refreshed. She requested and received a 45-minute break in the middle of the session, during which she had tea in a small room by herself while she relaxed. Overall she appeared serious and motivated to do her best on the tests, which are considered valid indices of her current optimal functioning.

HISTORY:

Ms. White is the youngest of four siblings. Her father (age 78) is a retired eye surgeon with insulin-dependent diabetes but otherwise good health, who separated from her mother (age 73), when Ms. White was nine years old. Her mother is currently a part-time accountant (she has mild hypertension). Her siblings are all working professionals, married, with children.

Delivery was difficult due to the fact that she lay in a transverse position, with no reported complications at birth. She thought she might have been early in attaining various developmental milestones. She denied any early injuries or medical problems growing up. She did well in school, skipping the third grade. After high school Ms. White attended The University of California in Santa Barbara, graduating with a degree in English Literature. Following graduation she traveled in the South Pacific, eventually settling in Hawaii, and marrying a Japanese cook. They divorced after two and a half years, and on her return she spent several years working at a museum shop. Seeking to pursue a law degree, she quit her job and took part-time jobs to support herself, but eventually left law school. Subsequently she worked for several years as a cataloguing assistant at a library. Finding herself bored and socially isolated, she eventually turned to waitressing and baking six mornings a week at a Japanese restaurant.

Two years into her job she experienced headaches of increasing frequency and intensity (mostly left-sided), burning in her eyes, and visual hallucinations (consisting of bright stripes of color and, once, a "rat-like animal moved across the table"). She also had unpleasant episodes of being in a dream-like state, and began to have memory difficulties. She had smelled gasses in the kitchen and knew there was poor ventilation, but was unaware of how toxic this was. Finally, it was discovered that carbon monoxide was leaking into the kitchen. She went to the ER the following day, and a carboxyhemoglobin level was done, but she was told it was too late for detection. Based on the burning eyes and throat it was thought that she might have been exposed to sewer gasses as well, and was referred to a neurologist, Dr. Martin, who reports that an EEG (3/28/99) showed abnormalities in the temporal region similar to those observed in childhood petit mal, and that an MRI done on the same day revealed "minimal white matter pathology in the periventricular and subcortical white matter and in the left external capsule region." She was referred for further assessment to Dr. Foley, who is currently following her for her seizures.

Past medical history is positive for mild hypothyroidism (for which she has taken Synthroid). In addition she had appendicitis at age 21, and was diagnosed with possible Crohn's Disease. Her X-rays are currently fine. She also sought help for mild depression in college, and off and on since then. She started seeing a new therapist, Dr. Naomi Wolf, last winter, following the carbon monoxide poisoning. Family history is positive for depression in her brother, requiring inpatient treatment for a year while he was in high school.

A neuropsychological assessment by Dr. Ris in June of 1999 revealed verbal problem-solving in the superior range, whereas she scored in the average range on several Performance tasks (in part because she dismissed certain correct responses as being too obvious). Difficulties in word fluency, naming, and in verbal as well as nonverbal learning and memory were found, consistent with left temporal involvement.

Ms. White reports that in the past year she has had spells up to five times a week, with the bad spells (occurring between once a month to once a week) resulting in significant fatigue. More frequently she experiences lighter spells with déjà vu and vibration of her jaw, and numbness to touch, again followed by fatigue. Since the spells started she has experienced fairly persistent left-sided headaches, which vary in severity, along with pain and stiffness in her hip and lower back. Appetite and weight are unchanged, despite occasional nausea episodes. While previously averaging eight hours, sleep now varies, with occasional nightmares. Mood is depressed (3 on a 10 point scale); she denies active suicidality but worries that she may get to that point. Difficulty articulating her emotional state was evident.

Ms. White noted that she is unable to multi-task effectively, and that she currently burns things, whereas previously she was quite good at divided attention tasks and could track six different things baking at once. She has found it more difficult to concentrate on learning and complex issues, and has noticed word-finding difficulties and, on the Phenobarbital, experienced increased clumsiness. She complains of being in a mental fog at times, and while having spells she also gets a sharp abdominal pain. She has experienced ringing in her right ear; a recent test indicated that she has a 20% conductive hearing loss in that ear. She has been told she may need a stapedectomy. No other sensory problems were reported; her sense of smell is unchanged, and vision is good.

Ms. White has been on several medications for her seizures. First she was on Phenobarbital from April '99 to November '99, then briefly on Tranzene, then Neurontin (which worsened her headaches). She will try a different version of Neurontin now that her assessment has been completed in the hope that it will have fewer side effects. At the time of assessment she was taking only Pepcid for her stomach and an occasional Tylenol.

TEST RESULTS:

In the following section, results are reported by area of cognitive functioning. A Summary and Recommendations section with diagnostic impressions follows.

Activation and Attention:
On an uncued computerized continuous performance test (Vigil), Ms. White scored well within the normal range with respect to both time to react and errors. On another computerized set of tasks (MicroCog), her reaction times on a simple reaction time subtest (Timers) fell in the superior range on auditory reaction time tasks and in the average range on visual reaction time tasks. However, her information processing speed across the board fell in the low average range (12th percentile) compared to others of her age who have more than a high school education. Accuracy on the same tasks fell in the average range. Thus when she is aware of the need to respond rapidly she is generally able to mobilize, but otherwise she tends to process information more slowly than expected.

On a visual cancellation test, Ms. White was systematic in her approach on both conditions (letters and symbols), but took a long time to check her work (impaired range). She still missed three letter targets (within normal limits, but they were in the top right quadrant, which is consistent with left temporal involvement).

On an auditory continuous performance task presented by tape, Ms. White correctly identified all targets both on the A condition and on the more challenging Alphabet Trails condition.

Mental control was assessed by means of span tasks and the PASAT, a divided attention task. On the latter she scored at the 95th percentile on the 3 seconds condition and at the 91.5 percentile on the 2 seconds condition.

On the span tests, Ms. White scored in the high average range on all but visual span backward, where she scored in the average range (48th percentile). There was little variability. Her scores are consistent with her performance a year ago, and demonstrate intact working memory. On the MicroCog computerized test she also did well on the visually presented digit span test, but she was in the low average range with respect to accuracy and response time on simultaneous visual span (Tic Tac).

Overall, Ms. White's activation level and ability to attend and respond to information over time is intact, although she approaches tasks carefully and slowly, and appears to be relatively better on auditory than visual tasks. Mental control is good.

General Intellectual Ability:
Ms. White obtained a score at the 92nd percentile on the Vocabulary subtest of the Shipley Institute of Living Scale and at the 93rd percentile on the Abstract Reasoning subtest, resulting in a total score at the 94th percentile (high average). This corresponds to an estimated WAIS-R FSIQ of 118, although this is likely (due to the psychometric properties of the test) to be an under-estimate. On the untimed, nonverbal Matrix Reasoning subtest of the WAIS-III she scored at the 95th percentile, despite her complaint of feeling very tired on this test (she took a break immediately afterwards). These scores are consistent with her performance of a year ago, and her educational history.

On the Analogies subtest (MicroCog), Ms. White obtained a total score in the superior range, but her response times fell in the below average range. A similar pattern was observed on the nonverbal Object Match subtest, where she had to indicate two different ways in which three out of four objects were alike. While her scores fell in the average range, her response time fell in the low average range initially (she improved and scored in the superior range subsequently, presumably because she had solved both aspects of the problem in the beginning). Thus, while she may be slower than expected on certain tests, her actual reasoning skills appear to have been unaffected.

Executive Functions:
Ms. White had no difficulty establishing, maintaining, or shifting set on tasks. Thus she scored in the average range on a task requiring her to simply sequence numbers on a page rapidly (Trail Making Test A, 62nd percentile) and then to alternate rapidly between numbers and letters in sequence (Trail Making Test B, 38th percentile). These scores are roughly comparable to her performance last year.

On a task that measures one's ability to inhibit responses (the Stroop test), she scored in the average range on all three conditions with respect to time and made only one self-corrected error on the interference condition, thus demonstrating both intact ability to inhibit as well as good self-monitoring.

On the WCST, a card-sorting test she had been administered last year, Ms. White again did very well. However her attention was momentarily diverted and she lost set briefly at one point (as she did a year ago). Nonetheless, her ability to infer the rules based on feedback, and to monitor and alter her responses appropriately, was intact. She was easily able to articulate what the rules were.

Planning was assessed by asking her to draw a clock, copy a complex figure, and write a brief description of a picture. She failed to number her clock by quadrants, which resulted in skewed numbers with irregular spaces; nor did she change her strategy after observing the examiner's approach on copy. Her copy of the Rey-Osterrieth Complex Figure, on the other hand, was carefully planned and accurate, perhaps because she saw this task as more challenging and, therefore, was more careful in her approach. Her approach to the narrative description of the picture (the Cookie Theft) was straightforward and rather descriptive, but captured the fact that the characters depicted were inattentive to the circumstances they were in. Overall, executive skills appear to be quite intact.

Motor Functions:
Ms. White is fully right hand dominant and there is no family history of sinistrality. On praxis items she had no difficulty with buccofacial commands, but her angle was off bilaterally on a transitive command. On a test of motor speed (finger tapping) she scored at the 11th percentile with the dominant right hand (RS = 40.6) and at the 50th percentile with the left hand (RS = 43.8). This finding is consistent with her scores a year ago, although at that time she reported "a little carpal tunnel and tendonitis, especially on the right." Thus the significance of her worse performance with the right hand is unclear. On the Digit Symbol subtest of the WAIS-III, a test of eye-hand motor speed, she scored at the 75th percentile.

Visuospatial Functions:
Gross acuity appears to be intact, judging from the absence of false positives on scanning tasks and the absence of perceptual errors. There was no indication of significant hemi-neglect, although her errors tended to occur in the upper right quadrant. Perception of angles was intact, as indicated by her average performance on the clock drawing subtest of MicroCog.

Ms. White's drawings were easily recognizable and relatively unremarkable; her attempt at three-dimensional perspective for the house, while not 100% successful, was nonetheless adequate, and probably represents mild improvement over her attempt a year ago. On clock drawing, she correctly rendered the time requested without difficulty, correctly placing the hour and minute hands (in contrast to her attempt a year ago). Drawings to copy for the same figures were unremarkable. Her copy of the Rey-Osterrieth figure was correct and she approached it in terms of the basic structure first.

Linguistic Functions:
Speech and comprehension were unremarkable. On a verbal fluency task, she hesitated on one letter (A), producing only one word in the first fifteen seconds, and scoring at the 25th percentile (F = 19, A = 11, S = 15). When asked to produce categorical exemplars she initially did quite poorly (15 animals, 5th percentile), without producing any items during the last fifteen seconds. She managed to improve considerably on the next two categories, producing 23 fruits and vegetables and 24 first names (average to low average). Overall, her ability to generate words is significantly lower than expected, particularly in the context of her predilection for languages and her good vocabulary. These results are similar to those obtained a year ago, and suggest that this is an ongoing area of difficulty.

On the Boston Naming Test, she correctly identified 57/60 items, with three items that she could describe but indicated that she didn't know the specific name for (and could not name with semantic or phonemic cues). Unlike last year, no semantic or paraphasic errors occurred; however, last year she was able to name 59/60 items with phonemic cues, indicating that she knew all but one of the words.

Narrative writing was straightforwardly descriptive of the picture she was given (the Cookie Theft from the BDAE). Her handwriting was legible and cursive, as requested, and she made only one minor self-correction. Her production was neat, and lines were straight. Overall her writing was within normal limits. Reading was also intact, as indicated by her ability to proceed without difficulty on written tasks such as the Shipley and the Personality Assessment Inventory. Reading speed on the MicroCog test was average.

Learning and Memory:
Incidental learning was assessed for verbal material with the Digit Symbol subtest of the WAIS-III. On this measure, she retained only 2/9 pairs on free recall and four unmatched symbols (impaired).

On a word list learning test (the CVLT), Ms. White demonstrated improvement relative to her performance a year ago. She recalled 12/16 words after the first trial (despite relatively little semantic clustering, but with a normal primacy and recency effect), a performance in the superior range. Thus, word span is consistent with her good digit span. After five trials, she recalled 15/16 words (average), with steady improvement across each trial. On a second list, she scored in the above average range (11/16 words), but on short delay recall of the first list could only produce 11 words, a performance in the low average range. With semantic cuing, she improved to 14/16 words (average), with one intrusion from the second list, and after a filled delay of twenty minutes she recalled an additional item, bringing her recall to 15 words (above average). She did not improve further with cues, as she had already organized the words by category, but on delayed recognition she correctly identified all of the words from the first list and made no false positive or source recall errors (a normal performance).

Memory for stories presented on the MicroCog computerized battery fell in the above average range on immediate multiple choice, and in the average range after a delay. This task differs from word list recall in that the material is organized for the respondent and the retrieval demands are minimized with a multiple choice task.

Memory for nonverbal material was assessed by means of the Rey-Osterrieth figure, which she was first asked to copy, and her ability to recognize faces (Faces subtest of the WMS-III). As indicated above, her approach to the copy of the ROCF reflected good planning and was an accurate representation. Difficulties became apparent on immediate and delayed recall, which were almost identical. In both instances, she produced a base rectangle with diagonal and horizontal crossing lines. The diamond on the right was suspended from a line hanging diagonally from the lower right corner. No details other than the circle with dots were provided. Thus, her recall on both occasions reflected significant failure to retrieve information. On multiple choice delayed recall, she correctly identified the original figure, remembering the details when they were before her. Thus, her primary difficulty appeared to stem from a retrieval rather than an encoding deficit. Retrieval deficits for nonverbal details are usually associated with left hemisphere involvement.

Recognition of faces, both immediately and after a filled delay was intact, with a score in the high average range on immediate forced choice recognition (91st percentile) and in the average range (75th percentile) on delayed recognition. This good performance is another indication that encoding is intact, whereas her ability to freely recall visual information is impaired.

Personality Assessment:
On the 344-item Personality Assessment Inventory (PAI), Ms. White responded consistently to the questions. However, her profile indicated a tendency to minimize any common shortcomings to which most individuals readily admit, suggesting a level of defensiveness that may have resulted in an under-representation of any difficulties that she experiences. Her profile was characterized by a pronounced elevation on one clinical scale, indicating an unusual degree of preoccupation with physical functioning and health matters. This, in the context of her actual symptoms, would seem to be a reasonable and predictable response. Symptoms consistent with relatively mild or transient depression were also reported. More specifically, she reported experiencing occasional and transient thoughts of self-harm, and is undoubtedly unhappy and pessimistic about the future. (This is consistent with her report during the history, although at that time she denied any active suicidal intent, but worried that she might eventually get to that point.) Her responses reveal notable stress, and she experiences her level of social support as somewhat lower than that of the average adult.

Ms. White's self-concept appears to be reasonably self-confident and her assertiveness, friendliness, and concern for others are typical for normal adults. Her responses indicate that she sees herself as more wary and sensitive in interpersonal relationships than others, whereas others may perceive her as tough-minded and skeptical.

SUMMARY:

Current testing was consistent with prior testing in documenting intact reasoning ability, although her speed of information processing is considerably slower than expected. At this time, Ms. White continues to demonstrate the reduced endurance for sustained effort and fatigue that was observed a year ago. Although she did not cancel any testing sessions, she did require significant breaks and the sessions had to be limited to two hours maximum in length.

Overall, Ms. White's activation level and ability to attend and respond to information over limited periods of time (approximately twenty to thirty minutes) is intact, although she approaches tasks carefully and slowly, and appears to be relatively better on auditory than visual tasks. Mental manipulation of visual information (spatial span; average range) was also less proficient than of verbal information (digit span; superior range). Errors on a visual scanning task occurred in the upper right quadrant, which is consistent with left temporal lobe involvement.

Mental control is good, as judged by above average performance on tasks of divided attention. Executive functions, including the ability to inhibit responses, to establish, maintain, and shift set on tasks, and to use feedback to modify responses were all unremarkable.

Motor speed was significantly slower with the right hand, which is consistent with her scores a year ago. At that time, she attributed her pattern to tendonitis and carpal tunnel problems. Although these may be continuing problems, she did not complain of them at this time, and the persistence of the pattern of results, together with some difficulties in the ability to sequence and plan motor acts (praxis), suggests ongoing dysfunction of the left motor area.

Speech production and comprehension were normal. Reading and writing were unremarkable. Verbal fluency continues to be an area of weakness, with relatively little improvement noted since last year. In the context of her strengths in the verbal area, her naming problems a year ago indicate that she would have done better before her toxic exposure. Although no errors of approximation (paraphasias) on a naming task were observed this time (as opposed to last year), her current lower score constitutes continued difficulty and possibly even a mild decrease in functioning.

Incidental learning (i.e., recall of material presented without express expectation to memorize) was impaired for both verbal and nonverbal material. Memory for stories and for a word list was intact, and her working memory was above average. Although her ability to recognize faces was average, difficulty in recalling a complex figure was observed, indicating impairment in her ability to retrieve nonverbal details. This is consistent with her performance a year ago.

On the Personality Assessment Inventory, Ms. White responded consistently and somewhat defensively. The profile was remarkable for preoccupation with health issues, and reflected mild depression. More specifically, she reported experiencing occasional and transient thoughts of self-harm, and is undoubtedly unhappy and pessimistic about the future. Her responses revealed notable stress and she experiences her level of social support as somewhat lower than that of the average adult. Ms. White's self-concept appears to be reasonably stable and self-confident and her assertiveness, friendliness, and concern for others are typical for normal adults.

In sum, Ms. White continues to demonstrate significantly reduced verbal fluency, incidental learning, retrieval of visual information, and generally slowed speed of information processing. Errors on a scanning test indicate inattention to the right upper quadrant, which is consistent with left temporal involvement. Right motor speed continues to be significantly slower than expected, and she demonstrates difficulties with motor planning. Fatigue continues to be a major factor, limiting the amount of time she can perform effortful tasks to two or three hours, and her mood is depressed. This pattern of deficits suggests subcortical involvement in addition to specific left temporal lobe dysfunction.

RECOMMENDATIONS:

- Continued therapy with Dr. Wolf for emotional support and to address and monitor Ms. White's level of depression. Anti-depressant medication is recommended. Given her level of social isolation, group therapy may also be quite helpful. Dr. Hurlihey at City Hospital runs such a group, and I would be happy to make a referral.
- Fatigue and symptoms related to seizure disorder are the greatest barriers to Ms. White's current ability to work. Her cognitive profile reflects many strengths that would otherwise enable her to find meaningful and challenging work. While it is unlikely that she will be able to function successfully in a job setting at this time, she should be encouraged to participate in rewarding and mentally stimulating activities (e.g., acquiring computer skills, or enrolling in continuing education courses) that can be performed in short spurts of time lasting up to an hour or two on a daily basis, in order to provide a measure of structure and purpose to her day.
- Ms. White might find it helpful to work with a vocational counselor and/or her therapist to explore and clarify her future occupational goals and interests, and if possible to come up with a specific plan to pursue in this regard, while taking into account her current limitations. A referral to the State Rehabilitation Agency would enable her to obtain such counseling and put her in contact with other vocational services that they provide.
- Ms. White will continue to be followed by Dr. Foley for her neurological issues, in particular her seizure disorder.
- Repeat testing in nine months to a year will help to clarify her status and ability to re-engage in competitive employment at that time.

DIAGNOSTIC IMPRESSION:

Axis I:
300.4 Dysthymia
296.3 Major Depression, mild to moderate, without psychotic features
294.9 Cognitive Disorder due to toxic exposure

Axis II:
V71.09 No diagnosis or condition

Axis III:
Seizure disorder due to carbon monoxide exposure and/or possible sewer gas exposure, mild hypothyroidism (per records); mild conductive hearing loss in the right ear; h/o possible Crohn's Disease.

Axis IV:
Stress related to medical problems, cognitive difficulties, social isolation, and unemployment.

Axis V:
GAF current = 50 (serious symptoms)

______________________________, PhD
Clinical Neuropsychologist

School Setting Report

The next report is an example of an assessment that was requested by the Director of Special Education of a public school. It concerns a fifth-grade student (Scott Taylor), who was going to be transitioned to middle school the following year. The assessment provides not only a helpful analysis of Scott's behavior and abilities in the context of a diagnostic discussion, but also focuses on recommendations to facilitate his transition to the next school, as requested. Although it is true, as pointed out in chapter 11, that teachers are often quite aware of the behaviors demonstrated by their students, a careful analysis of underlying cognitive functions is helpful in explaining and providing an integrated understanding of how those behaviors are generated. Thus, as Guare and Dawson indicate, the importance of the Summary and Impressions section cannot be overemphasized, as it provides a basis for the recommendations that follow. Importantly, behavioral observations are also solicited from the boy's teacher as well as from his parents.

NAME: Scott T.
DOB: May 18, 1989
DOT: January 13 and 16, 1999
CA: 10 years, 7 months
GRADE: 5

TESTS ADMINISTERED:

Wechsler Intelligence Scale for Children – III, Raven's Coloured Progressive Matrices Tests, Weintraub-Mesulam Cancellation Tests (letters and symbols), Automatized Series, Word Fluency, Boston Naming Test, Cookie Theft, Gray Oral Reading Test III, Kaufman Test of Educational Achievement (K-TEA), Spelling from the IOWA Test of Basic Skills, Test of Language Competence-Expanded Edition (TOLC), California Verbal Learning Test – Children's Version (CVLT-C), Sentence Memory and Story Memory from the Wide Range Assessment of Memory and Learning (WRAML), Rey-Osterrieth Complex Figure (ROCF), Hooper Visual Organization Test, Stroop Color and Word Test, Trail Making Tests A & B, Sensory Motor Exam, Grooved Pegboard Test, Beery Developmental Test of Visuomotor Integration (VMI), Achenbach's Child Behavior Checklists (CBC), Child Attention Profile (CAP).

REASON FOR REFERRAL:

Scott was referred for neuropsychological testing by the Director of Special Education of the Public Schools at the request of Mr. and Mrs. T. to assess Scott's current educational needs. Mr. and Mrs. T. are concerned about their son's social skills, anxious learning style, and transition to the middle school next year. Scott is presently a fifth grader at the Pinewood Elementary School. He currently receives classroom support by a Special Education Aide on a daily basis, and counseling once weekly in school.

RELEVANT BACKGROUND:

History was obtained by a review of medical and educational records provided by the parents, an interview with Mr. and Mrs. T., and a telephone conversation with the school counselor.

Developmental Milestones:
Scott is the second of three children born to caring parents; father is in management (telecommunications) and mother is a Learning Disabilities Specialist. Family history is remarkable for Attention-Deficit Disorder (Scott's older brother), learning disabilities, and seizures in the paternal family.

Scott is the product of a full term, uneventful pregnancy. Delivery was complicated by a long labor (weight=8 lbs., 4½ oz.), with no further complications. Developmental milestones were achieved within normal limits for language skills and motor development. He was an easy baby and slept through the night at 3-4 months old. He was toilet trained at age three years, but continues to experience mild enuresis and soiling.

Medical history is significant for surgically corrected undescended testicle at age 9 months. At age 8 years, he fell out of a tree, landing on his mouth and chin, and requiring stitches and subsequent dental work (three root canals and oral surgery). No head injuries, seizures, or loss of consciousness were reported. Scott's pediatrician is Dr. Wyman. His last physical, in June 1998, revealed no concerns. Scott does not take any prescribed medications.

At age three years, Scott entered preschool and began to experience social interaction problems. His adjustment may have been complicated by his grandmother's death. In school, Scott had difficulty understanding spatial relationships, particularly judging personal space, and was "on top of other children." He clung to walls when he walked and had an awkward gait. He experienced tactile sensitivity to such items as tags and socks. Scott has a history of anxious behavior, sometimes appearing hyperactive, oppositional, and agitated.

Scott was first evaluated in kindergarten, and found to have gross and fine motor difficulties. Adaptive physical education and occupational therapy were recommended, although service delivery was not entirely consistent. Teachers also reported that in kindergarten he had difficulty controlling his behavior. He had temper tantrums, was unable to sit still, and experienced social interaction problems. Midway through first grade, he was placed in a substantially separate classroom for children with behavioral and emotional problems as part of a diagnostic plan (502.9). This was not an appropriate placement, and he was subsequently placed in a regular classroom with more appropriate special education services. Scott has also received psychotherapy since second grade. Due to several family moves, he has been with several therapists and therapy groups. He currently receives in-school counseling by Mr. Andrews.

During the interview, Mr. and Mrs. T. described their son as musical and artistic. He has a wonderful sense of humor but often does not "get it" when others try to communicate with him. Scott's parents remarked that he is very literal in interpreting what people say and has a limited range of affect. He is not able to effectively problem-solve or consider alternate approaches to different situations (e.g., when he is angry, he acts aggressively). Scott has a sense of what acceptable behavior should be, but he is often unable to interpret the behavior of others (e.g., why people might be angry with him).

Presently, Scott does not have any friends his own age and will occasionally play with children in the neighborhood who are considerably younger than he. Mr. and Mrs. T. reported that he has poor self-esteem. Scott can be "rigid" and will over focus if not "obsess" on a certain topic or event. He screams when under stress and has difficulty negotiating relationships. He occasionally speaks in a "robot-like" voice. In addition, his need for perfectionism often results in frustration and subsequent anger with tantrum-like behavior. Scott can "misread" people and social cues. He exhibits a great deal of anxiety, particularly around daily changes and transitions. Eye contact with others is inconsistent, but has improved over the years.

On the *Child Behavior Checklist*, the following scales were rated in the clinically significant range (98th percentile or above): Anxious/Depressed, Social Problems, and Obsessive Behaviors. Withdrawn Behavior, Inattention, and Aggression were rated at the 95th percentile.

Scott's 5th grade teacher and teacher's aide completed the *Teachers Report Form* of the *CBC*. Consistent with the home report, Anxious/Depressed behavior and Social Problems were rated above the 98th percentile. Thought Problems (93rd percentile) and Aggression (90th percentile) were rated in the borderline clinical range. Withdrawn Behavior was also rated at the 90th percentile. On the *CAP* rating scale, Inattention was rated at the 84th percentile and Overactivity at the 93rd-98th percentile. In a telephone conversation with the classroom teacher, she remarked that Scott has "come a long way since the Fall." He can cooperate with groups, although he still gets frustrated and has frequent outbursts. Changes in routine (when homework is assigned, or when Scott does not understand something) are situations when he is likely to feel overwhelmed. He subsequently experiences stress and extreme anxiety resulting in tantrum-like behavior (e.g., screams and hollers). Scott wants to get along with other children but "doesn't know how."

Previous Evaluations:
In looking over the records, Scott has been seen by many different clinicians. Diagnoses vary across evaluations and include: Developmental Disorder, NOS, a nonverbal learning disability, Attention-Deficit/Hyperactivity Disorder, and Oppositional Defiant Disorder. What remains consistent is his difficulty relating to people, both peers and adults.

In addition to school evaluations and reviews, Dr. Green saw Scott almost four years ago, in March 1993, for psychological and educational testing. A visual/spatial learning disability and adaptive/social difficulties in addition to attention deficits were found, suggesting a developmental disorder with anxious features. Symptoms of ADHD were noted, although the etiology of his attention and overactive features was unclear.

In May 1996, Scott was referred for projective testing by his therapist. The evaluation revealed "emotional distancing," "low self-esteem," and oppositional tendencies. Aggressive themes also emerged.

BEHAVIORAL OBSERVATIONS:

Scott is a right-handed, 10-year-old boy with a freckled face and light brown hair. Eye contact was initially nonexistent, but gradually became intermittent. He tended to avoid eye contact, then suddenly look right at me, then quickly look away.

Scott was very talkative, and yet, impaired with respect to the pragmatics of social communication, such as initiating conversation (rather than "chatter"), and sustaining a meaningful conversation. Despite an excellent vocabulary, he was often inattentive to nuances in communication. His voice tone was mildly flat and his speech occasionally "robot-like."

Scott was physically awkward (e.g., he frequently bumped into the table and accidentally kicked the examiner under the table throughout the assessment). He was also unaware of space (e.g., he came too close to the examiner).

During the testing, Scott was quite anxious about his performance. He "regressed" without warning, becoming silly and fidgety. He could not easily modulate or regulate his behavior. And yet, during the parent interview, he sat in the waiting room for over an hour, kept himself busy drawing, and did not interrupt at any time.

Scott's problem solving style was variable. At times, he was very attentive, but occasionally he was impulsive and agitated. On one or two occasions, he paced the room. He had difficulty tolerating ambiguity and had to be cajoled to complete a task (e.g., the *Comprehension* subtest). Scott needed to "talk-through" or verbalize his actions on almost every task. For example, on the *Coding* subtest and *Trail Making Test*, he named every target as he circled or identified it.

Scott is right-handed. He holds the pencil with the thumb wrapped under the first finger. He held materials very close to his face suggesting possible acuity problems or, more likely, inaccurate judgment of distance.

Today's results are considered a reliable estimate of his current cognitive functioning.

TEST RESULTS:

Cognitive Functioning:

On the *WISC-III*, Scott earned a Verbal IQ of 118 (128 when prorated to exclude the Comprehension subtest) and a Performance IQ of 99. Given the significant discrepancy in Scott's verbal and performance scores, an "average" IQ score was not computed, as it would not adequately represent his intellectual potential. There was considerable variability within and across Performance subtests, as noted in previous evaluations.

Verbal	SS	%ile	Performance	SS	%ile
Information	15	95	Picture Completion	7	16
Similarities	15	95	Coding	11	65
Arithmetic	13	84	Picture Arrangement	6	9
Vocabulary	16	98	Block Design	15	95
Comprehension	6	9	Object Assembly	10	50
(Digit Span)	(19)	99	(Mazes)	(6)	9
			(Symbol Search)	(12)	75

On the *Raven's Coloured Progressive Matrices*, a visual spatial reasoning task, Scott was asked to conceptualize spatial designs ranging from the very obvious and concrete to the very complex and abstract. He performed within the 75th to 90th percentile.

Scott excelled on tasks that require rote learning of factual knowledge and logical reasoning. Particular difficulties were noted in areas requiring good understanding of social situations (i.e., *Comprehension* and *Picture Arrangement*), and planning (*Mazes*). Scott's anxiety and poor social reasoning affected his performance on tasks. For example, on the *Comprehension* subtest, his common sense judgments of social situations were highly variable in quality and his formal score reflects his difficulty connecting with "real life" situations (*WISC-III Comprehension*, 9th percentile). He became very silly and regressed, frequently responding with one-liners from television shows or commercials. He was also unable to inhibit aggressive responses. For example, when asked, "What is the thing to do when a boy smaller than you starts to fight with you," he replied, "knock him down." His affect was disconnected from his words, sometimes giggling as if the questions were part of a game, not to be taken seriously.

When asked to arrange cartoon-like pictures to tell a sensible story (*Picture Arrangement*), he showed a poor understanding of the stories and arranged picture cards impulsively and erratically (9th percentile). Of note, when asked to tell a story to go with the sequences, Scott described isolated details but often missed the point of the story. On one occasion, after the cards were placed in the specified disarranged order, he looked at them and said, "I think you put them in the right order."

Attention:
Scott's ability to sustain his effort and attention was adequate as seen on his persistence in canceling *"A's"* on a *Visual Search Task*. His approach was mostly organized and his three omissions are within normal limits for his age (163 sec). Time to completion was also average. He "verbalized" each target letter using self-talk to keep his place and stay focused. On a second visual search task, *Unstructured Symbol Cancellation*, Scott was also systematic in his approach and completed the task in a timely manner (98 sec, no omissions, one error of commission that he self-corrected).

On a computerized task of sustained attention (*Vigil*) Scott scored within the normal range on both cued and uncued conditions. Thus his response times reflected adequate activation (arousal) and, while a mild tendency toward impulse errors was noted on the cued condition, overall his performance was well within the normal range.

His immediate attention for auditory information was superior (*WISC-III Digit Span*, 99th percentile). He recalled 8 digits forward and 6 digits backward (better than most adults!). He was extremely anxious during this subtest, repeating the digits frenetically, and continually shifting position, e.g., knees against the table, legs over the table, or leaning backwards.

On tasks involving orally presented mental arithmetic problems, Scott performed in the above-average range. Overall, despite variability on the *WISC-III*, Scott did well on tasks explicitly requiring him to stay focused and pay attention.

Executive Functioning:
Scott was able to understand task demands and to maintain set without difficulty. On the *Trail Making Tests* Scott did well, both on the simpler number sequence, *Trail Making Test A* (where he connected numbers in sequence 1... 2... 3... etc.), and on the more demanding *Trail Making Test B* (requiring keeping track of, and alternating between, two automatized verbal sequences – 1...A... 2... B... etc.).

When Scott had to impose or create his own organizational structure, he encountered difficulty, particularly on nonverbal tasks (e.g., the *ROCF* and the *Object Assembly* subtest of *WISC-III*). In contrast, when structure was offered (e.g., models for *Block Design*) or when choices were available (e.g., *Raven's Matrices*), he performed best. Nonetheless, on a verbal fluency task Scott performed in the superior range, both when required to generate words beginning with specified letters and to organize his output efficiently, as well as when categories were provided.

When asked to plan a route through a visual maze, his performance was impulsive, in a sense "leaping before looking," resulting in a low average performance (*WISC-III Mazes*, 9th percentile).

On tasks requiring speeded color naming and the capacity to inhibit automatized responding (*Stroop Color and Word Test*), Scott performed above average on the Word Reading portion of the test (90th %ile), but one standard deviation below average on the *Color Naming* portion (11th – 16th %ile). When required to inhibit reading the word in favor of naming discrepant color, however, his performance was in the average range (54th %ile). This performance indicates that when the parameters are clearly specified, Scott is readily able to inhibit overlearned responses.

Language Processing:

On the *Vocabulary* subtest, Scott displayed an excellent repertoire of word knowledge (WISC-III *Vocabulary* 98th percentile). His responses were succinct and accurate. He took pride in his knowledge and was quite pleased with himself. At times, however, his responses had a "mechanical" quality, as if he were reciting from a dictionary.

On *Verbal Automatized Series*, Scott easily recited the alphabet, days of the week, and months of the year. On the *Boston Naming Test* his performance was very good, one standard deviation above age level (84th percentile). On the *Word Fluency Test*, where he was asked to generate words beginning with specific letters rapidly, he performed in the superior range (98th percentile), which is consistent with his *Vocabulary* score from the *WISC-III*. Given semantic categories, *Animals* and *Things To Eat*, he also performed well above average.

On the *TOLC Figurative Language Test*, Scott scored at the 16th percentile, with difficulty understanding the meaning of expressions such as "The team couldn't win, even with new blood." He selected a concrete interpretation: "That team couldn't even win with a blood transfusion."

On *Sentence Memory (WRAML)*, a task of short-term recall and syntactic comprehension, Scott earned a scaled score of 11 (63rd percentile).

Academic Functioning:

On the *Gray Oral Reading Test* – 3rd Edition, Scott's rate of oral reading given contextual material was very fast and mildly dysfluent. Nevertheless, he scored well above grade level for Rate and Accuracy. When asked to complete multiple choice questions, his performance was variable. He could easily respond to "factual" questions but had relatively more difficulty on questions requiring inferences or judgment, such as, "What does not fit in the story?" or "What is the best name for this story?"

GORT-3

	SS	%ile
Rate	15	95
Accuracy	16	98
Passage Score	15	95
Comprehension	11	63

On the *Spelling* subtest of the *K-TEA*, Scott's performance was at the high school level with a Standard Score of 138 (99th percentile), which is consistent with his *Spelling* score on the *IOWA Tests of Basic Skills*.

Scott's written narrative describing the *Cookie Theft* picture was concrete and brief, consisting of two full sentences. Given the limited sample obtained, a grade level could not be ascertained. Spatially, he evidenced difficulty maintaining the left-side margin, and spacing between words was inconsistent. On a second paragraph, where he could generate his own story line, he was more elaborate. Punctuation, grammar, and capitalization were satisfactory. Handwriting was smaller than on the previous sample, but legible. Letter and word spacing were again marginal (too close together). The left-side margin was better maintained, with only mild unevenness.

On the *Computation* portion of the *K-TEA*, Scott obtained a standard score of 100 (50th percentile; 4.9 Grade Equivalent). He evidenced many careless errors. When given the opportunity to correct careless errors, he performed at grade level (Grade Equivalent = 5.7). He has knowledge of addition, subtraction, multiplication, and division of whole numbers.

Sensorimotor Skills:
On *Finger Identification* (finger recognition with his eyes blindfolded), Scott performed within normal limits. He identified right and left on himself but evidenced confusion on a model. On *Fingertip Writing* (recognition of letters or numbers written on his fingertip with a pointed instrument), Scott made several errors bilaterally.

Gross motor performance was observed but not tested. Scott has an awkward gait, and frequently bumped into furniture. He is reportedly clumsy at home and at school. On the *Grooved Pegboard* test, a task of fine motor dexterity, Scott performed within the average range with his right hand, but 1½ standard deviations below average with his left hand. On the *Coding* subtest from the *WISC-III*, a timed motor task relying on fine-motor speed, visual scanning, and incidental learning, his performance was within normal limits, obtaining a scaled score of 11 (63rd percentile).

In sum, fine motor dexterity with his dominant hand is intact, but moderate difficulties are seen with the nondominant hand.

Visual-Spatial and Construction Skills:
On a task that involves using three-dimensional, colored blocks to copy abstract designs, Scott's performance was excellent (*WISC-III Block Design*, 95th percentile). He could also construct puzzles of familiar, concrete objects but not as quickly or accurately as seen on the *Block Design* subtest, in part, because there was no model to follow (*WISC-III Object Assembly*, 50th percentile).

On a more complex task of visual spatial construction, the *Rey Osterrieth Complex Figure*, Scott evidenced organizational problems. This figure is composed of a base rectangle divided internally by a cross and diagonals and has different details in each quadrant. Most of his copy errors were related to poor integration of internal features.

On a visual spatial task without a graphomotor component, the *Hooper Visual Organization Test*, Scott was asked to look at segmented line drawings of objects and decide what they might be when put together. He performed well above average for his age (28/30 items were correctly named). As noted previously, he scored in the above-average range on the *Raven's Coloured Progressive Matrices*, a visuospatial reasoning task.

Learning and Memory:
Scott's performance on tasks of new verbal learning was average when compared to his chronological age group. Asked to learn a list of 15 words from 3 semantic categories (e.g., rooms in a house, animals, clothing),

Scott's learning curve was at the 47th percentile (*CVLT-C*: 7, 7, 9, 10, 12/15 items over 5 learning trials). He recalled 7 words after an interference trial (16th percentile), but after a 20 minute delay, he recalled 9 words (31st). On a recognition trial including phonemically and semantically similar words, he recognized 14/15 (69th percentile) original list words but evidenced three false positives (31st percentile).

Scott was asked to recall two short stories (5-6 lines each) from the *Story Memory* subtest of the *WRAML*. He performed within the low average range recalling 8 out of 23 items on the first story and 12 out of 28 items on the second story (16th percentile). On a recognition task, his performance was also low average for his age (9/15 questions were correctly answered).

When asked to draw the *ROCF* from memory immediately after having copied it (see above), Scott drew one detail from the left side, then 2-3 details from the right side of the figure. As an afterthought, he drew a few lines representing the rectangle. The delayed recall (20 minutes later) consisted of a few details encased in several smaller triangles, suggesting a lack of appreciation of the overall shape of the figure.

SUMMARY AND IMPRESSIONS:

Scott T. is a 10 year, 7-month-old, 5th grader who was referred for an assessment due to his parents' concern about his social skills, anxious learning style, and transition to middle school next year. Scott presents with a history of having attained developmental milestones normally, but has experienced both gross and fine motor difficulties since kindergarten, difficulty interacting with his peers, and temper tantrums. Social difficulties appear to result from perfectionism leading to frustration, difficulty interpreting what people say, and modulating his own affect and voice. Scott has been in psychotherapy since second grade, and currently receives daily assistance in classroom from a Special Education Aide. Previous assessments have diagnosed him with a nonverbal learning disability, ADHD, and Oppositional Defiant Disorder. Medical history is noncontributory. Family history includes an older brother with an Attention-Deficit Disorder, and learning disability and seizures in the father's side of the family. Scott has never been on medication.

Scott cooperated adequately with the current assessment and appeared to have put forth his best effort on tasks that he was good at, but needed encouragement to complete tasks where he experienced great difficulty (particularly those involving social understanding and reasoning). He often demonstrated significant motor restlessness.

Test results indicate that intellectually Scott performs in the high average range on verbal tasks, and in the average to high average range on nonverbal tasks. He excels on tasks of factual knowledge and logic, and does best when structure and organization are provided.

He was able to establish, maintain, and switch set on tasks, and while some variability within and across tests was noted, he was able to sustain his attention over time when explicitly required to do so. His digit span both forward and backward was excellent. Verbal fluency was also in the superior range (both with and without the structure provided by categories). Naming was above average. When provided with structure or a model to copy from, Scott demonstrated adequate visuospatial ability. (e.g., *Hooper Visual Organization Test*, *Block Design*, and *VMI*).

Memory for both verbal and nonverbal material fell in the low average to average range. He had some difficulty with integration of the overall percept when copying a complex figure (*ROCF*), which in part resulted in recall of fragments without an overall contour.

Academically, spelling and reading were above average. Scott was able to answer factual questions about passages easily, but had difficulty when inference or judgment was required. Writing was adequate, although mild difficulties with spacing of words and margins were noted. Math (both written and oral) fell in the average range. Interpretation of figurative language was poor (see *TOLC* results).

As noted, Scott's greatest weaknesses were in the areas of social cognition (e.g., poor eye contact, poor conversational turn-taking skills, impaired performance on *Comprehension* and *Picture Arrangement* subtests of *WISC-III*, and by history and parent and teacher ratings). His difficulties with social situations (currently manifested by the fact that he has no friends of his own age) may stem in part from his difficulty with inferential reasoning (cf. *GORT-3 Comprehension*) and "getting the big picture" (cf. *ROCF* copy and recall). Thus he also had relative difficulty organizing and imposing structure on nonverbal tasks (cf. better performance on *Block Design* than *Object Assembly*).

In addition to difficulties in social cognition and integration and organization of nonverbal material, Scott has difficulty in the regulation of affect (ranging from silliness to aggression), prosody (relatively uninflected), and level of motor activity. Scott was observed to be quite restless during the assessment (fidgeting constantly, rocking in his chair, pacing the room, and unintentionally kicking the examiner under the table). In addition, he demonstrated poor awareness of personal and physical space. Attention was variable unless explicitly directed to a specific task. Fine motor ability was poor in his nondominant left hand.

This pattern of findings, together with the history, point to difficulty in functions typically thought to be mediated by the right hemisphere, and fall under the rather vague and nonspecific rubric of a nonverbal learning disability. More specifically, Scott's profile shares features with Asperger's Disorder as defined by the *DSM-IV*. This syndrome is characterized by qualitative impairment in social interaction, significant impairment in social, occupational, and other areas of functioning, the absence of a significant delay in language or cognitive development, and restrictive, repetitive and stereotyped patterns of behavior, interest and activity. Others (e.g., Pennington, 1991) have characterized the speech of individuals with Asperger's as often stilted and pedantic in nature; Scott's vocal characteristic and style appear to fit this description. Rosenn has also emphasized the difficulty that individuals with Asperger's Disorder have in dealing with change and with nonverbal communicational cues; social situations epitomize the situations where such skills are required. Thus, social situations can often lead to significant anxiety, avoidance, and low self-esteem. One area that does not fit the diagnosis perfectly is that there is no clear evidence of Scott having demonstrated restricted or stereotyped patterns of behavior or interest, or motor mannerisms (his parents did note, parenthetically, that Scott spends hours on the computer).

In addition to Asperger's Disorder, Scott's motor restlessness and variability in attention raise the likelihood of an Attention-Deficit/Hyperactivity Disorder. It should be noted, however, that level of arousal or activation appears to be normal, as indicated by his good performance on both a computerized vigilance task (Vigil), and a verbal fluency task.

RECOMMENDATIONS:

1. In order to facilitate transition to the middle school, every effort should be made to reduce the sheer amount of change and new information that Scott has to deal with at once. This can be accomplished by orienting Scott to the new school before classes start (e.g., showing him the new classroom, orienting him to the hallways, the playground, the cafeteria, etc.), preferably over several visits until he demonstrates a sense of familiarity.

   Secondly, it will be helpful for Scott to meet his new teacher(s) and teacher's aide before classes as well, to ensure that the teaching staff understand and are familiar with the nature of his difficulty in integrating and organizing material, his difficulties dealing with change, and his social difficulties. Their assistance will be critical both in helping Scott to adjust to a new environment and new classmates, and in preventing misunderstandings that result in labeling his behavior as willful and oppositional, rather than a product of his neuropsychological limitations. Because Scott does not always know how to negotiate with others and because his voice and facial expression do not reflect his anger and frustration, it may be hard for others to discern his growing frustration. To the extent that staff can become aware of, and identify in advance, precursors to his behavioral outbursts, they will be able to intervene before the outbursts occur. A teacher's aide will continue to be an important aspect of his IEP.

2. In conjunction with the above steps, Scott will also continue to benefit from ongoing counseling from an individual whom he has met and established a relationship with prior to the transition, if that is at all possible. Counseling will be beneficial in helping Scott to understand social pragmatics, reduce anxiety, and to develop more adaptive coping skills. [A resource for social skills training programs is *Skill Streaming the Elementary School Child*, Research Press, 2612 North Mattis Ave., Champagne, Illinois.]

   Scott would also benefit from language "pragmatics" training in a small group. This type of training is usually provided by a certified Speech and Language Therapist. [There are excellent tapes and scripts offered by Edcom Publishers: *Classroom Language Interventions: Developing Scripts and Schema for School Success*, by Nancy Creighead. There are other programs created by Wayne Secord by the same publisher. Edcom Publications: 800-458-7900.]

3. To assist Scott in developing better awareness of his body and physical space, he may benefit from exercises taught by a school physical and/or occupational therapist.

4. Finally, Scott should be referred to a pediatric neurologist or psychiatrist familiar with Asperger's Disorder for treatment of his anxiety and depression. I would be happy to assist in this referral.

DIAGNOSIS:

Axis I:
299.80 Asperger's Disorder
Rule out: 314.01 Attention-Deficit/Hyperactivity Disorder, combined type

Axis II:
V71.09 No diagnosis on Axis II

Axis III:
No current medical issues

Axis IV:
Interpersonal and educational difficulties

Axis V:
GAF = 60 (moderate symptoms)

_______________________, EdD, ABPP
Clinical Neuropsychologist

DATA SUMMARY

COGNITIVE FUNCTIONING:

WISC-III:

Verbal	SS	%	Performance	SS	%
Information	15	95	Picture Completion	7	16
Similarities	15	95	Coding	11	63
Arithmetic	13	84	Picture Arrangement	6	9
Vocabulary	16	98	Block Design	15	95
Comprehension	6	9	Object Assembly	10	50
(Digit Span)	(19)	99	(Mazes)	(6)	9
			(Symbol Search)	(12)	75

VIQ	118
PIQ	99
VCI	117
POI	97
FDI	189
PSI	109

ATTENTION, SET & MENTAL CONTROL:

Span:
Digit Span SS=19 (8 forward, 6 backward)

Sustained Attention:
Cancellation (A's) = 3 omissions
(Symbols) = no errors

Selective Attention: WISC-III

Picture Completion	SS= 7
Picture Arrangement	SS= 6
Symbol Search	SS= 12
Arithmetic	SS= 13

EXECUTIVE FUNCTIONS:

Planning:
WISC-III Mazes SS= 6

Shifting:

Stroop Test	Word: *T* score = 63
	Color: *T* score = 38-40
	Interference: *T* score = 51

Trail Making Test A	Raw score: 15 seconds
	Average score for age: 18.59 (*SD*=7)
Trail Making Test B	Raw score: 32 seconds
	Average score for age: 42.53 (*SD*=16)

LANGUAGE SKILLS:

Boston Naming Test:

Raw score:	51
Average score for age:	45.56 (*SD*=5.9)
Phonemic cues:	2 additional responses

Word Fluency:

FAS	Raw score:	41
	Average score for age:	23.8 (*SD*=8.2)
Animals	Raw score:	19
	Average score for age:	14.27 (*SD*=3.7)
Food	Raw score:	24
	Average score for age:	13.97 (*SD*=2.2)

Sentence Memory (WRAML):

Scaled Score: 11

LEARNING/MEMORY:

Story Memory (WRAML):

Scaled Score: 7

Recognition Raw score: 9/15 (low average)

California Verbal Learning Test-Children's Version:

Immediate Memory Span	70 %ile
Level Learning	47 %ile
Immediate Recall	14 %ile
Delay Recall	45 %ile
Recognition	WNL
Intrusions	WNL

VISUOSPATIAL/CONSTRUCTIONAL SKILLS:

Beery Visual Motor Integration Test:
Age Equivalent: WNL

Rey Osterrieth Complex Figure:
Organizational Score = 6 (Age Equivalent = 8 years old)

Raven's Coloured Matrices:
75th to 90th percentile

Hooper Visual Organization Test:
28/30 Superior range

MOTOR/SENSORY:

	Right hand	Left hand
Grooved Pegboard:	76 sec	94 sec
Finger Identification:	no errors	no errors
Fingertip Writing:	6 errors	4 errors

In addition, Scott has difficulty with body representation and representation of extra-personal space. Taken together, these findings point to less functional efficiency of right-sided brain areas.

Forensic Report

Finally, we provide an example of a forensic report (Mrs. Banting) that describes the findings of an assessment that was performed at the request of a lawyer to support a personal injury lawsuit. Thus, the neuropsychologist was retained in the role of an expert, on the basis of specialized education, qualifications, and experience (in this case, the neuropsychologist is board certified in clinical neuropsychology and has 20 years of experience working with traumatic brain injuries). As discussed in chapter 12, the report serves several functions. One is to describe and organize the findings in sufficient detail to facilitate preparation for a deposition that may not take place until much later. In addition to explaining, in non-jargonistic terminology (thus fulfilling the didactic function emphasized in chapter 12), the different cognitive functions and the relevance of test performance to different aspects of these functions, the discussion systematically takes into account and evaluates the contribution of potentially confounding influences (e.g., pain, depression, medication, motivation). It explicitly lists the preexisting records that were reviewed in order to obtain an objective and comprehensive history. These records not only provide a basis for estimating premorbid level of function (critical in determining proximal causality), but in this case, inaccuracies and omissions in prior experts' reports could only be corrected after examining their raw data. Consistent with ethical principles, the report includes information that could potentially complicate the plaintiff's position (i.e., Mrs. Banting's elevated responses on the Personality Assessment Inventory), but also seeks to incorporate these findings within an integrated explanation of her behavior. As befits a forensic report, no recommendations are provided; the emphasis is on diagnosis and causality. This is in stark contrast to reports written for clinical, vocational, or school settings, where the emphasis is on recommendations.

The tests selected for this report are maximally sensitive to the long-term effects of mild TBI (i.e., measures of divided attention and speed of information processing). To this end, as discussed in chapter 9, computerized tests (i.e., MicroCog; Vigil; Colorado Malingering Test; Personality Assessment Inventory; and Wisconsin Card Sorting Test) were selected. The first three provide reaction time-based indices, whereas the last two were used for scoring and interpretation purposes only. This allowed for the assessment of cognitive functions that paper and pencil measures do not readily provide and ensured accuracy and ease of scoring and manipulation of large data sets. For the WCST, a combination of standard administration and computerized scoring ensures both accuracy of input and appropriate use of normative data that are based on a standard administration of this test.

Forensic Report

Name: Mary Banting
Date of Birth: 05/27/42
Date of Eval.: 12/2/00 and 12/3/00
Age: 58 years
Referred by: J. Peters, Esq.
Examiner:

REASON FOR REFERRAL:

Mary Banting is a 58-year-old, married, mother of three adult children, with a high school education, who was referred for an expert opinion regarding the possible sequelae of a fall in a restaurant on 7/3/95. At that time Mrs. Banting fell backward on a chair that broke and hit her head on the floor. After being driven home one hour away by her husband, she presented at Mercy Hospital with contusions, headache, and blurry vision, and was diagnosed with a concussion and probable brachial plexus injury, and was sent home with head injury precautions.

Mrs. Banting was initially seen for a neuropsychological evaluation on 3/8/98 by Dr. D. Willowby. Dr. Willowby is currently indisposed and was therefore unable to provide a follow-up evaluation in person. She was also seen recently by neuropsychologist Dr. Jennings on 9/11 and 9/18/00. Reports and raw data from both evaluations, together with extensive other records, were available for review at the time of this assessment.

PROCEDURES:

- Record review: including records from Mercy Hospital; Dr. Thomas of Neurological Associates, Inc.; PT notes from Physical Therapy Network; Orthopaedics Professional Association; Dr. Zelnick; Dr. Eckor; Dr. Jennings; and Dr. Willowby; employment records of Mrs. Banting.

- History; Vigil (computerized continuous performance test); MicroCog (computerized assessment battery); Auditory Consonant Trigrams (ACT); WMS-R Digit and Visual Span; Shipley Institute of Living Scale; Wide Range Achievement Test-3 (WRAT-3); Rey-Osterrieth Complex Figure Test (ROCF; including copy, immediate and delayed recall, delayed recognition); Warrington Recognition Test; Wisconsin Card Sorting Test (WCST); Finger Tapping; Smell Identification Test (SIT); Colorado Malingering Test (Priming test); Personality Assessment Inventory (PAI).

BEHAVIORAL OBSERVATIONS:

Mrs. Banting came with her husband to both sessions. Both she and her husband were friendly and interactive, and answered questions readily. Mrs. Banting is a middle-aged woman appearing approximately her stated age, with light complexion and gray hair, wearing glasses. She came casually and appropriately dressed in slacks and sweater, with sneakers. She focused on the testing and was able to sustain attention to the tasks for several hours at a stretch, although she did report having a headache on both testing sessions. Affect was generally euthymic and pleasant. Speech and comprehension were unremarkable. She did not bring her cane, but while leaving the office for lunch held out her hand to steady herself against the walls. Gait was unremarkable. Results from the current assessment are considered a valid reflection of current abilities.

HISTORY:

Mrs. Banting was born as the third of four siblings, and grew up in Providence, Rhode Island. Her father died approximately fifteen years ago in his early 70s from lung cancer. He had a sixth grade education, and worked as a home builder. Her mother died approximately ten years ago at age 78 due to congestive heart failure. Mrs. Banting thought she had a sixth grade education as well. Her mother was employed as a foreman at a factory. Mrs. Banting's three brothers all graduated from high school; her youngest brother also completed two years of college.

Mrs. Banting reported that her birth was unremarkable and that she weighed 6 lb. Developmental milestones were reportedly achieved at the usual time. Early childhood was unremarkable for concussions or head injuries. She noted a fistula operation toward the end of high school. Prior to getting glasses she apparently also had headaches as a child. When the family moved to another town, she and her brothers all repeated one grade (the second grade in her case) due to the difference between the schools. She denied academic problems other than being a slow reader, for which she later took speed reading classes, but she had no trouble learning to read and received no extra help in any subject. Favorite subjects were English, French, and Math (especially algebra). She could not recall any subject she particularly struggled with or disliked. She made friends and got along well socially with her peers. She graduated at age seventeen or eighteen.

After graduating Mrs. Banting would have liked to attend college but her parents didn't think this was appropriate for girls. She worked instead as an assistant secretary, then as a secretary, and then as a secretary supervisor at an insurance company, where she stayed for four to five years. She married her current husband, a businessman, on 8/16/64, and after she had her first child they transferred to a different state for his job, where they lived for a year. They then moved back to the Northeast, and have lived in the same town ever since. Other jobs include working in a secretarial/administrative capacity for a school, and at a hospital. She has also assisted her husband in his business consulting firm on a part-time basis. Her husband is prone to depression and has been on disability for the last years for this reason. They are currently supported by his disability insurance.

Mrs. Banting denies any history of being charged, arrested, or sued. She reports having been ticketed only once for speeding, and noted that fast driving bothers her head now. She has taken legal action vis-à-vis several past accidents, but denies any past history of head injuries. She reports having been in four prior auto accidents, but was not at fault. She has won small settlements that essentially covered legal costs (this was confirmed by Mr. Peters, her attorney).

Leisure activities include sewing, although she does little of that now, and walking the dog. In the past she used to go horseback riding, swimming, and enjoyed reading. Mrs. Banting and her husband also used to go on hiking and bicycle trips with their children. She still reads, but finds that she is unable to concentrate well and now tends to read short stories in magazines, or skims the paper. She also watches TV. Much of her day is spent doing regular housekeeping activities, such as cooking and cleaning, although vacuuming bothers her back and she gets dizzy going up the basement stairs with laundry. Occasionally she will drive short distances and she goes shopping with a friend and her daughter. She appears to enjoy very much their dog, which she takes out for short walks. Mrs. Banting denied any history of excessive drinking, and drinks a glass of wine very occasionally, due to her diabetes. She does not smoke cigarettes. She denied any history of illicit substance use.

Mrs. Banting was raised a Catholic, but for the last ten years has attended a Unitarian church in her home town.

MEDICAL HISTORY:

Medical history is positive for diabetes, asthmatic bronchitis, hypertension, hyperlipidemia, and history of fistula repair, appendectomy, melanoma removal from the left arm in 1983, and an umbilical hernia repair in 1991. In addition she suffers from “dry eye syndrome” as a consequence of having been exposed to chemicals at one of her jobs. Although Mrs. Banting reported having been in several other accidents, there is no report of any head injury and they are considered noncontributory.

MEDICATIONS:

At the time of the current assessment Mrs. Banting reported taking the following medications: Ibuprofen prn, Naprosyn (prn for pain), Meclizine (for dizziness, dosage unknown, supposed to be taken daily but Mrs. Banting indicated that she keeps forgetting it and needs a new prescription), Glucophage® 500 mg and glyburide 5 mg twice daily for diabetes. In addition she has an inhaler, Albuterol, and a prescription for amitriptylene (for sleep) given to her a year ago, although she states that it makes her groggy in the morning and consequently takes it very infrequently. In the past she has been treated with a variety of other medications, including Zoloft.

MENTAL STATUS:

On the day of the first testing session Mrs. Banting rated her mood a 5 on a 10-point scale (10 is the positive end of the scale), but noted that she did have a headache and rated her pain an 8 on a 10-point scale (10 is maximum). She had taken 800 mg Ibuprofen in the morning before coming to her appointment. On the morning of the second day she rated her pain a 5. Mrs. Banting has had periods since her injury when she has experienced passive thoughts of suicide and wonders, "God, why not just take me?" Her chronic pain makes it frustrating and difficult to do things, and her husband's depression upsets her.

Appetite is good, and she eats regular meals and controls her diet because of her diabetes. She reported that after the last auto accident she had gained 100 lb. but had since lost it and now weighs 170 lb. Sleep has been poor since her head injury, averaging two hours a night by her own estimate. She has difficulty getting comfortable at night, and her head hurts. Occasionally she falls asleep sitting up, and she dozes while watching TV. (Her husband spends most of his day in bed and stays up at night watching TV.) She wakens feeling tired, and drinks an average of two cups of regular coffee in the morning, which helps her to wake up. Her sleep has never been formally evaluated. In addition to poor sleep she reports a loss of sexual drive or libido for the last several years, which contrasts with prior to her injury. Vision is poor in the left eye, and she has "dry eye syndrome" (reduced ability to tear, which is painful and which requires eye drops and ointment) since her eyes were exposed to a spray that burned them at one of her jobs (they had to be flushed out). Vision is corrected with bifocal glasses. In addition to constant headaches, she occasionally experiences numbness in her hands. She feels that her sense of smell is a little duller than it used to be, and that her sense of taste is less acute than before. Hearing is reported to be good.

Mrs. Banting was fully alert to her surroundings and the purpose of her being seen. There was no indication of disorientation or confusion. Speech was clear and goal-directed, with no significant tangentiality or evidence of delusional or hallucinatory thinking.

TEST RESULTS:

In the following section results from the current assessment are reported by area of functioning. Results from the recent testing done by Dr. Jennings are reviewed where relevant, as a deliberate effort was made to avoid duplication (and hence practice effects) wherever possible. Comparisons are also made to previous testing by Dr. Willowby. A summary section follows, with an interpretation and diagnosis that integrate prior findings.

Activation and Attention:
On simple computerized reaction time measures (Timers, MicroCog) Mrs. Banting scored in the low average range (compared to others of the same age and education) in response to visual targets, and in the average range in response to auditory targets. Her response time on the visual task fell in the impaired range in comparison to the general population, indicating that she has difficulty processing rapidly presented visual material. Thus on a visually presented computerized test of sustained attention (Vigil) she commented in consternation that "I can't keep up with this!" and made numerous errors of omission (but the expected number of false positives).

With visual cues she was unable to improve (Vigil, cued condition). With cross-modal cuing (auditory warning for visual cue), on the other hand, she demonstrated improved response times (Timers, MicroCog). Since her response times to uncued auditory stimuli were normal, her level of activation is also considered adequate. Her deficits lie in processing rapidly presented visual information.

No equally sensitive test of auditory information processing speed was administered previously, but when tested by Dr. Willowby on the Paced Auditory Serial Addition Test (PASAT), a test which measures mental control and divided attention, she was able to score in the expected range for an individual of her age.

Mrs. Banting was able to sustain her attention over time on the Alphabet Trails test (MicroCog). Her digit span forward (span = 5; 18th percentile) appears fairly constant, being unchanged since she was seen by Dr. Willowby in 1998, and again by Dr. Jennings in September. Digit Span

Backward was 2 and variably 3 (16th percentile; low average for her age), a performance that is comparable to that seen by Dr. Willowby but worse than observed by Dr. Jennings (4, variably 5; 31st percentile). Visual Span Forward was 4 (13th percentile) and Backward was 4 (48th percentile).

On the Auditory Consonant Trigrams test (ACT) Mrs. Banting scored in the impaired range in comparison to her age peers, recalling 5/15 letters at 3 sec, and only 1/15 letters at 9 sec and 18 sec. This test is very sensitive to problems with working memory and divided attention. It had not been administered before.

General Intellectual Ability:
Mrs. Banting was administered the Shipley Institute of Living Scale to determine whether her current level of reasoning ability represents a decline in ability (measured by the reasoning subtest) relative to premorbid level (estimated by the Vocabulary subtest). Her score on the Vocabulary subtest was at the 70th percentile (T = 55), while her score on the Reasoning subtest was at the 88th percentile (T = 62). Thus the discrepancy between the two subtests is well within the expected range and demonstrates no decline in ability. Her total score produced an estimated WAIS-R FSIQ of 108, an average score, and consistent with her scores on prior testing by Dr. Willowby and Dr. Jennings. Thus there has been no discernible change (as would be expected) in her level of general intellectual ability over time or as a consequence of her injury in 1995.

In addition to the Shipley, various reasoning tasks were administered as part of the MicroCog battery. Mrs. Banting performed in the average to above average range on these tasks as well (e.g., Object Match, Analogies, and Math). On Dr. Jennings's testing, her scores on the WAIS-R fell solidly within the average range, with the exception of Block Design (84th percentile, or above average compared to others of the same age), and Digit Symbol (25th percentile; Peer Scale Score = 8). Her score on the latter subtest was nonetheless not significantly different from her score at the time Dr. Willowby assessed her (50th percentile; PSS = 10), and is in the range that is considered normal.

Executive Functions:
Mrs. Banting had no difficulty establishing set on tasks (i.e., grasping task requirements), or maintaining set. On the Wisconsin Card Sorting Test (WCST) she was able to complete six sorts in 88 trials, with scores on the various indices in the normal range (55th to 77th percentile). This task required her to infer sorting rules based on feedback from the examiner. She used feedback efficiently, despite some difficulty understanding the basis for the fourth sort and her inability to explain the rules fully (she named two instead of three rules).

Prior testing by Dr. Willowby indicated that Mrs. Banting scored in the impaired range (3rd percentile, T = 30) on the Trail Making Test B, indicating that her ability to switch flexibly and rapidly from one automatized set to another (numbers to letters) was affected by her injury. Dr. Jennings's testing indicated that she has improved on this task over the last two years to within the average range. It is important to note that Mrs. Banting scored in the normal range on Trail Making Test A with both Dr. Willowby and Dr. Jennings. This less demanding condition (which simply requires sequencing numbers on a page) is considered a baseline condition against which Trail Making Test B is measured. The fact that her score on Trails A remained constant while her score on Trails B improved is consistent with improved functioning. It also belies Dr. Jennings's assertion that her improvement on Trails B was due to "her relatively low pain level at this administration of Trails B," since it does not account for her selectively impaired performance on Trails B with Dr. Willowby.

Motor Functions:
Mrs. Banting is predominantly right-handed, although she reported mild ambidexterity. Family history is positive for a left-handed brother. Praxis (the ability to program motor movements) screening was essentially unremarkable, although she made an error in the angle at which she demonstrated using a hammer bilaterally. Dr. Jennings reported that Mrs. Banting had difficulty acquiring set on the Luria Three Step, a sequence of hand movements, but improved with verbal mediation. This is consistent with mild apraxia. [Her reported ability to perform the so-called Go-No Go task and Reciprocal Motor Programs is unrelated to the issue of apraxia and instead reflects good inhibition and ability to switch set (considered executive functions).] Motor speed (Finger Tapping) was in the average range bilaterally (RH=42, 46%; LH=38, 34%). Motor dexterity was measured by Dr. Willowby (Grooved Pegboard) and found to be in the low average range.

Linguistic and Academic Functions:
Speech was unremarkable, with no indication (or complaint) of word-finding difficulty, problems with fluency or prosody. Comprehension was also unremarkable. Vocabulary is in the average range (50th percentile for her age on WAIS-R and 70th percentile on the Shipley multiple choice subtest).

Spelling (WRAT-3) was at the 45th percentile. Single word reading was at the 58th percentile. She was able to mentally perform simple math problems presented on MicroCog without difficulty, scoring at the 84th percentile. Written math on the WRAT-3 was at the 25th percentile (sixth grade level), with difficulty on fractions and failure to reduce answers. Difficulty with multi-digit multiplication was also observed. Thus, while she is able to carry out basic operations, she struggles with more advanced operations.

Visuospatial Functions:
Based on her performance on various written and other visually presented tasks, gross visual acuity appears to be intact. Visual processing speed, on the other hand, fell in the low average range on MicroCog (Timers), and her complaints after the accident included blurred vision. Prior testing with Dr. Willowby indicated that she did very poorly on speed of information processing tasks (simple reaction time) on the ANAM (a visually presented computerized battery).

Mrs. Banting was asked to copy the Rey-Osterrieth Complex Figure. She proceeded in a rather disorganized manner, and lines were poorly aligned in the center. Nonetheless she correctly copied all elements of the figure, and her performance is within normal limits.

Olfaction:
On the Smell Identification Test (SIT) Mrs. Banting correctly identified 37/40 scents, a score at the 51st percentile and within the normosmic range (olfaction is within normal limits).

Learning and Memory:
After copying the ROCF, Mrs. Banting was asked to draw the same figure from memory both immediately afterward and after a twenty minute delay. On both recall conditions, which were highly similar, she retained the base rectangle but lost much of the detail, and perseverated mildly. Her drawings reflected the disorganized approach demonstrated while copying the figure. Using the Denman (1984) scoring system, she scored at the 16th percentile on immediate recall (low average) and at the 25th percentile on delayed recall. On delayed recognition she was able to correctly identify the original design, despite some hesitation regarding one of the details. Her performance is within normal limits, and is relatively unchanged from her performance on this task when administered by Dr. Willowby.

This contrasts with her performance on the WMS-R Visual Designs subtest administered by Dr. Jennings, where she was able to recall all five designs both immediately and after a delay. It should be noted that the ROCF is a much more complex figure (hence its name), and the respondent is not informed in advance that she will be asked to draw it from memory. When tested by Dr. Willowby in 1998, her pattern was the same, with adequate scores on the WMS-R but very poor performance on the ROCF. As noted by Dr. Willowby, when she is required to impose organization on a visual retrieval task, she does worse than when the organizational requirements are minimal.

Mrs. Banting was asked to read stories as part of the MicroCog battery and then answer multiple choice questions about them both immediately afterward and after a filled delay. On both conditions, her scores were in the average range for someone of her age and education. On the Word List task, which combines sustained attention with subsequent recognition, her performance was again average. Spontaneous recall of prose passages from the WMS-R when administered by Dr. Jennings was also average (around the 50th percentile), with mild improvement from her scores in '98, when she scored at the 18th percentile. Her scores on the California Verbal Learning Test-II, administered by Dr. Jennings, also fell in the average range except for her performance on the interference list, where she scored in the impaired range (<3rd percentile, rather than the 25th percentile incorrectly reported by Dr. Jennings). This latter finding is an indication of *proactive interference*, a form of "overloading" such that the person has difficulty absorbing more information when large amounts are presented all at once. Furthermore, although Dr. Jennings does not comment on this, examination of the protocol indicated that her spontaneous organization of words into categories (semantic clustering) was quite limited, a reflection of her disorganized approach to certain tasks.

On the Warrington Recognition Test (WRT) Mrs. Banting scored at the 63rd percentile (44/50) in her ability to recognize words on a forced choice procedure, but only at the 9th percentile (low average; 36/50) on face recognition. These stimuli are exposed briefly in succession while the respondent rates each one for pleasantness.

Overall, therefore, Mrs. Banting's ability to encode and retrieve verbal material is intact, but her ability to impose organization is limited, as is her ability to absorb new information. This pattern is consistent with that observed by Dr. Willowby two years ago.

Motivation:

Several tests were administered to assess the possibility, given the legal aspects of the case, that she was not putting forth full effort during testing. As described above, her level of activation (wakefulness) during the assessment was adequate, despite her complaints of poor sleep. Furthermore, she rated her mood as average, and in any event there is evidence in the literature that depression does not affect scores on the MicroCog battery. Thus depression is unlikely to be a factor affecting her performance on the visual reaction time measures of information processing speed, nor would one expect depression to selectively affect rate of visual (vs. auditory) information processing or auditory consonant trigrams.

Although Mrs. Banting did complain of a headache, for which she had taken Ibuprofen prior to each session, she was able to complete testing without complaint or needing to take a break, and there is no reason to assume that her profile of test scores can be accounted for by this factor (pain) only. For example, the auditory and visual reaction time tests are presented twice over a period of approximately 45 minutes, one after the other, yet the results were identical from the first presentation to the second.

On formal tests of malingering (i.e., the Colorado Malingering Test-Priming Subtest, and the Warrington Recognition Test) Mrs. Banting performed as expected, with scores in the normal range on the former and well above chance on the latter. Her responses to the Personality Assessment Inventory are described in the following section on Personality Assessment.

Personality Assessment:
On the Personality Assessment Inventory (PAI), a self-report measure that has not been standardized on head-injured individuals, Mrs. Banting produced a profile that is unusual in the sense that her response patterns suggested both defensiveness about personal shortcomings as well as an exaggeration of certain problems. Bearing in mind that results are likely to have been distorted as a result of these response tendencies, the degree of elevation on certain clinical scales is often considered a "cry for help" or "an extremely negative evaluation of oneself and one's life."

Her highest score was on the Somatic Complaints – Somatization subscale ($T = 89$), which inquires about routine physical complaints such as headaches, back problems, gastrointestinal problems, or pain, and which are diagnostic more by their frequency than by their presence. The other two subscales on the Somatic Complaints scale (Conversion, measuring physiological symptoms such as paralysis, blindness and anesthesia, and Health Concerns, which measures preoccupation with the self-perceived complexity of one's health problems) were elevated but still within normal limits. Other elevated subscales included Thought Disorder (a subscale of the Schizophrenia scale), and all three subscales (Cognitive, Affective, and Physiological) comprising the Depression scale. In addition to her feelings of worthlessness, hopelessness, and personal failure, loss of sense of pleasure and disturbances in sleep, energy, and sexual interest, she is anxious and likely experiences continued distress due to a past traumatic event. She sees her life as severely disrupted by a variety of physical problems. There was no indication of a personality (Axis II) disorder.

These results are very similar to those obtained by Dr. Willowby in '98, using the Coolidge Axis II Inventory (CATI), and by Dr. Zelnick in 7/00 using the MMPI-2. Several comments are in order here. The CATI results indicated significant elevations on symptom scales suggesting brain injury, and the narrative protocol recommends further neuropsychological evaluation. Neither the MMPI (or other instruments used by Dr. Willowby and Dr. Zelnick, such as the SCL-90), nor the PAI were developed specifically for use with neurological populations, and it is critical that results be interpreted with this important caveat in mind. In other words, the results obtained from a head-injured person do not mean the same as those obtained from a non-head-injured person. As Lezak (1995) has summarized this problem:

> The pattern of MMPI profiles of brain damaged patients is an artifact of the test items and scale composition....Most of the "neurological symptom" items appear on the *Sc* scale, and many have double and triple scale loadings, particularly on scales *Hs*, *D* and *3* – Hysteria (*Hy*). As a result, neuropsychiatric patients with central nervous system disease tend to have an elevated "neurotic triad" (*Hs*, *D*, and *Hy*) and higher than average *Sc* scores. (p. 782)

In fact, it is precisely these four scales (*Hs, D, Hy,* and *Sc*) that were elevated on Mrs. Banting's MMPI-2 profile. Dr. Zelnick also failed to note that on p. 9 of his narrative printout, under the section headed Gass Head Injury Items, it clearly states: "The client endorsed 9 of the 14 Gass Correction items in the scored direction. The practitioner might consider the effect of reducing the designated raw scores in this case if there is a history of head injury that might account for the scale elevations," and the items and scale loadings are listed for convenience underneath. Thus, re-scoring the protocol without these items (which load on several scales) is likely to result in significant reduction on these scale scores.

SUMMARY AND DIAGNOSTIC IMPRESSION:

Mrs. Banting is a 58-year-old mother with a high school education and no prior head injuries, substance abuse, or previous psychiatric diagnosis. On 7/3/95, she hit the back of her head when the chair she was sitting on gave out unexpectedly beneath her in a restaurant. Loss of consciousness was momentary. Nonetheless, she sustained significant contusions and pain, with reduced range of motion of the neck and tenderness of the occipital nerves, and she complained of blurred vision off and on, together with dizziness and persistent headache. She was diagnosed with a concussion at Mercy Hospital. CT and MRI scans were negative. Despite physical therapy her complaints have persisted since the time of her injury, and Mrs. Banting has not returned to employment.

Mrs. Banting's first neuropsychological assessment occurred with Dr. Willowby approximately two and a half years after her injury. He noted impairments in speed of information processing, impaired sequencing, impaired executive functioning, impaired primary and working memory, impaired long-term verbal memory, and anxiety, depression, anger, and "other personality dysfunctions." Dr. Willowby's testing specifically indicated slowed visual processing.

Current testing confirms this finding almost three years later. Other medical experts (e.g., Dr. Zelnick, Dr. Eckor, and Dr. Jennings) have not assessed Mrs. Banting's speed of visual information processing. Difficulties in this area are not unexpected, given the fact that she hit the part of the head which is specifically dedicated to visual information processing (the occipital-parietal area), and she complains of occasional visual blurring. Visual difficulties are also often associated with dizziness and nausea, and with headaches, the main source of her chronic pain. Her difficulties on several tests, as well as her complaint that it bothers her when her husband drives very quickly, are accounted for by slowed visual processing. Slowed processing should not be confused with poor visual acuity or field cuts, neither of which appear to be present, or with reduced visual working memory.

Current testing, in conjunction with that performed recently by Dr. Jennings in September, indicates that Mrs. Banting functions intellectually in the average range. She demonstrated improvement on Trail Making Test B, from impaired in '98 to average in September, '00. She continues to demonstrate impairment on a highly sensitive test of divided attention and working memory (i.e., ACT and Digit Span Backward) even though she is able to process auditory material at a normal rate (e.g., PASAT given by Dr. Willowby; Auditory Timers from MicroCog battery). She also continues to manifest vulnerability in the area of organizing and imposing structure on stimuli (e.g., poor clustering on the CVLT-2; disorganized approach to the ROCF), that may affect subsequent recall (e.g., impaired recall of the interference list of the CVLT-2 and poor recall of the ROCF). On tests that assess effort (e.g., Colorado Malingering Test; Warrington Recognition Test) Mrs. Banting gave no indication of malingering.

Dr. Zelnick felt that Mrs. Banting demonstrated depressive affect during his mental status evaluation. However, his conclusion was that Mrs. Banting's profile on the MMPI-2 (uncorrected for possible head injury; see previous section), combined with her good effort on the Validity Indicator Profile, indicated a somatoform disorder. On the basis of this conclusion he dismisses all subsequent findings related to her injury that would suggest the presence of a mild brain injury. For example, he dismisses reaction time deficits reported by Dr. Willowby as being influenced by emotional factors. However, as noted earlier, there is at least one study which failed to demonstrate any significant slowing of MicroCog response times in a depressed population (Powell et al., 1993). Furthermore, depression does not account for her selective problems with visual versus auditory information processing on the MicroCog computerized battery, or her ability to perform the PASAT (a task which requires rapid processing of auditory information) when tested by Dr. Willowby. A similar argument can be made for the effect of pain on cognitive performance. Thus, contrary to Dr. Jennings's conclusion, it does not seem reasonable to attribute all her deficits to fluctuations in her level of pain.

As noted above, once the recommended Gass item corrections are made on the MMPI-2 it is likely that her profile will show significant reduction in psychopathology. On the Behavior Change Inventory, completed independently by herself, her husband, and her daughter Ann for Dr. Willowby, changes in personality characteristics were reported following the accident in 1995, from her being viewed as cheerful, optimistic, and enthusiastic to being discouraged, distractible, easily upset, fearful, forgetful, worrisome, and tired. This suggests onset of symptoms after the accident.

It is clear from the records that, at the time of her unexpected fall backward, Mrs. Banting sustained contusions and a concussion. She went to the emergency room at Mercy Hospital on the day of the accident with persistent parieto-occipital headache, dizziness triggered by lateral or upward gaze, and visual blurring, and was diagnosed as having had a concussion. Dr. Willowby noted that on the Multiphasic Pain Inventory (MPI) Mrs. Banting was classified as a dysfunctional type of pain patient, which is to say, someone with poor coping skills in dealing with her pain in everyday situations. The literature suggests that a persistent post-concussion syndrome is more likely to develop in women over age 50 who have poor strategies for coping with the consequences of their injury.

Thus, in the absence of information to the contrary, her symptom presentation represents an interaction of neurological and psychological factors, and as such constitutes, to a reasonable degree of neuropsychological certainty, a persistent post-concussion syndrome caused by her accident on 7/3/95.

______________________________________, PhD, ABPP
Board Certified in Clinical Neuropsychology

REFERENCES

Achenbach, T. M. (1991). *Manual for the Child Behavior Checklist/4-18 and 1991 profile*. Burlington, VT: University of Vermont Department of Psychiatry.

Adams, K. M., & Heaton, R. K. (1985). Automated interpretation of neuropsychological test data. *Journal of Consulting and Clinical Psychology*, *53*, 790-802.

Adebimpe, V. R. (1981). Overview: White norms and psychiatric diagnosis of Black patients. *American Journal of Psychiatry*, *138*, 279-285.

Allard, G., Butler, J., Faust, D., & Shea, M. T. (1995). Errors in hand scoring objective personality tests: The case of the Personality Diagnostic Questionnaire–Revised (PDQ-R). *Professional Psychology: Research and Practice*, *26*(3), 304-308.

Allen, C. C., Ellinwood, E. H., Everett, H., & Logue, P. E. (1993). Construct validity of a new computer-assisted cognitive neuromotor assessment battery in normal and inpatient psychiatric samples. *Journal of Clinical Psychology*, *49*(5), 874-882.

American Medical Association. (1992). *Guides to the evaluation of permanent impairment* (4th ed.). Washington, DC: Author.

American Medical Association. (1999). *The CPT Assistant*. Washington, DC: American Medical Association.

American Psychiatric Association. (1994). *Diagnostic and statistical manual of mental disorders* (4th ed., rev.). Washington, DC: Author.

American Psychological Association. (1992). Ethical principles of psychologists and code of conduct. *American Psychologist*, *47*, 1597-1611.

American Psychological Association, Committees on Professional Standards and Psychological Tests and Assessment. (1986). *Guidelines for computer-based tests and interpretations*. Washington, DC: Author.

American Psychological Association Practice Directorate (with Coopers and Lybrand, LLP). (1996). Washington, DC: American Psychological Association.

Anastasi, A. (1988). *Psychological testing* (6th ed.). New York: Macmillan.

Armengol, C. G. (1998). Attentional and self-regulation deficits in severe anoxia: Implications for rehabilitation. *The Rehabilitation Professional*, *6*, 24-29.

Armengol, C. G. (1999). A multi-modal support group with Hispanic traumatic brain injury (TBI) survivors. *Journal of Head Trauma Rehabilitation, 14*, 233-246.

Artiola i Fortuny, L., & Heaton, R. K. (1996). Standard versus computerized administration of the Wisconsin Card Sorting Test. *The Clinical Neuropsychologist, 10*, 419-424.

Axelrod, B. N., & Goldman, R. S. (1996). Use of demographic corrections in neuropsychological interpretation: How standard are the standard scores? *The Clinical Neuropsychologist, 10*, 159-162.

Barkley, R. A. (1998). *Attention-Deficit Hyperactivity Disorder: A handbook for diagnosis and treatment* (2nd ed.). New York: Guilford.

Barth, J. T. (1996, October). *Presidential address.* Paper presented at the 16th annual meeting of the National Academy of Neuropsychology, New Orleans, LA.

Beck, A. T. (1993). *Manual for the Beck Anxiety Inventory*. San Antonio, TX: The Psychological Corporation.

Beck, A. T., Steer, R. A., & Brown, G. K. (1996). *Manual for the Beck Depression Inventory-II*. San Antonio, TX: The Psychological Corporation.

Beery, K. E. (1997). *The Visual-Motor Integration Test (4th ed.): Administration, scoring, and teaching manual*. Austin, TX: Pro-Ed.

Bender, L. (1938). A visual motor Gestalt test and its clinical use. *American Orthopsychiatric Association, Research Monographs, No. 3.*

Benton, A. L. (1987). Evolution of a clinical specialty. *The Clinical Neuropsychologist, 1*, 5-8.

Benton, A. L., & Hamsher, K. deS. (1989). *Multilingual Aphasia Examination*. Iowa City, IA: AJA Associates.

Berger, S. G., Chibnall, J. T., & Gfeller, J. D. (1994). The Category Test: A comparison of computerized and standard versions. *Assessment, 1*, 225-258.

Berger, S. G., Chibnall, J. T., & Gfeller, J. D. (1997). Construct validity of the computerized version of the Category Test. *Journal of Clinical Psychology, 53*(7), 723-726.

Berry, D. T. R., Wetter, M. W., Baer, R. A., Youngjohn, J. R., Gass, C. S., Lamb, D. G., Franzen, M. D., & MacInnes, W. D. (1995). Overreporting of closed-head injury symptoms on the MMPI-2. *Psychological Assessment, 7*(4), 517-523.

Bieliauskas, L. A., & Matthews, C. G. (1997). American Board of Clinical Neuropsychology, 1996 update: Facts, data, and information for potential candidates. *The Clinical Neuropsychologist, 11*(2), 222-226.

Binder, L. M., & Thompson, L. L. (1994). The ethics code and neuropsychological assessment practices. *Archives of Clinical Neuropsychology, 10*, 27-47.

Blau, T. H. (1988, 1992). *Cue Book with 1992 Supplement*. Tampa, FL: Psychological Seminars.

Blessed, G., Tomlinson, B. E., & Roth, M. (1968). The association between quantitative measures of dementia and of senile changes in the cerebral gray matter of elderly subjects. *British Journal of Psychiatry, 114*, 797-811.

Bornstein, R. A. (1986). Classification rates obtained with "standard" cut-off scores on selected neuropsychological measures. *Journal of Clinical & Experimental Neuropsychology, 8*(4), 413-420.

Brooks, D. N. (Ed.). (1984). *Closed head injury: Psychological, social, and family consequences*. New York: Oxford University Press.

Brown, J. I., Fishco, V. V., & Hanna, G. S. (1993). *Nelson-Denny Reading Test*. Ithasca, IL: Riverside.

Butcher, J. N., Dahlstrom, W. G., Graham, J. R., Tellegen, A. M., & Kaemmer, B. (1989). *MMPI-2: Minnesota Multiphasic Personality Inventory-2*. Minneapolis, MN: University of Minnesota Press.

Butters, N., Grant, I., Haxby, J., Judd, L. L., Martin, A., McClelland, J., & Price, R. W. (1990). Assessment of AIDS-related cognitive changes: Recommendations of the NIMH workshop on neuropsychological assessment approaches. *Journal of Clinical and Experimental Neuropsychology, 12*, 963-978.

Caetano, C., & Christensen, A. L. (1997). The design of neuropsychological rehabilitation: The role of neuropsychological assessment. In J. León-Carrión (Ed.), *Neuropsychological rehabilitation: Fundamentals, innovations and directions* (pp. 63-72). Delray Beach, FL: St. Lucie Press.

Canter, M. B., Bennett, B. E., Jones, S. E., & Nagy, T. F. (1994). *Ethics for psychologists: A commentary on the APA ethical principles of psychologists and code of conduct*. Washington, DC: American Psychological Association.

Cavallo, M. M., Kay, T., & Ezrachi, O. (1992). Problems and changes after traumatic brain injury: Differing perceptions within and between families. *Brain Injury, 6*, 327-335.

Cermak, L. S. (1975). Imagery as an aid to retrieval for Korsakoff's patients. *Cortex, 11*, 163-169.

Chelune, G. J., & Edwards, P. (1981). Early brain lesions: Ontogenetic-environmental considerations. *Journal of Consulting and Clinical Psychology, 49*, 777-790.

Choca, J. P., Laatsch, L., Wetzel, L., & Agresti, A. (1997). The Halstead Category Test: A fifty year perspective. *Neuropsychology Review*, *7*(2), 61-75.

Chouinard, M. J., & Braun, C. M. (1993). A meta-analysis of the relative sensitivity of neuropsychological screening tests. *Journal of Clinical and Experimental Neuropsychology*, *15*, 591-607.

Coffey, C. E., Cummings, J. L., Duffy, J. D., Fink, M., Lauterbach, E. C., Lovell, M. R., Malloy, P., Nussbaum, R. D., Royall, D. R., & Salloway, S. (1995). Assessment and treatment outcomes in neuropsychiatry: A response from the committee on research of the American Psychiatric Association. *The Journal of Neuropsychiatry and Clinical Neurosciences*, *7*, 287-289.

Cohen, R. A. (1993). *The neuropsychology of attention*. New York: Plenum.

Cohen, R. F., & Mapou, R. L. (1988). Neuropsychological assessment for treatment planning: A hypothesis-testing approach. *Journal of Head Trauma Rehabilitation*, *3*, 12-23.

Commissaris, K., Verhey, F. R. J., & Jolles, J. (1996). A controlled study into the effects of psychoeducation for patients with cognitive disturbances. *Journal of Neuropsychiatry and Clinical Neuroscience*, *8*, 429-435.

Committee on Ethical Guidelines for Forensic Psychologists. (1991). Specialty guidelines for forensic psychologists. *Law and Human Behavior*, *15*(6), 655-665.

Committee on Psychological Tests and Assessment, American Psychological Association. (1996). Statement on the disclosure of test data. *American Psychologist*, *51*(6), 644-648.

Conder, R., Allen, L., & Cox, D. (1992). *Computerized Assessment of Response Bias*. Durham, NC: Cognisyst.

Conners, K. C. (1997). *Manual for the Conners Rating Scales–Revised*. New York: Multi-Health Systems.

Craig, P. L. (1979). Neuropsychological assessment in public psychiatric hospitals: The current state of the practice. *Clinical Neuropsychology*, *1*, 1-7.

Crook, T. H., & Larrabee, G. J. (1992). Normative data on a self-rating scale for evaluating memory in everyday life. *Archives of Clinical Neuropsychology*, *7*, 41-51.

Crum, B. M., Anthony, J. C., Bassett, S. S., & Folstein, M. F. (1993). Population-based norms for the Mini-Mental State Examination by age and educational level. *Journal of the American Medical Association*, *269*, 2386-2391.

Cummings, J. L. (1993). Mini-Mental State Examination: Norms, normals, and numbers. *Journal of the American Medical Association*, *269*, 2420-2421.

Cytowic, R. E. (1996). *The neurological side of neuropsychology*. Cambridge, MA: The MIT Press.

Dana, R. H. (1993). *Multicultural assessment perspectives for professional psychology*. Boston: Allyn and Bacon.

Daniels, A., & Deters, T. (1996). Recent changes in medicare reimbursement. *Massachusetts Neuropsychological Association Newsletter*, *1*, 2.

Daubert v. Merrell-Dow Pharmaceuticals, Inc., 113 S. Ct. 2786. (1993).

Delis, D. C., & Kaplan, E. (1983). Hazards of a standardized neuropsychological test with low content validity: Comment on the Luria-Nebraska Neuropsychological Battery. *Journal of Consulting and Clinical Psychology*, *51*, 396-398.

Delis, D. C., Kaplan, E., & Kramer, J. (1999). *Delis-Kaplan Executive Function System manual*. San Antonio, TX: The Psychological Corporation.

Delis, D. C., Kramer, J. H., Kaplan, E., & Ober, B. A. (1994). *California Verbal Learning Test–Children's version (CVLT-C): Manual*. San Antonio, TX: The Psychological Corporation.

Delis, D. C., Kramer, J. H., Kaplan, E., & Ober, B. A. (2000). *California Verbal Learning Test–Second Edition (CVLT-II): Manual*. San Antonio, TX: The Psychological Corporation.

Denman, S. B. (1984). *Denman Neuropsychology Memory Scale*. Charleston, SC: Author.

Derogatis, L. R. (1975). *Symptom Checklist-90–Revised (SCL-90-R)*. Minnetonka, MN: National Computer Systems.

Devivo, K., Rothland, J., Price, L., & Fein, G. (1997). Computerized assessment of arithmetical computational skills with MicroCog. *Journal of the International Neuropsychological Society*, *3*, 199-200.

Diller, L. (1994). Finding the right treatment combinations: Changes in rehabilitation over the past five years. In A. L. Christensen & B. P. Uzzell (Eds.), *Brain injury and neuropsychological rehabilitation: International perspectives* (pp. 1-16). Hillsdale, NJ: Erlbaum.

Duffy, J. D., & Camlin, H. (1995). Neuropsychiatric training in American psychiatric residency training programs. *The Journal of Neuropsychiatry and Clinical Neurosciences, 7*, 290-294.

Dunn, L. M. (1987). *Bilingual Hispanic children on the U.S. mainland: A review of research on their cognitive, linguistic and scholastic development*. Circle Pines, MN: American Guidance Service.

Expert disclosure in federal courts. (1997). *Expert Witness Journal, 9*(8), 1.

Faust, D. (1991). Forensic neuropsychology: The art of practicing a science that does not exist. *Neuropsychology Review, 2*(3), 205-231.

Faust, D. (1995). The detection of deception. [Special issue: Malingering and conversion reactions.] *Neurologic Clinics, 13*, 255-265.

Filley, C. M., Davis, K. A., & Schmitz, S. P. (1989). Neuropsychological performance and magnetic resonance imaging in Alzheimer's disease and normal aging. *Neuropsychology, Neuropsychiatry and Behavioral Neurology, 2*, 81-91.

Folstein, M. F., Folstein, S. E., & McHugh, P. R. (1975). Mini-mental state. *Journal of Psychiatric Research, 12*, 189-198.

Franzen, M., & Berg, R. (1989). *Screening children for brain impairment*. New York: Springer.

Franzen, M. D., Iverson, G. L., & McCracken, L. M. (1990). The detection of malingering in neuropsychological assessment. *Neuropsychological Review, 1*(3), 247-279.

Frederick, R. I. (1997). *Validity Indicator Profile: Manual*. Minneapolis, MN: National Computer Systems.

Freedman, M., Leach, L., Kaplan, E., Winocour, G., Shulman, K. I., & Delis, D. C. (1994). *Clock Drawing: A neuropsychological analysis*. New York: Oxford University Press.

Freides, D. (1993). Proposed standard of professional practice: Neuropsychological reports display all quantitative data. *The Clinical Neuropsychologist, 7*, 234-235.

Freides, D. (1995). Interpretations are more benign than data? *The Clinical Neuropsychologist, 9*, 248.

French, C. C., & Beaumont, J. G. (1987). The reaction of psychiatric patients to computerized assessment. *British Journal of Clinical Psychology, 26*, 267-278.

French, C. C., & Beaumont, J. G. (1990). A clinical study of the automated assessment of intelligence by the Mill Hill Vocabulary Test and the Standard Progressive Matrices test. *Journal of Clinical Psychology, 46*, 129-140.

Frith, C. D. (1992). *The cognitive neuropsychology of schizophrenia*. Hillsdale, NJ: Erlbaum.

Gaddes, W. H., & Edgell, D. (1994). *Learning disabilities and brain function: A neuropsychological approach* (3rd ed.). New York: Springer-Verlag.

Gardner, H. (1974). *The shattered mind: The person after brain damage*. New York: Knopf.

Gass, C. S. (1991). MMPI-2 interpretation and closed head injury: A correction factor. *Psychological Assessment: A Journal of Consulting and Clinical Psychology, 3*(1), 27-31.

Geisinger, K. F. (1992a). Fairness and selected psychometric issues in the psychological testing of Hispanics. In K. F. Geisinger (Ed.), *Psychological Testing of Hispanics* (pp. 17-42). Washington, DC: American Psychological Association.

Geisinger, K. F. (Ed.). (1992b). Preface. *Psychological testing of Hispanics*. Washington, DC: American Psychological Association.

Geschwind, N. (1965). Disconnection syndromes in animals and man. *Brain, 11*, 237-293, 585-644.

Geschwind, N., & Kaplan, E. (1962). A human cerebral deconnection syndrome. *Neurology, 12*, 675-685.

Gilley, D. W., Wilson, R. S., Fleischman, D. A., Harrison, D. W., Goetz, C. G., & Tanner, C. M. (1995). Impact of Alzheimer's type dementia and information source on the assessment of depression. *Psychological Assessment, 7*, 42-48.

Gilligan, C. (1982). *In a different voice: Psychological theory and women's development*. Cambridge, MA: Harvard University Press.

Goldberg, A. L., & McNamara, K. M. (1984). Internship training in clinical neuropsychology. *Professional Psychology: Research and Practice, 15*, 509-514.

Golden, C. J. (1981). A standardized version of Luria's neuropsychological tests: A quantitative and qualitative approach to neuropsychological evaluation. In S. B. Filskov & T. J. Boll (Eds.), *Handbook of clinical neuropsychology* (pp. 608-642). New York: Wiley.

Golden, C. J., Hammeke, T. A., & Purisch, A. D. (1980). *The Luria-Nebraska Neuropsychological Battery: Manual*. Los Angeles: Western Psychological Services.

Golden, C. J., & Kuperman, S. K. (1980). Graduate training in clinical neuropsychology. *Professional Psychology, 11*, 55-63.

Golden, C. J., & Strider, M. A. (Eds.). (1986). *Forensic neuropsychology*. New York: Plenum.

Goodglass, H., & Kaplan, E. (1972). *The assessment of aphasia and related disorders*. Philadelphia: Lea & Febiger.

Graham, F. K., & Kendall, B. S. (1960). Memory-for-Designs test: Revised general manual. *Perceptual and Motor Skills, 11* (Monograph Suppl. No. 2-VII), 147-188.

Grant, M. L., Ilai, D., Nussbaum, N. L., & Bigler, E. D. (1990). The relationship between continuous performance tasks and neuropsychological tests in children with Attention-Deficit Hyperactivity Disorder. *Perceptual and Motor Skills, 70*, 435-445.

Green, W. P., Allen, L. M., & Aster, K. (1996). *The Word Memory Test: A user's guide to the oral and computer-administered forms*. Durham, NC: CogniSyst.

Greiffenstein, M. F., Baker, W. J., & Gola, T. (1994). Validation of malingered amnesia measures with a large clinical sample. *Psychological Assessment, 3*, 218-224.

Grohol, J. M. (1997). *The insider's guide to mental health resources online*. New York: Guilford.

Gronwall, D. (1991). Minor head injury. *Neuropsychologia, 95*, 253-266.

Guilmette, T. J., & Faust, D. (1991). Characteristics of neuropsychologists who prefer the Halstead-Reitan or the Luria-Nebraska neuropsychological battery. *Professional Psychology: Research and Practice, 22*, 80-83.

Guilmette, T. J., Faust, D., Hart, K., & Arkes, H. R. (1990). A national survey of psychologists who offer neuropsychological services. *Archives of Clinical Neuropsychology, 5*, 373-392.

Haines, M. E., & Norris, M. P. (1995). Detecting the malingering of cognitive deficits: An update. *Neuropsychology Review, 5*(2), 125-148.

Hallowell, F. M., & Ratey, J. J. (1995). *Driven to distraction: Recognizing and coping with Attention Deficit Disorder from childhood through adolescence*. New York: Simon and Schuster.

Halper, J. (1997). The psychoeducational approach to complex protocols in neurorehabilitation. *Journal of Neurologic Rehabilitation, 11*, 149-154.

Halstead, W. (1952). The frontal lobes and the highest integrating capacities of man. *Halstead papers* (M175, p. 26). Akron, OH: Archives of the History of American Psychology.

Hannay, H. J., Bieliauskas, L. A., Crosson, B. A., Hammeke, T. A., Hamsher, K. deS., & Koffler, S. P. (1998). Proceedings of the Houston conference on specialty education and training in clinical neuropsychology. *Archives of Clinical Neuropsychology, 13*, 157-250.

Hartlage, L. C. (1985). Neuropsychology and the private practitioner. *Psychotherapy in Private Practice, 3*, 61-64.

Hartlage, L. C. (1987). Neuropsychology: Definition and history. In L. C. Hartlage, M. J. Asken, & J. L. Hornsby (Eds.), *Essentials of neuropsychological assessment* (pp. 1-11). New York: Springer.

Hartlage, L. C., & Telzrow, C. F. (1980). The practice of clinical neuropsychology in the U.S. *International Journal of Clinical Neuropsychology, 2*, 200-202.

Heaton, R. K., & PAR Staff. (1993). *Wisconsin Card Sorting Test: Computer Version-2* [Computer software]. Odessa, FL: Psychological Assessment Resources.

Heaton, R. K., Thompson, L. L., Nelson, L. M., Filley, C. M., & Franklin, G. (1990). Brief and intermediate-length screening of neuropsychological impairment in multiple sclerosis. In S. Rao (Ed.), *Neurobehavioral aspects of multiple sclerosis* (pp. 149-160). New York: Oxford University Press.

Hécaen, H., & Albert, M. (1978). *Human neuropsychology*. New York: Wiley-Interscience.

Heilman, K., & Valenstein, E. (1979). *Clinical neuropsychology*. New York: Oxford University Press.

Heinrichs, R. W. (1990). Current and emergent applications of neuropsychological assessment: Problems of validity and utility. *Professional Psychology: Research and Practice, 21*, 171-176.

Helms, J. E. (1992). Why is there no study of cultural equivalence in standardized cognitive ability testing? *American Psychologist, 47*, 1083-1101.

Hess, A. K., & Weiner, I. B. (Eds.). (1999). *The handbook of forensic psychology* (2nd ed.). New York: Wiley.

Hooper, H. E. (1983). *Hooper Visual Organization Test (VOT) manual.* Los Angeles: Western Psychological Services.

Hooper, S. R., Willis, W. G., & Stone, B. H. (1996). Issues and approaches in the neuropsychological assessment and treatment of children with learning disabilities. In E. S. Batchelor, Jr. & R. S. Dean (Eds.), *Pediatric neuropsychology: Interfacing assessment and treatment for rehabilitation* (pp. 211-248). Boston: Allyn and Bacon.

Horowitz, M. J., Wilner, N., & Alvarez, W. (1979). Impact of event scale: A measure of subjective stress. *Psychosomatic Medicine, 41,* 209-218.

Horton, A. M., Jr., Vaeth, J., & Anilane, J. (1990). Computerized interpretation of the Luria-Nebraska Neuropsychological Battery: A pilot study. *Perceptual and Motor Skills, 71,* 83-86.

Hyler, S. F. (1996). *Personality Diagnostic Questionnaire* (4th ed.). Scarsdale, NY: NiJo Software.

Ivnik, R. J., Malec, J. F., Tangalos, E. G., & Crook, T. H. (1996). Older person's reactions to computerized testing versus traditional testing by psychometrists. *The Clinical Neuropsychologist, 10*(2), 149-151.

Jacobs, J. W., Bernhard, M. R., Delgado, A., & Strain,, J. J. (1977). Screening for organic mental syndromes in the medically ill. *Annals of Internal Medicine, 86,* 40-46.

Jagger, C., Clarke, M., Anderson, J., & Battcock, T. (1992). Misclassification of dementia by the Mini-Mental State Examination—are education and social class the only factors? *Age and Aging, 21,* 404-411.

Johnson-Greene, D., Dehring, M., Adams, K. M., Miller, T., Shalini, A., Beylin, A., & Brandon, R. (1997). Accuracy of self-reported educational attainment among diverse patient populations: A preliminary investigation. *Archives of Clinical Neuropsychology, 12,* 635-643.

Johnstone, B., & Farmer, J. E. (1997). Preparing neuropsychologists for the future: The need for additional training guidelines. *Archives of Clinical Neuropsychology, 6,* 523-530.

Johnstone, B., Frank, R., Belar, C., Berk, S., Bieliauskas, L., Bigler, E., Caplan, B., Elliott, T., Glueckauf, R., Kaplan, R., Kreutzer, J., Mateer, C., Patterson, D., Puente, A., Richards, J., Rosenthal, M., Sherer, M., Shewchuk, R., Siegel, L., & Sweet, J. (1995). Psychology in health care: Future directions. *Professional Psychology: Research and Practice, 26*(4), 341-365.

Kane, R. L., Goldstein, G., & Parsons, O. A. (1989). A response to R. L. Mapou. *Journal of Clinical and Experimental Neuropsychology, 11*(4), 589-595.

Kane, R. L., & Kay, G. G. (1992). Computerized assessment in neuropsychology: A review of tests and test batteries. *Neuropsychology Review, 3*(1), 1-117.

Kane, R. L., & Kay, G. G. (1997). Computer applications in neuropsychological assessment. In T. M. Incagnoli & G. Goldstein (Eds.), *Contemporary approaches to neuropsychological assessment: Critical issues in neuropsychology* (pp. 369-392). New York: Plenum.

Kane, R. L., Parsons, O. A., & Goldstein, G. (1985). Statistical relationship and discriminative accuracy of the Halstead Reitan, Luria-Nebraska, and Wechsler I.Q. scores. *Journal of Clinical and Experimental Neuropsychology, 7*, 211-223.

Kaplan, E. (1983). Process and achievement revisited. In S. Wapner & B. Kaplan (Eds.), *Toward a holistic developmental psychology* (pp. 143-156). Hillsdale, NJ: Erlbaum.

Kaplan, E. (1988). A process approach to neuropsychological assessment. In T. J. Boll & B. Bryant (Eds.), *Clinical neuropsychology and brain function: Research, measurement, and practice* (pp. 125-168). Washington, DC: American Psychological Association.

Kaplan, E., Fein, D., Kramer, J. H., Delis, D. C., & Morris, R. (1999). *The WISC-III as a process instrument (WISC-III PI) manual.* San Antonio, TX: The Psychological Corporation.

Kaplan, E., Fein, D., Morris, R., & Delis, D. C. (1991). *The Wechsler Adult Intelligence Scale–Revised as a neuropsychological instrument.* San Antonio, TX: The Psychological Corporation.

Kaplan, E., Goodglass, H., & Weintraub, S. (2000). *Boston Naming Test.* Baltimore: Lippincott, Williams, & Wilkins.

Keefe, R. S. (1995). The contribution of neuropsychology to psychiatry. *American Journal of Psychiatry, 152*, 6-15.

Kelland, D., & Pieniadz, J. (1996, October). *To report or not to report (quantitative data, that is): A survey of actual practice and training in neuropsychology.* Poster session presented at the 16th annual meeting of the National Academy of Neuropsychology, New Orleans, LA.

Kennedy, R. S., Baltzley, D. R., Wilkes, R. L., & Kuntz, L. A. (1989). Psychology of computer use: IX. A menu of self-administered microcomputer-based neurotoxicology tests. *Perceptual and Motor Skills, 68*, 1255-1272.

Kennedy, R. S., Wilkes, R. L., Dunlap, W. P., & Kuntz, L. A. (1987). Development of an automated performance test system for environmental and behavioral toxicology studies. *Perceptual and Motor Skills, 65*, 947-962.

Kerns, K. A., Mateer, C. A., & Brousseau, S. (1998). Internet resources for neuropsychology. *The Clinical Neuropsychologist, 12*, 217-230.

Kittleson, M. J. (1997). *Web sites for health professionals*. Sudbury, MA: Jones and Bartlett.

Leach, M. F. L., Kaplan, E., Winocour, G., Shulman, K. I., & Delis, D. C. (1994). *Clock drawing: A neuropsychological analysis*. New York: Oxford University Press.

Lees-Haley, P. R. (1997). Attorneys influence expert evidence in forensic psychological and neuropsychological cases. *Assessment, 4*, 321-324.

Legal Information Institute. (2000). *Federal Rules of Evidence*. Ithaca, NY: Cornell Law School.

León-Carrión, J., Morales, M., Forastero, P., Domínguez-Morales, M. D., Murillo, F., Jimenez-Baco, R., & Gordon, P. (1991). The computerized Tower of Hanoi: A new form of administration and suggestions for interpretation. *Perceptual and Motor Skills, 73*, 63-66.

Lesser, G. B., Fifer, G., & Clark, D. H. (1965). Mental abilities of children from different social-class and cultural groups. *Monographs of the Society for Research in Child Development, 30* (Whole No. 102).

Levine, M. D. (1996). *Manual for the ANSER system*. Cambridge, MA: Educators Publishing Service.

Lezak, M. (1984). An individualized approach to neuropsychological assessment. In P. E. Logue and J. M. Schear (Eds.), *Clinical neuropsychology: A multidisciplinary approach* (pp. 117-134). Springfield, IL: Charles C. Thomas.

Lezak, M. D. (1988). IQ: RIP. *Journal of Clinical and Experimental Neuropsychology, 10*, 351-361.

Lezak, M. D. (1995). *Neuropsychological Assessment* (3rd ed.). New York: Oxford University Press.

Lishman, W. A. (1998). *Organic psychiatry* (3rd ed.). Oxford: Blackwell Science.

Locke, H., & Wallace, K. (1959). Short marital-adjustment and prediction tests: Their reliability and validity. *Marriage and Family Living, 21*, 251-255.

Lubin, B., & Sokoloff, R. M. (1983). An update of the survey of training and internship programs in clinical neuropsychology. *Journal of Clinical Psychology, 39*, 149-152.

Lucas, J. A., Ivnik, R. J., Smith, G. E., Bohac, D. L., Tangalos, E. G., Kokmen, E., Graff-Radford, N. R., & Petersen, R. C. (1998). Normative data for the Mattis Dementia Rating Scale. *Journal of Clinical and Experimental Neuropsychology*, *20*, 536-547.

Luria, A. R. (1963). *Restoration of function after brain injury*. New York: Pergamon.

Luria, A. R. (1966, 1980). *Higher cortical functions in man*. New York: Basic Books.

Magaziner, J., Bassett, S. S., & Hebel, J. R. (1987). Predicting performance on the Mini-Mental State Examination: Use of age and education-specific equations. *Journal of the American Geriatrics Society*, *35*, 996-1000.

Malloy, P. F., Cummings, J. L., Coffey, C. E., Duffy, J., Fink, M., Lauterbach, E. C., Lovell, M., Royall, D., & Salloway, S. (1997). Cognitive screening instruments in neuropsychiatry: A report of the Committee on Research of the American Neuropsychiatric Association. *The Journal of Neuropsychiatry and Clinical Neurosciences*, *9*, 189-197.

Mapou, R. L. (1988). Testing to detect brain damage: An alternative to what may no longer be useful. *Journal of Clinical and Experimental Neuropsychology*, *10*, 271-278.

Matarazzo, R. G. (1995). Psychological report standards in neuropsychology. *The Clinical Neuropsychologist*, *9*, 249-250.

McCaffrey, R. J., & Isaac, W. (1984). Survey of the educational backgrounds and specialty training of instructors of clinical neuropsychology in APA-approved graduate training programs. *Professional Psychology: Research and Practice*, *15*, 26-33.

McCann, R., & Plunkett, R. P. (1984). Improving the concurrent validity of the Bender-Gestalt test. *Perceptual and Motor Skills*, *58*, 947-950.

Melton, G. B., Petrila, J., Poythress, N. G., & Slobogin, C. (1997). *Psychological evaluations for the courts: A handbook for mental health professionals and lawyers* (2nd ed.). New York: Guilford.

Meyers. J. E., & Meyers, K. R. (1995). *Rey Complex Figure Test and Recognition Trial (RCFT)*. Odessa, FL: Psychological Assessment Resources.

Milberg, W., Hebben, N., & Kaplan, E. (1996). The Boston process approach. In I. Grant & K. M. Adams (Eds.), *Neuropsychological assessment of neuropsychiatric disorders* (2nd ed., pp. 58-80). New York: Oxford University Press.

Mild Traumatic Brain Injury Committee of the Head Injury Interdisciplinary Special Interest Group of the American Congress of Rehabilitation Medicine. (1993). Definition of mild traumatic brain injury. *Journal of Head Trauma Rehabilitation*, *8*(3), 86-87.

Millis, S. R., Putnam, S. H., Adams, K. M., & Ricker, J. H. (1995). The California Verbal Learning Test in the detection of incomplete effort in neuropsychological evaluation. *Psychological Assessment*, 7(4), 463-471.

Millon, T. (1994). *Millon Clinical Multiaxial Inventory-III (MCMI-III)*. Minnetonka, MN: National Computer Systems.

Minden, S. L., & Moes, E. J. (1990). A psychiatric perspective. In S. Rao (Ed.), *Neurobehavioral aspects of multiple sclerosis* (pp. 230-250). New York: Oxford University Press.

Mitrushina, M., Boone, K. B., & D'Elia, L. F. (1999). *Handbook of normative data for neuropsychological assessment*. New York: Oxford University Press.

Morse, P. A., Armengol, C. G., Carper, J. M., Cohen, R. F., Dowds, Jr., M. M., Levine, L., Mapou, R., Moes, E. J., Nelson, A. P., Orren, M. M., & Wilson, A. (1986). *Recommended neuropsychological testing protocol*. Boston: Statewide Head Injury Program.

Nadler, J. D., Richardson, E. D., & Malloy, P. F. (1994). Detection of impairment with the Mini-Mental State Examination. *Neuropsychiatry, Neuropsychology, and Behavioral Neurology*, *7*, 109-113.

Naeser, M. A., Palumbo, C. L., Helm-Estabrooks, N., Stiassny-Eder, D., & Albert, M. L. (1989). Severe non-fluency in aphasia: Role of the medial subcallosal fasciculus plus other white matter pathways in recovery of spontaneous speech. *Brain*, *112*, 1-38.

Naugle, R. I., & McSweeney, A. J. (1995). On the practice of routinely appending neuropsychological data to reports. *The Clinical Neuropsychologist*, *9*, 245-247.

Naugle, R. I., & McSweeney, A. J. (1996). More thoughts on the practice of routinely appending raw data to reports: Response to Freides and Matarazzo. *The Clinical Neuropsychologist*, *10*, 313-314.

Nelson, A., Fogel, B. S., & Faust, D. (1986). Bedside cognitive screening instruments. *Journal of Nervous and Mental Disorders*, *174*, 73-83.

O'Connor, D. W., Pollitt, P. A., Treasurer, A. U., Brook, C. P., Reiss, B. B., & Hughes, H. (1989). The influence of education, social class and sex on Mini-Mental State scores. *Psychological Medicine*, *19*, 771-776.

Ommaya, A. K., & Ommaya, A. K. (1997). Why neurobehavioral sequelae do not correlate with head injury severity: A biomechanical explanation for the traumatic disturbances of consciousness. *Seminars in Clinical Neuropsychiatry*, *2*(3), 163-176.

Orsini, D. L., VanGorp, W. G., & Boone, K. B. (1988). *The neuropsychology casebook*. New York: Springer Verlag.

Ozonoff, S. (1995). Reliability and validity of the Wisconsin Card Sorting Test in studies of autism. *Neuropsychology*, *9*(4), 491-500.

Padilla, A. M., & Ruiz, R. A. (1973). Latino mental health: A review of the literature. (DHEW Publication No. ADM 74-113). Washington, DC: U.S. Government Printing Office.

Paivio, A. (1969). Mental imagery in learning in memory. *Psychological Review*, *74*, 241-263.

Palmer, B. W., Boone, K. B., Allman, L., & Castro, D. B. (1995). Co-occurrence of brain lesions and cognitive deficit exaggeration. *The Clinical Psychologist*, *9*(1), 68-73.

Pankratz, L. D., & Taylor, J. D. (1982). Issues in psychological assessment. In J. R. McNamara & A. G. Barclay (Eds.), *Critical issues, developments, and trends in professional psychology* (Vol. 2, pp. 117-134). New York: Praeger.

Paolo, A. M., Axelrod, B. N., Ryan, J. J., & Goldman, R. S. (1994). Administration accuracy of the Wisconsin Card Sorting Test. *The Clinical Neuropsychologist*, *8*, 112-116.

Parker, R. R. (1990). *Traumatic brain injury and neuropsychological impairment*. New York: Springer-Verlag.

Peyser, J. M., Rao, S. M., LaRocca, N. G., & Kaplan, E. (1990). Guidelines for neuropsychological research in multiple sclerosis. *Archives of Neurology*, *47*, 94-97.

Potosky, D., & Bobko, P. (1997). Computer versus paper-and-pencil administration mode and response distortion in noncognitive selection tests. *Journal of Applied Psychology*, *82*(2), 293-299.

Powell, D. H., Kaplan, E. F., Whitla, D., Weintraub, S., Catlin, R., & Funkenstein, H. H. (1993). *Microcog: Assessment of cognitive functioning manual*. San Antonio, TX: The Psychological Corporation.

Prather, P., & Kaplan, E. (1991). *L'attenzione e i suoi disturbi: Fatti, fisiologia, e inquadramento teorico*. [Attention and its disorders: Facts, physiology, and a theoretical framework.] Venice, Italy: Fidia Biomedical Information.

Prigatano, G. P. (Ed.). (1986). *Neuropsychological rehabilitation after brain injury*. Baltimore: The Johns Hopkins University Press.

Prigatano, G. P. (1997). The problem of impaired self-awareness in neuropsychological rehabilitation. In J. León-Carrión (Ed.), *Neuropsychological rehabilitation: Fundamentals, innovations and directions*. Delray Beach, FL: St. Lucie Press.

Prigatano, G. P., Altman, I. M., & O'Brien, K. P. (1990). Behavioral limitations that traumatic brain impaired patients tend to underestimate. *The Clinical Neuropsychologist, 4*, 163-176.

Prigatano, G. P., & Schachter, D. L. (Eds.). (1991). *Awareness of deficit after brain injury: Clinical and theoretical issues*. New York: Oxford University Press.

Puente, A. (1994). Billing recommendations and CPT codes for neuropsychological assessment. *National Academy of Neuropsychology Bulletin, 11*, 14-15.

Puente, A. E., & McCaffrey, R. J. (Eds.). (1992). *Handbook of neuropsychological assessment: A biopsychosocial perspective*. New York: Plenum.

Putnam, S. H. (1989). The TCN salary survey: A salary survey of neuropsychologists. *The Clinical Neuropsychologist, 3*, 97-115.

Putnam, S. H., & Anderson, C. (1994). The second TCN salary survey: A survey of neuropsychologists, Part I. *The Clinical Neuropsychologist, 8*, 3-37.

Putnam, S. H., & DeLuca, J. W. (1990). The TCN professional practice survey: Part I: General practices of neuropsychologists in primary employment and private practice settings. *The Clinical Neuropsychologist, 4*, 199-244.

Putnam, S. H., & DeLuca, J. W. (1991). The TCN professional practice survey: Part II: An analysis of the fees of neuropsychologists by practice demographics. *The Clinical Neuropsychologist, 5*, 103-124.

Raven, J. C. (1938/1996). *Progressive Matrices: A perceptual test of intelligence: Individual form*. Oxford, England: Oxford Psychologists Press Ltd.

Reeves, D., Kane, R., Winter, K., & Goldstone, A. (1995). *ANAM V3.11 clinical and neurotoxicology subsets*. Irvine, CA: National Recovery Foundation.

Reitan, R. (1955). Discussion: Symposium on the temporal lobe. *Archives of Neurology and Psychiatry, 74*, 569-570.

Reitan, R. (1959). Impairment of abstraction ability in brain damage: Quantitative vs. qualitative changes. *Journal of Psychology*, *48*, 97-102.

Reitan, R. (1960). The significance of dysphasia for intelligence and adaptive abilities. *Journal of Psychology*, *56*, 355-376.

Reitan, R., & Fitzhugh, K. B. (1971). Behavioral deficits in groups with cerebrovascular lesions. *Journal of Consulting and Clinical Psychology*, *2*, 215-223.

Reitan, R. M., & Wolfson, D. (1993). *The Halstead-Reitan Neuropsychological Test Battery: Theory and clinical interpretation*. Tucson, AZ: Neuropsychology Press.

Reitan, R. M., & Wolfson, D. (1997). Emotional disturbances and their interaction with neuropsychological deficits. *Neuropsychology Review*, *7*(1), 3-19.

Reitan, R. M., & Wolfson, D. (1998a, March). Documenting brain damage in cases of mild head injury. *The Neurolaw Letter, 7*(7), p. 41.

Reitan, R. M., & Wolfson, D. (1998b, April). Documenting brain damage in cases of mild head injury–II. *The Neurolaw Letter, 7*(8), p. 49.

Rempel, R. G. (1994). Advocacy and support for victims of brain injury and their families. In M. A. J. Finlayson & S. H. Garner (Eds.), *Brain injury rehabilitation: Clinical considerations* (pp. 376-392). Baltimore: Williams & Wilkins.

Reports of the INS Division 40 Task Force on Education, Accreditation, and Credentialing. (1987). *The Clinical Neuropsychologist*, *1*, 29-34.

Retzlaff, P., Butler, M., & Vanderploeg, R. D. (1992). Neuropsychological battery choice and theoretical orientation: A multivariate analysis. *Journal of Clinical Psychology*, *48*, 666-672.

Reynolds, C. R. (1997). Postscript on premorbid ability estimation: Conceptual addenda and a few words on alternative and conditional approaches. *Archives of Clinical Neuropsychology*, *12*(8), 769-778.

Rogers, R. (Ed.). (1997). *Clinical assessment of malingering and deception* (2nd ed.). New York: Guilford.

Rosenn, L., & Weil, M. (1996). Psychologists and technology: A look at the future. *Professional Psychology: Review and Practice*, *27*(6), 635-638.

Rossi, F. F. (1991). *Expert Witness*. Chicago: American Bar Association.

Rumpf, H.-J., Hapke, U., Hill, A., & John, U. (1997). Development of a screening questionnaire for the general hospital and general practices. *Alcoholism: Clinical and Experimental Research*, *21*, 894-898.

Russell, G. K., Peace, K. A., & Mellsop, G. W. (1996). The reliability of a microcomputer administration of the MMPI. *Journal of Clinical Psychology, 42*(1), 120-122.

Ruthven, L. (1996). Psychologists as gatekeepers in mental health management. *Bulletin of the Division of Independent Practice, Division 42 of the American Psychological Association, 16*, 86-88.

Saling, M. (1994a). Neuropsychology beyond 2001: The future of diagnostic expertise. In S. Touyz, D. Byrne, & A. Gilandas (Eds.), *Neuropsychology in clinical practice* (pp. 3-14). Sydney, Australia: Academic Press.

Saling, M. (1994b). Report writing in neuropsychology. In S. Touyz, D. Byrne & A. Gilandas (Eds.), *Neuropsychology in clinical practice* (pp. 394-400). Sydney, Australia: Academic Press.

Salvia, J., & Ysseldyke, J. E. (1998). *Assessment* (7th ed.). Boston: Houghton-Mifflin.

Sattler, J. M. (1992). *Assessment of children* (3rd ed.). San Diego, CA: Author.

Sayette, M. A., & Mayne, T. J. (1990). Survey of current clinical and research trends in clinical psychology. *American Psychologist, 45*, 1263-1266.

Sbordone, R., & Long, C. J. (Eds.). (1996). *Ecological validity of neuropsychological testing*. Delray Beach, FL: St. Lucie Press.

Schinka, J. A. (1983). *Manual for the Neuropsychological Symptom Checklist in Neuropsychological Status Examination*. Odessa, FL: Psychological Assessment Resources.

Schmidt, R., Freidl, W., Fazekas, F., Reinhart, B., Grieshofer, P., Koch, M., Eber, B., Schumacher, M., Polmin, K., & Lechner, H. (1994). The Mattis Dementia Rating Scale: Normative data from 1,001 healthy volunteers. *Neurology, 44*, 964-966.

Schwamm, L. H., VanDyke, C., Kiernan, R. J., Merrin, E. L., & Mueller, J. (1987). The Neurobehavioral Cognitive Status Examination: Comparisons with the Cognitive Capacity Screening Examination and the Mini-Mental Status Examination in a neurological population. *Annals of Internal Medicine, 107*, 486-491.

Sedlacek, W. E., & Kim, S. H. (1995). *Multicultural assessment*. Office of Educational Research and Improvement: Washington, DC.

Seidman, L. (1990). The neuropsychology of schizophrenia: A neurodevelopmental and case study approach. *Journal of Neuropsychiatry and Clinical Neurosciences, 2*, 301-312.

Sellers, A. H., & Nadler, J. D. (1992). A survey of current neuropsychological assessment procedures used for different age groups. *Psychotherapy in Private Practice, 1*, 47-57.

Selzer, M. L. (1971). The Michigan Alcoholism Screening Test (MAST): The quest for a new diagnostic instrument. *American Journal of Psychiatry, 127*, 1653-1658.

Sheer, D. E., & Lubin, B. (1980). Survey of training programs in clinical neuropsychology. *Journal of Clinical Psychology, 36*, 1035-1040.

Siegal, A. W. (1996). Historical, phenomenological and observational data: A context for neuropsychological test findings. In R. J. Sbordone & C. J. Long (Eds.), *Ecological validity of neuropsychological testing* (pp. 43-71). Delray Beach, FL: St. Lucie Press.

Silver, J. M., & McAllister, T. W. (1997a). Forensic issues in the neuropsychiatric evaluation of the patient with mild head injury. *Journal of Neuropsychiatry and Clinical Neurosciences, 9*(1), 102-113.

Silver, J. M., & McAllister, T. W. (1997b, July). Forensic neuropsychiatric evaluation of the patient with mild traumatic brain injury. *The Neurolaw Letter, 6*(11), p. 153.

Slay, D. K., & Valdivia, L. (1988). Neuropsychology as a specialized health service listed in the National Register of Health Care Providers in Psychology. *Professional Psychology: Research and Practice, 19*, 323-329.

Slick, D. J., & Craig, P. L. (1991). Neuropsychological assessment in public psychiatric hospitals: The changing state of the practice–1979 to 1989. *Archives of Clinical Neuropsychology, 6*, 73-90.

Slick, D. J., Hopp, G., Strauss, E., & Spellacy, F. J. (1996). Victoria Symptom Validity Test: Efficiency for detecting feigned memory impairment and relationship to neuropsychological tests and MMPI-2 validity scales. *Journal of Clinical & Experimental Neuropsychology, 18*(6), 911-922.

Slick, D. J., Hopp, G., Strauss, E., & Thompson, G. B. (1997). *Victoria Symptom Validity Test*. Odessa, FL: Psychological Assessment Resources.

Snyder, D. K., Widiger, T. A., & Hoover, D. W. (1990). Methodological considerations in validating computer-based test interpretations controlling for response bias. *Psychological Assessment: A Journal of Consulting and Clinical Psychology, 2*(4), 470-477.

Sohlberg, M. M., & Mateer, C. A. (1989). Training use of compensatory memory books: A three stage behavioral approach. *Journal of Clinical and Experimental Neuropsychology, 11*, 871-891.

Solomon, G. S., Hale-Friske, R., McCaffrey, R. J., & Isaac, W. (1985). Neuropsychological assessment training in APA-approved counseling psychology programs. *Professional Psychology: Research and Practice, 16*, 22-25.

Spiers, P. A. (1981). Have they come to praise Luria or to bury him? The Luria-Nebraska Battery controversy. *Journal of Consulting and Clinical Psychology*, *49*, 331-341.

Spinhoven, P., Labbe, M. R., & Rombouts, R. (1993). Feasibility of computerized psychological testing with psychiatric outpatients. *Journal of Clinical Psychology*, *49*(3), 440-447.

Stromberg, C. D., Haggarty, D. J., Leibenluft, R. F., McMillan, M. H., Mishkin, B., Rubin, B. L., & Trilling, H. R. (1988). *The psychologists legal handbook*. Washington, DC: Council for the National Register of Health Service Providers in Psychology.

Sweet, J. J., & Moberg, P. J. (1990). A survey of practices and beliefs among ABPP and non-ABPP clinical neuropsychologists. *The Clinical Neuropsychologist*, *4*, 101-120.

Sweet, J. J., Moberg, P. J., & Westergaard, C. K. (1996). Five-year follow-up survey of practices and beliefs of clinical neuropsychologists. *The Clinical Neuropsychologist*, *10*, 202-221.

Sweet, J. J., Westergaard, C. K., & Moberg, P. J. (1995). Managed care experiences of clinical neuropsychologists. *The Clinical Neuropsychologist*, *9*, 214-218.

Tallent, N. (1993). *Psychological report writing* (4th ed.). Englewood Cliffs, NJ: Prentice Hall.

Taylor, J. S. (1996). *Introduction to Neurolaw* (Cassette Recording No. 3NL1N). Houston, TX: HDI Publishers.

Taylor, J. S. (1998, February). Rapid ascendency of forensic neuropsychology. *The Neurolaw Letter*, *7*(5), 29.

Teeter, P. A., & Semrud-Clikeman, M. (1997). *Child neuropsychology*. Needham Heights, MA: Allyn and Bacon.

Therapeutics and Technology Assessment Subcommittee of the American Academy of Neurology. (1996). Assessment: Neuropsychological testing of adults. *Neurology*, *47*, 592-599.

Tombaugh, T. N. (1996). *Test of memory of malingering*. North Tonowanda, NY: Multi-Health Systems.

Tramontana, M. G., & Boyd, T. A. (1986). Psychometric screening of neuropsychological abnormality in older children. *The International Journal of Clinical Neuropsychology*, *8*, 53-59.

Trexler, L. E., Webb, P. M., & Zappala, G. (1994). Strategic aspects of neuropsychological rehabilitation. In A. L. Christensen & B. P. Uzzell (Eds.), *Brain injury and neuropsychological rehabilitation: International perspectives* (pp. 99-124). Hillsdale, NJ: Erlbaum.

Uzzell, B. P. (1997). Neuropsychological rehabilitation models. In J. León-Carrión (Ed.), *Neuropsychological rehabilitation: Fundamentals, innovations and directions* (pp. 41-46). Delray Beach, FL: St. Lucie Press.

Varney, N. R., & Menefee, L. (1993). Psychosocial and executive deficits following closed head injury: Implications for orbital frontal cortex. *Journal of Head Trauma Rehabilitation, 8*, 32-44.

Voogt, R. D. (1997). Economic and legal aspects of neuropsychological rehabilitation. In J. León-Carrión (Ed.), *Neuropsychological rehabilitation: Fundamentals, innovations and directions* (pp. 531-552). Delray Beach, FL: St. Lucie Press.

Walsh, K. (1987). *Neuropsychology: A clinical approach* (2nd ed.). Edinburgh, Scotland: Churchill Livingstone.

Walsh, K. W. (1991). *Understanding brain damage: A primer of neuropsychological evaluation* (2nd ed.). Edinburgh, Scotland: Churchill Livingstone.

Watson, C. G., Manifold, V., Kleet, W. G., Brown, J., Thomas, D., & Anderson, D. (1990). Comparability of computer- and booklet-administered Minnesota Multiphasic Personality Inventories among primarily chemically dependent patients. *Psychological Assessment: A Journal of Consulting and Clinical Psychology, 2*(3) 276-280.

Wechsler, D. (1991). *Wechsler Intelligence Scale for Children* (3rd ed.). San Antonio, TX: The Psychological Corporation.

Wechsler, D. (1997a). *Wechsler Adult Intelligence Scale* (3rd ed.). San Antonio, TX: The Psychological Corporation.

Wechsler, D. (1997b). *Wechsler Memory Scale* (3rd ed.). San Antonio, TX: The Psychological Corporation.

Wechsler Individual Achievement Test. (1992). San Antonio, TX: The Psychological Corporation.

Wedding, D. (1991). Clinical judgement in forensic neuropsychology: A comment on the risks of claiming more than can be delivered. *Neuropsychology Review, 2*(3), 233-239.

Wedding, D., & Faust, D. (1989). Clinical judgment and decision making in neuropsychology. *Archives of Clinical Neuropsychology, 4*, 233-265.

Werner, H. (1937). Process and achievement. A basic problem of education and developmental psychology. *Harvard Educational Review*, *7*, 353-368.

White, D. A., Heaton, R. K., & Monsch, A. U. (1995). Neuropsychological studies of asymptomatic human immunodeficiency virus-Type 1 infected individuals. *Journal of the International Neuropsychological Society*, *1*, 304-315.

Wilkening, G. N. (1987). Brief and extended neuropsychological assessment of learning disabilities. In L. C. Hartlage, M. J. Asken, & J. L. Hornsby (Eds.), *Essentials of neuropsychological assessment* (pp. 122-137). New York: Springer.

Wilkinson, G. S. (1993). *Wide Range Achievement Test manual* (3rd ed.). Wilmington, DE: Wide Range.

Williams, A. D. (1997). Fixed versus flexible batteries. In R. J. McCaffrey, A. D. Williams, J. M. Fisher, & L. C. Laing (Eds.), *The practice of forensic neuropsychology: Meeting challenges in the courtroom* (pp. 57-70). New York: Plenum.

Wilson, B. A. (1987). *Rehabilitation of memory*. New York: Guilford.

Wilson, B. A. (1993). Ecological validity of neuropsychological assessment: Do neuropsychological indexes predict performance in everyday activities? *Applied and Preventive Psychology*, *2*, 109-215.

Wolfson, D. (1985). *Neuropsychology History Questionnaire*. Tucson, AZ: Reitan Neuropsychological Laboratory.

Woodcock, R. W., McGrew, K. S., & Mather, N. (2001). *Woodcock-Johnson Psychoeducational Battery manual*. Ithasca, IL: Riverside.

World Health Organization. (1992). *ICD 10: International statistical classification of diseases and related health problems* (Vol. 1, rev.). Geneva, Switzerland: Author.

Youngjohn, J. R. (1995). Confirmed attorney coaching prior to neuropsychological evaluation. *Assessment*, *2*, 279-283.

Youngjohn, J. R., Burrows, L., & Erdal, K. (1995). Brain damage or compensation neurosis? The controversial Post-Concussion Syndrome. *The Clinical Neuropsychologist*, *9*(2), 112-123.

Zakzanis, K. K., Leach, L., & Kaplan, E. (1999). *Neuropsychological differential diagnosis*. Lisse, Netherlands: Swets & Zeitlinger.

Zilberg, N. J., Weiss, D. S., & Horowitz, M. J. (1982). Impact of Event Scale: A cross-validation study and some empirical evidence supporting a conceptual model of stress response syndromes. *Journal of Consulting and Clinical Psychology*, *50*, 407-414.

NAME INDEX

** = et al.; ** = editor*

D

E

F

G

* = *et al.*; ** = *editor*

* = *et al.;* ** = *editor*

** = et al.; ** = editor*

** = et al.; ** = editor*

** = et al.; ** = editor*

SUBJECT INDEX

T

TEST INDEX